Woke Up
This
Morning

Woke Up This Morning

The Definitive Oral History of
The Sopranos

MICHAEL IMPERIOLI &
STEVE SCHIRRIPA
with Philip Lerman

4th ESTATE • *London*

4th Estate
An imprint of HarperCollins*Publishers*
1 London Bridge Street
London SE1 9GF

www.4thestate.co.uk

HarperCollins*Publishers*
1st Floor, Watermarque Building, Ringsend Road
Dublin 4, Ireland

First published in Great Britain in 2021 by 4th Estate
First published in the United States by William Morrow in 2021

2

Copyright © Archangela Productions Inc. and Noelani Inc. 2021

Michael Imperioli and Steve Schirripa assert the moral right
to be identified as the authors of this work in accordance
with the Copyright, Designs and Patents Act 1988

A catalogue record for this book is
available from the British Library

ISBN 978-0-00-851341-2 (hardback)
ISBN 978-0-00-851342-9 (trade paperback)

All rights reserved. No part of this publication may be
reproduced, stored in a retrieval system, or transmitted,
in any form or by any means, electronic, mechanical,
photocopying, recording or otherwise, without the
prior permission of the publishers.

This book is sold subject to the condition that it shall not, by
way of trade or otherwise, be lent, re-sold, hired out or otherwise
circulated without the publisher's prior consent in any form of
binding or cover other than that in which it is published and
without a similar condition including this condition being
imposed on the subsequent purchaser.

Set in Chaparral Pro
Printed and bound in the UK using 100%
renewable electricity at CPI Group (UK) Ltd

MIX
Paper from
responsible sources
FSC
www.fsc.org **FSC™ C007454**

This book is produced from independently certified FSC™ paper
to ensure responsible forest management.

Find out more about HarperCollins and the environment at
www.harpercollins.co.uk/green

For Jim

To Victoria, Isabella, Vadim and David: Love, forever
—*Michael*

To the loves of my life, Laura, Bria, and Ciara
—*Steve*

Contents

Cast and Crew Interviewed in
Woke Up This Morning

CAST

Ray Abruzzo	Little Carmine Lupertazzi
Jerry Adler	Herman "Hesh" Rabkin
Leslie Bega.	Valentina La Paz
Peter Bogdanovich	Dr. Elliot Kupferberg (also director)
Lorraine Bracco	Dr. Jennifer Melfi
Steve Buscemi	Tony Blundetto (also director)
Chris Caldovino	Billy Leotardo
Carl Capotorto	Paul "Little Paulie" Germani
Max Casella	Benny Fazio
Federico Castelluccio	Furio Giunta
Jason Cerbone	Jackie Aprile Jr.
Dominic Chianese	Corrado "Junior" Soprano
Matthew Del Negro	Brian Cammarata
Edie Falco	Carmela Soprano
Robert Funaro	Eugene Pontecorvo
Lola Glaudini	Agent Deborah Ciccerone
Dan Grimaldi	Philly Parisi /Pasty Parisi
Robert Iler	A. J. Soprano
Michael Imperioli	Christopher Moltisanti
Will Janowitz	Finn DeTrolio
Ariel Kiley	Tracee
Alla Kliouka	Svetlana Kirilenko
Oksana Lada	Irina Peltsin
Marianne Leone	Joanne Moltisanti
Louis Lombardi	Skip Lipari
Joe Lisi	Dick Barone
Angelo Massagli	Bobby Bacala Jr.
Kathrine Narducci	Charmaine Bucco
Arthur J. Nascaraella	Carlo Gervasi
Vincent Pastore	Salvatore "Big Pussy" Bonpensiero
Richard Portnow	Harold Melvoin
David Proval	Richie Aprile

Peter Riegert .... Assemblyman Ronald Zellman
Michael Rispoli .... Jackie Aprile
Al Sapienza .... Mikey Palmice
Steve Schirripa .... Bobby "Bacala" Baccalieri
Paul Schulze .... Father Phil Intintola
Annabella Sciorra .... Gloria Trillo
Matt Servitto .... Agent Dwight Harris
Suzanne Shepherd .... Mary De Angelis
Jamie-Lynn Sigler .... Meadow Soprano
Aida Turturro .... Janice Soprano
Frankie Valli .... Rusty Millio
John Ventimiglia .... Artie Bucco
Maureen Van Zandt .... Gabriella Dante
Steven Van Zandt .... Silvio Dante

CREW

Phil Abraham .... Director of Photography
Jack Bender .... Director
Peter Bogdanovich .... Director (also actor)
Henry Bronchtein .... Director
Peter Bucossi .... Stunt coordinator
Steve Buscemi .... Director (also actor)
Mitchell Burgess .... Writer
Martin Bruestle .... Producer
Allen Coulter .... Director
David Chase .... Creator, Executive Producer
Robin Green .... Writer
Sheila Jaffe .... Casting Director
Todd A. Kessler .... Writer
Ilene Landress .... Executive Producer
Jason Minter .... Location Manager
Mathew Price .... Production Sound Mixer
Juliet Polcsa .... Costume Designer
Alan Taylor .... Director
Georgianne Walken .... Casting Director
Matthew Weiner .... Writer
Terence Winter .... Executive Producer

Woke Up
This
Morning

Introduction

THIS ALMOST NEVER HAPPENED.

This book grew out of our podcast, *Talking Sopranos,* which started airing in April of 2020 and quickly found a great following of wonderful, dedicated fans. They've been enormously supportive of us from day one—actually, from before day one.

Because if it weren't for them, we wouldn't be here now.

The Sopranos has been off the air for nearly fifteen years now, but the fascination with the show has never ebbed. In fact, there seem to be more people watching it now than when it originally aired. The support of the fans, both those who are watching it again and those who are discovering it for the first time, has been fantastic.

We started noticing it around the time we were celebrating the twentieth anniversary of the show's premiere, early in 2019. Michael was working on a pilot in New York that March and shooting a scene in Central Park when a young man, maybe all of twenty years old, walking through the park with his father, politely approached him. He said they were from Scotland, visiting the city for the first time, and were so excited to see a cast member from their favorite show. Suddenly, the young man rolled up his pant leg—and revealed a tattoo of Michael's face on his calf! He explained that he had discovered the show in the past year and it had quickly become a huge part of his life, to the point where he felt the need to have one of the show's main characters permanently etched into his flesh. It gave us both pause: what the heck was going on out there?

It was about that time we both entered the wide, wild wilderness of social media via Instagram and Facebook. Before long, it became evident to us that *The Sopranos* had found an entire new flock of passionate followers. We found tons of fan pages, meme pages, *Sopranos* fashion pages, *Sopranos* food pages, *Sopranos* music pages—you name it. It was obvious that social media was the domain of the young—and these teens, twentysomethings, and thirtysomethings were now streaming *The Sopranos* on their iPhones and Androids.

We'd known for a long time that we had legions of loyal fans—most of them close to our own age, give or take a decade or two—but the fact that we were being taken up by a whole new demographic gave us an idea. Not many shows have the ability to be passed down to a younger generation that embraces it as wholeheartedly as their parents did. And so we wondered, what if we tried to meet these newfound devotees on their own turf—the podcast?

The two of us had worked together on a ton of projects, both *Sopranos*-related and otherwise. We did a movie called *Nicky Deuce,* based on a book by Steve; the movie *The Hungry Ghosts,* written and directed by Michael, which Steve starred in; and a number of other films.

We also did a stage show, along with Vinny Pastore—you know him as Big Pussy—called *Conversations with the Sopranos,* which we toured around the country and as far away as Australia. And we're very close friends in real life—when one of us gets to go on vacation, the other's the first one to get a call to come along and bring the family.

So when the idea came up to do a podcast in which two buddies would sit down and chat, rewatch all eighty-six episodes of *The Sopranos,* and bring on all the other cast members, directors, writers, everybody—from the sound guy to series creator David Chase—it seemed like a natural. It was announced, we did a whirlwind press tour, and were ready to go into the studio to record together starting March 25.

And then COVID hit.

On March 13, the day a national emergency was declared—the day the world stopped turning for all of us—Michael was stuck in California, sick as a dog. Later, we realized he and his wife probably had come down with COVID. Steve was holed up with his family in his apartment in New York, depressed as hell. The thought of doing the podcast remotely never occurred to us—we didn't even know it was possible. None of us had even heard of Zoom yet.

And besides, to be perfectly honest, we didn't think we should do it anymore, either. We thought doing a podcast in the midst of all this tragedy was totally tone-deaf. After all, who could possibly want to hear us talk about a TV show, with all the suffering that was going on in the world?

But then we started hearing from the fans, both the older generation who'd watched the show back in the day and the legion of new young followers. We're stuck at home, they told us. We're sheltering in place, like we're supposed to. We're binge-watching *The Sopranos*. We're waiting for the podcast. We want you to watch it with us.

Where the hell are you?

And so, reluctantly, we started talking to our producers about trying to do the podcast from our homes. We had a crash course in virtual programming, in creating home studios, in setting up our lights and mikes and backgrounds. We didn't even have time to talk about what the hell we were going to do once the tape started rolling. On March 30, we just jumped into the deep end and recorded our first show.

We were both depressed, and worried as hell. We had a mutual friend who passed away just before we went to air. But here's what Steve said on that first podcast:

"If we could give you a moment of joy, I guess that's what we're doing. I'm in the house twenty-three hours a day. I know people have it a lot worse than I do. Listen, we'll do it for the fans. We'll do it for ourselves. We'll see what happens."

And here's what happened: As soon as that first episode aired, we heard from a ton of people, saying they wanted more. They told us that listening to the podcast buoyed their spirits, and hearing their kind words buoyed ours. More than they'll ever know.

Our depressions started to lift. We did another episode, and another, and soon all the old gang started showing up. Lorraine Bracco, Edie Falco, Vinny Pastore, John Ventimiglia, everybody. It was like homecoming week, every week. Pretty soon, we got to the point where we couldn't wait to do the next episode. Being with the *Sopranos* gang always had a kind of Rat Pack feel to it—whenever we got into the studio or met on location, it was always just like hanging out with all your old friends on the corner. And this podcast brought that all back to us. It was like no time had passed at all. Only this time, we got to bring all our fans along for the ride.

So once a week, we all got to forget about our troubles for an hour or two. In the time of COVID, that meant everything to us.

In the process, we got to revisit the greatest TV show ever, and, in doing so, realize what made it so great. In rewatching the series all these years later, we came to an appreciation and understanding of how unique a moment in time this series represented. What an unparalleled gathering of talent. And how it changed the world of television forever. There isn't a dramatic series anywhere, on network or cable, that doesn't owe something to *The Sopranos*.

And so what you're about to read sprang from that podcast, and, more directly, from the renewed passion for the series that we first encountered when that young man rolled his pants leg up in Central Park and showed Michael a tattoo of his own face. Some of this is drawn from conversations we had on the podcast; a lot of it stems from conversations we had once the cameras and microphones were turned off. On the podcast, we went episode by episode; we won't do that here, but we will delve deep into the key moments, the best scenes, the astounding acting, and the brave eyes-wide-open look at the moral choices we all have to make, as embodied by Tony and Carmela and Christopher and Adriana and good old Bobby Bacala. We'll rediscover the incredible writing, the unparalleled direction, the stunning cinematography, the side-splitting humor, the brilliant use of music—all the things that went into the making of *The Sopranos*. These are the inside stories, the behind-the-scenes tales, the how'd-they-do-that insider info, that only the folks who created it and lived it can tell.

And we decided not to hold anything back—because, after more than twenty years, we figured, what the fuck? Let's just let it all out.

And so we did.

In one sense we did this for selfish reasons: It has been a wonderful gift to be given the chance to go back and visit with all our old friends. And we had a ball watching the shows. They not only stand the test of time; they've somehow grown better with age.

But mostly, we did it because you asked us to.

Happy to oblige.

—Michael Imperioli and Steve Schirripa
October 2021

ONE

Getting the Band Together

BY THE TIME IT WAS OVER, The Sopranos had garnered 112 Emmy nominations and 21 wins; it was nominated for Outstanding Drama Series over and over, and finally won in 2004, a first for cable television.

But let's begin at the beginning. Or, more precisely, a year before the beginning. When Steve and I sat down to do Talking Sopranos, *the first thing I realized was that I'd never really heard the full story of how Steve wound up on the show. Turns out, Steve wanted to know the same about me. It led to a discussion that we had with all of the old gang. And everybody's story was different. It's hard to believe, after all these years, how many twists and turns and odd coincidences went into creating the strange alchemy that was* The Sopranos. *What follows is a synthesis of those conversations, melded with the story-behind-the-story as told by the only two people who were always in the rooms where it happened: the casting directors, Georgianne Walken and Sheila Jaffe. —Michael*

WHAT THE HELL is "strange alchemy"? How do you meld a synthesis? Who says that? Forget that crap. Let's just tell the stories. —Steve

Steve: Take me back. It's 1997, you are an actor in New York. You're what, thirty-one years old? You get the call from your agent.

Michael: I really have to give credit to the casting directors, Sheila Jaffe and Georgianne Walken. They were champions and advocates for me for a lot of projects and they always had me in mind. We became friends, and so anything I'd be remotely right for, they'd bring me in. And they said, "There's this series casting for HBO. Come meet the director and the writer." There were no real series on HBO at the time; it was a very new thing. So I read the script, and I'm gonna be honest, I can't say I was blown away or it knocked my socks off. Partly because from the pilot script, it's not easy to get the tone completely. For one thing, it was very funny—I wasn't sure if it was a spoof. There was a movie on Showtime called *The Don's Analyst,* with Robert Loggia, which was terrible. It was a bad spoof. And another script was floating around for a movie that was in the works, *Analyze This.* They were all being made around the same time. So when I first read the pilot of *The Sopranos,* I wasn't sure if it was another spoof.

Steve: Where were you in your career?

Michael: I had done a lot of movies. Mostly independent movies. And theater. So I'm paying the rent. I had just done a big Hollywood movie the year before called *Last Man Standing,* and I had done a couple of leads in two independent movies. But you know, the idea of a series—you read one script and you sign on for maybe a hundred scripts. I had never done that. So when I read the script, I was kind of, "Do I want to do it? Do I not?"

Steve: Did you know David Chase? Or any of the other actors?

Michael: I didn't know David Chase, the creator and writer. But I did know some of the actors they were talking about, like Edie Falco, Tony Sirico, Vinny Pastore, and Lorraine Bracco, who I knew a bit from *Goodfellas.* Lorraine was the only star at this point. She was nominated for *Goodfellas.* Jim Gandolfini, I didn't know, but he had a good reputation.

So I went and auditioned for David. My character, Christopher Moltisanti—his name in the original pilot script was Dean Moltisanti, which never would have worked as well. Nothing would have worked except for what worked, you know what I mean? Nobody else would have worked. What it is, is what it should have been.

Steve: How long is this after you did *Goodfellas*?

Michael: That was maybe eight years before.

Steve: You were Spider in that movie. Not a huge role, but a very memorable role. Everybody remembers Spider.

Michael: In the business, everybody knew who I was. People on the street would recognize me.

Steve: What were they saying, "Hey, Spider, get me a drink"? Is that what they were doing?

Michael: Ha! No, thank God. That would have been horrible. I would have been miserable.

Steve: Before we move on—didn't something really strange happen after your big scene in *Goodfellas*?

Michael: So when I did the second scene in *Goodfellas*, when I get shot in the chest, I decided to do the stunt myself. They attached all these squibs to me, for where I got shot.

Steve: Explain squibs, for people who don't know.

Michael: They're little explosive devices, almost like a little weak firecracker. They're attached to you, and they puncture the clothes to make the bullet holes. They're remotely controlled, so the special effects guy can set them off as you're getting shot, and usually they have blood packs underneath that get exploded, and you react to them.

The shot required me to go flying back, hit the bar, hit the ground. They padded me up and we rehearsed it a little bit. I had a glass in my hand that I was bringing to the table and it was not a breakaway glass. When I hit the ground, the glass cut my fingers open pretty badly. Marty [Scorsese] yelled, "Cut! Don't move! Nobody move!" I'm on the ground and there was blood everywhere, and I knew I fucked my fingers up. I looked up and De Niro was looking down at me like, *Oh, shit.*

They rushed me to the hospital because I needed stitches in two fingers. It's Queens, and the production assistant drove me to the hospital; he brings me in, and the people in the hospital, they're like, "Code blue! Code blue! We've got an emergency!" They bring out a stretcher. They think I'm about to die because I have three bullet holes in my chest and I'm talking about my fingers, and saying that I'm in a movie—they think I'm delusional!

I keep trying to explain that I'm in a movie but they won't listen. They think I'm about to die. They bring me into the emergency room, they start cutting open stuff and they see all the squibs, and the wires and the blood packs. I said, "I told you. I cut my fingers. I'm in a movie with Robert De Niro!" They're like, "Okay." They put some tape on my fingers and said, "Go wait in the corner." I had to wait four hours to get stitches.

Then I went back and did another take. I think they used the first take. Here's the significance of that—when you're made into the Mafia, they cut your finger. They take your blood and then they burn it on [the picture of] a saint. This was me being made into movies, specifically gangster movies. Cutting my finger in the presence of the boss and the capo, Scorsese and De Niro, that was my initiation, right? There's something mystical to that, no?

Steve: Absolutely. So after *Goodfellas,* you had to go back to waiting tables, right?

Michael: Yeah. I wasn't quite making a living. What was I, twenty-three then? I would go back and forth. I'd go off and do a movie, I'd go off to do a play, quit my restaurant job, come back. It was back and forth 'til I was about twenty-five, and then I was pretty much paying the bills.

Steve: So anyway—you read for David Chase. What was that like?

Michael: I worked really hard on the scenes. I did the scene when Christopher kills "Email" Kolar. I read the scene with Pussy when we're trying to throw the body in the dumpster.

Now, David has a poker face. You can't really read him. He doesn't give a lot away. I thought I was kind of boring him because I really wasn't getting much of a reaction. And he would give me direction—I would do the scene and he said, "Can you do it a little more angry?" Or "A little less?" And when you're auditioning, when people give you direction, sometimes you think as an actor, because you're so insecure, you're not getting it, you're not doing it right. So I'm thinking, "This is not going too well," but, I'm acting my ass off, trying really hard, because I liked the character a lot. And finally he said, "Thanks a lot," and that was it. And I walked out of the room, convinced that I blew it, convinced that I bored him to tears and that I wasn't going to get it.

Steve: I'd rather have that poker face than some director, which we've all had: "That was terrific! You're fantastic! Oh my God!" Then you get home, you know, and your agent calls, "Oh, they loved you!" The minute that your agent tells you they loved you, you're dead. You're dead. "They loved you! (You didn't get the job.)" Anyway, so you go home, you get the callback.

Michael: I get the call that they want to fly me to L.A. to test for the network, which is a big deal. 'Cause they fly you first-class, they put you up in a nice hotel, and then you're going to go do the audition scenes in a screening room in front of a dozen executives for HBO. I was the only one testing for Christopher, or Dean at the time. Lorraine, who was reading for Melfi, was there.

Steve: She's an Academy Award nominee—and they made her read?

Michael: Yes. Then there were three guys reading for Tony Soprano—James Gandolfini; Michael Rispoli, who goes on to play Jackie Aprile; and one other guy who I thought looked familiar, but I couldn't place his face. And then Sheila Jaffe, the casting director, came up to me and whispered, "That's Steven Van Zandt"—from the E Street Band—but he was wearing the Silvio wig. No bandana.

Steve: So Michael Rispoli, James Gandolfini, Little Stevie Van Zandt, they all could have been Tony Soprano.

Michael: Yeah, and I'll be honest, I really thought Michael was gonna get it. Michael is an excellent actor and I was very familiar with his work. I thought he was about to take off. But obviously, they were all great actors, very talented, and they all wound up on the show.

Steve: In general, do you think you're a good auditioner, bad auditioner, or what?

Michael: I like auditioning for the most part. I used to like it a lot more. I like the stakes and the pressure of it.

Steve: Now, you won an Emmy—you were nominated five times, you won once. And Golden Globe, were you nominated?

Michael: Twice, yes. I lost the Golden Globe to William Shatner and Donald Sutherland. Donald Sutherland, I could swallow. But William Shatner? That was too much.

So how about you, Steve? What was your story?

Steve: I came on the second episode of the second season. I auditioned in June 1999.

Michael: Did you like the show? Did you watch it a lot?

Steve: I didn't watch it a lot. I was in Vegas. I didn't watch that much TV. I knew it was popular. A friend of mine really liked it. When I told him that I was going to read for it he was all excited.

I came to New York for a wedding. This is in June of '99. And I had been working a little bit. But I had a full-time job as entertainment director at the Riviera Hotel.

Michael: But you had done some acting too at this point.

Steve: Yeah, I had an agent helping me out, and I had done some stuff. I did a *King of Queens,* I did a *Chicago Hope.* I did little bit parts. I played a doorman in *Fear and Loathing in Las Vegas.* When we threw Benicio del Toro and Johnny Depp out of the club, me and Benicio rolled around on the floor. I broke my watch. Then I had a little part in *Casino.* If you really slow it down, and turn the volume way up, you'll hear me yell, "Joey, look out look out!" That was my big claim to fame.

So for *The Sopranos,* I came into New York for the wedding, like I said. It was a total accident. This is a Friday afternoon. So the wedding's the next day. They faxed me the sides. Which, for those who don't know, those are the parts of the script that you're going to read. They just give you those pages.

I went up to read for the role of Skip Lipari, the FBI agent. I go up there, Georgianne Walken's alone in the office. I read the Skip Lipari stuff. She goes, "Don't be nervous. You're nervous. What are you worried about? It's just me and you." Which relaxed me. I mean, I was green, man.

Michael: When you're starting out, nerves are a big thing to conquer, you know?

Steve: Tell me about it! And I gotta tell you I'm forever indebted to Georgianne. Because she calmed me down. So I read, and she said, "I don't see you as an FBI agent. We have this other part, we have someone in mind for it, but read it." And it was for the role of Bobby Bacala. It was the scene in the doctor's office with Dominic. So I read it. She said, "That's not bad."

So I go back to Las Vegas, and they call me. They said, "We want you to read for David." I wasn't going to do it. I didn't want to spend the money. Hotel, airfare, all that. My wife says, "Listen, you're only happy when you're doing this stuff." So I went back to New York. I went up to Silvercup Studios, I read for David Chase, the same doctor's office scene. There were fifteen people there. The only words David Chase said to me in the audition were, "That was really good." That was it. I said, "Thank you for seeing me," and I walked out the door. And the next morning Georgianne called me. She said, "I know I'm supposed to talk to your agent, but I gotta tell you, you beat out over a hundred people. You worked so hard." And that was it.

That was a good phone call. A good call. These moments in life, you know? You look back and you think, What if I zigged when I should have zagged? What if I didn't go to that wedding? Everything would have turned out different.

Michael: Tell me about it. You know I almost didn't take the part.

Steve: You're kidding me. Really?

Michael: Right before we shot the pilot, I also at the same time auditioned for Woody Allen. I'd always wanted to work with Woody Allen, and I finally got an audition with him. It was very nice. It was for a movie, one of his not-so-great movies that probably nobody saw, called *Celebrity*.

Steve: I was in *Wonder Wheel*. Not his best movie.

Michael: Well, *Celebrity* starred Leonardo DiCaprio. I'd already worked with Leo on *Basketball Diaries* and then my role would be to play one of his posse, and that sounded great. And I get the part! And now my agent's got to work it out.

Steve: The money for *Sopranos* was pretty good, I guess.

Michael: Yes, and the Woody Allen, not so good.

Steve: Woody Allen pays the bare minimum.

Michael: The part in the Woody Allen movie is not a big part, but it's a number of days. What agents do when you have two jobs at the same time, they try to work it out with the producers of both jobs. *Sopranos* was in what they call "first position," that the other job has to work around. It worked out for everything—except for one day. There was one day where both productions needed me on set. My agents say, "You got to make a choice. You want to do the pilot or you want to work with Woody Allen?" So you know which way I went. Sam Rockwell wound up doing the part I was offered in the Woody Allen film.

Steve: Boy. You made the right decision there.

Michael: Amen to that, brother.

WHEN IT *comes to how Steve and I—and all the other actors—got to be part of* The Sopranos, *what most people don't know is that it all starts with a little independent movie that Steve Buscemi wrote, directed, and starred in a year earlier, called* Trees Lounge. *I was lucky enough to have a small role in that movie, thanks to the two women we've been talking about—two women who were then pretty new to the casting business: Sheila Jaffe, who used to manage a café that I hung out at, and Georgianne Walken, who happens to be Christopher Walken's wife. They go on to become two of the most well-respected and sought-after casting agents in the business. Here's the story behind that story. —Michael*

Michael: How did you two get started?

Georgianne: I have to be honest. I had turned forty and I wanted to do something with the rest of my life other than being Mrs. Christopher Walken. I had the opportunity to meet these wonderful producers in Israel. They called me out of the blue. I called Sheila instantly. Sheila knew everybody because she worked at the café, Café Central. Everybody came into that establishment.

Sheila: I was the hostess, and then I became the manager of Café Central. The restaurant was very, very actor-friendly. It was a big actor hangout on the Upper West Side. Bruce Willis was the bartender before he was acting. He was acting, but Off-Broadway. Everybody went there, from Robert De Niro, to Robert Duvall, to Sean Penn, to Matt Dillon, to Cher—it was just unbelievable.

I met Georgianne at the restaurant. She came to me and she said, "Somebody asked me to do a movie in Israel, do you want to do it?" I was like, "I don't know how to do that. I have no idea how to do casting." She said, "Well, it can't be that hard. We'll figure it out."

Michael: And after that you started casting more movies, and eventually you start working with Steve Buscemi on *Trees Lounge*. What were you looking for when you cast that movie?

Sheila: The mandate was always, "Get me great faces, get me real people." Easier said than done, because sometimes real people freeze up in front of a camera, but there are actors out there with those faces, so we did gravitate to those faces.

Georgianne: It's like reverting back to really the old days where people looked like people. Where they weren't Californianized, you know what I mean? The people who moved to California became very beautiful because they were beautiful to start out with, and they had more beautiful kids. But I would pick up people on the subway if I had to. I would say, "Have you ever acted in a movie?" I'd be sitting there going to work, and I'd get into a chat with them. We would look for that kind of authenticity. I think that's what makes indie movies work. Authentic people.

Sheila: When Georgianne and I started the casting business, most of the directors we got to work with, like Steve Buscemi and Alex Rockwell, they were very influenced by John Cassavetes, so that shaped us a lot. That shaped our sensibility and our taste because that was their taste, so that's what we had to find for them. The John Cassavetes–type actors.

Michael: Like Ben Gazzara and Peter Falk, and Gena Rowlands, who were in a number of his movies. Gena Rowlands was also John Cassavetes's wife.

Sheila: I love those guys. Authentic people. Like, we were in love with Sam Rockwell. When we started casting, we called him into everything. Our taste was like that.

Michael: And *Trees Lounge* is what leads to *The Sopranos*.

Sheila: David had seen *Trees Lounge*. He said, "I want those girls that cast *Trees Lounge*," because it was so authentic and it was so good. All those characters, so many of them wound up being in *The Sopranos*.

David was based in L.A. I had gone to L.A. to do a movie called *Slums of Beverly Hills*. Georgianne did the New York end of it. While I was there doing that, I got a call from Susie Fitzgerald.

Michael: From HBO.

Sheila: She wanted to send me the script. I read it, and I thought it was really good. At that time, it was Tommy Soprano! It wasn't Tony, it was Tommy.

Michael: So he hired you as the casting directors, even though you'd never done television.

Sheila: We didn't know anything. We'd never done television. We didn't know what that would be like. The actors that we were approaching were also indie actors, movie actors, and they didn't really understand what television was either. People didn't want to do it. At that time, it was actually a bad thing, if you were a film actor, to be known now as a TV actor. It was a negative.

Michael: Very separate worlds in a lot of ways. Things have changed.

Sheila: Oh, my God, now everybody's on television.

Michael: But David did that because he wanted to bring a cinema-like quality to television. That's why he brought you guys in, because he saw how specific the casting was, how authentic, how New York it was. And real.

Sheila: Yes. He also liked my accent. [*laughs*] When I read Melfi and I had to say what kind of birds they were, from my Bronx roots, I didn't say "seagulls," I said, "What were they, Siegels?" He liked that, because I didn't say sea-gulls, it was Siegels.

Steve: So what was it like working for David in those early days? From our perspective he was totally poker-faced. You read for him, he said thank you, you left. Boom. No chitchat, no bullshit. What was it like once the door closed behind us?

Georgianne: David was extremely thoughtful. This was something that was ingrained in his DNA. The miracle about David is that he remembered everything about his childhood. Everything. He transferred it into *The Sopranos*. He remembered the names of streets. He remembered stores. He remembered street corners where things would go on. The man has a remarkable memory. But he's not an emotional guy. He lets you know what he wants, and then he walks away. He'd done major TV before, you know, he was an executive on *I'll Fly Away,* and *Northern Exposure,* and he did *Rockford Files,* all that. He knew the game. He knew what he was about and how he wanted to go about it. David just knows what he wants. He knows when he sees what he wants.

Sheila: He wanted to see it, one shot, thank you very much. Either you're going to nail it or you're not. There's different directors; some directors like to work with people, to see exactly what's in their mind. David, very rarely did he give a note. Sometimes during the pilot, I would say, "Can they do it again?" He would never initiate that they should do it again, or if he did, it was rare. I also think he was always nervous that we wouldn't find the right person.

Steve: When the actors leave, when the door would close on the way out, would he ever immediately say, "That was it"?

Georgianne: No, the only time he ever said that to me was about Nancy Marchand. It was one of those days. Nancy had emphysema, and she had to walk up two flights of stairs to the room. Her agent told me she would not read, but I brought her in anyway. She sat down, and the camera was sitting there. She started having a cordial conversation, and then a couple of minutes later she said, "Okay, what scenes are we reading?" Then she won David's heart. She *was* Livia. No ifs, ands, or buts about it. The fact that she had played all these incredibly erudite women just got washed away.

YOU'D THINK *finding the right Tony Soprano would be the hardest part of the process, but David Chase—who we'll talk to at length a little later— spoke about the enormous challenge of casting Livia. —Michael*

David: The hardest to find what I wanted was Livia. It was agony. I don't know how many actresses we saw and they all did this crazy Italian mama thing. Nancy Marchand came into the office, I looked at her and I said, "My God, that's my mother. She's channeling my mother." It was unbelievable. I was a happy guy. The cadence, the attitude, oh, Jesus God, and all my family went nuts when they saw her.

Michael: They recognized her right away?

David: Right away. "That's Aunt Norma!" That was just all her. At one point, she said, "I trust that this creature that I'm playing is deceased."

NANCY MARCHAND *was already a legend—an accomplished star of the Broadway stage, she'd already won four Emmys for her role on* Lou Grant—*so it's no surprise that she was able to blow David Chase out of the water immediately at her audition.*

But we all remembered that the rest of the casting didn't go that way. At all. —Michael

Michael: I remember the auditions at HBO. I remember that waiting room, being with all the other actors.

Sheila: That was the first TV show I had ever done, so I was not prepared for what it really is. Bringing everybody in at once. It makes not only the actors nervous, it made me nervous. Everybody's there at the same time looking at each other, and most of them know each other, and they're all reading for the same part.

Michael: And then we came in and read in front of all the executives. Chris Albrecht, Carolyn Strauss, Susie Fitzgerald, all the HBO bigwigs.

Sheila: Yes. Right next door to that waiting area was that room that's like a theater. It's like a box theater, a black box. All the execs sit on movie theater chairs, along with David, and whatever writers—there was a guy that was involved at the very beginning of *The Sopranos,* Frank Renzulli. Everybody was there. And I read with the actors. It's very nerve-racking. You hope as the casting director you're doing a good job; you want the actors to give David and the executives the best they can.

Michael: How did Jim Gandolfini become Tony Soprano?

Sheila: That begins with a thing at Sundance. The writer/director was a woman named Melissa Painter who knew Jim. She had this script, called *Wildflower* or something. She got accepted to the Sundance Lab to do a workshop on it to flesh out the script, and she needed to cast the two roles. The thrust of the story was really the girl, and she had a father that she had this relationship with.

We had to find a girl, and she wanted her face to be just very unique. Clea DuVall was working in a coffee shop on Sunset Boulevard that I used to get coffee from, and it was totally the face that Melissa wanted. She was so young—maybe eighteen or nineteen. I brought her in, and Melissa fell in love. Then we had to cast the father. And Melissa said, "I have a friend, and I really like him. I don't know—what do you think about Jim Gandolfini?"

We had only seen Jim Gandolfini play heavies, and this father was this hippie who was very different, but I thought he was a good actor. I'd seen him in *A Streetcar Named Desire* with Aida [Turturro]. I always thought he was really good, interesting, but I had never seen him do this kind of a thing. But it was a lab and it was like, "Why not?" He did it, and it was great.

So I knew this other side of him that I don't think the general public had seen yet, which made me know he was capable of so much, because he was a really great guy. It was a great role for him.

I saw more humor, and I saw a kindness, and I saw him being a caring father, a family man. When you think about *The Sopranos* and all this stuff that goes with it, we already knew he could do the tough stuff, but we hadn't seen him have all these other layers. But at Sundance, he played a loving father who had trouble with his daughter.

Steve: So that's how you guys get turned on to Jim. Then what happens?

Georgianne: Primarily, Sheila and I were casting out of New York City. At the same time, David would go back to L.A. This was such a movable feast. Wherever we could grab the actors, and wherever I had David or Sheila had David, is where we did it. There was a rental audition room on Seventy-Second Street, with a table and a couple of chairs, and I had the camera. Jim lived in New York. When he walked into that Seventy-Second Street upstairs room, he sat down; David and he chatted back and forth and he fessed up right there and then—he said, "I'm not ready to read this for you. This material is much more complicated than I thought it was going to be." He asked David if he could come back. Then by the time he's ready to come back, David's in L.A.

Sheila: They flew him to L.A. It was just me, David, and Jim at David's house, in the garage. David ran the camera and I read. It was the Melfi scene when he told her about the ducks.

Steve: Same deal—David doesn't say anything.

Sheila: It was just, "Thank you, safe trip. Thanks for coming in." Nobody says anything. David didn't say, "You're the guy," nothing. We have to run it past everybody anyhow. But we go up to David's house, and we put the tapes in—it was VHS tapes, that's how long ago it was—and we watched it and we both got really excited. He looks at me and says, "Is he the guy?" I said, "He's the guy."

David remembers it the same way. —Steve

Steve: Did you float big names for Tony? Because when the show started, really the only person that the audience knew was Lorraine Bracco.

David: If that had been a network show, which it came close to being, they would have wanted to put in big names. At HBO, maybe there was some talk about it. Not much.

Michael: Chazz Palminteri was one of the names?

David: Yes. There was a talk about that but very briefly. They were really open. I remembered Jim from *Get Shorty* but vaguely. I wasn't aware of the rest of his work. He came in to read, and he was doing fine, and halfway through he left. He was going to come back that Friday. I talked to his agent. "He'll be there on Friday." Friday came and I swear this is what I heard, that his mother had died. But his mother had been dead for years. He wasn't there on Friday.

Finally, I came back to California again, he came to my house in my garage, we taped the audition. I heard he was famous for saying, "This is shit, I can't do this." But once we saw that audition, it was the whole thing, obviously, there was no question.

SO AS *time went by, we got a chance to talk with just about everybody on the show, and we wanted to hear their "origin stories" as well. Can you imagine* The Sopranos *with Lorraine Bracco as Carmela, instead of Edie Falco? Turns out that very easily could have happened. Lorraine famously played the mob wife in Martin Scorsese's* Goodfellas, *one of the iconic predecessors to* The Sopranos, *so she was an obvious choice for Carmela. That's what David, along with the casting directors, was interested in her for. And it* almost *went that way.* —Michael

Michael: Did you ever actually audition for Carmela?

Lorraine: Here's what happened. Sheila Jaffe sends me the script, it's a Mafia thing. I said, "Listen, I have refused every Mafia script for the last ten years. I don't want to do that." Sheila begged me. "Please, please, read the script. Please, please, just meet him. David just wants to meet you." "No, no, no, no, no." Finally, she goes, "Listen, do I have to get on my knees and beg you to read this stupid script?" I said, "I'll read it, okay." I read it and I go, "Whoa, wait a minute. This is a great script." But I told my agents, "I don't want to play Carmela." They're pulling out their hair. "What do you mean?" I said, "I don't want to do it. I want to play Dr. Melfi." I remember their words: "The title is *The Sopranos,* not *Dr. Melfi.*" They begged me to go and meet him, but they said, "Don't tell him that you want to play Melfi."

So Chris Albrecht [head of HBO] brings Jimmy, me, and David to L.A. The three of us went. I don't know if it was really an audition, but Chris Albrecht just wanted to see us in person. I went in to read with Jimmy. That's when I threw the monkey wrench at David. I said, "I've played Carmela. I'm going to have a hard time doing that again in a different way or a better way. I'm a very different woman now. I want to play Dr. Melfi."

Steve: So you never read for Carmela.

Lorraine: No, I only read for Melfi. I said, "I want Melfi or nothing else." One of my big reasons with David was, "I've got to tell you. You never see an educated Italian woman. I would like to do that. I want to be that woman." We talked about being in therapy, talked about me going on meds. We had a lot in common for that. I convinced them.

Steve: We talked about when people were knocking the stereotypical Italian stuff in *The Sopranos*, we say, here is an Italian-American that's smart and educated. That was a really big thing.

Lorraine: I think David understood that, coming from a woman, a mother, an actress. I said, "We are more than just making pasta in the kitchen. Here is a perfect role." There's the other thing that I love about Melfi and Tony, was that it's a very intimate relationship. It's very personal. He has to trust her. I think he would trust somebody that's from the neighborhood.

So with Lorraine out of the picture for Carmela, that left the role open. Edie Falco was a perfect choice in everybody's mind. Except for Edie Falco's. —Steve

Steve: I've known you for quite a while, but I didn't know you back then, when you started on the show, of course. Did you always want to be an actress?

Edie: When I was a kid my mother used to do community theater. She would have her job during the day and at night, she'd go to her little rehearsals and she had all her actor friends. It was all unbelievably sweet. She took it very seriously, she worked her ass off, she was always running lines on her little tape cassette. I would go with her to all of these rehearsals, all these performances.

I just thought it was the coolest thing going. I was always getting crushes on these actors and I would flirt with them during rehearsal. It was such an alive, exciting time for me as a kid. I guess I always assumed I would probably do that too, but the way my mom did it. You get a job and at night you do your theater and then you do your performances on the weekends.

I guess that's what I thought, but it never occurred to me to do it for a living. I just thought, "Who the hell does that?" I don't know how any of this happened. It was not part of a larger plan at all, no.

Michael: But then you did start acting, of course. How did that lead to *The Sopranos*?

Edie: I was doing *Oz* at the time, which I loved. It was the beginning of my love affair with series television. It was irregular, a couple of days and episodes here and there, but I was doing that. I was just about functioning financially and in the midst of all that I get this call to audition for something called *Sopranos,* which I had heard about. I thought it was about singers. It never occurred to me it was something I would be called for. My agent said, "The audition is tomorrow."

I had to show up at the Mayflower Hotel and I've read the script and thought, "Well, yes, I know exactly who this woman is and I'll never get it." Because it's Italian-American and I thought it's going to be Annabella Sciorra or Marisa Tomei or one of the women who were getting all the parts that I thought I wanted at the time. I heard they were going to cast Cathy Moriarty as Carmela. I went to the Mayflower Hotel and David was there. Johnny V [John Ventimiglia] was reading the part of Tony. Georgianne was there. Chris Albrecht was there.

I went in, I read the parts. I was just not thinking much about it. Then David asked me to read a scene that I hadn't looked at and I was like, "Yes. Whatever." I didn't know who any of these people were or who they would come to be to me many years later. Then I left and didn't really think about it. There's something very empowering about feeling sure that you're not going to get the job.

I tend to bring my best self to those auditions because the caring piece is gone. You figure, "Oh, I'll just have fun." Then I got the call the next day that I got the part. It was beyond. It all happened very quickly.

SHEILA AND *Georgianne filled us in on the story behind the story of how Edie wound up with that role. —Steve*

Sheila: Everybody thought we were going to cast Cathy Moriarty. Because anybody who saw *Raging Bull* was like, "Cathy would be good. She's got a great accent, she'd go good with Jim." At the time, Edie wasn't a thought because she was on *Oz*. In our mind, she wasn't available.

Michael: So who suggested Edie?

Sheila: Cathy and Jim read, and there was a discussion afterward. Carolyn Strauss, who ran HBO with Chris Albrecht, said, "What about Edie Falco? Did you check on her?" I said, "I don't think she's available because she's on *Oz*." Carolyn said, "No, we didn't make her a series regular. She's recurring." A series regular, you're attached to the show, the show owns you. When you're recurring, they can only use you if you're available for the days they need you. They have no claim on you. So then I thought, "Well, she's great."

Michael: And one of the wonderful things about Edie in that role was that Carmela is so conflicted, and Edie managed to show that conflict, sometimes without saying a word.

Georgianne: Her great talent and ability is—I want to use the word "stoic," and I'm not sure that's the right word to use, but she is. This is a woman who in real life would carry her sick dog around—a dog that was very large, I might add. I watched her come from the parking lot one day and I thought, "She's carrying the dog, what's wrong?" It was a big dog. She's got it grasped in her arms, and she said, "He's not feeling well." I thought, "Oh, my God, this is an amazing woman." It's her character. It's her inner self. She's still like that. She hasn't changed. It's a quality that Edie has. Great strength and great vulnerability simultaneously, which shows in her face. She doesn't have to do a lot.

ONE THING *you might notice: Just about everybody in this chapter has a name ending in a vowel. Because just about every actor on the show was Italian—not everybody, of course, but pretty close. There's a reason for that.*

Georgianne: They had to be Italian. Pretty much. David insisted on it. It's not to exclude everybody else, it was the fact that it was this subject matter. You can't provide this subject matter with an Irish-American. It just doesn't work. The thing is that when he says, "You got to be Italian," I looked at him and I went, "Well, we can count on all four hands here how many Italian actors there are." As the show progressed, I started asking everybody about their families, about anybody who was interested. I drove everybody nuts, because I was running out of individuals.

I brought in Patty McCormack to play Adriana's mother. Patty's last name was Russo when she was a kid. She was the *Bad Seed* girl, from when she was a little kid. The first thing David said to me— "She's not Italian." I said, "Yes, she is. She's from New York. She's Italian. Honest to God, cross my heart, hope to die."

I SPENT *five years on a TV show called* The Secret Life of the American Teenager, *and I can tell you, of all the roles in television, teenagers are maybe the hardest to cast. You gotta not only find some kid who can do the part, and not be self-conscious and all that, but kids who have the discipline to do the hard work and balance everything else in a teenager's life, which, as a dad of two girls who used to be teenagers, I can tell you is a whole lot to deal with.*

Fortunately Sheila and Georgianne struck gold twice—even though they were among the very few actors who violated the "Italians Only" rule: Robert Iler, who did an amazing job playing A. J., and Jamie-Lynn Sigler, who absolutely owned the role of Meadow. We asked them about their auditions. —Steve

Robert Iler: After the audition, my mom was pissed when we left, because it was a roomful of a hundred Italian kids, and they all had the slicked-back hair, leather jacket, and they were trying to be like *The Sopranos.* Little Italian mob guys. And I was like, two hundred pounds with freckles, as Irish as can be. I always remember that every time I said "fuck" in the audition, David laughed. I would go do it, come back, do it. He laughed, he laughed, and then finally they said, "Yes, you got the role."

Steve: Did they tell you right there in the room?

Robert: No, I was actually at school, and my mom called. When we found out I got *Sopranos,* my family was going, "This is it. You're going to be famous, you're going to be on a TV show. It's going to be the biggest thing ever, Robert." Then, when we went and shot the pilot, I said that and Tony Sirico said, "No, that's not how this works. We shoot these pilots all the time. We're never going to see each other again." I had to go back and tell my family, "No, this isn't it. This isn't the thing." They were all bummed and everything. Then, the billboard came in Times Square.

GEORGIANNE WALKEN *told us more about that story. —Steve*

Georgianne: How could you not hire a kid that says, "Fuck it," in the casting room, unannounced?

Steve: He wasn't reading the script?

Georgianne: No, I don't think it was in the script. I don't think we would have put that in for a kid. How old was he when we cast him, ten, eleven? Again, I'm talking here a natural. Robert was Robert. He wasn't an actor-actor. He wasn't trying to be a child star. He just was going on auditions and getting jobs periodically. I just do regular kids. That was what was so important, that these kids not be—I was going to say not be stage kids, but that's not a nice thing to say. I didn't want anybody cute or adorable. I didn't want anybody you want to go pinch their cheek.

ALTHOUGH IT'S *hard to say that Jamie-Lynn Sigler wasn't adorable. But she was a lot more than that. —Michael*

Steve: Let me ask you, Jamie, how'd you get the gig?

Jamie-Lynn Sigler: I was sixteen years old. I had strictly only ever done musical theater. I'd maybe audition a couple of times here and there. I had a very small agent, a very small manager. I used to get most of my auditions from *Backstage* because it was just for Broadway and touring-type stuff. It was the summer when I was sixteen and I was going to go to sleepaway camp. I was going to try to be like all my friends. Right before I left, I got a call about a sixteen-year-old Italian-looking girl for a show called *The Sopranos*. It was the only information I got. Then the sides were Meadow arguing with Carmela about wanting to go on a ski trip with Hunter.

So I figured because of the title, *The Sopranos,* maybe it was a musical, and I figured I could pass for Italian, so I went in. My first audition was just with Georgianne, who is the warmest, loveliest person and makes everyone feel so comfortable. It was something I was very familiar with—fighting with my mother about wanting to do things that she wasn't going to let me do.

Then I got home, and this was the time with no cell phones, so I had a message on my answering machine from my manager saying, "They want you to come back tomorrow." I went back the next day and David was in the room. I read the same thing and then I asked, "Do you need me to sing?" And he said, "Why?" I said, "Oh, never mind."

Michael: But eventually you did sing?

Jamie-Lynn: I did. They wrote it in the show later, I guess for me. Then I had another callback two days later with the producers and at that point, there was a bunch of Meadows and A. J.s.

Steve: You had to audition three times?

Jamie-Lynn: Then a screen test. The fourth time was a screen test. It was down to two girls. It was now the scene again, the same scene of fighting with Carmela, and the other one was where she talks to Tony about his ancestors' building, the church. Johnny V read Tony Soprano with me.

They said that they had apprehension of how tan I was. For the week before my audition, I stayed out of the sun. I wore long sleeves, in the dead of August, to that HBO building in the city. It was very intimidating because again, I'm sixteen years old, I had really never auditioned for TV or film before, and this was all very scary and new.

HERE'S ONE *of the great untold stories of the casting of* The Sopranos. *The role of Hesh, who becomes something of a rabbi figure to Tony Soprano, almost went to a man best known for two things: arguing with his wife and comedy partner, Anne Meara, on* The Ed Sullivan Show *in the sixties, and screaming at his son George Costanza on* Seinfeld. —*Michael*

Sheila: This is a little-known thing about the role of Hesh, that Georgianne and I know. It was a Friday. You guys were going to shoot the pilot on Monday. They were trying to call Georgianne. I was in L. A., she was in Connecticut. She wasn't around, it was a weekend. They reached me in L.A. saying—can I say this?

Georgianne: Yes, you can. Absolutely.

Sheila: Jerry Stiller was Hesh.

Georgianne: Jerry Stiller was a David choice. Jerry Stiller and Stevie Van Zandt specifically were requested by David Chase.

Georgianne: I had gone home already. It was Friday. Somehow, HBO heard that Jerry took a commercial instead of the show.

Steve: You have two days to come up with a new Hesh, right? He was due on set that Monday?

Sheila: It was so scary. Just out of sheer—I don't know, luck, fate, purpose, destiny, whatever—I called Jerry Adler's daughter, Alisa Adler, who was an agent at Paradigm. I said, "Where is your father?" He happened to be in New York.

Georgianne: I didn't know anything about it until Monday when Sheila called me. She said, "Hey, did *we* just have a historical weekend!" She really pulled a rabbit out of the hat. It was amazing. Jerry Adler.

Steve: Yet when you look at it now, he's so perfect.

Sheila: Jerry Stiller, it would've been a whole different thing.

Steve: Absolutely. I can't even picture that.

Sheila: Jerry Stiller got a lot of money for that commercial.

Georgianne: It was a blessed accident.

Michael: And let's talk about casting Steven Van Zandt. That's got to be the strangest story of all. As we know, David Chase saw him give a speech inducting the Rascals into the Rock and Roll Hall of Fame and said he wanted that guy for the show. Originally, to play Tony Soprano. What did you think? Here's a guy who never acted before. What was your reaction?

Georgianne: My take on that was that anybody who could be in E Street Band, and do what they did all those years, could handle this without a problem.

WE ASKED *Steven Van Zandt what he thought when Georgianne and David brought up the idea of him acting in* The Sopranos. *—Steve*

Michael: I just watched that speech again, your Rock and Roll Hall of Fame speech. It was really amazing. I get what David was reacting to. But the question is, what did you think when he approached you about this? Did you almost not do it?

Steven Van Zandt: At first, I thought it was just only for music. I get a lot of requests for the music. So I was surprised that they wanted me to act. And I was very surprised at how good the script was. So, I was kind of in between. I really had nothing going on. And I thought, "Well, this must be destiny speaking."

Michael: You had left the E Street Band several years earlier.

Steven Van Zandt: Right. And really, I thought music was over for me at that point. Nobody wanted to sign me after "Sun City" had such success, because when you start bringing down governments, people get nervous.

Michael: You're talking about your creation of Artists United Against Apartheid, which really brought the situation in South Africa to a lot of people's attention. It really made a huge difference.

And God bless you for what you did.

Steven Van Zandt: Thanks. But I'm serious about that. It wasn't anything as dramatic as blackballing, but I was really kind of looked at as dangerous. So, I'm just walking my dog, and trying to figure out what to do with the rest of my life, and here comes David Chase, and I figured, "Could I picture doing something like this? Yeah, well, I kind of love the genre. I've read every book. I've seen every movie going back to the early thirties." You kind of grew up around it in Jersey. It just kind of felt like it was familiar to me, and I thought, "I'll give it a shot, man. Why not? Jump in. Give it a shot."

Steve Schirripa: Were you nervous?

Steven Van Zandt: I don't think I was knowledgeable enough to be nervous. I don't think I was intelligent enough to be nervous.

TWO

Season One

Cunnilingus and Psychiatry

WHEN DID THE BAD GUYS BECOME *the good guys?*

Some say the idea of the criminal as antihero in American cinema starts with Humphrey Bogart in High Sierra *in 1941. Roy "Mad Dog" Earle is killed in the end, of course, but not before he pays for surgery to help a young girl walk again (and then is spurned in his attempt to marry her), earning the audience's sympathy. The concept was raised to an art form by Martin Scorsese in* Mean Streets *and, later, in* Goodfellas, which I was lucky enough to be a part of. Those movies, and the many in that genre that followed, gave mob members complicated interior lives and normal-people problems along with the guns they had to stash, the money they had to launder, and the bodies they had to hide.*

But no one had brought any of this to television—the gangsters struggling with their Catholic upbringing, the daring attempt to get an audience to identify with a killer—before David Chase came along. Color TVs had appeared more than thirty years earlier, but when it came to crime, television was still very black-and-white: for the most part, the good guys were good and the bad guys were evil. The antiheroes of the big screen didn't cross over to TV.

*There had been many superb dramas with excellent writing and ensemble casts—*Hill Street Blues, Law and Order, Northern Exposure*—but no one had ever attempted to bring such a cinematic look and scope, and such complex themes and images, to an episodic show. Let alone to ask audiences to come to grips with the conflicts we all face—the questions of right and wrong, and the gray areas in be-*

tween—by sympathizing with a guy who, by the fifth episode, would kill a man with his bare hands.

It's hard to imagine these days, with literally hundreds of excellent dramas being produced by cable and streaming services, that there was a time when pay cable produced virtually no original programming, unfettered by the rules that govern broadcast TV. HBO's powerful Oz, featuring a wonderful young Edie Falco, is a notable exception, and Sex and the City, in a very different vein of course, started airing a few months before we did. But that was about it. That was the largely barren landscape that the Sopranos pilot landed in when it premiered on January 10, 1999.

And after that, nothing would ever be the same. —Michael

Steve: What was it like, shooting the pilot?

Michael: It was a lot of fun. We had a really good time. I knew a lot of these people. Like I knew Tony Sirico from doing the John Gallagher movie *Men Lie.* What made it so much fun was that so many of us had worked together before and so there was a kind of instant camaraderie, and here we were, a bunch of Italian-Americans, doing a TV pilot about Italian-Americans together! We all had this vibe that something really special was happening.

Steve: Tony is a great guy.

Michael: He was never very nice to me up until *The Sopranos.* After the pilot we became very, very close, tight friends on the set of *Witness to the Mob,* which we filmed after the pilot and before Season One. Up until then, I was a little reluctant because he could make really nasty comments—he could really stick the knife in. For example, at the premiere for *Men Lie,* which was way before *The Sopranos,* I was there with my girlfriend at the time, Lili Taylor, who had already appeared in *Mystic Pizza* and *Short Cuts* and a bunch of other movies. Tony came up to me and said, "I see your girlfriend is working all the time, and you, nothing. What, did someone put the *malocchio* on you?"

Steve: The *malocchio*. The evil eye.

Michael: Tony was like that. He was just that way. It was funny, but I was intimidated. But later, as I said, we became really good friends.

Steve: We have to talk about the wings. Tony has gray hair. But he would go to a barbershop in Brooklyn called Three Brothers, and they would dye his hair jet black and then put the silver wings in on the sides. If you look in the pilot, the wings are very small. They get bigger as the series goes on.

Michael: That was a good choice, too. Where would the show be without the wings? That was critical.

Steve: There are only two people with that hairdo. Only him and Grandpa Munster. It never caught on with the rest of America.

Michael: Even when *The Sopranos* was a big hit, the kids weren't running around getting the wings put in.

Steve: It wasn't like the Rachel on *Friends*. Or the Elvis.

Michael: Out of all the characters on *The Sopranos*, Tony Sirico, out of anyone I think, is the most similar to his character, no?

Steve: There was an episode where they were going to go to Paulie's apartment, and the set designers and producers were racking their brains to figure out what the apartment would look like. They were going on and on. "What would Paulie's apartment look like?" Finally, somebody said, "The guy is the guy. Let's go to Tony Sirico's apartment." That's what wound up being Paulie Walnuts's apartment. It was an exact replica of Tony's. I'm telling you, the guy is the guy.

Michael: Tony Sirico auditioned for Uncle Junior. Did you know that?

Steve: Yes, but he was too young. Only fifty-five at the time, and the Uncle Junior character was much older. Anyway, when do you find that the show has been picked up?

Michael: I got the call right before Christmas, and it was on the set of *Witness to the Mob*. My first son, Vadim, had just been born, on December 6. He had respiratory difficulties at birth and had to be transferred to Columbia Presbyterian hospital because the situation was so serious. He and my wife were in the hospital for two weeks. It was an agonizing time for me. They finally got home on December 20, and the very next day, I was in my trailer with Sirico and I got the call that we were picked up for a whole season. All I can say was that was the best Christmas I ever had.

THE SOPRANOS would not be The Sopranos *without Dr. Melfi. All the characters in the first season were top-notch, but I think it was having Tony seeing a shrink—and a female shrink on top of that—that really made people sit up, take notice, and realize something different was going on here. But I gotta say, if it weren't for Lorraine Bracco, I don't know how that would have gone. She did such an amazing job with that role. She was Tony's equal, and fought him tooth and nail the whole way. And then later, when we start to see Dr. Melfi's own problems, Lorraine made her so human and so real.*

Lorraine was born in Bay Ridge, not far from me, but she grew up on Long Island. She did a few movies early on but her big break came in Goodfellas, *a role that got her nominated for an Oscar and a Golden*

Globe. But before all that, she started out in modeling—not bad for a girl who says she was voted "ugliest girl in sixth grade." —Steve

Lorraine: I lived in Paris for a while. I modeled for a while there. All the art directors and big photographers that I worked with always said to me, "Go be an actress." Even one night at dinner with Catherine Deneuve, she said to me, "No, you're an actress." I was like, "No, I'm fine. I'm happy." I just felt that I could never make it. I'm a die-hard New Yorker, as we know. I didn't see myself in Hollywood anyhow. Who knew?

Steve: You lived in Paris for how long?

Lorraine: Ten years.

Michael: You speak fluent French.

Lorraine: *Oui, mon amour.*

Michael: How did you make the transition from modeling to acting? How did it happen?

Lorraine: When I was in Paris, I took some classes with John Strasberg, Lee Strasberg's son. I had done a lot of commercials in France. I was like the girl next door in France, let's put it that way. Then I started to get these calls from directors to come meet them to be the American in Paris. Also, it didn't hurt that I spoke French. I did a couple of really bad little movies. I was bored to tears, because all you do is, as we know, sit and wait. I didn't know about building a character or any of those things.

I met Harvey Keitel in Paris. He said, "Oh, my God. I can't believe I had to come to Paris to meet a girl who's from Brooklyn." We hooked up and we spent seven, eight years together. One day he turned around and he said, "Listen, I got to go home. My work, my life is in New York. Come with me." I went, and I sat at the Actors Studio for a year with Harvey. Special permission. [*laughs*]

Steve: Then you got into the movies. You did *Someone to Watch Over Me*. I love that movie. Before I even met you. I'm not kidding you. It was terrific, with Tom Berenger, and you played the blue-collar girl.

And then there was *Goodfellas*. How did that come about? Did Harvey introduce you to Martin Scorsese?

Lorraine: I had met Marty socially, yes. Dinner with Robert [De Niro] and Marty and whoever else. Then one day, he asked me to come read for the movie that he did before *Goodfellas* with Griffin Dunne, *After Hours*. I went in and I thought I gave a really good audition. I was happy with myself, which is very rare. I came home and I said to Harvey, "I did a really good job nailing this Soho artist." At the time I lived in Tribeca. It was my milieu, and Marty called me that night and said, "I really like you. I'm not giving you the part. One of the big reasons I'm not giving it to you is because you're not experienced enough and I have to bring this film in on time. I'm in trouble. I went over on lots of my other movies and I have to really behave and I'm a little nervous, but we're going to work together."

Steve: We've all heard that, Lorraine—"I like you, I love you, but you didn't get it."

Lorraine: A hundred percent. I hung up the phone, I looked at it and I'm going, "Fuck him. [*laughs*] That's never going to happen."

It's a funny thing. I've always had a sense of what kind of director would like me, because I'm not your normal kind of girl. I saw *Raging Bull* in Paris on the Champs-Élysées when it came out. I said, "This director would like me. This guy will get me." So after I get that call, I hang up the phone cursing and yelling.

Then later he called up about another movie and said, "Read this script," but Robert De Niro had given me the book before and said to me, "Read the book."

Michael: So that script was *Goodfellas*? And the book was *Wiseguy*, Nicholas Pileggi. The book that *Goodfellas* is based on.

Lorraine: I read the book, and I looked at Robert and Harvey and I was like, "I get it. I'm from Long Island. I was brought up in a Jewish neighborhood," which I thought was really good for the role. Marty called and asked me to come meet him at his apartment to talk. All right. Well, this is good. This can't hurt. I said, "I can only shoot myself in the foot at this point." I go up and Ray Liotta is there. Basically, he just wanted to see Ray and I together.

Ray and I got along really well. By the way, Ray was a rock for me through the whole movie. He would shove me to my mark. He knew I didn't have that much experience really. I'll never forget one day, when I was working on *Someone to Watch Over Me*. The script girl came over, and we were doing the scene in the café where I end up in the parking lot hitting somebody. In the café, we were eating, and the girl comes over after the first take and says, "Okay, you did this, and you did that." She's telling me that I have to repeat my actions exactly and match them with my words. I was like, "What?"

Steve: It's really hard. When they shoot you from different angles, you have to match your hand motions and everything, so the different shots will edit together. People don't realize that.

Lorraine: I was thinking, "What is that?" I started to cry. I didn't even know what it was. Ridley comes over, "What's the matter?" I said, "Well, they never told me that at the Actors Studio." God bless

Ridley Scott, which is one of the reasons I adore him, he said, "Just do whatever. I'll figure it out." That's a master filmmaker, instead of making you totally crazy in trying to figure it out. I was a novice, I didn't know. I learned a great lesson there.

Steve: This is your first big role, and you get nominated for an Oscar. That's crazy. That had to be a whirlwind of all the award shows, the whole press, the whole shit.

Lorraine: Yes, it's crazy and it's fantastic. I'm proud of myself for what I did. The best part was when I was nominated for a Golden Globe before the Oscars. Everybody was calling and sending flowers and sending cakes and coming over and everything. I whispered to Harvey, "What's a Golden Globe?"

Steve: That's hysterical. That's priceless.

Lorraine: I really didn't know.

Michael: Let's jump ahead to *The Sopranos*. Dr. Melfi. How did you prepare for that role?

Lorraine: I had two psychiatrists in real life, and I stole from the both of them.

Michael: That'll do it.

Lorraine: One man, one woman. I took the yin and the yang.

Michael: You did so well that the show got awards from psychiatric societies and all that kind of stuff, didn't it?

Lorraine: Yes. But you know what? I did tell David from the get-go, "Listen, I'm not sure I would be sitting here talking to you if I didn't have a good shrink and good medicine." I went through a really, really hard time in my life. I said, "If you're going to make her the psycho killer, sex addict, all that, I'm not your girl. Go get somebody else." For me, it was a very serious life-turning experience. I want her to be serious.

Steve: Lorraine, you were the only known actor on the show. You had *Goodfellas,* one of the biggest movies, especially of that genre. Not a whole lot of people could have played Melfi except you.

Lorraine: Thank you, Steve. But this role was my gut. It was who I was, in front of David, talking to him about his script, his character that he wrote.

Steve: Along the way, did you give David any input?

Lorraine: No. I asked him one thing. "How does he pay her?"

Michael: [*laughs*] That's a good question.

Lorraine: That was my thing. I asked him, just once, "How does he pay her? Does he have insurance?"

Michael: He might through the union, through one of the unions.

Lorraine: David was hysterical. At one time, you see him throw the money at her, which I thought was great.

Michael: So, let's talk about you two. Did you hit it off with Jim right away?

Lorraine: Yes.

Michael: You didn't have to build that relationship so much, you guys clicked?

Lorraine: Absolutely. For me, when we did all those Melfi scenes, I didn't have all you guys. I just had him. Sometimes what he would ask for was for the film to be really long, so he could do most of his part like in a monologue. He would ask for four, five minutes to have the camera just keep rolling, so he could just do his part as one thought. Once in a while, I would catch myself not being Dr. Melfi, but just being Lorraine Bracco watching this actor in awe. Then all of a sudden, it'd be, "Oh, my God! It's my part!" I caught myself with my mouth open.

Michael: The majority of your stuff was such a pressure cooker, you and him in that room, in those chairs. It was a crucible. It was a specific intensity I would imagine, right? All the time.

Lorraine: Absolutely.

Michael: Did you usually shoot his side first or did you do a master with both sides at once? How would that work?

Lorraine: This is where I get to curse him. We would always shoot him first, because he was the storyteller. You always do that. When Jim was doing his part, he didn't want to see any of the camera people or anybody moving, to take his attention off of what he was doing, so they set up these black screens behind me. Then they would turn around to shoot my side, and they would move the screens around. And that bastard would moon me! Nobody could see him except for me.

Michael: So the screens were behind the camera while it was shooting you, and he'd hide behind them? So you could see him, but no one else could?

Lorraine: Right, because they were all facing me. I would be saying, "Yo, you have no idea what this fucking guy is doing to me." They were going, "Ugh, Lorraine, come on, let's go." I am the one who always got in trouble. They got angry at me! Meanwhile, he's taking his pants off, showing me his tushy, which I would say, "Stop that! Put that away! Put that away!"

Michael: But I heard you got him back once.

Lorraine: One day I took Anabella Sciorra's hair extension, and I stuffed it in the front of my pantyhose and hid it. So when I crossed my legs, there was all this hair. Jim was totally grossed out. The look on his face was worth a million dollars. He goes, "You're disgusting." And my response was, "I learned everything from you."

Steve: This was all late at night, right, a lot of times? Because on location, there would be a set time you had to wrap, but on the set, they could shoot as long as they needed to, so sometimes it would go late at night.

Lorraine: It was late at night, and he always had a huge amount of dialogue. One time he picked me up, I was all nice and pretty and suntanned in a little nice summer dress and he would growl at me: "Who died and gave you this role?" [*laughs*]

Steve: Because you only would work one day an episode, usually. You had the best job in show business. I remember you telling me one time, when I was working fifteen, sixteen days, "You'll work more in this episode than I will all season."

David saw how good you were, because Melfi becomes more and more complex as the series goes on. Pretty early on we find out that she's seeing a psychiatrist herself. Played by Peter Bogdanovich. How did you like working with Peter?

Lorraine: I liked Peter. He is old-school. He enjoyed himself, which was fun. Originally, they wanted to cast James Lipton—God rest his soul—from *Inside the Actors Studio*. Now, I happened not to really like him. I think he's very pretentious, and I would have had a hard time with him.

Michael: Peter was a much better choice. Peter was really wonderful in that role.

Lorraine: He's a delicious guy. He's so smart and so knowledgeable about filmmaking.

Michael: What was the most difficult and challenging episode for you?

Lorraine: I want to say the pilot. I always felt I was the weak link in the show.

Michael: That certainly is not true. That's your own actor's neurosis and stuff.

Lorraine: There were great scenes in the pilot.

Steve: The three of us obviously never had any scenes together, but we all got to be good pals.

Lorraine: And the fact is I consider us all still pals. We have stuck together. I love that about us. I've had other successful things. I don't believe it was just the show. I really believe it's who we are innately.

Steve: I also think David somehow consciously or subconsciously put us all together, a lot of us are from the same background. We would see you at the read-through, we did a million appearances and things together and charities and all kinds of stuff.

Lorraine: I always said I was the Shirley MacLaine to your Rat Pack. [*laughs*]

Steve: Do people still come up to you, do they still react to you as Dr. Melfi?

Lorraine: Yeah. They all call me Doc. "Hey, Doc!"

Steve: They do still?

Lorraine: Oh yeah. I still get Karen from *Goodfellas*!

WE SHOT *the pilot in early fall of 1997, but we waited months to find out if we were picked up. It was an agonizing wait. When we finally got the call in late December, it was like a big Christmas present. But what we didn't know until we talked to Lorraine was, it turns out that she was Santa Claus. Or at least, one of the elves.* —Michael

Lorraine: I called up David eight, nine, ten months after we did the pilot, and I said, "What's going on? Don't they have to pick us up or let us go or whatever?" He said, "Yes." He goes, "You know, it's very expensive, the show. But why don't you call Chris Albrecht?"

I said, "All right. You have his number?" He gave me his number. I was walking around my house. I'd never called an executive before. I don't know, who am I? Nobody. I called up, "May I please speak to Chris Albrecht?" He gets on the phone right away. I was sweating. I said, "Hi, Chris." "Hey, Lorraine, how are you?" I said, "Chris, what's going on? We all need to know." He goes, "It's very expensive." I said, "Okay." I said, "Can I see it? Will you send me a copy of it?"

Right away, I get the copy, I watch the show, and I find myself screaming, jumping up and down on my bed. I was beyond thrilled. I called back Chris Albrecht, I said, "Are you kidding me? This is the best. This is unbelievable. I've never seen anything so good. Pick it up. Pick it up. Do it."

Steve: Well, he must have listened to you.

Michael: Thank God.

Lorraine: I don't know if he listened to me, but I said, "This is the best thing I've seen in ten years. No movie touches this."

GANGSTER MOVIES *and TV shows, by their nature, are male-centric: the main characters, like the mobsters and killers they portray, are all men.*

The women in these films, by and large, are pretty one-dimensional—lots of strippers and girlfriends, but not a lot of depth (Faye Dunaway's Bonnie Parker in Bonnie and Clyde, *and, of course, Lorraine's character, Karen Hill, in* Goodfellas, *being some of the notable exceptions).*

But The Sopranos *changed all that, bringing the women characters to the fore, exploring their conflicts and aspirations and hopes and fears as deeply as those of their male counterparts. In addition to Lorraine's Dr. Melfi, Nancy Marchand's Livia brought us a female character as powerful, conniving, and dangerous as any Scarface or Little Caesar.*

And the emotional heart of The Sopranos, *especially in that first season, lies in the character of Carmela. Edie Falco created a character as fully formed, as real, and as emotionally torn as Tony Soprano—and the electric scenes between them, starting with the first episode, made it clear that we were watching something thoroughly unique. —Michael*

Steve: Edie, I would assume you loved playing Carmela.

Edie: I loved it, yes.

Steve: It's so unlike you. You're nothing like this. You're not your typical Italian mob wife stereotype. The nails, the hair, the clothes, the decorations in the home, the whole shebang.

Edie: Right, which is why I loved it. Who wants to play themselves over and over again? Which a lot of people do, and do well. But for me, I'd rather play someone really completely different. I loved that she was so high-maintenance, with the hair and the nails, the jewelry, the clothing—it was all a big part of who she was, and that was really fun. For the first five years. But then, the amount of time I spent in hair and makeup! It was a fair amount of lead-in time before work. But it was great. Nothing was more exciting than playing someone so different from me.

Steve: Do you cook, Edie?

Edie: Not at all.

Steve: But Carmela is the ultimate suburban housewife. The ultimate hostess. You're really acting here? There's none of that in real life?

Edie: [*laughs*] No, that's not me.

Michael: A lot of the fans think you cook, I bet.

Edie: Of course they do.

Michael: People come up to you all the time and say, can they have recipes.

Edie: They want my recipes. It's really hysterical.

Michael: Let's talk about how you created the character of Carmela. Because it's really remarkable. The tension between her indulging in the benefits of being in this life, and also knowing the cost of it, the karmic repercussions. She's both accepting that, and also fighting against it, and wrestling with it in her conscience—it's really amazing the way you were always able to dance around and in between both of those things.

Edie: Thank you. I think it's what a lot of people do in their real life. If you really have to come to terms with the various pieces that make up what you call your life, if you really have to admit to the things that you're not okay with, then you're going to have to make some changes, right? I think there was a big part of her that was in denial on some level about the way her husband made money. It's as if she could pretend she didn't know. Of course, she knew everything, but she had to keep it in a closet way the hell in the back of her brain, or she'd have to do something about it. Change her life, take the kids, get in the car, and go to her mother's house. None of that was something that she was willing to do, because she loved the life.

Michael: She thought about it. She thought about doing those things at times.

Edie: I think so. When the payoff wasn't as good as what she was putting herself through, when the ratio started to get a little iffy, she had some doubts. But they didn't last long. She always came back to him.

Michael: Georgianne Walken talked to us about how you could show all of that conflict, and all of Carmela's strength, and her vulnerability, all at the same time, without even saying a word. I think she's absolutely right.

Edie: David Chase was brave enough to write scenes where there wasn't a lot of dialogue, which was kind of unheard of on series television. You've got to keep the plot moving. But David would occasionally give Jim and I a scene where we didn't say much. Jim was such a great actor to work with, because speaking or not, you were getting so much from him. It really was like playing. That's the way we did it in college, we were taught that acting is kind of like when you were a little kid, and you would play cowboys and Indians or something. You didn't think about it, you were just playing, weren't you? That's always what it felt like with Jim, that he was always there with me.

There was one scene, it was in the kitchen, he came home late, and he hadn't eaten, so I walked in, and I go to the kitchen and get something out, I cook it up. He's sitting, and then I put it in front of him, and then I sit down next to him. I don't think a word was said through the whole thing. All I kept thinking was, first of all, how weird it is to shoot something like that. You continually feel like you've got to say something, like it's not okay to actually just *be*. But it ended up being just so moving, and so rich. It was one of a number of scenes that Jim and I had where we didn't talk, and I just loved that. It was such an opportunity. I hadn't had it before, nor have I had it since then.

Michael: Let's go back a little ways. To where it started for you. You went to SUNY Purchase—the State University of New York at Purchase—and NYU always gets the credit for being the premier film school in New York, but I truly think Purchase had more to do with the indie movie explosion in nineties New York than NYU did.

Edie: There was something about the fact that you couldn't buy your way into Purchase. It was a state school. It was cheap, so you had eight million people auditioning. You really have to take it seriously and work your ass off with your audition stuff. I would like to think it was based on merit as opposed to whether or not you could afford it. Even though it was cheap, I still couldn't afford it, by the way. I was in debt forever. It was actually the *Sopranos* pilot where I was finally able to pay off my student loans.

Steve: So many big stars went to Purchase. Stanley Tucci; Parker Posey; Melissa Leo, who won an Academy Award a few years ago; Wesley Snipes; Ving Rhames—the list goes on and on.

Michael: Not to mention directors too, like Hal Hartley and Nick Gomez.

Edie: Right after I graduated, Hal Hartley asked if I could have coffee with him, and he asked me if I would do one of his movies. That was *The Unbelievable Truth*. I was reluctant—I was doing every student film I could get my hands on because I loved it, but I had a waitressing job and it was money that I could not afford to do without at the time.

I did it anyway. We went out there to do it on Long Island. He promised he'd reimburse me for the train ticket, which he didn't.

[*laughs*] Anyway, that's when the whole little "Purchase Mafia," as it has been referred to, got going.

Steve: Then you got *Bullets over Broadway*. Was that your first big movie? How did that come about?

Edie: It was because my friend Eric Mendelsohn, who is now a directing professor at Columbia University—he also went to Purchase—he was working in the costume department for Woody Allen.

He's a godfather to my kids. He got me a job as an extra on the Woody Allen film *Bullets over Broadway*. Then it was something like, "Who can we give some lines to?" Somehow my name got through. It was like that. Suddenly, my character has a name, I'm getting fitted for costumes—I was in a blackout for that whole thing. I was beyond excited.

Michael: What were your interactions with Woody like?

Edie: Well . . . minimal, shall we say? I was a nervous wreck because he was a god in my house. My father, we watched his movies, and he was worshipped. All I remember is he was in the middle of the theater and we were on the stage. I heard him say to somebody, "Who's the girl next to so-and-so?" Then he goes, "Edie. Hey, Edie." I turned around and it was like Charlie Brown's teacher—you know, "Womp-womp-womp." He said something to me but all I could think was, "Wow. Woody Allen just said my name."

Steve: Getting back to *The Sopranos,* I was in the makeup trailer with you one time, and you were just learning your lines in your makeup chair. You have an easy time learning your lines, don't you?

Edie: I do. I don't know if it's photographic or what it is. I've always done that. I still do that. I just learned them in the makeup chair.

It's like it's a muscle. If you use it a lot it gets better. Jim used to hate that about me. He used to really struggle with his lines, but I'm very lucky because if I learned them the night before or even earlier than that, by the time I'm saying them, they're old.

Steve: That is a gift, because I got to work really hard and if I don't know my lines the night before when I go to bed, I am screwed.

Edie: I know. I understand it. But since *Sopranos* was pretty early on in maybe all of our careers, it was all those years ago, I didn't realize how easy it was to memorize because it was just so well written. The words just flowed based on this character that we'd all created together. It doesn't happen like that for the most part.

Steve: So when did you first start getting recognized on the street? Was it from *Oz*?

Edie: No, not from *Oz,* but it was funny, one time, in particular, from *Laws of Gravity.*

Michael: A movie you did in the early nineties, written and directed by Nick Gomez, one of your Purchase Mafia.

Edie: Yes. I was with my dad. He had driven in from Long Island to get lunch with me. We were going back to his car, and someone said, "Oh my God—*gasp!*—are you EDIE FALCO???" They said this in front of my dad, which was the ultimate, because when you tell your dad you want to be an actress, you just wait for the other shoe to drop, but here was someone recognizing me from *Laws of Gravity.* That happened a couple of times, but the fact that it happened the first time in front of my dad will forever be a gift.

Michael: Did your dad say anything to the person who came up to you?

Edie: No. He's a very quiet guy, and he got in the car, and he just looked at me in the passenger seat like, "Woo-hoo-hoo!" It was really a big deal. It was really nice.

Michael: I seem to remember that you told me David Chase reminded you of your dad?

Edie: I love David. I love David well beyond what he knows, partially because of this thing that he made and the artist that he is, but also, yes, he reminds me of my dad and always did. My dad was a drummer when he was a kid and my whole childhood was my father having his hands on a table doing some kind of drumming thing, not even knowing he was doing it. It was at some read-through, I turned, and David was doing that same thing on the table. I guess David, I don't know, he was in a band or something when he was young.

Michael: He was a drummer.

Edie: A drummer, there you go. I had a relationship with David that was much bigger in my imagination. There's a familiarity with him that means the world to me. I haven't seen him in a long time, but when I do I feel like I want to crawl up on the couch next to him and laugh my head off and tell him stuff. I really do love him and I love what he was able to do with this thing.

Steve: When did you know that *Sopranos* was really taking off? You shot the first season, you're waiting for it to air, when do you know?

Edie: It was a slow dawning on me that this show was something bigger than I had anticipated. When we got picked up for the second season, Jim told me, "Well, now we got to go do it again, whatever it was we were doing." Clearly, he didn't know what he was doing, I didn't know what I was doing, but we were going back to do that again. If I had thought about it too much, you always think someone is going to come with a hook and pull you off the stage like, "How the hell did you get in here?"

OF COURSE, *no one ever came with a hook and pulled Edie off of anything. Before we move on from Edie I wanna bring up one more thing: Allen Coulter, who directed a lot of* Sopranos *episodes, talked to us about one scene that showed her incredible talent.* —Steve

Allen: Edie, I always said, was a lunch box actress, one that shows up, puts a time card in, lights go on, does it right. I think she's truly one of the greatest of her generation of American actresses, for sure.

Michael: No doubt.

Allen: We were doing an episode where they're having an engagement party for Richie and Janice. They're in the living room. Carmela gets upset, and she leaves the living room and walks back into the kitchen, and she breaks down crying. It's a very interesting moment for her.

I was using the Steadicam and I said to her, "Don't break down until you get to the kitchen." She said, "Okay." We did seven takes. Every one, she would hold it back, and the camera would swivel around, and she would get to where she couldn't be seen by the others, and then she would break down. She did that for seven takes.

Steve: Seven takes of breaking down. Wow.

Michael: But that's who Edie Falco was. And is. Just the ultimate professional.

Steve: How was it working with Jim?

Allen: I used to come on the set and Jim would look at me like he didn't know who I was. It was the most unsettling thing. He would have this look of, "What are you doing here?" It was not until "The Test Dream"—in Season Five—that he ever asked me a single thing, or we ever had a single exchange of anything personal. Maybe I wasn't his kind of guy. I had no idea. Finally I just thought, after five fucking years, if you can't just be decent with me, at least just ask me something. We were shooting something and I said, "Come on, let's just shoot for Christ's sake," or something like that. I was just fed up with him. And after that, we were on break, and he said, "What are you doing this summer?" That was the first time that he ever said anything.

Then one night I went to the theater with Kim, [my wife,] and we ran into him. I said hi, and I couldn't get away! He was just talking, he was so open and so friendly, and so just curious, and then I went to get a drink or something, and I couldn't find Kim, and then she comes back, she's saying, "I couldn't get away. Jim wanted to just keep talking."

ONE OF *the things people focus on when they talk about Season One of* The Sopranos *is how David Chase made these mob guys' problems relatable for the average viewer. Tony Soprano had work troubles and family troubles and psychological troubles just like anybody else. But what sometimes gets overlooked is how pervasive this was throughout the first season. Each character had specific real-life issues that went much deeper than who they had to whack or who wasn't paying protection. The character of Jackie Aprile was central to this concept. Who had ever seen a gangster movie where the head of the mob was dying of cancer? For me, those scenes with Jackie Aprile were one of the main things that humanized this show for viewers. And it wouldn't have happened without the power and grace and humility that Michael Rispoli brought to that character.*

Michael Rispoli and I have been friends ever since we worked together on a movie called Household Saints *that came out in 1993. We went on to do another movie,* Summer of Sam, *that I cowrote, which was shooting the same summer that the first season of* The Sopranos

was shooting. Even though he lost out to Jim for the lead role, David Chase recognized what an immensely talented actor Michael is and cast him as the incredibly sympathetic dying mobster Jackie Aprile.
—*Michael Imperioli*

Steve: Before *The Sopranos*, you've done a ton of work up until then. And 1997 comes, you get the call. Your agent says they want to see you for this new HBO show. Do you go right to David Chase at this point?

Michael Rispoli: I auditioned for David in New York and then, by the time I took the subway back home, they go, "They're going to want to see you again." I said, "All right. Great." I went out to St. George, Utah, to a place to go get in shape, hike the mountains, that kind of thing, and I get a call, "They want to see you. They want to test you in L.A." I flew to L.A. and they picked me up and they brought me to Century City, one of the hotels there. I walked across the street to HBO and we did the test there. I saw Jimmy there.

Steve: You'd known Jimmy?

Michael Rispoli: I met Jimmy on a movie called *Angie*. Then we became friendly running around New York a little bit. Jimmy and I, we were kind of coming up at the same time, and it would come down to the two of us for many roles. I got to be honest with you. Jimmy took more of those than I did.

Steve: But now you're both up for the same role in *The Sopranos*.

Michael Rispoli: Right. So I'm going to go back to Century City, and I went in to read, then Jimmy's going in, and I saw Jimmy and I go, "Look. Jimmy, I'm across the street. When you're done, let's have lunch." I went back to the hotel. He came over, and then we sat down and had lunch. I said, "Look. If it ain't me, it will be you, and good for you." He said, "Yes. If it's not me, it'll be you, and good for you." He was very generous, Jimmy.

The next day I flew back to St. George, Utah, and while I was there, my manager kept calling. One day she'd say, "Look. They really want you," then, by the evening, she'd go, "They really want Jimmy." Then the next day it was like, "Ah, they're back with you."

Steve: Oh, God, as an actor, you're waiting for this job, it's torture.

Michael Rispoli: It is torture, and here's the thing. My wife, Madeline, we're expecting our first child, and I'm thinking, "Let me get this fricking thing. I can do the pilot and then I can just cruise through the birth 'til the end of the year, whatever, until it gets picked up," because I knew this show was going to get picked up. I knew it was going to go just because the writing, to me, it was already brilliant.

Anyways. It goes to Jimmy, so I call up Jimmy and I say, "Congratulations, you fuck. You're going to be great in this," and he laughed, he goes, "Yes, thanks. Listen. I don't know what to do. I never did TV," and I had done a few TV shows, so I said, "Don't worry about it. You're going to take to it like a duck to water."

Steve: You're both such great guys and great actors. One of you had to get it. So they liked you, and they wanted to cast you in something. So how does that come about?

Michael Rispoli: So they shoot the pilot. Obviously, I wasn't there, but then they go to series, and David calls me up and he said, "Look. I got this part and, I'm gonna take him down from being an older guy to be a contemporary with Tony Soprano." I said, "All right." I said, "Great," and he says, "But he dies."

I said, "Ah. Come on, man. I don't want to die in the show." I said, "Make me a boss from Philly or South Jersey. I'll come in every once in a while. I don't got to be a regular." He goes, "We only got thirteen episodes. I don't even know how long it's going to go," and you've got to remember David came from network TV and they would can a show just like that [*snaps fingers*], you know? I said, "David, this is a marathon, not a sprint. I'm telling you. This is going."

Steve: As the series goes on, are you just really unhappy or upset, or what? I mean, you wind up doing just fine for yourself.

Michael Rispoli: Yes, thank God. Look, here's the thing. Jimmy got tied up with the show, which was a great thing to get tied up with, but it opened up other roles for me because he wasn't on the market. One night I went out with Jimmy and he said, "You know they tell me when you do TV, all this work starts coming in. I got no work coming in." I said, "I'm getting all the work you're not available for!"

Steve: You're being very humble, but you're getting the work because people know you're a very talented guy.

Michael Rispoli: Look, I would have loved my shot at playing Tony Soprano. We all would've, right? But Jimmy took that pilot. When you're doing a pilot, the producers, the network, they want to get the right lead for that pilot, the guy flying the plane, someone who could take that plane where it's going to go. Honestly, and may he rest in peace, James did more than that with that pilot. He flew that plane up into the stratosphere. He became the first television astronaut.

Michael Imperioli: Let's talk about how you created the character of Jackie Aprile. One of the great characters, not only on this show, but in the whole pantheon of crime dramas. A unique character.

Michael Rispoli: Any actor, when you're in an ensemble—obviously you had the leads, but it was an ensemble—it's like being in an orchestra. So you got to figure out what section you want. Are you woodwind, or are you in the brass? Are you in the strings? Are you percussion? That kind of thing.

So this was an ensemble. That would include Jimmy as well. Any good actor feels that way. Michael, you had your own sound. Whatever it was, the music that was made sounded great. I had to figure out what kind of instrument I was. I couldn't play the same instrument somebody else was playing. I had to add my own sound. I just found where I could blend into the rest of the musical composition.

Michael Imperioli: But what you created, you made Jackie this very sympathetic, very human character. He was the leader, he was feared, but you didn't play him as a tough guy.

Michael Rispoli: Yes, absolutely. My character was built by the fact that David Chase and the rest of the writers would talk about Jackie as though he was this great leader. "Oh, when Jackie was around, Jackie would know what to do." There's an old saying, and I want to say it's Peter O'Toole, or maybe it's Laurence Olivier or something. They played kings.

Michael Imperioli: "When you play the king, you don't play the king. You play the man inside the king."

Michael Rispoli: Exactly. Guys would come in to play the king—and every actor is guilty of this—they all come in, and they play the mean king who's going to take your head off if you displease him. But all the other characters on the stage have already told you how tough and mean and horrible this king can be. If they've already set you up as being that kind of king, and you come out and go, "Hey, the flowers are nice out here today. Whoa, I got to make sure I water those flowers," they all go, "Holy shit. He's *really* nasty."

Steve: One of your last scenes, you're in the hospital, Tony is trying to talk business with Jackie, and Jackie isn't listening, he's only worried about his temperature. That was an incredible scene. What was it like playing that?

Michael Rispoli: Let me tell you why that scene worked. I'm saying the words, but it's the look on Jimmy's face. As he sees me, he's trying to keep me in the living world, and I'm not there anymore. It's me and the thermometer and what's happening to me. They end on Jimmy's face. There's a look of, "He ain't here. He ain't listening. He's gone." It's all in Jimmy's face.

Steve: That's a really good point. Sometimes it's about the other actors in the room.

Michael Imperioli: So we were talking about the choices you made in creating Jackie Aprile. Did you ever make any choices that you regretted later, or did you feel like you did it the way you wanted to?

Michael Rispoli: There was one scene, it might have been the first one I ever shot with them outside the pork store. Junior and Tony. I have to settle it between them. I was playing it as though I was thinking, "Well, I'm very ill, and I had all the treatments." I was supposed to be nauseous and stuff like that, and I played into it. I went for the weakness of the character, when right there, he should have been fighting through the weakness. There were a few lines of dialogue that I figured, "Let me do this, giving in to it." I made that choice and as soon as I fucking go back to my trailer, "Why the fuck did you play that? Why did you go down that path?"

Steve: But I just watched that scene. I think you played it strong.

Michael Rispoli: That's because finally, when the show comes out, those shots come out! They had cut that little bad choice I made, and I said, "Oh, that's a good editor."

Steve: The editors save our asses all the time.

AS WE *said in the beginning, we're not gonna go episode by episode through all the shows. But we are gonna talk about some of the best moments in each of the seasons. And when you talk about Season One, of course, you gotta talk about the pilot.* —Steve

Steve: David directed and wrote the pilot. He only directed two episodes. The first one and the last one. Going back and watching it after all these years, there's so much you missed the first time. For some reason in my head, I'm always thinking that the first scene is Tony getting the newspaper.

Michael: Which it's not.

Steve: No. He is in Melfi's office. He had a panic attack. He wants to know why. Cusamano, his neighbor, sent him to Melfi. Obviously tipped off Melfi that he's a mob guy.

Michael: There's a lot of things that I'm trying to figure out, as I go through it now again. That first shot, he is staring at the statue of a nude woman in Melfi's waiting room, and you see him framed between the legs of the statue—it kind of sets the stage for everything that's going to come, the way Tony feels boxed in by all the women in his life, his mother, Carmela, Melfi. And the statue itself—the face— later you see a photograph of the young Livia, brilliantly played by Nancy Marchand. The statue in some ways resembles the young Livia.

I don't know if Tony is making that connection. There is something with him relating to a woman, and he's going to talk to a woman and reveal his innermost secrets. Very interesting moment. As I watch the series again, I'm making some connections you couldn't have made the first time—unconscious things.

Steve: Like the ducks. You and I were talking at one point about how the ducks represent his family. I always wondered about that. I just realized that.

Michael: That's one of the reasons why the show really works so well. When I went back to watch the pilot, I wanted to make a conscious effort to compare the first scene, the very beginning of the series, to the end, and see if you could connect the dots. Was there an arc? Was there some through-line? And it's really about family. His fears, which come out later in the pilot, about how he's going to lose his family. The ducks come as a couple and then they have babies. That rocks his world and he winds up with panic attacks and in therapy and then on Prozac. Then in the very last scene of the last episode when the Journey song "Don't Stop Believin'" comes on: It's the family. They're coming together. They're going into the diner, there's a lot of tension. Then it goes to black. Did he keep the family together? Did he not?

Steve: And it ties into the last scene of the first season too, which we'll get to in a minute, but before we get off the pilot I wanna ask you about Christopher, because this is when we first meet him. How did you create that character?

Michael: I modeled Christopher on a guy I know, who does not know that I did that, and will never know, and nobody knows who I modeled him on. But he was a guy who was involved a little bit with the mob in New York. There was something in his personality that was almost larger-than-life. With Christopher, nothing is subtle. Everything is high drama. And this guy was like that. To the point sometimes I'd watch him behave and it almost didn't seem real, in a weird way.

Steve: Well, some of what Christopher does and says doesn't seem real. He's not the brightest guy.

Michael: He's not the brightest guy, but he is very ambitious and works really hard. He wants to please Tony. Although in the pilot, he's very immature. He's lazy, he overslept, he didn't make the call he was supposed to make.

Steve: When he says, "My mother said I shouldn't even have come in today." And he was nauseous. That is comedy. You're a mob guy, but you're saying, "My mother said I shouldn't have come in," because you don't feel good. But let's talk about that scene. When you're driving Tony. Because that's a really funny story. It's your first day on the set, and it coulda been your last.

Michael: Yes, that's a whole thing in itself because I lived in New York my whole life, I didn't have a driver's license.

Steve: Did you ever drive? Because you looked like you knew what you're doing.

Michael: Not really, but I didn't tell anybody that. They just assumed, you're thirty-one years old, you have a driver's license. I wanted the job; I didn't say anything. I figured I could wing it.

Steve: You don't know Jim. This is your first scene with him.

Michael: At some point, I'm driving backward down the sidewalk, with Jim next to me, with extras getting out of the way, trees on both sides. And I have to look at the mark in front of me at the same time, and talking. Even if you know how to drive, that's a lot to do. I did it four or five times and, finally, the AD—the assistant director—says, "Go twice as far and twice as fast." So, I go twice as far, twice as fast, and *boom*! I go right into a tree, really hard. The airbags go off, Jim's head goes back. I'm thinking, "I'm done. They're going to fire me. This guy is the star of the show, he must think I'm an asshole." I'm horrified. I mean, it's your first day. It's a big deal. It's a series. I was mortified. Then I look at Jim, and he just starts hysterically laughing. Then I'm thinking, "All right, he's a good guy."

Steve: Jim always liked when shit went awry. When the wheels fell off the bus, he found humor in that.

Michael: Now, the prop person who was in charge of the cars was Barbara Kastner, a very tough New Yorker, and she's furious at me. So when she finds out I don't have a license, she gets *really* pissed off! She wants to file a union violation complaint, and I'm like, "Oh my God." But they just bring over another Lexus. They had another one that I guess they were going to use to rig up on the flatbed truck for when we were driving around. They bring it over and say: "All right, do it again."

Steve: I gotta ask you about one more scene in the pilot. David Chase, famously, didn't ever want anyone to change a line. But in the pilot, you were in a scene with Vinny where he did an ad-lib that stayed in, right? One of the few?

Michael: Yes, in the pilot, Vinny, who is playing Big Pussy, he and I had a scene after I killed Emil Kolar, where we have to get rid of the body. We were going to throw the body in a dumpster that was owned by that family to send a message. But the dumpster was pretty high. The prop person—I think to mess with us—made the body, or whatever was in the body bag, really heavy. We're rehearsing, and we're trying to throw this thing into the dumpster, and then we start doing takes, and we can't get it near the top of the dumpster, because it's so freakin' heavy.

Finally, Vinny just improvised and said, "You know what? Put it in the trunk. We'll take it out to Staten Island." We opened the trunk, tossed the body in, and drove off, and rewrote the scene on the spot.

ONE OF *the big surprises for fans, when they saw the pilot, was spotting Steven Van Zandt in the role of Silvio. Steven was a huge celebrity in New Jersey, of course, as an alumnus of Bruce Springsteen's band. Turns out, Steven told us, the one had a lot to do with the other.*
—*Michael*

Steve Schirripa: Stevie, unlike the rest of us, you really kind of came up with your own character, the character of Silvio, or you had a lot to do with it, right? You wrote a whole biography of him, a whole backstory.

Steven Van Zandt: I wrote that biography. And I also figured if I can look in the mirror and see the guy, then I can be the guy. So I found out where John Gotti got his clothes made. I decided what he looked like, and the fact that he romanticized the earlier years in the mob, the forties and fifties, all that. And designed the hair to be more of a throwback, old-school, fifties hair. Those guys never did change their hair. I wasn't thinking about my age, so I had him growing up with Tony Soprano and they were best friends.

Steve Schirripa: But the character, Silvio Dante, that actually came out of a story or a treatment that you wrote, way before *The Sopranos*?

Steven Van Zandt: Yeah. I now have finished the actual script. But at that point it was just a treatment of a retired hit man who opened a club. And again, he was living in the past, with a Copacabana type of club set in contemporary times. But you walked into this club and you were back in the fifties; it had the big bands and the Jewish comics and the dancing girls.

Steve Schirripa: And the guy, the owner of this club, was named Silvio Dante. You came up with that. Did you give that to David, and he turned it into a strip club? Or did he see the treatment?

Steven Van Zandt: I just told him about it, I just said, basically I was rewriting *Casablanca*. A lot of things happened within the club. The five families had their tables, the police commissioner had his table, everybody had their table. And then Silvio Dante would be hired to do special jobs.

Steve Schirripa: What was David's reaction?

Steven Van Zandt: He said, "Well, this is a great idea. I think this show could use a club." And then he comes back a couple of days later and says, "We can't afford what you're talking about, but we'll make it a strip club."

Michael: Of all the characters, Silvio is the one who has the most confidence in terms of being honest with the boss. He's the most fearless in that respect. Where does that confidence come from? How did you bring that to the role?

Steven Van Zandt: In the end, I used my relationship with Bruce Springsteen, which was kind of the role of the adviser, the consigliere, kind of the underboss.

Steve Schirripa: I never thought of that. You were Tony's second in command, and kinda you were the same with Springsteen. You were the underboss to the Boss.

Steven Van Zandt: And I thought part of that job is to watch the boss's back, to protect the boss. Which gives you a fearlessness, because it's not about you, it's about protecting somebody else. It's easier to be fearless about protecting someone else than it is about yourself. And so, I decided this guy is going to be a real tough guy, even though he ended up a bit more in the diplomacy part of the family. At that stage of his life, he had gone through being the muscle, being the hit man, and now you're going to graduate to an executive position. But he still had that toughness. So I just wrote it into the character.

Michael: Do you recall any scenes with Jim that were particularly memorable, or that reminded you of that relationship with Springsteen?

Steven Van Zandt: Every scene I had with Jimmy was memorable, but mostly there was one where I had to bring him bad news, and he gets mad at me, which was directly out of my life with Bruce. I was one of the very, very few people who could bring him bad news, and very often he'd get mad at me. It's part of the job. It's part of the job of being somebody's best friend, or in this case being the consigliere, being so close to the boss. So there's one scene in the back room of the Bing, and I had to tell him something that was not what he wanted to hear, and he gets mad at me.

Michael: Fantastic scene. You have to tell Tony that the crew is upset that he won't give up his cousin. Tony gets really pissed at you, and you give it right back to him.

Steven Van Zandt: It's a really great, very, very realistic scene. It was useful that I actually lived that thing in real life.

SHE'S NOT *always the first character people think of now, when they talk about the pilot of* The Sopranos, *but here's something that people don't know: When HBO started screening the pilot, to see if they were going to pick it up for the series, they would give these questionnaires to the test audiences, to see which characters were the most likable. And Kathrine Narducci's character, Charmaine Bucco, who is married to the restaurant owner Artie Bucco, was the highest-testing character. And when I say a lot of people don't know that—I mean a* lot *of people. —Steve*

Michael: Charmaine, your character, was the highest-testing character, the most likable character in the tests. Did you know that?

Kathrine: No way, I didn't know that.

Michael: They felt that she stood up to the mob, and they liked that, the fact that she had principles and wasn't afraid to live by them.

Kathrine: So funny. At the end, everybody ends up loving Jimmy and hating me, because I was so mean to him all the time.

Steve: Yes. Listen, people thought you were a bitch, but you were the voice of reason for the show, you were anti-mob, you were a businesswoman trying to raise her family, you didn't do anything bad.

Kathrine: It always confused me, that character. I was always breaking David Chase's chops. I understand there's a voice of reason, but I always felt like, I wish they would have drawn the kindness side more for Charmaine Bucco.

So I gave it to myself. One day I said to David Chase, "I have to justify why I can't stand Tony," because he's always being nice to me. Why do I hate him so much? He comes, he brings me business. I had to rectify it for myself, so I gave myself a backstory. I said, "When Carmela went away that summer, I fucked him. I slept with Tony, and really, it wasn't for me. And I really wasn't for him, and he dumped me when she got back."

For me, that made it stronger than just "I don't like the mob." Then it made sense to me why I had this hate, because he made me screw my best friend over and then he dumped me.

Steve: When you told David that, what did he say?

Kathrine: I said, "I made myself a backstory, and that's going to happen," and he went, "Nah."

Michael: But that makes sense to you.

Kathrine: Yes, in my mind.

Steve: And it must have made sense to David too, because he wrote it into the script. In the third episode. It was after the scene where she waves you on when you're catering the party, you're supposed to be one of her closest friends and she treats you like you're just a worker, and then you give her the big touché that you banged Tony. That is a wonderful moment.

Kathrine: Yes. I even felt bad doing that. I really did.

THERE WAS *a ten-month gap between shooting the pilot and coming back to shoot the second episode in June of 1998. I asked Michael how things had changed. —Steve*

Steve: Was there anything different with the shooting of Episode Two, after you shot the pilot?

Michael: Just you had less time. We did the pilot in a month, and now we're doing an episode in maybe ten days or something like that. Production schedules got longer as we went on—as you get more successful, you can ask for more days. But it was still much more than network television, which was a strict seven days.

Steve: Back then, when you were shooting in New Jersey and New York—all the studio stuff was in New York, but the exteriors were all in New Jersey. David would say that New Jersey was like another cast member.

Michael: I really enjoy shooting on location. That was always exciting. And really, while we were shooting that first season, you started seeing, script after script, how much deeper it got, more intricate, more interesting, more bizarre, more funny. That's when I realized this is really, really special. Whether or not it's going to be a hit, who knows? Because we shot all the first season's episodes that summer and they didn't go on the air until January. But I did get the sense we were doing something really fantastic.

Steve: Also they added a new character. Kind of an important one.

Michael: Of course you're talking about Adriana. Drea de Matteo was just a hostess at a restaurant in the pilot. It was supposed to be a one-shot deal. But David liked her so much that he created the role of Adriana, starting in Episode Two.

Steve: I can't imagine *The Sopranos* without Adriana.

Michael: Or Christopher without Adriana. I can't imagine that either.

YOU CAN'T *talk about the first season and not talk about Episode Five—* *"College." It was ranked number two on* TV Guide's *list of the all-time greatest episodes ever on television. And with good reason. A lot of people, when they talk about* The Sopranos, *say this is the episode they remember the most. This is when the conflict in Tony's life really gets hammered home—trying to pretend to live a normal family life and keep that separate from what he does for a living, which, not to put too fine a point on it, sometimes involves murdering people.*

Taking Meadow to college and tracking down a guy to kill him—there was incredible tension in this episode. And there was incredible tension behind the scenes, too, because the network didn't want it to happen. *—Steve*

Michael: Episode Five won an Emmy for the script written by James Manos and David Chase. James Manos went on to create *Dexter*. Very good writer. This episode is very interesting because it's a very self-contained episode. It's almost like a little movie. It stands alone. I think it's very dear to David Chase's heart for that reason, the way the "Pine Barrens" is—although "Pine Barrens" is much more comedic and this one's much more dramatic and intimate, in terms of the family stuff and the affairs of the heart. Also, most *Soprano* episodes, as with a lot of TV hour-long dramas, are structured with three stories intertwined: an A story, B story, and C story. This episode really only has two.

Steve: This one, the A story is Tony taking Meadow to college, they get to visit three schools in Vermont; and the story of Carmela and Father Phil, that's the B story. In this one, there's no Junior, no Livia, no Silvio, no Pussy, no Paulie.

Michael: And I think it's because the writers really wanted that very narrow focus.

Steve: HBO did not want Tony to kill the guy, right?

Michael: When they read this script, they were afraid that the fans would turn on Tony Soprano. The first few episodes are about getting into him and liking him a lot, and then HBO was afraid that fans would turn. And David Chase said, no, the fans are going to turn if he *doesn't* kill this guy because it's going to make him look weak, it's going to make him look like he's not an honorable mob guy. Because this is the code that they're living under. This guy that Tony was hunting down was a rat, this guy turned on the family, and to live by that code, Tony's got to do this.

Steve: Is this the first time a main character in a TV series murdered someone? I mean, Dick Van Dyke didn't kill nobody; Gilligan, I don't remember.

Michael: I wish he did. That might've been interesting.

Steve: Really. I can just see Gilligan pulling a gun on the Skipper and going, "Now you say hello to *my* little buddy."

Michael: Right. That just never happened. Maybe on a cop show they'll kill a bad guy. But this is a cold-blooded killing. Up close and personal. A crime of passion and a crime of vengeance.

Steve: Now, you only have a couple of scenes in this episode but they're really crucial. You're Tony's tie back to the real world in Jersey. You were great in those scenes, on the pay phone, in the rain.

Michael: There's a metaphor with the storm and the dark night of the soul and all that. If it was just a regular sunny day out and Christopher had to do the phone calls, it wouldn't have that power, that sense of danger. And it's not just raining. It's pouring rain. It's a deluge.

Steve: Let me ask you something, because I've never been in a scene where it's raining except for when it's really raining. How did they do that?

Michael: It's a rain machine. Rainmaker. It's like a giant sprinkler. It's a big tall post with big propellers and it spins around and it's just a shitload of water coming down on you. We shot that very close to Silvercup Studios. Down the block or something, on the pay phone. It's an obstacle for Christopher. It's not just that he's on the phone with Tony; it's pouring rain, he can't hear so good, it's long distance, he's on a pay phone. It's an excellent scene. This is something people should understand about *The Sopranos,* and about David Chase: Nothing's ever just cut and dried and just generic or taken for granted. It's always very specific.

Steve: And the murder, of course, is very cold-blooded. That's intentional. David doesn't want to make this easy for you to watch.

Michael: It takes a long time for Tony to kill the guy. It's not an easy just-shoot-him-in-the-back-of-the-head thing. He's up close and personal. Then after the killing, the ducks fly away—so again, the ducks represent the family unit, the safety of his family, and that safety is out of reach now. When you read that quote from

Nathaniel Hawthorne, on the wall of the college: "No man can wear one face to himself and another to the multitude without finally getting bewildered as to which may be true"—that's Tony. If he's gonna do this, then this is who he is. That's his conflict.

ROBIN GREEN *and Mitch Burgess told us where the idea for this episode came from. No surprise: it was David Chase and one of the terrific writers and producers in those early years, Frank Renzulli. —Steve*

Robin: After the pilot, David had definite ideas for the next three episodes. Then he came in one day. We were about to break Episode Five.

Michael: When you say "about to break," we should say, that means break down the episode into its various beats, the scenes that will make up the episode.

Robin: Yes. We were about to break Episode Five and David said, "I can't stand it anymore. I've got to get out of here." We thought he meant he had to get out of the writers' room. But what he meant was, he had to get Tony out of New Jersey. He wanted to do that college trip. We wanted to leave Carmela at home, so that was a good chance to do the priest. What is the Richard Chamberlain movie, there's a priest?

Mitch: *Thorn Birds.*

Robin: Mitch and I went home that night and we beat that out. It was a very simple story to beat out. It was really fun, and Mitch is Catholic, so we had fun with that. David had the idea that Tony wanted to take his daughter on this college tour. That is a very amusing conceit, because you have this thug taking his sweet daughter to all these Ivy League institutions in New England. It was just fish out of water.

Mitch: But that's not a story. That's not enough of a story.

Robin: Yes, David said, "Something has to happen." We were stumped. We all sat around. It took about a minute and a half for Frank Renzulli, who was just a fantastic presence in the room— he was the real marinara, he grew up with these guys in Boston— Frank says, "Tony sees somebody in the witness protection program." At that moment, it was, "Boom." David saw the whole thing.

Mitch: David disappeared, went into his office, and then about an hour later, he came out and wrote down every single beat of that story. I mean, on a whiteboard, just one after the other.

Robin: Yes, he had it.

Mitch: David is a master at this. He really is. We beat this story out, but David wrote it. Along with James Manos.

Michael: They won the Emmy for that script.

THIS EPISODE, *besides being a definitive one in the course of the show— because you have the leading man killing somebody, which was a very risky move—was groundbreaking for another reason. The camerawork in this episode is daring and bold, and while David Chase had already established a cinematic look that was beginning to distinguish* The Sopranos *from what came before, Allen Coulter's direction of this episode set a tone and a vibe and a feel that took it to a whole new place. We talked to Allen about it. —Michael*

Michael: Allen, your camerawork in this episode is really remarkable. There's a lot of very stalking, voyeuristic moments, particularly in the scenes with Febby Petrulio, the guy in witness protection. A lot of handheld shots where you move the camera from the point of view of somebody watching someone else, stalking them. Very cat-and-mouse. It's very distinctive.

Allen: Thank you, Michael. What was an advantage to me was, I really hadn't done that much television, so I hadn't been indoctrinated in the way that people shoot TV. What I did was a minor-key variation on David, who did all those years of television and then wrote *The Sopranos*. I think, given his wonderful caustic nature and his deep cynicism, he somehow resisted being seduced by the world of television. That's why *The Sopranos* looks nothing like television up until that point.

I was not on that level, but I really didn't watch television. I shot it as much as I could like a little movie. I think that that's what David liked.

Michael: You did some pretty daring things with the second story in this episode as well.

Allen: In the communion scene with Carmela and the father, there's the moment where he gives her the wafer, and I was feeling pretty loose. I said, "Let's do that in front of the fireplace, so it looks a little pornographic." The fact that she's on her knees, and the fire behind her, and he puts the wafer in her mouth. That quality that you're describing, Michael, really resonated with David. I know, because he told me. That's why he asked me to stick around.

Steve: And you wind up directing eleven more episodes.

Allen: What happened was, I was shooting "College." We were in Jersey somewhere at one of those colleges filming the scene when Tony comes out smoking the cigar and the camera circles around, or something like that. David came on the set. He said, "I've just seen the dailies from what you've been shooting. You get it. I'd like you to stay on as an executive producer, a producing director." That was it.

One more thing about this amazing episode. We talked about how Meadow shows her maturity—but I thought Jamie-Lynn Sigler, who played Meadow, really came into her own on this one as an actress, as well. I asked her if she felt the same way. —Steve

Steve: The fifth episode, you had a lot of big scenes with Jim, it was basically you and him the entire episode. I read somewhere that you were nervous and a little uncomfortable and Jim calmed you down. What was that about?

Jamie-Lynn: That was in the scene where the two of us went out to dinner, and Tony's basically opening up about maybe he didn't have a choice as to what he was doing with his life. I remember Jim could feel that I was wanting so badly to do a good job and he said, "Jamie, just look in my eyes and trust me, just talk to me." He just gave me such great lessons about being an actress, during that whole episode. When we shot the scene in the car about asking if he was in the Mafia, after I finished my part of the scene, Allen Coulter was like, "Jamie, you're good. Let's wrap it up, we can move on." Jim said, "Wait." He looked at me and said, "Do you feel good?"

I said, "What do you mean?" He said, "Do you feel you have more to give, or you want to do something different?" I didn't know I could ask for that. He gave me a lot of gifts during that time. It was a special bonding time, just being the two of us. He really made me feel confident that I had a place in the show.

Michael: He did that all the time. He made sure actors got another take if they wanted. He wanted everybody to feel comfortable. Both the crew and the cast.

Steve: Yes, he really cared. That wasn't a show. He did it to me all the time also. He gave a shit if you were happy.

AS SEASON *One unfolded, it became clear that David was trying to push the boundaries of what was done on television, in every way—the writing, the cinematography, the direction, the pacing, everything. Stunt coordinator Pete Bucossi said that extended to all the stunt work, as well.* —*Michael*

Steve: The stunt work you did on *The Sopranos,* was that different from stuff you'd done on TV before?

Pete: A beating's a beating—but *The Sopranos* became more movie-like in how we shot things. Everything about *The Sopranos* is more movie-ish than TV-ish.

Michael: From a stunt coordinator's point of view, can you tell me what that means?

Pete: Movies have big budgets, and they take the time, and spend some money on big "gags," as we call them. And *The Sopranos* was kind of proud of that also. They didn't cut corners toward anything at all. They're expecting what was on the written page to be shown on camera. So whether we needed rehearsals or elaborate kinds of things that went on action-wise, we moved forward on that. And just being on HBO, you could get away with a lot more gruesomeness in what was shown. So it was definitely fun.

There were just so many great fights. Artie Bucco beating up Benny Fazio in front of his house; that was a great fight. But just starting from the pilot, when Tony was chasing down this gambler, and Christopher gets kicked in the groin, and Tony jumps in the car and chases after the guy and ends up clipping him, and gives him a good little beating—I was like, "Okay! Here we go!" And we were all looking forward to what was going to be coming up in the next script.

WE HAVE *to take a moment to talk about one of the best quotes in Season One. Tony says, "Uncle June and I, we had our problems with the business, but I never should have razzed him about eating pussy; this whole war could have been averted. Cunnilingus and psychiatry brought us to this." —Steve*

Steve: "Cunnilingus and psychiatry." Where did that whole story line come from, with everybody razzing Uncle Junior about going down on his girlfriend?

Michael: Robin Green told me the story. She was one of the writers on Episode Nine, "Boca," where that story line begins. David apparently brought in a guy who had left the mob and would lecture at Quantico for the FBI. The guy came in as an adviser on the show, back in Santa Monica when they were in the writers' room for the first season.

He told them the mob stance on cunnilingus was very negative. David and everyone thought that was both very bizarre and very hilarious, and they worked it into the script.

Steve: "Boca," the name of the episode, that's part of the joke, by the way. It's about going to Boca Raton, but "Boca" also means "mouth."

Michael: Junior and his girlfriend Bobbi are in bed in Boca, which, yes, means "mouth." "Boca Raton" is usually translated as "rat's mouth." So the whole question of who the rat is comes up as well. But the word "Boca," "mouth," has a totally new significance for this episode when it's revealed in the scene that Uncle Junior is an expert cunnilingus practitioner. So "mouth" has two meanings.

Steve: Plus Junior's going to Florida and going down on her, so he's going south in more ways than one.

Michael: Right.

Steve: That's the big joke of this episode, that Uncle Junior loves performing oral sex and apparently, he's very good at it. I have a friend of mine, an older guy. He said he's never done that in his life.

Michael: That's a real old-school Italian thing—not just a mob thing. You wrote a bestselling book called *A Goomba's Guide to Life,* which explored Italian-American, neighborhood-guy culture. I guess *A Goomba's Guide to Oral Sex* would be a very short book.

Steve: That would be really short, but listen, I'm sure guys have been doing it since the beginning of time.

Michael: In the closet. You have to get the goomba out of the closet.

"BOCA" ALSO *marked the appearance of a terrific character, Junior's lawyer Harold Melvoin, played by Richard Portnow, a veteran actor who broke in way back in the 1980s. He had some nice things to say. Of course, Michael had to spoil it. —Steve*

Steve: You had a lot of scenes with Dominic, obviously, as did I.

Richard: Dominic was what I would consider a true gentleman. A really lovely man. He was just so giving and so gentle. He would entertain at senior citizens' homes on the weekend with his acoustic guitar. He gave me advice on the set. Which you did too once, Steve, and I really appreciated it.

Michael: You didn't actually listen to Steve, did you?

Steve: What'd I tell you?

Richard: Steve, I learned from this and I've taken it with me and I do it all the time. You and I are standing at Uncle Junior's bed. He's in the hospital. And we start with dialogue. I had the first line and the director calls "action." And I said my first line immediately. Then during the cut, you told me, "Don't come in so fast. Let the camera land on us. Let the camera get to know us, and then talk."

Steve: Michael, there you go.

Michael: You should be a director, Steve.

Steve: You gotta be sarcastic. Richard, Michael would never listen to me because I'm way beneath him. In the totem pole of life, I'm on the bottom. Michael's on the top. You've worked with enough Hollywood stars. We're just fucking small-timers compared to a guy like him, you know what I mean?

Richard: I don't want to get in the middle of this.

Michael: Smart thinking.

Steve: Michael, before we go on with the episodes, I wanna ask you something. We had some really good times going out as a gang, all through *The Sopranos*.

Michael: That's the biggest understatement in the book.

Steve: I wasn't around the first season. When did that begin?

Michael: When we started the first season, we had a bar. My wife and I owned that little speakeasy-like place on Seventh Avenue in Chelsea, between Twentieth and Twenty-First, called Ciel Rouge, which means "red sky" in French.

Steve: I remember it well, my friend. It was still there when I came along. We had some terrific times in there. Tell about what it was like.

Michael: It had no sign. It had curtains. You couldn't look into the place from the street. It opened at seven o'clock at night, and it basically stayed open until we wanted to close it, and I had the keys to the place. It was a kind of place you can just go hide out. It was small. It was intimate. Nobody would bother you there. The smoking laws hadn't come into effect so you could smoke all the time there.

So that's where it started. I took Jim there after shooting one night. We went to the bar and hung out. And it just became a thing. At four A.M., we'd lock the doors, and whoever was there that we wanted to hang out with, we'd let them stay, and whoever not, we'd get rid of them, and we'd hang until we got tired.

Things got out of hand sometimes. One night me; my wife, Victoria; Drea; and Drea's boyfriend at the time were hanging out really late—it might have been after a premiere or something—and at five A.M., somebody gets the idea of going up to the Conservatory Garden in Central Park and climbing the fence to go swim in the fountain. So we all got in cabs, along with the bar staff, brought some bottles of booze, and went up to 105th Street and Fifth Avenue. The entrance to the Garden is locked at night but we climbed the tall wrought-iron fence, and all the guys stripped to their underwear and went into the fountain. Like that line in *My Favorite Year*, with Peter O'Toole: "What were you doing in the fountain in Central Park at three in the morning?" "The backstroke."

Steve: Do not try this at home, kids. Illegal and dangerous.

Michael: But fun. Another thing that was funny about Ciel Rouge— even after *The Sopranos* started shooting, I would still work at the bar sometimes.

Steve: Even after I came along, even after the show was a hit, you would still wait tables.

Michael: Yes, so one night a bunch of theater students came in, who just moved from California to New York to be actors. I was waiting on them. They kind of looked at me funny and asked, "Are you the guy on *The Sopranos*?" I said, "Yes." They said, "We're theater students from CalArts and we're wondering, is show business that tough that you're on this hit show and you're still working as a waiter?" So I said, "It's a tough business, kid. You can hack it or you can't, and if you can't, you better go back to where you came from."

Steve: You may have scared them out of a career in show business. Those poor kids. Who knows?

ONE QUICK *note on Episode Ten, "A Hit Is a Hit." It's a fascinating episode that alludes to the corrupt history of the music industry. Jerry Adler, who played the inimitable Hesh, told us that the episode could have been more important than any of us knew.* —*Michael*

Michael: Hesh was based a little bit on Morris Levy, the famous gangster in the music industry, wasn't he?

Jerry: That's right. As a matter of fact, David told me one day that the original idea for the whole show was about Tony Soprano's father and Hesh, because David wanted to do a show about music. It became the impetus for *The Sopranos*.

THERE ARE *so many great episodes in Season One. There was the whole "Where's Pussy" phenomenon, for one thing, which we'll talk more about. And I loved "The Legend of Tennessee Moltisanti," where Michael does such a terrific job showing all of Christopher's emotional problems—up to the point where he shoots a guy in the foot in a pastry shop for no reason, which of course is an echo of what happens to Michael as Spider in* Goodfellas, *where he gets shot in the foot by Joe Pesci.*

But for a lot of us, Episode Twelve—"Isabella"—was the highlight of the season. It's about Tony's infatuation with this beautiful woman next door, only it turns out she doesn't exist. And in the same episode, we have the hit on Tony, the fantastic scene on the street. It's all amazing. We talked to Edie Falco and Allen Coulter about it. —Steve

Edie: Tony has a crush on this woman who lives next door. He's watching her hanging the laundry. It's like it harkened back to his childhood, his younger self and his mom hanging laundry. I was so moved by that because Jim's performance in it was so great. I was thinking, "I can't believe I'm on this show. It's so good and I'm so moved by these performances." That was one of my earliest times of going, "Holy shit. This is good stuff."

Steve: By the end of the first season, Carmela knows everything. What he's going to do to Junior, how's he going to get back at him—she goes with it. She's conflicted constantly, she talks about how this is their chance to get out, but she's all in. She loves the lifestyle.

Edie: That's it. On some level, she talks a good game about wanting to get out because it's almost like, as long as God hears her say those words, she's covered. There's a bigger part of her that really was very attached to their status in the community, status within the family-with-a-capital-F, knowing her kids would be taken care of. That was all a big part of what she agreed to early on.

Michael: Yes, and the power in subtle ways too. Like when the teacher's car gets stolen and Carmela says, "Oh, can you do something about that? Pussy has got a garage." The power of being able to do favors and you know you're going to get a favor back and they're beholden to you in that.

Edie: That's right. It's all a big game. It's like chess.

AS WE'VE *said—and we'll probably say a whole lot more times—one of the things that distinguished* The Sopranos *was that it was the first show to really bring a cinematic eye to the small screen. It's hard to pick out any one scene that typifies that, but I did ask Allen Coulter about one of the ones he created in Episode Twelve. —Michael*

Michael: In the episode that centers on Tony's hallucination of Isabella, you created this very dreamlike texture, and it had a flowing, lyrical mood to it. Like you said, it wasn't textbook TV, which is master shot, medium shot, over-the-shoulder, closeup, closeup. You're breaking that mold and making it cinematic, making it reflect the theme of the script.

Allen: That's great. I'm glad you guys liked that. I generally don't like whatever I do. But after I heard you talk about it, I looked back at it, and I thought, "It's got some stuff."

Michael: Is there one scene that stands out for you, as an example of that?

Allen: The final shot of that episode, Tony where he's on the phone with Melfi, talking about getting shot, and he says, "I'm going to find out who did it," there's the final shot of him, and he's really small in the frame. That shot was inspired by a Fellini film called *Juliet of the Spirits.* In that film there's a final shot of Giulietta Masina where she's walking, and there's the trees just towering over her, and she's just this tiny figure. I thought it was right for that moment because Tony says this threatening thing, but the truth is, he's powerless. There are things beyond his knowledge. Things that he can't do anything about. I tried to actually make him not look powerful in that final shot. That was the kind of thinking I was doing throughout that episode.

THERE ARE *two other notes we should add about Episode Twelve. First, in addition to being one of the outstanding creative achievements on TV to date, it also marked the first time we got thrown out of a location. Not the last, of course. But the first. Ilene Landress, who was with David right from the beginning and was credited as a producer and then later as executive producer on the show, told us the story. —Steve*

Ilene: Did I ever tell you about how we got thrown out of the funeral home?

Steve: No, I never heard that story. It was this episode, Episode Twelve of the first season?

Ilene: Yes. We were always shooting in New Jersey, but I lived in Chelsea and I was just thinking, "Oh good. We're shooting in an Italian funeral home in Little Italy. I can grab a coffee. I can walk to work. This is going to be great." And I show up an hour after call, after everyone else was called to the set, and I'm there for about ten minutes and the location manager comes to me and says, "We're getting thrown out of the place."

Steve: Why? What happened?

Ilene: It's the scene where the guys are paying their respects to some old lady who's in the coffin. You see Uncle Junior peering into the coffin and he turns to somebody and says, "She gave me my first hand job." And we got thrown out of the place.

Steve: Because he said that?

Ilene: Yeah, they were pretty proper so they didn't want us there. So, we got thrown out. After that, specific to the scene, we built the same funeral parlor on the stage, because we had shot part of it. We matched that onstage. But the other problem was with shooting in Catholic churches. They don't like us that much either. So, it was pretty hard finding churches to go to. It's not the individual churches themselves, but in terms of getting permission from the archdiocese, they want family-friendly. Kind of like Major League Baseball.

Steve: The Catholic Church I get. Major League Baseball?

Ilene: There was a line in the script where they're about to watch a baseball game. We couldn't get clearance on using Major League Baseball footage in the show because it's not a family-friendly show, so to speak. There's a line in the script where Artie says, "Fuck Major League Baseball. Let's watch ballet." When David would get pissed off, if we couldn't clear something we wanted, we kind of worked it right into the dialogue.

EPISODE TWELVE *was also the one that started the biggest fight between me and Michael. —Steve*

Michael: Episode Twelve of the first season, out of thirteen, is the first example of what David liked to do often. Episode Twelve usually would be the shocker. You'd expect thirteen as the finale to be the shocker and the cliffhanger but very often something very unexpected would happen in Episode Twelve, and this continued throughout the seasons. We see it in this episode. It's a pattern that he established.

Steve: Why do you think that is?

Michael: I think it's David just trying to play against expectations. Not doing what had always been done.

Steve: It works. Because when Tony gets shot, the hit comes out of nowhere. It's a great moment when they shoot the bottom of the orange juice out.

Michael: This scene is very much like the scene in *The Godfather* when they shoot Don Corleone at the fruit stand. Tony is buying orange juice. Corleone was buying oranges. Tony seeing the hit men coming out of the corner of his eye; it's very, very similar.

Steve: Tony sees him in the reflection, he comes running, and Tony grabs him and he is fighting for his life. He's been depressed, but all of a sudden, he snaps out of it. This is the jolt that he needed. He's grabbing this guy, the other gunman comes running up and tries to shoot Tony but accidentally shoots the first gunman instead. Tony manages to get away and then crashes the car. Tony is laughing. It's a really good scene.

Michael: Excellent choreography. Pete Bucossi, the stunt coordinator, did a fantastic job on this. Jim's double was a guy named Frank Ferrara. He doubled him when they crashed the car there, and he was with Jim as his stunt double through the whole series.

Steve: Now, in the episode, they think it's a carjacking at first, correct?

Michael: Tony doesn't really, but he's saying that. Now, there's a theory out there, Steve. This is a big one. Certain pundits, theorists, *Soprano* experts, have floated this theory that Tony actually died at this shooting. That the whole rest of the show is him in this near-death state, or during the time transitioning to death.

Steve: That's bullshit. Who said that? Some asswipe critic that doesn't know anything?

Michael: That's what I've heard.

Steve: That's complete nonsense, so let's move on. That shit annoys me. When people weren't there and they don't know, that shit annoys me.

Michael: It's a theory. I don't know. It could be.

Steve: But by who? That's what I'm saying. By what theory?

Michael: I don't know. I mean, I'm considering it.

Steve: Really? Okay. Well, you're wrong.

IN ANY *case, the season ended on a wonderful scene of the Soprano family walking into Artie's restaurant during a storm. It's dark and cold outside but it's warm and candlelit inside. The whole crew is there, cozy and romantic—almost Christmasy, in a way. For the moment the conflicts are at bay. Tony proposes a toast: "To my family. Someday soon, you're going to have families of your own, and if you're lucky, you'll remember the little moments, like this, that were good." They all wondered what the future held for them—as did everyone in the cast and crew. Allen Coulter summed it up for us. —Michael*

Allen: It was not obvious that this was going to be a hit. I remember thinking, "It's too good. It's not going to succeed." I do remember talking to David. The first season was basically in the can; we were shooting the title sequence. I was standing there with David while Phil Abraham went up for the camera—he had a camera up in his apartment in the West Village—and David and I were standing out there and I said, "What are you going to do?" He said, "I don't know. If the show's a flop, maybe I'll go to France and write novels." Then he said, "What are you going to do?" and I said, "I'll probably go back and do some shitty television." That was it. It wasn't like, "I can't wait till this is a big smash hit." Basically, the vibe was, it's not going to work. This has been great, but we're going to have to go on with our lives.

And that's where we left it at the end of Season One. At the beginning of the season we were mostly movie actors who had no experience committing to a TV series with all that entailed—including agreeing to perform scripts that hadn't been written yet, for episodes that hadn't been dreamed up yet—so signing on had been a leap of faith. Now we had seen and performed a season's worth of scripts, and watched them become darker and more intricate, sometimes funny, sometimes violent, sometimes absurd, sometimes sublime. And we were hungry for more. I was so turned on by The Sopranos *that I was inspired to try to write a spec script, because I wanted to be involved with all the characters; my second child had just been born, and here I was with a chance for regular work in New York City, so for both professional and personal reasons I was really hoping it would be a hit.*

But remember, we shot the whole season before any of it aired. So we all went home, knowing we'd done something incredible, and having not the slightest idea if anyone out in the world would feel the same way. We had a long time to ponder that, to go off and work on movies and live our lives and know there was this possibility, hanging out there in the universe, that this might be the start of something big.

We spent a long time waiting for that shoe to drop. —Michael

THREE

Bada Bing Back Room
with David Chase

DAVID CHASE IS A LOT OF different people. And they're all interesting guys.

He's a poker-faced guy, for one. Nobody ever quite knew what he was thinking, until he told you. Then you had absolutely no doubt. Because he was a guy who never minced words, either. Not for a second.

He's a very, very smart guy. Jim Gandolfini told me, on more than one occasion, that David was the smartest guy he ever met.

He's a funny guy. He's got one of the silliest senses of humor of anyone you'll ever meet. He's the first one to say that there's a lot of stupid toilet humor, real eighth-grade stuff, in The Sopranos. And he's the first one to admit that that's all him. He just finds it funny.

He's also an incredibly dedicated guy. Dedicated to his artistic vision, dedicated to his work, dedicated to getting every single detail right.

But more than anything else, here's who David Chase is:

He's a guy who knows what he wants.

He's not afraid of anyone. He's as tough as Tony Soprano.

I can't say enough about David Chase. So I won't try. Let's let David speak for himself. —Steve

Michael: When you conceived the idea or had the germ of the idea, what were you trying to achieve artistically through *The Sopranos*?

David: I was just trying to make a show that I would want to watch and that my friends that I respected would want to watch, that you hadn't really seen on network TV. That doesn't really sound artistic but that's what I wanted.

Michael: What would the qualities of that be, that show that you wanted to watch or that your friends wanted to watch but that you hadn't been seeing?

David: A slow pace, if you wanted it. A comedy mixed with drama. Language like people speak. Believability in the way conversations happen, which is: people very seldom say what they mean; they say something else. That was kind of it. I just wanted to get out of network.

Steve: You worked many years as a writer in network TV. You did *Rockford Files,* and *I'll Fly Away,* and of course the excellent *Northern Exposure.* Did you absolutely hate it, or as the years went on, were you just tired of listening to the network executives? There are so many variables, there's so many hands in the pie on network TV. Did you just get tired of all that?

David: When I first started, it was very exciting to drive through the gates at Paramount. "Paramount Pictures! Oh my God, here I am!" And the process of making films was very exciting. I didn't hate the medium. When I was really young, I loved it.

The meetings were a drag. Somehow those people know how to find just the thing that you really want, that you really love, and go, "Why did you have to do that?" I don't know how, but they have an unerring instinct for picking the one thing that was the whole reason you were writing for. You know what I mean? They smell it.

Michael: What did you see in TV that made you think it was at all possible to do what you really wanted to do?

David: I didn't see it in the TV business as it was structured then. That's why, when HBO came along, I grabbed that. In the beginning, you take a big pay cut because you're used to making twenty-two episodes, and now you're making thirteen. I didn't care. I used to say [at the networks], "Why don't they just take ten percent [of all their programming] and call that research and development, and make weird shows or shows that they're scared of or whatever?" That never happened.

But I want to say something, which is, I was really lucky. I worked with, and for, really good, talented people. I never worked on a show that I was ashamed of. I worked on shows that I thought were really good.

Michael: You had worked on *Rockford* for a number of years, right? You started a couple of years into its run?

David: Yes, that was a lot of fun.

Michael: That was a very good show and very unique in a lot of ways. And human, despite the genre.

David: Yes. I hadn't watched it on the air, but when they showed me *The Rockford Files*, I said, "Well, this really looks like, this really feels like Los Angeles." It had that quality. It was more human. All the details were right.

Michael: Detail is something that we've talked about a lot. You watch *The Sopranos* and nothing's ever taken for granted. You cut to a character and they're always doing something specific, whether he's fixing a trophy or cutting his toenails or whatever. There's nothing like "He's just sitting in a chair." It's something that I really learned from working with you. Everything has a specificity, and you're communicating who these characters are through those details.

David: That's what's behind it. Putting those details in. At some point I heard the expression "God is in details." I thought, "Yes, right." I've always thought that way.

Michael: I've also heard the "devil is in details" too, that expression.

David: Yes. That's true too, he's in there also.

Steve: David, did you grow up around mobsters? Did you know that world? Did you have relatives who were involved?

David: I did have one cousin who was involved. He was connected with the Boiardo family, the big mob family in Newark. He's gone now. People used to say, "Oh, him and his Cadillacs." The cops came for him at three o'clock in the afternoon one time, just as his kids were getting home from school. My mother was scandalized. That was that guy. I had an uncle Tommy, my father's brother, who I just realized recently was probably connected, although I didn't realize it at the time. He was called the black sheep of the family, who had a habit of disappearing and going somewhere that nobody knew for long periods of time. Then he came back. So yes, there was some of it around. I guess there were kids in high school whose fathers were in the numbers business.

Michael: How long did you live in Mount Vernon?

David: Until I was four and a half.

Michael: David and I were born in the same hospital, Steve. We were both born in Mount Vernon Hospital. I lived there most of my childhood. Remember that one episode when I wrote in, "Meet me at Webendorfer's parking lot"? It was a factory in Mount Vernon. David, when you first read my script you said, "Webendorfer's, huh?" I said, "Yes, my grandfather worked there, he was a tool and die worker in Webendorfer's," and it turned out your father worked there.

David: Yes. It was a factory that manufactured printing presses. My father was a draftsman. He's one of the few people in the family that went through higher education.

Michael: My grandfather used to sell shit on the side to the employees at Webendorfer's, like stockings and condoms. And Howdy Doody dolls at one point when they were a big deal.

David: Where did he get them?

Michael: He would go down to the city and buy them wholesale or something like that, and then sell them in the parking lot at lunchtime. That was how he made money on the side.

David: Oh my God. That is great. One of the episodes of *The Sopranos* was based on a story in my family, my mother and father, while my father was working at Webendorfer's. There were guys in there who were going to California to start a printing press thing, and he wanted to go really badly. My mother just wouldn't hear of it. Didn't want to leave her sisters. There was an episode, it was actually the "Down Neck" episode, where Johnny wants to go to Reno.

Steve: Just to remind everybody, that's the episode where Tony tells Melfi about the time his father, Johnny Boy, got a chance to move to Reno to manage a supper club for a big mobster. Livia, Tony's mother, refused. But it could have changed Johnny's life. So you based that on your family? David, you also told me years ago that a lot of the names of the characters were your relatives' last names.

David: Yes, Bucco was my mother's maiden name. Melfi was my paternal grandmother's maiden name. Satriale was my cousin Theresa—like that.

Steve: The Sunday dinners you had as a kid—you had those big Sunday dinners—didn't you have an uncle Junior?

David: I did have an uncle Junior. Actually, he was my cousin. What is it, cousin once removed or something? My mother was about the same age as my oldest aunt's daughter. They were contemporaries. So my uncle Junior was actually my cousin Joe.

Steve: Was he as grumpy as Uncle Junior on the show?

David: No. Nobody is that grumpy. No. He actually played the character of Beppy on the show. My uncle Joseph was called Beppy.

Michael: When you started the show, did you have an ending in mind?

David: No. Well, first of all most pilots don't go to production. Then if it does go to production and they look at the film, most things don't get bought. Then if it goes on the air, most things fail, and they're taken off their air. The idea that you're going to have an ending is like, nobody troubles to think about that because it happens so seldom. At least that's the way it was then. No, I had no ending in mind.

Steve: Did you have a favorite character? Was there a guy you liked to write for more than another?

David: I have to say my favorite characters to write for—I loved them all, I loved writing them all, and they were all so different. I really did. I loved writing Tony, I loved writing Chris, Bacala, absolutely, but I guess my favorite was Junior. Junior could just say anything.

Michael: Yes. His dialogue is very specific, and the way he delivered it too.

David: I know. Dirty, old-fashioned, and intellectual. He would use words that you wouldn't expect him to use. I loved Livia too, obviously, that was a great character, another one who could and did say whatever came into her mind. With those two characters, there was no self-censorship at all.

Michael: So what would you say was the germ of *The Sopranos*? Was there a eureka moment when this thing came into your head? What did the whole thing erupt out of? Was there a vision, a scene, a moment, a character that really gave birth to the whole shebang?

David: I used to tell people stories about my mother. My wife, Denise, was the first one to say, "You got to write a movie about her, or you got to write a TV show about her, because she's so funny." I said, "Well, how do you do that? A western or what?" Then Robin Green said to me, "You have to write something about your mother." And so I started thinking about it. Robin said, "Make it a TV producer and his mother." I thought, "Who cares about a TV producer and his mother?" I thought, "The guy has got to be a tough guy, or something." That's when the idea came, "Oh, a mob guy, yes." That's what happened.

Steve: A lot of people say that you're Tony Soprano. That you based him on yourself. Lorraine Bracco told me she thinks you were Melfi. That you identify with Melfi. What do you think about that?

David: Am I Tony? Yes, a lot of that is me. I feel that. Melfi, no. Melfi was based on a therapist that I went to. That's who she was. She was very much like that therapist, a woman named Lorraine Kaufman, whose husband, Millard Kaufman, wrote *Bad Day at Black Rock*. She was great. It was probably my third or fourth therapist, and I based Melfi on her. Most of the ideas were me trying to think like Lorraine.

Michael: When you had the idea to do the show, you're dealing with a mobster and his mother, at what point did the themes that you wanted to explore start to emerge? By the themes I mean, a lot of what the show is about, to me, is America itself, and about the American dream, getting satisfaction out of life in an American context, and what that means.

David: That's really the only theme that I had, once I started to write it. I didn't know that when I was talking about it, pitching it. When I sat down to write it, that's what started to come out: "It's good to get in at the top, but I got in at the bottom." Painting this picture of America lost, and consumerism, certainly. That happened right away. I don't know how or why, but it just did.

Michael: Connected to that, there's this running theme of people who always feel slighted, they feel underappreciated, they feel like they're not being respected or given enough credit. That seems like a running commentary.

David: Yes, it is. Now that you mention it, it is true. That's probably me right there. Certainly, my mother was like that, resentful. You see that a lot in people, don't you? "They don't get me. Nobody gets what I'm trying to say here." It's just always very funny to me. I hadn't thought about that, but that's true. They were all pissed off and annoyed and felt slighted.

Steve: Tony always feels underappreciated by everyone in his family. We see that in Silvio. Paulie is slighted by Ralphie. Carmela always feels that way.

David: Yes. I don't think Bacala ever felt that way, did he?

Steve: Bacala was easygoing. I don't think so.

Michael: Oh yeah? When he got bumped up in the Nostradamus scene, he said, "It should have happened a long time ago."

Steve: "I thought it would happen sooner." [*laughs*] Even good old Bacala was annoyed.

David: The mob was a good place to put that motive in. Because those guys are easily offended. And you don't want to offend those guys.

Steve: When you had to tell someone they were getting killed off, was that hard for you? Did anybody try to talk you out of it? When you had to make that call or tell the people face-to-face, how was that?

David: Yes, it was hard. I tried to pretend I was an oncologist or something, "Yes, you have cancer. I'm sorry, but you do," and tried to be as nice as I could about it. The only person who ever really took it bad—well, I don't know, a lot of people could take it bad. Like John Fiore, who played Gigi. He died on the toilet. And he was really not happy. The guy who really tried to talk me out of it was Al Sapienza.

Steve: Al, who played Mikey Palmice. He gets whacked at the end of Season One.

David: Al Sapienza. He'd never stop. It was funny because he was always coming up with ideas and things. I'd say, "Al, you got to go." Then we had a read-through, it was his final episode, and everybody's around the table, and he's sitting there. Sirico comes into the room, and sees him and he goes [*imitating a gun*], "bap bap bap bap bap." [*laughs*]

Steve: That sounds about right.

Michael: He did that to you, Steve, didn't he?

Steve: Yes.

Michael: On your first day or something?

Steve: My first episode, when Bobby meets Tony, gives him the envelope, and Tony says, "If I were you, I would seriously consider salads!" When he pulls away, I spit, and I go, "You insensitive cocksucker." I didn't know Sirico. I had just met him, and after the scene is over, he said, "You're dead. No one spits at the boss, you're dead. You're a goner."

Michael: David, when did you know Pussy was going to become a rat?

David: Before we started the second season. What happened was, we did the first season, and unlike most TV shows at the time, we were finished writing and editing, and it was all done before the series went on the air. With network series, you're working on it all year long. Show number one is airing, and you're working on show number six.

So we were all done, and I thought, I said it before, like most TV shows, we're not going to come back. It was so much fun; it was so great. I talked to Edie about it and I said, "No. I don't think they think it's supposed to be fun. We probably won't be coming back." It was a guess.

Then I went on vacation in Europe, it was maybe a month or something. I came back, and everybody in America was talking about, "Where's Pussy?" Somebody said to me, "You're not aware that everybody's saying 'Where's Pussy'?" I said, "No." I educated myself, and I thought, "Wow." Obviously, that's a big question, and he should be the focal point of Season Two.

Steve: Did you tell Vinny about it early on, that it was going to happen?

David: Yes, I said to him, "Listen, this is going to be your last season, but I swear to you, it's going to be a really good season for you. You're going to really get to do stuff." He did, and it was great.

Steve: He told me also when I first met him on the show, "They're killing me off. I guess you're going to take my place. How many fat fucks could they have on the show?" That's what he said to me.

David: Turns out it was a lot. [*laughs*] It was a successful season, and people were really interested in it, and it was sad. I remember the episode "D-Girl," I guess it was, when he was in the bathroom sitting on the toilet crying?

Steve: Yes, it was sad, very sad.

David: That was real.

Michael: Also, killing off a main character. The show established that main characters are going to die early on in the series. That was a big thing, and really broke a lot of boundaries. It was a good way to keep a lot of tension.

Were some of the more stylistic elements of the show part of your vision from way back? Like for instance dreams, or even like when Ralphie starts saying lines from "Sympathy for the Devil"—adding those kinds of flights of fancy. Was that part of your impulse? Or, for another example, using music to the effect that you did, was that something you always wanted to do with the show?

David: Yes, I did see them. When we were setting up the show, I forget what it was, we asked for $50,000 an episode for music, and they said, "What do you want that for? This is a show about the mob." I said, "I just do. I think we're going to use it and need it." It turns out I was right. Did I have any other plans for things I wanted to do? Well, I told you I like to have the pace of the shows be different, and to not tie everything up.

Michael: That was a big thing, and that was a very new thing for TV. The lack of closure. For instance, "Employee of the Month," "Pine Barrens," and of course the ending—things where audiences really were expecting a certain closure, and they didn't get it. Your idea behind that was, life is not like that, right?

David: Well, yes. I did think that, but really I just thought, "This is the best story. It's really interesting, and there *is* an ending—but you don't like the ending." [*laughs*] For all those that you mentioned.

Michael: I get asked about the series finale all the time, and I always say, "There's no punctuation mark, no final thing that would make everybody happy." Anyway, what would it be? Tony getting killed? Tony killing everybody? There is nothing that's going to satisfy whatever that need is.

David: The way I started thinking about it was, you don't want to do "crime doesn't pay," because crime does pay. You don't want to do "crime does pay," because crime is crime, it's wrong. That was what most gangster movies were, I guess before *The Godfather*. Actually, it was all those from *The Godfather* on, somebody is suffering at the end. Doesn't mean they die on the steps of the cathedral like Jimmy Cagney. But the protagonist is suffering, that's what I feel.

Steve: I'm sure the question you're constantly asked—you're tired, I'm sure, of answering—have you ever said what the ending of the series is? Is there a definitive answer?

David: No. I really shouldn't talk about it at all because when I say anything, people interpret it some way, and then it starts up again. For a long time, I was really upset because that's all they talked about, they didn't talk about the rest of the episode.

Michael: I started seeing it like a book. When a book is done, it ends where it ends. It's over, there's nothing left to read.

David: That's true. I've been accused—I don't know if that's the word—of being too much into European film. I like a lot of European film but in a lot of those movies there really wasn't some "Okay, here we are. This is the end of the movie." They just didn't do things that way. You're supposed to reflect on what's happened and think about it.

Michael: I think what people got stuck on is that there was tension building in that last scene and people questioned what it was building to—Meadow was struggling to park, there's music starting, there was a sense of urgency—people were trying to make sense of what that meant.

David: The car-parking thing, I hear about that all the time. I don't know why. I didn't write that because I had some plans where it's supposed to mean *this*. I just thought this will be interesting film, that we're worried Tony's going to get shot, and she's having trouble parking her car. Or we're wondering what's going to happen to Tony, and she's busy parking her car. That's all I ever saw. It didn't mean anything.

Michael: And everyone knows this is the last scene of the last show, so you know something is happening, or you're expecting something.

David: We're almost at ten o'clock.

Michael: When did the idea for the Journey song come into play?

David: We were driving around during prep in a van. There's [production designer] Bob Shaw and the whole gang, all the department people, and I had three that I was considering. One was "Love and Happiness," Al Green. I forgot what the second one was. And I asked people in the van—and this is the first time I've ever done it—I asked, "Well, what do you think? I'm thinking of these three songs." The third one was "Don't Stop Believin'," and everyone was, "Oh, Jesus Christ, no!" It got a reaction. I had always considered that song a guilty pleasure of mine. I always liked that song, but other people think it's, I don't know, corny eighties shit.

Michael: The other song that's great in the finale is the Dylan song, "It's Alright, Ma." That sequence was fantastic, from A. J. and the new girlfriend Rhiannon listening to music in the car, through the end when the car blows up—breathtaking.

David: What a masterpiece that song is. It's even more relevant now than it was then. I just can't believe Bob Dylan. I've been thinking about him a lot lately. I liked doing that scene. I thought people would reject it because people would say, "Oh, come on, nobody's car catches on fire from parking in the leaves." But nobody ever said that.

Steve: Dylan sang the Dean Martin song "Return to Me." Did you talk to him about that or he volunteered?

David: No. I've never talked about it with Dylan. His manager, Jeff Rosen, said Bob wanted to do a song on the show. I was like, "Oh, my God." Then he said it's going to be that Dean Martin song. I went, "Oh, shit." You think, "Well, Dylan's going to write a song for our show." Well, no. Hold on, it's not going to happen that way. But I really like what he did, it was great.

Steve: Would you change anything from the show now that you look back? Is there anything you would change and do differently?

David: Not too much. There were episodes that we should have done, and maybe themes also. Stevie [Van Zandt] once told me a prostitution story, which would have made a great episode. I just said something to Denise the other day. I said, "That should have been on *The Sopranos*. How did we miss that?"

Steve: Michael doesn't want me to ask you this, but I'm going to anyway. Is there a significance with mayonnaise on the show? Because numerous times we see and hear "mayonnaise." The "Pine Barrens," toward the end, Tony yells, "You got mayonnaise on your chin! Mayonnaise, mayonnaise!" to Paulie. At one point Carmela tells Tony that they're invited to a barbecue and he says, "Oh, the mayonnaises up the street," meaning I guess white people, white-bread Americans. Does mayonnaise mean anything? Do you love it? What's mayonnaise mean?

David: Yes, there's something about mayonnaise that just seems really white.

Steve: Yeah, like saying "Wonder Bread wop," or "vanilla"—not real Italian. My grandmother would not have mayonnaise in her house. My mother did, but my mother was Jewish. My grandmother was from Calabria, and that was a huge no-no.

David: When I was eight or nine years old, me and my cousin, our parents would serve us spaghetti and meatballs, and we'd drink milk. These were people whose parents had immigrated here, and their parents would go, "How can you kids drink that milk with the tomato sauce?"

Steve: That's another big no-no.

David: You just don't drink milk in Italy.

Steve: Tony, numerous times we see him with a dish of macaroni, drinking milk.

Michael: Yes, there's that scene where you see Furio with his wine, he's made his own pasta, he's tossing it properly, and eating it. Then it cuts to Tony microwaving something and drinking it with milk. Which is a magnificent moment.

Steve: Do you have a favorite episode, David?

David: I really don't. I've never seen the whole show since it went off the air. I've seen an episode or two, maybe three, but I've never seen the whole show. But in my memory, there's so many of them that I really love. Sometimes you like the ones that people don't like because you're thinking, "Okay, that's the runt of my litter. That's my worst kid, I know. He's not cool, he can't play sports, but I love him most."

Steve: Everyone loves "Pine Barrens," but "Whitecaps" is just an incredibly acted show between Edie and Jim.

David: I was on the stage at two thirty in the morning when they did that, it was just unbelievable. I wish I could have done—what she should have said instead of, "I have been dreaming and wishing about Furio," she should have said, to get him, "I have been dreaming and masturbating about Furio." But it's too late. That was a good one. "The Ride" is one of my favorites. I just love that. Everybody was great. It was just mind-boggling. I don't think most people would think of "The Ride" when they think of the series.

Michael: No, but since I've been doing this stuff on social media, I've found that it's a big fan favorite, actually. Season Six.

David: Right. What was the deal? Bacala came in and beat the guy up who runs the rides, right?

Steve: Yes. Then, he got mad, he went after Paulie because Paulie cheaped out on the rides at the festival, and some people got hurt. Me and Tony really got into it.

Michael: I saw Tony after I moved to California in 2012. I hadn't seen him in a while, and the first thing he said to me was, "I heard you lost your mind." [*laughs*] I said, "You heard that from who?" He says, "People are saying you lost your mind, it's all right." I never got to the bottom of it, but he was convinced that I had gone insane or something. He never minced words, Tony. He never holds back.

David: Toward the end, maybe in the last season, he said to me, "You know what you ought to do? Remember you used to give us those really great presents at Christmastime? Little pieces of jewelry and stuff? They were great. You ought to do that again." I said, "You never gave me one fucking thing." He just was stunned. He said, "You're right!" That week I got all this stuff. Perfumes, leather goods, it all came from one place. A lot of stuff.

Steve: We love him to death. He did not mince words. Once we were out at one of the premieres, I was with my wife, he told her, "If he ever gets hit by a bus, make sure I'm the first call."

David: It's really a pleasure for me when I think back about Tony. I have seen him develop over that time as an actor. He had one line in the pilot, and then little by little he was so good that we began to give him stuff. He would refuse to do things in the beginning, and then he softened up, he would get into it. I love seeing that progression. By the end of the show, he was one of the real features.

Michael: Without a doubt.

Steve: What's your favorite memory? Is there one memory that stands out from the entire show for you?

David: It sounds corny, but I have so many great memories. My favorite memory? Well, this is before we started shooting. Jim and I went out to dinner to the Old Homestead Steak House. We came out of there; we've been drinking and stuff. He picked me up, lifted me off the ground. I don't know, I just felt very warm toward him. It was fun, it was like we were kids. I liked that a lot.

Michael: I felt that way all the time. I always say it was like walking down the street and hanging out with your friends every day. It's never really felt that way since on any show, or even before that. It really was that sense of warmth.

David: What was your favorite memory, Steve?

Steve: David, somehow you put all of us together. I don't know if you had that in mind or if it was a coincidence, but you put this group, guys and girls, all similar, from the same background. It sincerely was like a family, with the cast, with the crew. We had so many laughs, we had so many drinks, so many parties. But everyone was really serious with the work. There was no fucking around then.

David: Absolutely. The only thing, I really tried to hire only true Italian folks because that detail—whatever those details are—meant so much to me. Michael Madsen, apparently, was pissed off at me because I wouldn't hire him. He's a great actor, but he has a Chicago accent, and I couldn't see it. It was like a family, I guess. Probably almost all from the same class, right?

Steve: Yes. That's it, I told people that, whether you did it subconsciously or consciously. You saw thousands of actors for these roles over the years, and the ones that wound up, we're all cut from the same cloth to a degree.

Michael: Wonderful experience.

Steve: It was a once-in-a-lifetime.

David: [Executive producer] Brad Gray said to me, "This is it. This is not going to happen again."

Michael: No. It's not.

Michael: The movie, the prequel that's coming out, *The Many Saints of Newark*. I know you don't want to talk about the movie specifically, but did the idea for the movie come out of story lines in *The Sopranos* that you never did? Or is it a different animal altogether?

David: A different animal altogether.

Steve: Did you have the movie in mind for a long time?

David: No. This was an interesting story. I didn't want to do a *Sopranos* movie at all, especially when it ended the way it did, and it ended really well. Everybody loved it and agreed it was good. I thought, "Why risk all that?" That was one of the reasons. I just didn't want to do it. But I had an interview with Tom Fontana—

Michael: Great writer, great producer. He created *Oz*.

David: We were talking, and he said, "Do you want to do a movie of this?" I said, "No, not really," and he said, "Because you know what would be good is if we saw Junior and Johnny when they were younger, back in Newark. Do Newark back in the fifties." I thought, "Oh, yes. That would be interesting," because that's where my parents grew up, I was there in Newark in the fifties and sixties.

The thing that's interesting about it is that Toby Emmerich, now the head of Warner Bros., pursued me, and pursued me, and pursued me, and never gave up, for probably fifteen years. I swear. Finally, I said yeah. I thought, "Yes. We could do that."

Steve: Before you go, I have to say, your eulogy at Jim's funeral was just magical, it was so real.

David: I'd never done a eulogy before, I didn't know what to do, how to go about it, or what it even meant. It was difficult to do because Jim and I did not get along that well toward the end. All that thing about how we were like brothers—I thought, "You can't say that," but then I realized brothers often don't get along.

Steve: There's something you said—I'm gonna quote you—you said, "I feel you're my brother because of the things we both loved. Family. Work. People in all their imperfection. Food. Alcohol. Talking. Rage. And a desire to bring the whole structure crashing down. We amused each other." I just really love that.

Michael: The eulogy, David, we all needed it, being his friends, colleagues, and coworkers. The sentiment that you expressed was for all of us, and we needed it because it was really hard.

Steve: For people who never read it, they should look it up. It's just so perfect.

David: You thought it was expressing your feelings too? And you too?

Steve: Yes.

Michael: Yes. Because I felt like his brother too, and I'll be honest too, there were moments when I didn't get along with him either. It wasn't always Shangri-la. I could be difficult, and so could he. We hung out, and there were times when it was really late at night and maybe one of us was a little too messed up. I could be an asshole, and so could he.

Steve: Make that three of us.

Michael: I'm not ashamed of that, that's being human.

David: Jim had a problem with authority, and I was the authority on that show. I have a problem with authority too, so I understood all that. In the end, we patched it all up, and it was fine.

Steve: It was just about two months before he passed away, when we had the party at his apartment, remember? Jim was so much more relaxed. Once the show ended, time had passed, he wasn't overworked, I think he finally came to terms with everything. Before he died, he was in a much better place with his new wife, and his baby, his son was growing up.

David: We made this movie together.

Michael: *Not Fade Away,* brilliant movie. A couple years after *The Sopranos* ended. You directed it.

David: We made that movie, and it was smooth, just great, working together again, directing him. All that other shit went away.

Michael: It was a big responsibility to be Tony Soprano. All of a sudden, people just recognizing you everywhere you go, which started to happen, with him even more so. I think he found it difficult to adjust to that.

David: I don't think people would know about me if not for him. He did not want to go out there in the press and be the face of the show.

Michael: He didn't do a lot of press.

Steve: He didn't want to do any talk shows. I said, "Jim, why don't you pick one, whether it be Leno, Letterman, Oprah, or the *Today* show, go on one of them and show people who you really are and that you're not Tony Soprano." He would go, "It's not me. I don't find myself interesting."

David: Maybe like many people, he didn't like who he was. So, saying that, he was saying, "Yes, they're going to see all my faults and weaknesses."

Steve: He did a movie for Harvey Weinstein later on and he wouldn't do any press. And Harvey Weinstein continued to badger him and he told me, "If he fucking calls me again, I'm going to beat the fuck out of him. I swear, my hand to God."

David: That's Jim.

Michael: That's Jim.

FOUR

Season Two

A Cultural Phenomenon

SEASON TWO IS REMEMBERED, OF COURSE, *for one thing: the appearance of Bobby Bacala.*

I'm kidding of course. I did debut on the show as Bobby in the second episode of Season Two—and we'll get to that—but so many things had changed since the show first appeared. The main thing was, The Sopranos' cast and crew shot the first season in obscurity. Nobody knew anything about it; they could go on location and no one would notice. By the time we started shooting the second season, the show was extremely popular. As Michael said earlier, it was already changing the landscape of television, and Emmy season proved it. It was nominated for the Emmy for Outstanding Drama Series in 1999—the first cable series to get the nomination. But more important than any award was that the fans were going crazy. Everybody was talking about it.

All of a sudden you couldn't go anywhere without people going nuts. It was amazing. The great Terry Winter, who wound up writing twenty-five episodes of the show, reminded Michael of a night in Jersey with Drea de Matteo, who played Christopher's girlfriend Adriana. It was the moment that Terry realized that the world had changed. —Steve

Terry: Basically, I started as a writer as the series was starting to air in reruns. It was in the first rerun that the groundswell started.

Michael: Because at that time, there was no streaming, no on-demand. If you missed it the first time around you had to catch the reruns when they were on.

Terry: People started telling their friends, "Did you see this thing? You got to check this thing out." As that built, by the time we started shooting Season Two, it was crazy. Michael, you may remember this. We were on location shooting an episode for Season Two and you and Drea came out of a trailer somewhere in New Jersey at night. There was a crowd of people that just started applauding.

Michael, you and Drea looked at each other like, "What the fuck is going on?" This was one of the first times, because you guys shot Season One in anonymity. Nobody knew who the hell you were or what you were doing. You guys came out and you were already Chris and Adriana. We started to need security. It was pretty crazy.

Michael: I remember getting on the subway around the holidays, a few weeks before the Season Two premiere, and I sat across from this big picture of myself—they did individual ads of the characters. It was a little bit freaky. That was a big revelation moment for me.

MY OLD *friend John Ventimiglia, who played Artie Bucco, remembers his revelation moment as well. —Michael*

John: Michael, you and me, when we started out, you were seventeen and I was nineteen and we did little things before I got my SAG card. We just shared these experiences. One time we went to Radio City Music Hall and it was Roy Jones's fight. We walked in with Jimmy and Tony, Stevie, and maybe Lorraine. People stood up and turned around and we were all trying to figure out what they were looking at.

It was the first time we realized, "Hey, they are talking about us!"

You turned around and you looked at me and I'm going, "Wow!" That experience of being two kids and then having that at Radio City Music Hall—it was a feeling of respect.

Michael: Whitney Houston was sitting right in front of us. We met her that night. It's not that long after we were just two kids, struggling to get a line here or there—that moment was completely surreal.

————

Michael: It was fun being on location shooting *The Sopranos*, especially after the show was a hit. People would invite me sometimes into their homes to relax, or have dinner, or get something to eat.

Steve: It was incredible, the way people reacted. I didn't get to the locations as often as you did, obviously, so what was it like?

Michael: Once, we were in New Jersey in a working-class neighborhood, and there were crowds of people around. It was a Friday night. I was sitting in my set chair on the sidewalk, and this Italian grandmother comes up to me and says, "Christopher, why you gotta wait out here. Come inside, I got some pasta *lenticchie*," which is pasta with lentils, something I really like. It's kind of almost like a soup, but not quite. More like a pasta. I had some time between scenes, so I go in the house, she lives alone, I sit at her kitchen table, she serves me the pasta *lenticchie*, which was amazing. And then after I ate, she says, "You look really tired, why don't you go relax on the couch." I sit down on the couch, she turns on the Yankee game, and I fall asleep!

Steve: You're sleeping on the couch in this grandma's house, and meanwhile they're setting up for your scene?

Michael: Yes, and the PAs come to get me to shoot the scene, and she says, "Christopher is tired. He's taking a nap. Come back later."

Steve: She's protecting Christopher! Not Michael. To her, it's Christopher.

Michael: The PAs didn't know what to do. They came back, they knocked, they had to convince her that it was very important that I had to go and shoot the scene so she came and woke me up.

Steve: That's the thing. The people in Jersey loved us. They were very proud.

Michael: Yes, we were the home team.

Steve: A lot of people say *Sopranos* put New Jersey on the map, because before that, Jersey got a bad rap, but now, you're seeing Jersey in a different light. Suddenly, people want to go to New Jersey. People go on those *Soprano* tours. People want to see the spots, they want to see where Tony's house was. The sporting goods store, and the pizzeria, and the pork store.

Michael: It was good for Jersey all the way around.

Steve: But you know, by this time, *The Sopranos* was such a big hit, it was sometimes hard to be around big crowds of people.

Michael: You get people who see somebody famous or on TV, and maybe they're drunk, and they want something from you. And if it doesn't go the way they want it to go, they might have an attitude.

Steve: We like to hang out with each other but it doesn't mean we want to entertain some drunk.

Michael: There's this one bar, the Spring Lounge on Mulberry Street, which is also known as the Shark Bar, because there was a shark on the wall. I don't know why, but in that bar, there was always some weirdness.

Steve: Just seemed as though in that place there would be some drunk coming up who wouldn't let us alone. It was never fistfights. It never came to that.

Michael: No. But there were situations that could have gone that way that had to be gracefully exited from, let's put it that way.

LOCATION MANAGER *Jason Minter, who later became David Chase's assistant, remembers that things began to change in a lot of different ways starting in Season Two. —Steve*

Michael: After the show aired and became a hit, how was the interaction with the public? How did that change?

Jason: We hired these off-duty Newark police as a security detail, and they were pretty hard-core. They were tough guys. We had a bunch of them with us at all times. We went places and people were chanting, "No fucking ziti!"

Michael: One of A. J.'s most famous lines, from the pilot, when he finds out Livia's not coming to his party.

Steve: And how about things like location fees, did that change?

Jason: Of course, people wanted more money, but that was understandable. The show had more money. Not so much in Season Two. But as the years went by.

Steve: What are we talking, what kind of money?

Jason: This is many years later, but I would buy out restaurants.

Michael: Say I own a deli in Harrison, you want to shoot there for half a day, what are you going to pay me?

Jason: If you open for half a day? I'm going to offer you $6,000, and if you go up to ten, fine, then you'll get it.

Michael: If I owned a house, the same thing if you come to my house and shoot in my house?

Jason: It depends on the caliber of the house.

Michael: What was the most expensive location that you remember booking or that we booked?

Jason: My location work ended at the end of Season Four. "White-caps" was my last episode being on set. I had the time of my life on that one when we were shooting at the beach. It was wonderful. I don't know, we probably paid that house on the beach $10,000. Back then, that was a lot of money. The Sopranos' house in North Caldwell obviously was very, very expensive because those home-owners knew that we had the money and we needed the house. We couldn't get around that. All told, they probably got, oh, more than $250,000 over the years. Probably $500,000.

Michael: What about when we had to go in the city, like Mulberry Street, Little Italy, would that be expensive? Is the city more expensive?

Jason: Yes, because you're blocking other businesses, and then people come out, and they want money. When we were shooting in Newark, we shot on one block and we were there for half a day. I had to pay $9,000 more to various stores because people came out screaming that we were blocking the street.

WE DODGED *one bullet, going into Season Two: a lot of us didn't realize it at the time, but we almost lost Silvio. Either that, or fans of Bruce Springsteen and the E Street Band might never have seen the return of the amazing Little Stevie. —Steve*

Michael: Now, you talked earlier about how you'd been out of music for a while. But just as Season Two was starting, you thought you were gonna have to make a choice between acting and music?

Steven Van Zandt: Yeah, unfortunately, the E Street Band went back together in the second season. I really, really had to consider, should I go back into the band or not, because I really thought, "Okay, this acting thing is going to be my future. I'm completely into it. I want to evolve into writing for TV, directing TV." I just fell in love with the whole process. And it was a very, very, very hard decision for me to go back to the E Street Band. But I felt I needed closure there. It was a very, very, very tough decision, but miraculously I ended up doing both simultaneously. I don't even know how to this day. But David, fortunately, booked my scenes on days off.

Michael: At that moment in time, when you came to that fork in the road, if you would've had to choose, you would have gone to the band?

Steven Van Zandt: One or the other? Maybe not. If I literally had to choose one or the other? Maybe not.

Michael: You might've stayed with the acting?

Steven Van Zandt: Yes.

Steve Schirripa: Good thing for everybody that you got to do both.

Steven Van Zandt: Yes.

WHEN YOU *talk about Season Two, there are a few characters that absolutely stand out in people's minds. One, of course, is Big Pussy. People were drawn in by the arc of his story. The name attracted attention, of course; David Chase was the first one who told me that "pussy" is a slang term for a cat burglar, and that's how Salvatore Bonpensiero—*

Big Pussy—started out. But it was his character, really, that people were drawn to. From the big, lovable teddy bear of a guy who then starts selling heroin to help send his kids to college—perhaps a rationalization on his part, but Vinny Pastore was so good he made you believe it—to the moment Tony takes his life. They were drawn in by the art and skill of the writing, the sheer audacity of a show daring to kill off a beloved character in such a shocking fashion, and, I believe most of all, by the talent of Vinny himself. We can't talk about Season Two without talking about Vinny Pastore. —Michael

Steve: You started acting late, as I did. Let's go from the beginning. Your story begins right near Michael, right?

Vinny: I grew up in the town right over from Michael. I grew up in New Rochelle. Michael was in Mount Vernon. David Chase grew up in Mount Vernon as well. It's ten minutes from my house. I was running nightclubs, and I was doing a lot of rock and roll. I used to sneak Michael in to come see the bands.

Michael: At the Crazy Horse! That was a club in New Rochelle. Steve, I'm going to tell you this: When we were teenagers in Mount Vernon, Vinny was a legend. People knew who he was, they knew his club. Some kids would get in under the drinking age and hang out, including me. We all thought he was a wiseguy, even though he wasn't. People thought he was a stand-up guy and a good guy, but always larger-than-life.

And I used the names of all those clubs from those days. I wrote this episode when Christopher gets the club for Adriana. The name of the club is the Lollipop, which was another bar that Vinny was involved in in New Rochelle. So when I wrote it, it was the Lollipop, and then when we took over it became the Crazy Horse. These names are all homage to Vinny Pastore.

Vinny: An honor.

Steve: How do you go from the Crazy Horse to being an actor? Didn't the Dillon brothers, Matt and Kevin, didn't they suggest it to you?

Vinny: I was getting burned out. Matty suggested it. Matty said it to Kevin. We were sitting in my bar one night. We were watching *Pope of Greenwich Village*, and Matty said, "Why don't you set him up?" Kevin sent me down to Astor Place, to Curtis Brown management.

Steve: That's where his agent was.

Vinny: The agent got mad at me. He holds up some headshots and says, "Look. I could bring any one of these guys into my room, but you're here because of Kevin." He was a little grumpy. "Come back in a month," he says, "and give me a monologue."

I didn't know what a monologue was. But I came back about a month later, I did a monologue. He was sending me out, but he also gave me some good advice. He said, "Go to NYU and start doing student films." And that was the beginning.

Steve: And you did that, and you start working as an extra.

Vinny: I got lucky. The first job I did that was of any significance was *True Love*, and I was Annabella Sciorra's father. It won Sundance. And because of that, Ellen Lewis brought me in and she says, "You're not going to get a big part, but I'm going to put you in *Goodfellas*."

Michael: Ellen Lewis, the great casting director.

Vinny: Right, she said, "I'm going to put you in *Goodfellas*." I got "the Man with the Coat Rack."

Steve: That was in the big scene in the Bamboo Lounge, the big POV shot from Ray Liotta's point of view as he walks into the club.

Everybody remembers that shot. Nobody had ever done a shot like that before. What was that like?

Vinny: Marty did fifteen takes on that. It was a Steadicam shot in the Bamboo Lounge. By the time they got to me, it was the last part of the sequence. Ray Liotta, he had to do a different take each time, and one time, he smacked me.

Steve: In your face?

Vinny: Yes. He said, "Why'd you bring me these clothes for?" Then he hit me. "Come on," I said. "What'd you hit me for?" He said, "I felt like it." [*laughs*]

Steve: But that part leads to other parts, and then to *The Sopranos*. Not bad for a guy who burned out on the Crazy Horse.

I ONLY got to be in a few scenes with Vinny. But he was always such a presence. We were all a little shocked when we found out that he was going to get whacked. I mean, I know, it was Pussy who got whacked, not Vinny. But I gotta say, sometimes it felt the other way around. —Steve

Vinny: This is a true story, and we always bring this up. We're in Italy. You were there, Michael; David and Timmy Van Patten created the scene. There was a look-alike guy who was walking through Italy. Tony Soprano and you guys thought it was me. That's why I was over there. I was sitting around when David was doing his cameo in the coffee shop outside, and Sirico says, "You're really going to get rid of Vinny?" David said to him, "I'm not getting rid of Vinny, I'm getting rid of Big Pussy. He's got to go."

Michael: But they never used the shot in Italy, right?

Vinny: No. I kind of think Timmy did that just to get me over there, because he felt bad that everybody was going to Italy and I wasn't.

Steve: So obviously your character, he gets killed off in Season Two, but everybody remembers him. You're called Big Pussy every day of your life.

Vinny: Only if I leave my house. Nobody calls me Big Pussy in my house.

Steve: What about your granddaughter? What does she call you? Grandpa Pussy?

Vinny: No. She calls me Grandpa, but there are funny stories with me and her. Like when I take her to the National Zoo. People are jerks. They yell out, "Hey, Pussy!" She's looking at me. I say, "They're looking for the pussycats." One time we were in Baltimore having dinner in the Italian section and some lady I don't know, she kept saying, "Hey, Pussy! Hey, Pussy!" I finally had to get up and walk away. My granddaughter's here, will you relax? Because the kids don't get it. I don't think she gets it now. She gets *Shark Tale*. That's her favorite movie, Michael.

Michael: A lot of kids love that movie. You did an outstanding job in that, voicing Luca, which none of the kids get is a reference to Luca Brasi from the original *Godfather*. Or "from One," as the Sopranos would say.

Steve: You have such a funny line in that movie, "We got your girl. You gotta come to the sit-down if you don't wanna see her sleeping with the fishes," and then he thinks it over because, I mean, they're all fish! So he says, "I mean the dead ones!" That always cracks me up.

Vinny: They love *Shark Tale*. She hasn't been able to watch *Sopranos* yet so I don't think she knows why they call me Big Pussy. The other day I was talking with Chazz Palminteri. He said, "Everybody knows you. Because of the name."

Michael: It's not just the name. It was your performance, your beloved character. People loved Pussy. People are just not used to main characters of a show, one of their favorite characters, getting killed off in Season Two. It never happened before. Even though we know he's working with the feds, seeing them kill you is such a big deal. A, because the audience loves you by then. B, because the guys loved you and it was so hard for them to do that, both as the character and as the actors. It's so powerful. You were so powerful.

Vinny: Thanks, Michael. Appreciate you saying so.

WITHOUT A *doubt, Season Two would not be Season Two without Aida Turturro. Her character, Tony's sister, Janice, bursts on the scene like a hurricane blowing in from the coast. She's every bit a match for Tony—and that's in part because Aida was every bit a match for Jim Gandolfini. Aida of course became my TV wife in the later seasons—but it was in Season Two that the unstoppable force of Janice Soprano hypnotized everyone. Me and Michael included. —Steve*

Steve: Aida, I have to tell you, when you came on, it was amazing. Janice is the most evil, crazy lunatic.

Michael: She is very complicated and has a lot going on.

Aida: She is complicated. I never looked at her like that because you can't look at her objectively that way when you're filming, when you're being her. They wrote great stuff for her. Come on, who gets to steal a leg? Not many people.

Steve: You were engaged to a nineteen-year-old, you tell Tony, "He's nineteen and he can go all night long." And you did it with such a straight face. It was brilliant. And I also loved the way you played off that character Aaron—the one Turk Pipkin played.

Aida: He was the narcoleptic, right? That was funny. I remember shooting that because everybody was at the dining room table, and everybody was laughing about it, and I couldn't laugh. I had to be angry and serious about them picking on him. About being a narcoleptic, and then born again. I was like, "Will you guys stop? I'm trying to freaking stay in character here!" [*laughs*]

Steve: Where did it start for you, the whole acting thing? Were your father and John and Nick Turturro's father, were they brothers?

Aida: Oh, yes. John's father, he was the oldest one. John's father actually grew up in Italy and then came over at a young age. My father was born here. John and I are really close.

Steve: Did John get into the acting first? Did you do it together?

Aida: Basically, John is five years older than me. John and my other cousin Ralph, they would always do imitations. All the uncles loved all the old movies, so they'd watch the old films and do imitations. Nicholas too, who's more my age, they all were doing theater and shows. I was the shy one. John went off to SUNY New Paltz, and years later, I finally started getting into it.

Steve: Where did you go to college?

Aida: I went to SUNY New Paltz. A great theater department. Then John and I ended up doing some Off-Broadway together. John and I have this nice bond of working together, and so I've done some of his movies. Call it nepotism if you want.

Steve: That's all right. I'm all for nepotism. And how do you wind up auditioning for *The Sopranos*?

Aida: When it first started, James actually called me because he and I met during *A Streetcar Named Desire* on Broadway in 1992.

Michael: Yes. You're one of the few who'd worked with Jim Gandolfini before.

Aida: Right, and we had done a movie, *Angie*. We were friends, and he called me up and said, "Hey, there might be something in this show I'm doing." So the first year, it never panned out. He calls me up, and now, I'm watching *The Sopranos*, and I love it and the opportunity comes to audition, and now everybody wants it.

Steve: This is when they were casting for Janice.

Aida: And the audition came up, but everybody else was up for it. I'm a huge Marcia Gay Harden fan. She was up for it. I will say one thing, I go to Jimmy and Jimmy is going, "Hey, why don't we just go over this scene? I really want you to get this." I said, "Listen, Jimmy, of course, I want this, but what are you going to do? If it's meant to be, it's going to be. I just have to say, if I don't get it, you have to lend me my rent money." [*laughs*]

Michael: Georgianne Walken told us that it started at the wrap party for Season One. Robin Green went up to Georgianne and said, "I don't want to surprise you, but there's going to be a sister." And she went, "Oh, my God, it's got to be Aida."

And then it came down to you, Marcia Gay Harden, and somebody else. Sheila Jaffe said you told her you loved Marcia Gay Harden and you told her, "Give it to Marcia. She's brilliant." But she wasn't Italian, and she wasn't right for the part. And she said that you and Jim just had great chemistry.

Aida: Luckily, she wasn't right for the part, or else I probably wouldn't have gotten it.

Michael: What was your way into Janice? How did you approach it? Was it based on somebody real?

Aida: Definitely not based on anyone. You do the homework, take a little bit of what's there in the script and what they say about her. So I put it all together and I came out with what I came out with.

Steve: I see Janice as very much Tony's sister. They're very similar in so many ways. You totally believe they're brother and sister. Janice is basically Tony in a wig.

Aida: Oh, yes, they did come from that family, don't forget. They're still siblings by birth. They come from a really sick mother and are trying to survive that, and each one does it differently.

Steve: A sick mother and a gangster father. A murderer father.

Aida: A murderer, yes. When you grow up learning that it's okay to murder, then, where are the boundaries? If you're going to kill someone and it's okay, then whatever you do is really okay as long as you take care of yourself, she thinks.

The beauty of the writing and with David was, there were no one-dimensional characters. These were people, and between the writing and the actors, it's not one-note. You could be funny, you could be boring, you could be scary, you could be tender. That's real life. Therefore, that's also what's wonderful about all the characters, because they were real people first and foremost.

Steve: Let's talk about your relationship with Jim. Like Sheila said, there was amazing chemistry there.

Aida: I talk to Jimmy all the time. Nobody believes it.

Steve: Now? Still?

Aida: I talk to him, and I have been talking to him. I don't feel distant from him because I know he's with me. He was such an unselfish person. I'm going to get sad, but he really was. He was so talented. James was harder on himself than anyone. But if you needed him, he was there for you no matter what.

Michael: Of course, 100 percent.

Aida: With James, I didn't feel like we were acting. We were just . . . talking. One of my favorite scenes—I haven't seen it since maybe twenty years ago, but when I go to anger management and we're sitting around the dining room. Tony doesn't like that I'm so calm, so he ends up provoking me and I lose it on him.

Steve: But I remember that scene, where you have the big argument and he's yelling about you blowing roadies and all that. First it was your characters arguing, but then you and Jim got into an argument. You got mad because you thought he wasn't looking at you, right? They were shooting your part of the scene, the camera was turned around toward you, and you wanted him to be paying attention, so you could play off him, and he was just kind of ignoring you. And you got mad.

Aida: I got *really* mad!

Steve: You were the only one who called him "James." And you were going, "Don't fuck with me, James!" And I got caught in the middle. Jim was going to me, "Am I wrong? Am I wrong?" I didn't know what to say. You're going, "Would you, Steve, tell him?" I just wanted to get the hell out of there.

Aida: I actually was really sick that day, I swear to God. I had some major flu or whatever it was. Jimmy was the most giving actor, so he never wasn't there. Now, maybe I was sensitive because I was ill, but I went bananas. He got so mad at me, he walked away. He goes, "I don't fucking give a shit." Everybody wasn't sure. At first, they thought it was part of the scene, and then they were like, "I think they're really fighting!"

Steve: You kept saying, "Don't fuck with me, James." [*laughs*] Like, maybe other people think he's a big star now but you couldn't give a shit.

Aida: I was going, "I don't give a fuck who you are. You're not the fucking boss of me." One thing James loved is that I would say, "I knew you when you used to move with all your clothes in garbage bags."

Steve: But in the end, it all blew over. You took a break and came back and you guys hugged and did the scene and you were terrific. These are the things that happen with good friends.

Aida: Exactly.

Michael: So you had all these amazing scenes with Jim. You also had some amazing scenes with Janice's mother, Livia, played by the legendary Nancy Marchand.

Aida: You want to hear a Nancy Marchand story? It's my second episode in my first year. I'm getting to do a scene, I'm looking at the script, and it's the scene where it flashes to where I'm throwing her down the stairs. It was a very strange Hitchcock-y scene.

Steve: Janice looks at that "In case of fire" sign with a stick figure going down the stairs, and then she pictures Livia falling down the stairs.

Michael: Livia brings up *Kiss of Death,* a movie with Richard Widmark. Happens to be one of Sirico's favorites. Widmark plays Tommy Udo in that movie, where he pushes the old lady down the stairs in a wheelchair. That's what Livia is referring to.

Aida: Yes, right. And I swear to God, I'm reading it and I'm thinking, "Oh, my God, I don't understand this, but who am I to say? It's my second episode, I better shut my mouth." We go to rehearse a little bit and Nancy goes, "I don't understand this, what the hell?" Thank you, Nancy. I thought, "Okay. I don't feel so bad." She goes, "What the fuck is this? I don't understand this shit." I said, "Me either." I was thinking, "Oh thank God."

Steve: Now, the episode where you kill Richie, and then Jim puts you on the bus, that was an amazing episode, but you didn't know if you were gonna come back, is that right?

Aida: Right. David Chase calls me up. It was right before Thanksgiving, and he says, "Hey, we have this great episode for you." He tells me about the episode, I say, "Oh, my God, this is great, David." He goes, "Then you get on the bus and you go to Seattle." I said, "Oh, do I come back?" He says, "You know, Aida, I don't know that." I don't find out until basically June. Oh, my God. It was excruciating because you get this job, you get to know these people, you get this fantastic opportunity to be part of this whole world, and now I don't know if I'm coming back. It was really, really hard.

Steve: You had to go from November to June? You just had to hang on, you didn't know if you had a job or not?

Aida: I had no idea and I couldn't get another job until they completely let me go.

Michael: They had you under contract.

Aida: Yes.

Steve: But then of course you came back. And you became my screen wife. Aida, of all your lovers on the show, I know that Bobby was your favorite. I'm sure of that.

Aida: By far.

Michael: Bobby was the nicest, that's for sure.

Aida: The sex I had with Bobby, let me tell you, he seemed like a little pussycat, but he was an animal. [*laughs*]

Steve: I knew you before they put us together, but I didn't know you that well. You called me, and I came over to your apartment in Gramercy, and we ran the lines, and you couldn't have been nicer. Then we went on Second Avenue in the park. Sitting in the park and running lines. That way we got to know each other better.

Aida: That's right. Yes, that was nice.

Steve: There was one scene in the kitchen, later on. When you wanted me to eat the last ziti that Karen made. You said, "This is a hard fucking scene." And it was because there was so much emotion, we had to get to that place. And then we got it, and it was great. Once you learn your lines, that doesn't mean that it's so easy, and it was a hard scene.

But if you remember we shot the scene, but then David was editing it and decided to change the dialogue and we had to come back months later, that July, and shoot it again. And David saw me and screamed, "Are you *tan*!?"—because it wouldn't match the other scenes. And I said, "No, no!"—but of course I was tan. It was fucking July. And so I ran to makeup and said, "Lighten me up! Lighten me up!"

Aida: So not only was that a hard scene, but then we had to do it again.

Steve: But me and you never had a problem ever. Not one second did we have a problem.

Aida: No. Because when someone works honestly and they're good people, there's no problem. It's when people start with a big ego, that's when you get a big problem.

Michael: Yes. That didn't fly on our show. If people tried that, they got the message pretty quickly that it was not the place for that.

Aida: Oh, yes. That's not going to happen.

THERE'S ONE *other person we have to talk to before we get to specific episodes in Season Two. There were so many twists and turns and developments in the plot and characters, and the writing became deeper and the production became more complex—but nothing could have propelled the season forward with more force, and more terror, than the appearance of Richie Aprile. The power and the understated danger that David Proval brought to that role was, in my mind, among the most compelling elements of the season, if not the entire series. —Michael*

Michael: You were in *Mean Streets,* you played Tony, you were kind of one of the originals, the OG of the whole modern mob genre. We've been talking about how *Mean Streets* was maybe an inspiration for *The Sopranos.* I've watched it a hundred times.

David: I agree with you. David Chase probably watched *Mean Streets* as much as you did. I think that *Mean Streets* was an inspiration.

Michael: That whole question of, how do you reconcile what mobsters do, the life they live and the Catholic beliefs, and how do you deal with that?

David: Exactly. Right. I mean, people miss that for some reason. There's a scene in *Mean Streets* around a pool table where my character is telling all these characters that the church is a business. It's something that these people hustle you on retreats and all that baloney, and if you want to be saved, you got to be like me. We're shooting pool, and Johnny Boy says, "Well, I'll never go on any retreats." That's the key in the movie, how these characters struggle with Catholicism.

Steve: You worked nonstop after that obviously, but then you actually read for the part of Tony Soprano. Like everybody they were auditioning, you were Italian, or at least part Italian, right?

David: Yes, there's Italian in the family. But my mother and my grandmother raised me Jewish, and that's what I am.

Steve: So after you read for Tony, what happened?

David: Then I get a call to read for Richie. It was at Silvercup Studios, in Queens. So I read, and then they say, "Could you stay a moment? We want to get Jimmy from the soundstage." Jim Gandolfini.

They took him out of a scene he was shooting downstairs at Silvercup and brought him up to the office to read with me. He comes up, he's complaining to somebody about something—"I don't know what the fuck they want!"—and I realized, this guy's in a bad mood, and he's going to sit with me. I'm dead.

Steve: You'd never met him before?

David: Never met him. The star is pissed. I think, "I can't handle this." He sits down and we read a little bit and we finish. But here's what happened.

I wore a shirt that day intentionally, a particular gaudy wiseguy shirt. It was a checkerboard thing, it was terrible. He looks at me, and goes, "Where'd you get the shirt?" I say, "Why, you don't like this shirt?"

He goes, "It's not that I don't like this shirt." I said, "Why'd you ask it that way? You sound like you don't like my shirt." He said, "No, Richie, I like the shirt, the shirt looks great." I go, "No, don't bullshit me. If you don't like the shirt, tell me you don't like the shirt. What are you, afraid to tell me you don't like the shirt?" We go into an improv, it was great. It was just like jazz musicians, each tying into each other. He was right there.

After that reading, I left. I was staying at a hotel across the street from the Museum of Natural History. I went into the museum and—you know the big dinosaur in front?

Steve: Yes.

David: I stood in front of that dinosaur and I knew how small I am. I'm looking at this dinosaur and I thought, "Look, okay, I can't live up to any of this."

What I was feeling was that I'd been a journeyman actor at that point for a lot of years, from say 1973 to the year 1999, when I went in to read. There was something within me that felt 100 percent entitled to do this, to be on this show. It's very hard to verbalize, but entitlement and rage and anger at the whole thing. There's a line they wrote for Richie, "You can't give me what's already mine." It's a great line in the thing, and Richie understood that completely, and so did I. I always felt, we gave our life to this, and we love it. There's a point in life where you say, "I'm entitled to this work. It's precious. I'm privileged to be able to do it, but it's mine. I love it, and it's mine."

So I go up to the room after the dinosaur, and I'm at the door and my phone's ringing and I'm trying to open the door. And the fucking card doesn't work on the door. Finally I get it opened and I get to the phone. It's my agent: "Hey, you got it!" I said, "I got what?" He goes, "You're on *The Sopranos*. They gave you seven shows, David."

Did I cry? Of course, I cried, like a fucking baby.

Steve: Working with Jim, you went nose to nose with him—he's six-one, two hundred fifty and whatever pounds, and so much bigger than you, but you don't blink. Richie Aprile does not blink. He's not the least bit intimidated by him. I'm sure you must have loved going on the set and doing those scenes with Jim.

David: Oh, it was fun. It was the classic David and Goliath. The first day of shooting—the first day I worked with James Gandolfini—we drive up to his trailer. We're parked in Jersey in a mall, so you had to go over to his trailer to pick him up. Guy gets out of the van, knocks on the door, comes back in the van, and we're waiting five, ten minutes. Guy goes out again, knocks on the door, Jimmy is not coming out. And I'm biting at the bit. I was up all night. I can't sleep. You know that one, you're going to work the next day, you can't sleep. I'm sitting there and then he comes out and screams, "Can't anybody take a shit anymore in the morning?" He screamed at everybody. I said, "Okay, right. This is perfect."

Steve: What was it about? Was he kidding around, or was he getting psyched up to do the scene, to get into character?

David: Both. It was part joke and part Tony Soprano. He screamed at everybody, then we get to the place and we do this long walk-and-talk. It's my first fucking day. I'm standing there in the clothes, Members Only, and I'm wearing the pants high. I look down at myself and then people walking by who are going shopping.

I look up at Jimmy, and I say to him—I'll never forget because I always feel this way—I say, "Do you feel a little silly right now? Silly like we're going to go pretend something right now?" He just whipped around at me and he said, "Always. I always feel very dumb doing this." And then the guy says, "Action," and we spilled into it.

Steve: That's Jim all the way. He could get crazy serious and in the next second say something funny and then snap back. He was amazing. But let me ask you. That character, Richie Aprile, he's so intense. So evil. How did you create that character? How did you get into that?

David: I was raised in Brooklyn, the Brownsville–East New York section of Brooklyn. It came from just watching guys on the streets. It was actually specifically two guys I knew who frightened everybody. I used to call them fear peddlers. They just knew how to frighten you without saying a word, just by what was going on with them, the rage within them. It's people who feel the world owes them something or denied them of something.

Michael: We've talked about that a lot too—that sense throughout *The Sopranos* that everybody feels they've been snubbed, or cheated, in one way or another. These particular guys, were they connected? Were they mobsters?

David: They became that. One of the guys got made.

Steve: Terry Winter said, and a lot of people said, that what came across in your performance was that look in your eyes. Let me ask you, was that something you did consciously, or did that come from internally, from getting the rage inside? Did you ever practice in front of a mirror?

David: No, never. It was 100 percent internal. Never in front of a mirror. And in fact, when that was pointed out, when I started hearing "The eyes, the eyes, the eyes," I said, "What the fuck are they talking about?" David labeled it "Manson lamps"—which I hated, by the way. I hated to be compared to that guy, and these two guys I knew from the streets would have hated that, too. I mean, they're not that kind of aberrant, you know, the fucking violence.

Michael: Interesting. So the internal rage, where did that come from? How did you create that for Richie Aprile?

David: My family grew up struggling. We were on welfare. We were very poor people. And I reach back for those feelings, of feeling "less than." Having welfare investigators visit your home. And you have to sit politely on the couch. And they're looking into your icebox that you don't have a steak or expensive food. My mother trembling from the investigators coming into the house.

Steve: I know what you mean, pal. I grew up like you grew up. It was demeaning. Especially the way you knew that other kids, other people were looking at you.

David: Right. The entitled people. I remember being taken by rich people from Long Island to go shopping for my school clothing. It was a charity organization. And I'd go with them and their children. They would take me, and I would stand there, and listen to their kids complain about the jackets they wanted. And I would say to myself, "My God, I'd be so grateful to have a mom and dad who can do that."

Steve: We can't say enough about your performance. You were only on for that one season, but no one ever forgets that character. Did you know that you were going to just be around for one season? Did you know? Did they tell you it was just one season?

David: No. I had a meeting with this HBO girl. She said, "You know, we have an idea of Richie Aprile moving to Philadelphia and he's got a crew in Philadelphia, and every few episodes he'll come in," and I said, "Hey, I'm thrilled." But David said no. And he was right. Which I respect. Look, do I want to choke him? Yes, of course, I want to choke him [*laughs*], but I understand his principles and what he felt about the show.

One of the writers, Robin Green, she wrote the scene to kill me, and she said, "I felt terrible doing that because we love what you were doing." Was it the right choice? I don't know. They went on for another four seasons, five seasons. They did pretty good without Richie.

Steve: Was it hard for you to watch the show, after you were off it?

David: Yeah, very, I didn't take it well. When David called me to tell me—there's that call he makes—and I said to him, "Did I get a reprieve?" And he said, "I'm sorry, David, no reprieve." And I said, "Well, thank you for the work. And maybe someday I'll be able to say your words again." And then I hung up the phone. I looked at the phone and I said, "Fuck you!" And that stayed with me. I was so upset about being off that show.

Steve: When did you get over it?

David: Yesterday. I think I resolved the thing yesterday. [*laughs*]

SO LET'S *get to the episodes. It was an amazing season—starting with the long montage that opens the first episode, "Guy Walks into a Psychiatrist's Office." —Steve*

Michael: I think the montage is a phenomenal way to show the passage of time, and reintroduce the characters, and bring everybody back up to speed. The song is "A Very Good Year," Frank Sinatra.

Steve: Fantastic song.

Michael: It was a very good year for the show on one level, right? And a very good year for the characters, and for us as actors.

Steve: Tony was the boss again, everybody did okay. Everything is back in order. You see A. J. is grown up, he cares about his appearance, he's no longer the chubby little kid. The montage starts with Livia in the hospital, and Tony's playing solitaire at the Bada Bing. Paulie Walnuts is there, Carmela cooks—you see her kind of just living a humdrum life. Junior's in prison. Paulie's having sex with a stripper.

Michael: The hair not moving, even while he's having sex.

Steve: They probably asked him, "Would you mind taking your shirt off?" or something, and he probably said, "No." I would almost bet that he refused. He's fully clothed.

Michael: Because he didn't want to mess up his hair, maybe.

Steve: That's probably right.

Michael: The montage really establishes the tone for the season—there's an epic feeling to the characters. Even though it's just one season we've been through with them, coming back like this, it's almost as though everything's larger-than-life in a way, in terms of how the success of this show affected the audience's relationship to the characters. The montage is really fantastically done.

EPISODE TWO, *like I said, was when I made my grand appearance. A lot of people don't know that the most important person in my life that day was Juliet Polcsa, the costume designer. It was also the day that David Chase saved my ass. Literally.* —Steve

Steve: Juliet, I don't know if you remember, but my first episode, I got a call last-minute that I had to wear a fat suit, which I don't even know if you knew about, because there were all these fat jokes in the script—Tony calls Bobby a calzone with legs, calls him "that blimp," says "consider eating salads," and on and on. In real life I wasn't that much bigger than Jim. I was a little bigger, but not that much. I had to put the fat suit on. I come to see you upstairs. You felt bad for me, I think.

Juliet: [*laughs*] I did. It was horrible.

Steve: I don't know why Lorraine Bracco was there, but there was Lorraine and David Chase. The fat suit you made was a makeshift thing, with a T-shirt and stuffing, and I was parading up and down the aisles where all the clothes were, and you were being so compassionate. I didn't know anyone; I didn't know you. I had never worked in New York before. But you were really being nice. I appreciated that. Then you fitted me for the fat suit.

Juliet: I was aghast, like, "You have to wear *WHAT*?" Writers write things, and they really need to underline it, and they really want to make sure, I guess, that those jokes landed. Visually, that was right for the character, so we had to do it.

Steve: Whatever happened to that fat suit?

Juliet: The original one, we had a wardrobe sale at the end of the season, and God rest her soul, Karen Reuter, who was one of our makeup people, she bought it and she said her kids would play with it. They would put it on and pretend they were like sumo wrestlers. It's hilarious.

Steve: For Season Three, you gave me a nice one. We went to a Broadway costume shop and got a real one. I still have that one. But the original one—I don't know if you remember this, but I do: you had put a fake ass on me, just a tremendous ass. It was comical.

Juliet: I'm sorry!

Steve: No, it's fine, and I remember, I was wearing it, and David Chase walked by, and said, "No, get rid of the ass."

BY COINCIDENCE, *it wasn't just my first episode. It was the first episode directed by Martin Bruestle, one of the big producers on the show. We'll talk to Martin a lot more later about the music on the show, because he had the biggest hand in that. But I wanted to check in with him on our starting out together. —Steve*

Steve: I always felt a little bond, Martin, because it was your first episode as a director. Obviously, very intimidating for you. It was my first episode. Intimidating for me.

Martin: Yes, I totally agree. I've worked on three series, *Thirtysome-thing*, *Northern Exposure*, and *The Sopranos*, from the beginning. When you work on something from the beginning, you're blessed because then you don't have to deal with hearing people say, "This isn't how we do it. We don't do it like that." It's nice to be there in the beginning to set the tone on everything.

Steve: You were there from the beginning because even though you didn't direct until Season Two, you were already producing. But how did you like directing?

Martin: I loved it. I was fearless. It was fun. Allen Coulter, one of the regular director-producers on *The Sopranos*, said something to me that really calmed me in the preparation. He said that you can show up to the set basically drunk and the episode will get done.

Steve: Did you try that?

Martin: [*Laughs*] I didn't. I didn't drink at all.

Steve: But he was basically saying, don't worry, everybody around you is a professional, they know what the hell they're doing.

Martin: Right. It's like the feeling that you don't have to go and re-invent the wheel. It was just a really great experience. But the funny thing about directing is, when you direct, you can't even walk to a convenience store without an assistant director following you and talking on a walkie-talkie about where you are. The minute your episode's done, you're chopped liver. It's like, get in the car and go to the airport.

Steve: Were you in on the casting?

Martin: I was. I walked into casting and I had some ideas for the part of Bacala but David just plopped down an eight-by-ten glossy of Steve Schirripa and said, "This is Bacala. You don't have to cast this one."

I WAS *happy for Steve that he got the part on* The Sopranos. *The first time we were in a scene together was the big fight scene at the construction site in that same episode, where we're breaking up the strikers. We met that day, and we've been good friends ever since. But let's just say he and I remember our first meeting . . . a little differently.* —Michael

Steve: The first time I met you, you were aloof to me.

Michael: I was aloof?

Steve: Very aloof. Somebody introduced you, "You know Michael?" You were, "Uh," kind of like you couldn't be bothered.

Michael: No, I didn't. I don't do that.

Steve: You kind of big-timed me. You high-hatted me.

Michael: No way.

Steve: That's the only time that I saw you all Season Two. I had never seen you. I never worked with you. Maybe you were concentrating. It's possible. It was a very hot day.

Michael: Really hot and really chaotic. Not an easy scene to shoot. It was kind of a mess.

Steve: One thing on *The Sopranos,* whenever a guest star or somebody would come in, everyone made him feel at home. Except for you, when I came on.

Michael: You might have deserved it, Steve. I didn't have lines with you. I don't know if I knew what you were doing there. What do I know? You didn't say nothing to me.

Steve: I said, "Hello. Nice to meet you." You gave me the fish handshake.

Michael: Get the fuck out of here.

Steve: You put me on the pay-no-mind list.

Michael: Maybe I needed to put you on edge a little bit.

Steve: We've talked about this before. You always deny it instead of just fessing up and going, "You know what, Steve? I was in a bad mood that day." Or whatever.

Michael: No, I wasn't in a bad mood. I don't know how long you're going to be around. What do you want me to do? "Oh, hello. Welcome aboard. Nice to see you." Is that what you want?

Steve: If there's an actor that you don't think is going to be around, you don't bother to get to know him?

Michael: It's not like we were playing the scene together. You were on the other side of the protest. We were in the same scene but we didn't interact.

Steve: At least I admit when I am wrong. I'm not wrong that often.

Michael: I'll tell you what, I don't even remember that day. You remember it. It's some big event that you can't get over. I'm already past it. I'm way past it.

Steve: Because it wasn't done to you.

IN ANY case, Michael and I got to be good friends. But we didn't have a lot of scenes together. The one I had the most scenes with was Uncle Junior—Dominic Chianese. When I first joined the show, I worked exclusively with him, and he could not have been nicer. I was really green, but I knew enough to know that some actors aren't that generous. They *could bury another guy. But not Dominic. He was really kind to me, and as the new kid on the block, I'll never forget it.*

Not like that goddamn Imperioli, I can tell you that. —Steve

Steve: Dominic was so great to work with. He really became a mentor to me.

Michael: So can you remember anything specific Dominic told you that helped you with the part?

Steve: A lot of things. I'll tell you one thing specifically: I had the fat suit on and I was trying to work around it, but he would say, "Use it. Use it. Use your belly."

Michael: Use it as an actor. Yes.

Steve: To move as though I really have a big belly like that. You know how in *The Irishman,* they digitally made De Niro's face look like a young man, but he still moved like the seventy-six-year-old guy that he is? Here I am looking like I added seventy-five pounds but I'm still moving like myself. So Dominic taught me, use the belly. I started to lumber around. I made it like I could barely get out of a car. He really helped me create the physicality of that character.

Michael: Jim really loved working with Dominic.

Steve: He did. Everyone loved working with Dominic. We're gonna have a big interview with him later in the book. If you're not a Dominic Chianese fan, there's something fucking wrong.

All right, Michael, now let me ask you something about acting in Season Two. By that time we see Christopher doing a lot of drugs. One of the fans wrote in and asked—and we get this question a lot—"Did you ever drink or smoke anything beforehand for added realism or was it all natural? Also, was the intention always for

Christopher to go down that road or was it something that as the seasons continued, it was written in more?"

Michael: I don't know what the intention was from the beginning. I think it was something that David Chase thought would make for interesting story lines, and it worked for the character. In that scene in Season One when he tells Tony about the regular-ness of life not being enough—that really speaks to addiction. Season Two is the first time we see him doing heroin, which means his drug use obviously is progressing. He was doing coke before and pot and drinking a lot and maybe speed. Heroin is a big step in the wrong direction, obviously.

But no, I'd never ever drink or get high to play scenes like this. I never would use some kind of mind-altering thing in order to play an altered mind.

Steve: I also don't think anyone could perform better high or drunk. I don't buy that for one second. Not at all.

Michael: They say Rock Hudson was drunk for three days when he did a drunk scene in *Seconds,* that John Frankenheimer movie in the sixties. You hear that sometimes. But no, I've never known anyone who could do that. Or would.

I will say, being high was a lot of fun to play. I did a lot of research about the effects and I've seen the effects in the real world. It's the kind of thing where you need even more control over yourself to act, because it's a very specific physical and mental state. You have to almost be even more sober to really portray it properly. Besides, you may do the scene for four, five hours. You have to have your wits about you.

FOR ME, *one of the big things that started with Episode Two of Season Two was my first exposure to the major pregame event: the read-through. —Steve*

Steve: I remember my first read-through. I had never been to one before. We would have a big square table, you'd spend some time talking before it begins, getting to know each other, which was nice for me because I never worked with a lot of these people. Then you go around the table. People that have one line would come. I had heard stories of people getting fired at the read-through.

Michael: Oh, really?

Steve: Oh, yes. For one reason or another, now that they came in, they weren't what the producers expected. I was paranoid that I was going to get fired. The purpose of the read-through is so the writers could hear the words. A lot of times, you'll get some notes, we're going to change this and that. We had a read-through for every single show.

Michael: It was mandatory. Even if it was your day off.

Steve: All the producers were there, all the writers.

Michael: Jim Gandolfini was always there. Jim was much more like the captain rather than the boss. He wanted everybody to feel comfortable and welcome.

Steve: I had a great time at the read-throughs.

Michael: As time went on, and the show got more and more popular, the read-throughs got more secretive. The press would try to find out story lines, and then the cast and crew had to sign confidentiality agreements.

Steve: After the read-through we would sit around and bullshit. Then a lot of times we would go out. That's when I first really started hanging out with you guys. It started at your bar in Chelsea. I spent many a night in there.

Michael: We had my place, and we also hung out at Pastis, which was in the Meatpacking District. There was Peter's on the Upper West Side. We had our haunts where the owners knew us, the bartenders knew us, so we could sit at the bar and be relatively undisturbed.

There was Edward's in Tribeca which was next to my house. The Ear Inn on Spring Street. Pão, also on Spring Street, where my brother, John, worked. He was the bartender. And as I said earlier, the Spring Lounge in Little Italy, which for some reason, every time we went, there'd always be like a problem, some kind of argument breaking out. I don't know why.

Steve: But it was fun. It was mostly you, me, Jim, and John Ventimiglia. We were the core four.

Michael: Roger Haber, our lawyer, hung out with us a lot too. Sometimes, if there was an event, we would go out after the event, and then you have Tony Sirico and Vinny Pastore, and maybe Steve Buscemi and David, Drea de Matteo, whoever else was hanging out.

Steve: I was the lightweight of the group. I don't use the word "lightweight" about myself a lot. But I was the lightweight. I went home early a lot.

Michael: You were pretty good. You would get home early most of the time. I would usually stay. It usually would wind up being me and Jim until about four A.M. I liked to get home before the sun went up. Sometimes Jim didn't, but usually it would wind up being me and Jim in the wee, wee hours.

Steve: Yeah, you guys liked to keep it going.

Michael: But look, it was New York. Nobody was driving a car and it was safe. I certainly wouldn't do that if I had to wake up at seven o'clock in the morning. I only did that once, and I learned very quickly that I needed my rest. The good thing about those times—people didn't have iPhones then, so nobody was videotaping anybody. Thank God. You could pretty much be in the bar and be famous. People come up and say hello, and it's kind of under the radar. Nowadays, you got to be on your best behavior because somebody could be videoing you without your knowledge and it'll wind up in the *New York Post*.

Steve: It was a very Rat Packy kind of a thing. We would travel together a lot, doing appearances and events at the casinos in Atlantic City and Vegas, Foxwoods, all over the country.

Michael: Those were really fun. They got to be a really big deal after a while.

Steve: Huge. There were maybe eight or nine of us who would go— you, me, Jim, Stevie, Tony Sirico, Lorraine, Johnny V, Vince Curatola.

Michael: You should describe what those appearances were like.

Steve: It was kinda like visiting Santa Claus at Macy's. People would come sit in a chair and get their pictures taken with us. It was just for the highest of high rollers. I want to say, for example at Foxwoods, you needed to have at least a hundred thousand dollars' credit line at the casino to come. And they would have a private party and then the main party.

Michael: And we would have some parties of our own.

Steve: It was a great time. And they paid us a ton of money for that. They would fly us down first-class, and put us up in suites with butlers, and we would eat and hang out and drink very heavily.

Michael: But the thing of it was, we liked each other and liked to hang out. Working together and drinking together and hanging out together. It was always a lot of fun.

Steve: Most of the time. Every once in a while some drunk would get out of hand. Remember that guy at the Las Vegas Hilton? It was in this big fifteen-thousand-square-foot suite, this smart-aleck asshole starts berating us, insulting us. We bit our tongues and moved on. Then the next year, at the Golden Nugget in Vegas, who walks in but the same guy.

Michael: That's right! Jim went ballistic.

Steve: He said, "There's that fucking scumbag from last year. He says one word, I say we beat the shit out of him." And we were gonna do it. I went up to the guy in charge of the party, Rich Wilke, and I said, "If you don't get him out of here, this whole thing is gonna be a mess." And they escorted him out. I think that's as close as we ever got to actually beating the shit out of someone.

THE MOST *fun we had—and sometimes too much fun, I will be the first to admit—was when the show would go shoot at remote locations. I have to take my hat off to Ilene Landress, one of the executive producers. OG, really—she was there from the beginning and was like David Chase's right arm. She had the job of wrangling the cast when we were on the road. Tough job. —Michael*

Michael: What was it like, Ilene, keeping everybody in line out on the road? Was it like herding cats?

Ilene: Ours was more like puppies in the box. When we were out of town, at a hotel, it usually wasn't a fancy hotel, because it's usually out in the country someplace. One time, you were all like, "Hey, we're going to get in cars and we're going to go here, we're going to go there." Like a bar or a strip club or something. You were just going out to get in trouble. And I said, no, no, no. No, we're not doing that. I said, "I don't care if you destroy this hotel, but anything that happens tonight happens in this hotel." I just didn't want people in cars.

Michael: I remember that very well. You know, we had just as good a time. That was the thing—we just enjoyed hanging out with each other, wherever it was. But I understood why you felt you needed to do that.

Ilene: It's just that you were all so easily recognizable. You don't want the publicity. I was like, you all like each other. Let's go for some good clean fun at the hotel, you know? It's like, everybody can go to the bar. In my role when we were shooting, I'll be honest, I probably could have had a lot more fun if I didn't have the job I had. I didn't want to be the schoolmarm, but at the same time, it was my job. And like I said, it's like as long as everybody stays in this bar, I don't care what you do.

THERE ARE *so many incredible moments we could talk about in Season Two—the episode in Italy; Big Pussy beating Elvis to death because he saw Pussy with an FBI agent; so many incredible scenes between Janice and Tony. One of my favorite episodes was "Big Girls Don't Cry," for a number of reasons. Not the least of which is that it introduced us to Terry Winter. Terry had been working in network TV for a while on shows like* Diagnosis Murder *with Dick Van Dyke, and later became famous for writing* The Wolf of Wall Street *and creating the incredible* Boardwalk Empire. *As we said earlier, Terry wound up writing twenty-five excellent* Sopranos *episodes. This was his first. —Michael*

Steve: *The Sopranos* wouldn't have been *The Sopranos* without you, my friend. "Big Girls Don't Cry" was your first episode. How did that story come about?

Terry: David and I met. It was me, David, Robin, and Mitch.

Michael: Robin Green and Mitch Burgess, the writers and producers.

Terry: We started talking about a potential story. The idea was, David was going to give me a script to write. They said, "Yes, we're thinking about Christopher Moltisanti. Maybe Chris wants to get into Hollywood and acting." I said, "When I started out writing, I took an acting class." They always say that writers should take acting classes just to understand what actors are asked to do. That morphed into this story of Christopher taking the first acting class. That was the first script I wrote, "Big Girls Don't Cry," that whole story line. So much of what we put into the show came right out of our lives or your life. You would tell me something and I would end up putting it in the script.

Steve: There's that one amazing scene in "Big Girls Don't Cry," where Furio—played by Federico Castelluccio—he goes in to beat up the woman and her husband in the whorehouse. That was all done in one take, right?

Terry: We shot that at four in the morning. We were pulling the plug at four thirty. It was a Friday night and it was a long, long day.

Michael: We should point out that Friday nights could be the longest, since there wasn't a "turnaround"—there's a mandatory twelve hours between the wrap and the next day's call, but since there often wasn't a shoot on Saturdays, there was no turnaround.

Terry: Right, and it was a location in New Jersey, so it wasn't anything we could go back to on a set. We needed to get it. It was a very complicated shot and Tim [Van Patten] was directing the episode.

Steve: Another thing people don't know, when you write the episode, you're on the episode. You're producing the episode. That's why you're there.

Terry: Right. They wanted to do it in one shot. As it turned out, we only had time to do it once. That was Federico's first episode—even though he appeared in the Italy episode. The Italy episode was actually shot out of order, after "Big Girls Don't Cry" in the schedule, so this was one of the first days that Federico ever worked. He was asked to do an incredibly sophisticated stunt sequence. Starts with Tony in the car, camera's over his back, follows him into the door of the whorehouse. *Boom,* smack this person. Another guy comes out, knock him down, pick up a gun, go into the back—and what you see on TV was one take. The only take of that. We got it at exactly four thirty and boom, that's a wrap, go home. It was really magical. Tim, Federico, the camera department, everybody was perfect. Every actor in that scene just was flawless. I don't think that I've ever been so proud of anything that I've worked on or shot since.

Steve: Federico is a great actor. How did he wind up on the show?

Terry: It was interesting casting Federico. We went through so many guys because, of course, we wanted them to speak Italian. Every guy sounded like Mr. Bacciagalupe from *Abbott and Costello*. It was horrible. Then finally, this guy walks in—and literally, I've said this to Federico and it's the God's honest truth, he is exactly what I thought about when I wrote that character. He is precisely the image of the guy I thought of. He walks in, he's big, he's physical, he speaks Italian, and he does the scene—and then I thought, "Okay, here's the deal. He's not going to be able to pull off the violence, the physical stuff." But he mimed the violence and I thought, "Holy shit! This guy is the guy." David says to him, "Where in Italy are you from?" And he breaks accent and goes, "I'm from Paterson, New Jersey."

We almost fell out of our chairs. This is what I thought to myself: "This show is blessed." How fucking lucky are we? That cast was already Mount Rushmore to me. To add another face in there—it just fit beautifully.

FEDERICO REMINDED *us of a funny story that happened when we were in Italy.* —Michael

Steve: Federico, tell me about the story since I wasn't in Italy, that somebody pickpocketed David, and then you caught the guy and smacked him around. Is that true?

Federico: Yeah. You know, I feel bad, you know, in retrospect I shouldn't have hit the guy. It was as though all of a sudden my Paterson days came back. I'm thinking, "What the fuck am I doing? I'm slamming this guy in the head." But you know, we got his wallet back.

Steve: How did you find the guy?

Federico: We had this guy that was working with us in Naples. His name was Max. He was working in the prop department, but he was a local in the neighborhoods we were shooting in. And he was, whenever you needed, if you needed something or to talk to somebody, he was the go-between with everything. He was a character. You know, I'm almost wondering if he had something to do with that whole pickpocket thing.

Steve: It was a setup.

Michael: I think Max paid that pickpocket.

Steve: He wanted to get his foot in the door.

Federico: I just thought of that.

ONE OF *my favorite episodes of the season—one of everybody's favorites, really—was "From Where to Eternity," where Christopher's been shot and he thinks he died and came back. I love that episode—and I'm not just saying that because it happened to be written by my coauthor on this book.* —Steve

Steve: This episode is the one where Christopher had been shot, and now he's in the hospital in sort of a coma, and he has some kind of dream or whatever that he's in the afterlife. It's the first one you wrote. I'm not blowing smoke up your ass, it's one of the funniest, if not the funniest, of the eighty-six episodes. It's bizarre, it's hilarious, it's serious. It's just so good.

Michael: Thank you. I hadn't seen it maybe in twenty years, until we started our rewatch. I was pleasantly surprised. I was surprised how far out there it was, compared to the other episodes up until that point. It was an effort really to explore how these mob guys see and deal with the karmic repercussions of their actions, in light of Catholicism and what that means.

If you really believe in all the tenets of Catholicism, and your actions, instincts, and desires go against that, what does that mean? Does that mean you're going to go to hell? Does it mean you're a bad person? It's definitely something that I wanted to explore.

If you think about it, it's a question that runs through a lot of the great mob movies. The contrast between what they do and what they believe. Starting with *Mean Streets,* probably, but it's always the question: Do these guys believe in heaven and hell? Do they fear that? Do they even think about it? So I got to write about that. I got to write some really funny stuff for Paulie Walnuts.

Steve: Paulie has been making donations to the church almost as an insurance policy. He's thinking, "I'm going to take care of the priest. I'm going to donate to the church, because when it comes my time I'm going to go to heaven."

Michael: He thinks it's going to balance off the negative things that he's done.

Steve: Tell me about writing this script. What's your way of writing? Do you write the same time every day, same place, or what?

Michael: Often the writing happened before the season started shooting. If it was during the season, most of it was done really late at night, usually at the bar that my wife and I owned in Chelsea. I'd work on set during the day, then go down the basement around one A.M., and I'd stay till after they closed.

Steve: You were drinking?

Michael: Not too much. You can't write if you're drunk. I'd listen to late-night talk radio in New York. I don't really write at night much anymore. I'm usually more of a day guy now, but this one was written in the wee hours.

Steve: Now, did you come up with this name?

Michael: I did, yes. "From Where to Eternity."

Steve: My favorite line in the episode, probably one of my favorite lines in the whole series, is the line about St. Patrick's Day.

Michael: "Hell is an Irish bar, and it's St. Patrick's Day every day." I was just playing off the fact that there's always been an attraction and repulsion between Italian and Irish. They often live in the same city and usually work together on the police force or firemen and stuff like that, but they're very different culturally. The idea of an Italian having to eat corned beef and cabbage every day would be a nightmare.

Steve: This wasn't the first thing you wrote. When did you start writing?

Michael: I started writing not long after I started acting, but I didn't finish anything until *Summer of Sam*, which fortunately got made.

Steve: So where did you come up with this idea, of Christopher dying and going to the afterlife and coming back?

Michael: It started with a spec script I wrote, about Christopher OD'ing.

Steve: A spec script means on speculation, you weren't hired to write it, you just wrote it and gave it to them to look at.

Michael: Right. The spec script was Christopher OD's and then all of this afterlife stuff happens. It took me about three weeks to write. I gave it to David between Season One and Two. David said, "I like what you wrote." He said, "I'm planning on Christopher getting shot, so we can use all this afterlife stuff." I was thrilled that he liked it. I just loved all these characters, and I loved that I was going to get to write for all of them.

Steve: Is that when you started going into the writers' room?

Michael: No, I did not go into the writers' room at that point. I did later on in the production. In the writers' room, they'll break out thirteen episodes, the idea being, "This is a general story line of Tony and of Carmela, and of the wiseguys, or whatever." Then they'll break down each episode, the A story, the B story, the C story. In the writers' room, you'll outline it together with the other writers. But I didn't with this episode.

Steve: Out of the whole spec script that you turned in, how much do you think wound up being used?

Michael: Quite a bit actually. Because the A story is Christopher and the afterlife and the stuff with Paulie, all that stuff was in the spec script. When Paulie is grilling Christopher about the afterlife—did the bouncer have horns, whether it was hot, whether Christopher was in hell or purgatory. All that.

The other story lines, hunting down Matt Bevilaqua, the whole business with Tony's vasectomy, those weren't in there. Those were story lines that David had broken out, and then he gave them to me. Then you go off with an outline and write a first draft. Then you get notes, and then you write a second draft. I was really excited to do this. I had never written for television. Robin Green was very helpful to me in the beginning because she just taught me about concision. In television, it's an hour or less. Things have to be really concise. It's not like a movie where it's two hours and scenes can be a lot longer. It has to move, you have two to three story lines. The idea here was, "Get into the scene late and get out early." She was really good, she was really helpful.

Steve: The stuff you wrote for Paulie is outstanding. I love when he's trying to punch holes in Christopher's story. Chris says he saw the devil, and Paulie goes, "Did he have the knobs in his head? Did he have horns? Did he have the beginning of the horns?" He's trying to punch holes. Paulie is worried about what will happen to him after he dies.

Michael: I did write a scene where you actually see the afterlife, a kind of dream sequence, and it was Mikey Palmice wearing a gangster suit pretending he was James Cagney in the bar or something like that. We got rid of it in the drafts.

Steve: So after that, were you in the writers' room every episode?

Michael: I was in the writers' room for Seasons Three, Four, and Five.

Steve: So last thing. This is the episode where three o'clock keeps showing up. Christopher brings a message back from the afterlife, "Mikey Palmice told me to tell you three o'clock," Paulie wakes up at three o'clock, Michelle, who he's in bed with, tells this story how she got married at three o'clock. It keeps showing up, here and then later, through the seasons. What's the meaning of that?

Michael: I'm not allowed to ever say.

Steve: But you know?

Michael: I am not allowed to ever say, Steve. I've got to go to my grave with what three o'clock means.

Steve: Michael, come on. You gotta give it up. People paid good money for this book. We want to know.

Michael: Well, we don't always get what we want, do we?

Steve: You know, you really fucking piss me off sometimes. You know that?

Michael: Yes, I do know that. You've made that very clear.

WE CAN'T *leave this episode without talking to the man who directed it, Henry Bronchtein. He directed four episodes of* The Sopranos, *and got an Emmy nomination for two of them, including this one. —Michael*

Michael: Your direction on this episode was terrific, Henry. You were always so precise, getting all the details just right.

Henry: Thanks. It's always a challenge. David Chase had very high standards. Really, the challenge was, the directors would try to meet those standards. Everybody wanted more. We wanted it to be high feature-film level. You have to understand, it was a time of huge transitions. *Sopranos* started a whole huge transition in the quality of television. That first season, we were supposed to do eight-day episodes, and we had some eight-day twenty-hour days in order to do the work.

Steve: And every year it got a little bit more, right?

Henry: It grew. Everybody's sense of what the production level should be kept growing. The directors wanted more. People were liberated, to not fit into to the television box, but to do more, and so it was bigger numbers of extras, bigger locations. We made big company moves. David always wanted the show to be location, New Jersey–driven. We would sometimes start in Patterson one day and move to Newark with the whole company. You couldn't cheat one city for another in David's mind. It was very hard. At a certain point, I probably should've stopped worrying about what it was costing because nobody else cared. [*laughs*]

Steve: HBO made it all back and then some.

SO LET'S *get to the climax of Season Two—the killing of Big Pussy. I always thought that was one of the ballsiest things David ever did— killing off one of the most beloved characters on the show, and not only that, but having his best friends do the killing. It's so painful. I always thought it was David's way of saying: This is serious. I've made you get comfortable with these characters but don't get too comfortable.*

We talked to Terry Winter about how it all went down. —Steve

Steve: I always thought it would be Paulie or Pussy would get killed, one or the other. Was there a choice at any point, or it was just Vinny?

Terry: No, it was always Vinny. It was interesting, when I came onto the series, in the beginning of Season Two, we started plotting out the season. Pussy had disappeared at the end of Season One and David Chase went off to France, to have a long vacation, and he was away for the groundswell of popularity of the show. He didn't understand the chatter that was going on around people. It was a hit, but he didn't understand what people were talking about. Everybody wanted to know, what happened to Pussy? Where's Big Pussy? What's going on? But when we started plotting out Season Two, Pussy wasn't even on the radar.

I brought it up. I said, "What about Pussy?" and David was,

"Nobody cares about him. He's just a minor character." I said, "David, I don't think you're aware how much people want to know about this guy."

Michael: It did become this huge thing on the Internet. Steven Tyler from Aerosmith had a T-shirt made. We did an appearance at Foxwoods, and he showed up with the T-shirt—"Pussy is not dead." It was one of the first big Internet phenomena around the show that I remember. "Where's Pussy?"

Terry: David asked around and he's like, "Holy shit, yes, this is what we need to write to. That's the mystery." The whole season was now, "Okay, where was Pussy?" Now we answer that question, unfortunately for Vinny, and the conclusion was he was taken in and flipped by the FBI, and that whole season slowly unraveled where we find that out and then, of course, Tony finds it out, and there's only one thing that can happen. Sadly, that was the answer and it had to end the way it ended. There was never a question.

TERRY IS right—it seemed as though the whole world wanted to know. And no one knew.

But Vinny knew. —Steve

Steve: Vinny, my first day on the set, if you remember, you came to me and said, "You're going to replace me. They're killing me off." You told me that. That was before Italy. You knew already that they were killing you off. How did you know?

Vinny: David called me after Season One was totally aired. He said, "Vinny, it's David. Everybody on the internet wants to know 'Where's Pussy?'" He told me, "We really don't know yet, but this is what we're thinking. Vinny, you're going to be the rat. You're going to die, but you're going to have a good season." He said, "I promise

I'm going to try and bring you in as much as possible." He did. He kept his word. But I was a ghost.

Steve: We used to joke with you about why David killed you off. You used to say, "He saw me smoking weed at a concert. I think that's why he killed me."

Vinny: [*laughs*] Tony Sirico said, "You left the set one day to work with Danny Aiello, and that's when we knew you were going to get fired." I said, "What?" He said, "You went up to David and said, 'I got to leave. Let Tony do my line,' and David said he was going to kill you off."

Steve: None of that's true of course. There was nothing personal at all. It was all to make the best story, the best show. In most shows the audience wants the snitch to be killed. There's a bad guy ratting on everyone. Kill him. But you broke the audience's heart, Vinny. People were crying because they were going to kill this gangster. Big Pussy was a murderer, a drug dealer, and a snitch—yet the audience loved him. That was from your performance.

Vinny: I killed Elvis. Do you remember? I killed Elvis, and they still liked me.

Steve: You know what's so funny to me, all those guys at the social club up in the Bronx, they were so proud of you. And then when you became a rat, they never spoke to you again.

Vinny: That's true. That's a true story.

Steve: But, Vinny, when you finished your season, the cast was really sad. The show went on, and it kept on going on for five more seasons. You were, of course, a part of it, and our friend, and we did appearances, but that had to be a tough pill to swallow. I know it would've been for me.

Vinny: It was hard. When the third season started to air, I wasn't even watching them for a while. I'll tell you the truth, I was devastated. This show became a huge hit, but financially and career-wise, I wasn't a part of it. But on the positive side, I was the first Soprano, with the exception of Rispoli, to be available for projects. And I was grabbing them. I went to Hollywood, and I knocked off a bunch of movies, and it was so cool. My life really changed because of this show.

Steve: We were all really sad to see you go off the show. But everybody was glad it at least led to good things for you. Listen, let's talk about your last scene. It took quite a while to shoot that scene, right?

Vinny: Yes. Actually, it was more days on that episode than any other episode that season. They added four or five more days. They really wanted to get it right.

Steve: Give me the whole layout. You're on the boat. They're going to kill you. Where? What boat? Where was it? What was in the studio?

Vinny: First, they shot the scene of me walking up the gangplank with Paulie, Silvio, and Tony. And they built a boat in the studio. We went in there all week, shooting the interior. If you pay attention, the interior of that boat looked a little bigger than what that boat should look like inside.

Michael: It was rocking. How did they do that if you weren't on the water?

Vinny: You had the crew rocking it. It was like Noah's Ark and they were rocking it. We were there for a while, and then we went out to Jones Beach to shoot the scene of me sitting up on the boat and going down below, and the scene when they brought the body bag out and they threw it in. They couldn't make that bag sink. They were shooting all day to make that bag sink. It wasn't going down.

Steve: Were you in the body bag?

Vinny: Some people think I was and some people think I wasn't. It depends on the person.

———

Michael: Steve, there's one more thing we gotta say about the end of this episode, and the end of this season. Some people consider it among the greatest moments of *The Sopranos*. It ends with a long montage, all slow motion. Lots of warmly lit shots of Tony and his family celebrating Meadow's graduation.

Steve: They're toasting their good life, their good fortune.

Michael: Right. Toasting their good fortune with gold-rimmed champagne glasses. But it's intercut with all the depressing scenes of how Tony makes the money to support that lifestyle: the garbage trucks, the calling-card scam, the businessman whose life he ruined, all of that.

Steve: And it ends on the ocean. Where he just dumped Pussy's body. Even in this happy moment, your daughter's graduating, you see Tony's face, you know just what he's thinking.

Michael: Incredibly powerful. And the music there is the Rolling Stones' "Thru and Thru." Keith Richards wrote that song and sings it. His voice is just filled with weariness. It's such a beautiful, haunting song. And it underscores just how bittersweet this moment is for Tony. All the shit he has to put up with, and all the shit he has to do, just to get to this place.

FIVE

Bada Bing Back Room with Michael Imperioli

YOU THINK YOU KNOW A GUY.

I've been friends with Michael Imperioli almost since the day we met. I say almost, because to be honest he was kind of a jerk to me the first day I showed up on the set, as I said. But I mean after that, we were friends.

Pretty soon we started hanging out, going drinking after the shooting would wrap, getting a little crazy in between seasons. We worked together a bunch too—I'll always be grateful to him for giving me one of the big roles in the movie he wrote and directed, The Hungry Ghosts, *which I knew was a labor of love for him.*

But for all that time—until we began recording Talking Sopranos— *there was a ton of stuff I never knew about the guy.*

This is my attempt to make up for that. —Steve

Steve: So, Michael, I gotta say, I've learned a whole lot that I never knew about you since we've been doing the podcast.

Michael: Like what?

Steve: Like you have some pretty weird ideas.

Michael: What do you mean? Give me an example.

Steve: Like, you think *Midnight Cowboy* and *The Wizard of Oz* are the same movie.

Michael: They are, if you think about it.

Steve: I don't wanna think about it. What are you talking about? One is the first X-rated movie to win the Oscar. The other is the greatest family movie of all time. I think sometimes you say these things just to piss me off.

Michael: There is that.

Steve: Maybe we'll get into that later. Now, a good place to begin is Mount Vernon, where you grew up. There was one episode we talked about, where Melfi says to her ex-husband, "Your Calabrese is showing." And you said you had Calabrese in the family.

Michael: That's a funny line. My grandfather was Calabrese, yes.

Steve: So am I.

Michael: My grandfather on my mother's side. My grandfather on my father's side is from Rome.

Steve: So okay, take me back. You grew up like that, all the generations living together, right? Tell me about that.

Michael: When I was three, my parents moved into the house that my grandfather owned, which was a three-family house. We lived on the second floor. Also my uncle was living with my grandparents, and my grandmother's sister and brothers all lived in Mount Vernon, so there was a big extended family. There were always lots of parties at people's houses and lots of relatives coming in, and my grandmother was the center of a lot of family and friends.

Steve: And your dad, he was a bus driver, but he did community theater, too, you said. I didn't know that.

Michael: Yes, my dad, one day, I must have been about thirteen, so he was in his late thirties, maybe forty, and he decided he wanted to do community theater. He had never acted. He was into movies, took me to see a lot of movies when I was young, or turned me on to cool movies on TV when I was a kid. So he does this play called *Night of January 16th,* which is a courtroom drama. I thought that was very courageous for somebody who's never done it, and does something else for a living.

Steve: Do you think that had an influence on you, in the path you took?

Michael: Oh, yes, without a doubt. But maybe, even more, being exposed to a lot of good movies. His love for it, definitely, he passed on to me. I grew up watching really good movies and that's what really did it. Particularly *Dog Day Afternoon* and *Midnight Cowboy.*

Steve: Those were great movies.

Michael: Those two movies probably changed my life. They'd be on late-night TV and I'd watch, and I just never saw anything like them. These characters had a little-guy-against-the-world kind of thing, like Pacino's character in *Dog Day,* and then Hoffman and Voight in *Midnight Cowboy.* These little guys struggling. There was something about these characters and the way they were portrayed, something very real about them.

In both films the characters are outcasts, living outside society. Even though Al Pacino is a criminal, robbing a bank, there's something very sympathetic and vulnerable about him. Obviously, he's robbing a bank to pay for his lover's gender reassignment surgery, but that's not the only thing that makes him sympathetic, it's who he is as an actor. What he brought to that situation was very honest. You're rooting for him even though he's a bank robber. It's bizarre.

Those two movies were a very clear-cut path for me, seeing them—especially Pacino, he's Italian-American, he's from the Bronx. Mount Vernon is right next to the Bronx. It was something about seeing him do it that made me think I could do it. There was a logical path from that movie or from that type of actor, and even Hoffman as well, to me wanting to do it—I wanted to be in film, I wanted to be an actor, because of those two movies.

Midnight Cowboy became like a Christmas Eve tradition with me, my brother, and my father. You know, I worked with Jon Voight in a movie called *Five People You Meet in Heaven*. Working with him was just like a dream. He was so creative and fun and we were watching Sid Caesar's *Show of Shows* in his trailer between scenes. I had the best time with him and I told him, at one point, "You know, for years we would watch *Midnight Cowboy* every Christmas." He goes, "Wow, that's really sweet . . . it's a little sick but it's very sweet."

Steve: Sweet I don't know. Sick, I get.

Michael: It was those movies that made me want to be an actor, and probably *The Wizard of Oz*. Which may be my favorite movie ever. When I was a kid, *Wizard of Oz* was on TV once a year. This is before videos, VHS, and cable and all that. That movie really just captivated me as a kid. And in some ways still does.

Steve: Okay, I guess we gotta get into this. On the podcast, you said *Midnight Cowboy* is *The Wizard of Oz*. What the hell is that about? What, is Ratso Rizzo supposed to be a munchkin? What are you talking about?

Michael: I compare *Midnight Cowboy* and *Wizard of Oz* a lot. Joe Buck and Dorothy are very similar in a way. He's looking for something else. He leaves his home, and he goes to this strange and scary world that's populated with all these bizarre characters.

Joe Buck's character is this wide-eyed innocent from the country. He wants to find himself and be fulfilled so he goes to New York, which is like Oz, and he's excited, and then he realizes that it's very scary and there's a lot of danger. He's almost too innocent and too naive to navigate it. And then he finds help. At the end, he realizes that he doesn't have to pretend to be somebody. In the *Wizard of Oz,* it's "There's no place like home," but in *Midnight Cowboy,* it's, there's no one but you, who you really are. He's pretending to be this cowboy, pretending to be this gigolo, or pretending to be this hustler, and he's not. He's really just a good guy who wants to be loved and wants to love, and he does that at the end.

If you track the two journeys of those main characters, Dorothy and Joe Buck, it's very similar. Oz is like New York and it's very colorful, and it's otherworldly, scary, and unlike anything the character has seen before. I find a lot of common ground with those two.

Steve: I hate to admit it, but that actually kinda makes sense. A little bit. Maybe.

Michael: Very big of you.

Steve: Anyway, lemme pick up your story again. All the times we've known each other I don't think I've ever asked you, when did you decide to become an actor? Because you never went to college, right?

Michael: No. I was going to go to college. My best friend and I both applied to Columbia. I didn't get in. The next choice was SUNY Albany. I got accepted. I agreed to go there. I went upstate for the orientation weekend. It just didn't feel right. But I felt I had to go to college. I figured it was expected of me.

I didn't want to go but I was afraid to tell my parents. Finally, the night before I was supposed to move up there—this is now the beginning of September, everything was packed, we were ready to drive up in the morning—I just said, "You know what, I don't want to go up there. I don't want to go to college. I want to go to acting school."

Steve: If I'm your parents, I think you're going to college, premed or whatever, and you tell me acting school, I'm having ten heart attacks.

Michael: I'd heard about the Actors Studio. I said I want to go to this Lee Strasberg school, and my parents, God bless them, were very supportive and said, "Listen, it's your life. Why don't you check out this Strasberg? But you should go to college anyway. You should get an education. It is important."

I'm thinking, "Maybe I'll look into other colleges in New York that have good theater programs," because I wasn't totally sure about Strasberg. I didn't even know where it was and how to get in. So I went to check out NYU. I took the train to the city, went down to the Village, went to NYU, got some brochures, and just started walking north, back toward the train. It was the first time I was ever alone in the city, by myself. I was just wandering the streets. I was really enjoying it. And finally, I come to Union Square and I see this Irving Place. I had never heard of Irving Place, so I walk up, and all of a sudden, I look and I see this big flag, "Lee Strasberg Theater Institute." And I walked in.

Steve: Holy shit. It's fate. So you just walked in.

Michael: That's exactly how it happened. I walked in and I got an interview and started going there. I met John Ventimiglia right away. I was a little bit intimidated because I'm going from high school with teenagers, now I'm in a class with adults. It was very interesting, though, suddenly being around adults studying the same thing as you. I really loved it.

Steve: You loved it, but at some point you quit.

Michael: I was at Strasberg for two years. During those two years, I was also trying to get acting jobs. See, I was very deluded. I figured, "I'll go to school for three months, and then, I'll start doing TV and movies and stuff." You have to have that—it's blind confidence, but it's also a bit of delusion—because it's such a hard business to get started in. I didn't know anyone in show business at all. It just seemed like this incredibly impenetrable world.

Backstage and *Show Business* were the trade newspapers. They published auditions, mostly, for NYU, Columbia student films, and off-off-Broadway plays. I was going on these auditions as much as I could, especially for these plays that were pretty much put up in shitholes. You'd go on a Saturday morning, there'd be a couple of hundred people auditioning for a crap play that didn't pay, and you'd spend half your day waiting in line to be seen and do a monologue and not get it. I was also trying to get an agent; I got headshots and résumés and was constantly sending them out to agents. I got thrown out of an agent's office once because he was saying, "I can't do anything with you. You'll never do anything in this business. It's not going to work for you."

After two years, I was thinking, "What if this never happens?" I did not get one job. Not one. I'm working in restaurants as a cook and as a waiter and as a busboy, whatever, moving furniture, hanging lights in the theater, and I'm wondering, "Is this going to be the rest of my life?" I was frustrated and full of despair, and I stopped going to classes.

I spent a summer really lost and really depressed, and then, I went to an REM concert at Radio City, and I ran into my friend Tom Gilroy, who had left Strasberg with a teacher who opened her own studio: Elaine Aiken. He said, "You should come to this class. She's really great." And I started going there.

Steve: You've told me about it, that was some all-star acting class. It was yourself; John Ventimiglia; Sharon Angela, who played Rosalie Aprile; John Costelloe—four actors who wind up on *The Sopranos*—and then Alec Baldwin was also there.

Michael: It was a good class. She was a terrific teacher. She said to me—and remember, I'm a kid, I'm nineteen—she said, "You're going to do much more than act in this business. You're also going to write and direct and produce." She just had an instinct about that. She was a great mentor.

Steve: Now, all this time of course you gotta make a living, you're not making a dime on the acting, what are you doing?

Michael: I mostly worked in the restaurant business. In the eighties I was making a lot of money in restaurants, between $100 and $200 a night, cash.

Steve: That was a lot of money then.

Michael: Yes. For a twenty-one-year-old. I moved furniture for a while; I hung lights at La MaMa, an off-off-Broadway theater in the East Village. The worst job I ever had was market research, where you'd have to cold-call people and get them to do surveys about products. They would only pay you if you kept someone on the phone for a half an hour. One survey was about liqueurs. You had to say, "Now, tell me which do you drink on a regular basis? Creme de menthe, often, not often, not at all? Amaretto?" The only people who wanted to stay on for half an hour were lonely people who just wanted to talk to you about their lives. But most people would hang up on you. There were guys in the other cubicle crying, begging people to stay on the line with them. It was a terrible job. Worst job I ever had.

Steve: And you and your buddy Johnny V are living in the East Village, middle of the 1980s, like the heyday of CBGB's and that whole thing, what must that have been like?

Michael: I'll tell you one story. Around 1985, we were in acting class with this guy who was a duke or a count from Austria. He came to America to study with Elaine Aiken. He rented an apartment on Eleventh Street between B and C, which was a very bad neighborhood in the early eighties. Very dangerous, and he loved it. He loved this experience of being this aristocrat who's now living on the Lower East Side.

Steve: He had money?

Michael: Yes. His uncle was the archbishop of Vienna or something. He came from a lot of money, but he wanted this New York punk rock experience. At some point he had to go to Austria for a few months. He offered to sublet the apartment to Johnny and me for very cheap. Johnny and I move in. It's one of those railroad tenement apartments, the tub was in the kitchen, the whole thing.

One night we threw a party in the apartment. We invite everybody we know and it's just insane. It goes all night long, there's music, the neighborhood's wild, the party is just as wild. At around six in the morning, there's people crashed on the floor, sleeping, fucking, throwing up. It's a mess. Suddenly the duke shows up two months early because he kind of had a meltdown and needed to get out of Austria. He knocks on the door. I wake up, I swear there's people on the floor, the place is trashed. I opened the door and he just stands there and goes, "I should laugh, really." He's kind of excited but kind of horrified because he just wants to come home and chill out.

Steve: Of all days, of all mornings.

Michael: Of all days, he shows up, and right before, while he's at the door—this is all true—the neighbor across the hall opens the door and is OD'ing on speed, foaming at the mouth. Before he even got to our apartment, he had to call 911 for the neighbor who was naked and OD'ing on speed and is asking him for help. That's life in the East Village in the eighties.

Steve: But finally you get your big break. A little role in a big movie, *Lean on Me*. And that's almost your last movie too, right?

Michael: So another student in my acting class got an audition for an agent. We had been working on a scene together in class and she asked me to do it with her for the agent, who winds up signing both of us. Now, this is five years after I started, by the way. Anyway, this agent starts getting me auditions. He said, "There's this movie *Lean on Me*. They need a kid, a white high school kid." I looked very young at twenty-two, so I auditioned. It was an extra role, but I had to give somebody a gun.

Steve: That's what they used to call a silent bit. It's called a "featured extra" now.

Michael: It's one notch above an extra, but it would get me my SAG card if I did it. I was thinking, "Oh, that's great." I go out to Jersey, and they're shooting in a high school with five hundred kids as extras in the audience. When I got there they told me they wrote in a new character who had one line. They said I could audition for the director. Now, it's the lunch break in the cafeteria, and there's hundreds of kids, and there's the director. It's John Avildsen, who directed the first *Rocky* and *The Karate Kid*. And he made me audition right there in the cafeteria, with hundreds of people around.

I got the line, but I had never been on a movie set before. I'd been studying acting for five years but had never been in front of a camera. This is a very different experience. And this is before digital, so these are big thirty-five-millimeter film cameras. They're huge. That big lens just coldly staring at you. It was very intimidating. I don't know where to look.

We rehearsed the scene. The principal, played by Morgan Freeman, is calling the kids' names, and when he calls my character's name I walk onto the stage. That's the scene. When they call my name, I stand up and I'm supposed to say, "Hey, I'm going to be a star." That's the line.

I don't know who to say the line to, I don't know where to look, and I'm terrified. The first take, I figured, "Well, if you mumble it, maybe they won't notice me or something." So I say, under my breath, "Heyimgoingtobeastar," and I just shuffle up onstage.

Director cuts. He comes over. "You with that line, 'I'm going to be a star,' you got to give me something or you're out of here." And I felt awful. I just felt just like garbage. Then we did it again and I probably blew it again because the line is not in the movie. I am in the movie, you do see me on the stage, but my line was cut.

It was a horrible experience, to be honest, because you want to be great. I've been studying for five years and for the most part, my life was only about acting. I was really into it and it was my first movie, and it was terrible.

Steve: But you hung in there.

Michael: Yes, I had an agent at that point, so it was really, just wait for the next job.

Steve: And then you got your big shot. A year later. Martin Scorsese puts you in *Goodfellas*. Everybody remembers your scene as Spider.

Michael: I'm always grateful to Marty. He made me feel that I really belonged there—and nobody knew me from anywhere. He made me feel like I was an actor and I should just have fun. I'm forever grateful for that experience, because he could've destroyed me if he was not who he is. He made me feel I could do whatever and try stuff, and I felt so welcomed by him. And by the cast too. By Joe Pesci and Ray Liotta and Bob De Niro. It was wonderful.

Steve: And you worked in his office too. Was that before or after *Goodfellas*?

Michael: That was after. About a year later I met the woman who ran the development office for Martin Scorsese. We had mutual friends in the theater and she hired me to be her assistant. My job was to answer phones. His video collection was right next to my office and it was like a video store. He had thousands of movies, and nobody did at that time. People would borrow movies from Marty, other directors, journalists, writers. I would have to make sure they would go back where they belonged and keep track.

Steve: Is Martin Scorsese your favorite director?

Michael: I love Marty. I love his movies. But my favorite director by far is John Cassavetes. The stuff that he did independently, especially like *Faces* and *Woman Under the Influence, Opening Night, Love Streams,* those are some of my favorite movies ever. I can watch them over and over again and I always see new things. I knew *Gloria,* which is probably his most commercial movie, but the first time I saw his independent stuff was at the Anthology Film Archives in New York. I was probably about twenty-two or twenty-three. When I saw *Opening Night* or *A Woman Under the Influence* I didn't know what I had just seen. *Killing of a Chinese Bookie* is probably one of the best movies ever in the whole crime genre. Anybody out there who has not seen those movies, I urge you to do it.

Steve: What was it about Cassavetes and those movies?

Michael: It was the complexity of the experience, the ability to completely get lost in those worlds and those characters. Most movies have a beginning, a middle, and an end, and you pretty much know where you are and where you're going the whole time. His movies, you can't tell where you are—it's the equivalent of being in a dream. Also his compassion for the characters, his understanding of the frailty of the human soul, and of people's struggles. Of what it means to be a human being.

Steve: We talked before about how you wound up on *The Sopranos* and all that. But I wanna know how at the same time you're starting on *The Sopranos* you wind up writing a whole other movie.

Michael: Cowriting. With Victor Colicchio. And Spike.

Steve: Spike Lee. *Summer of Sam.* How does that come about? How do you wind up writing a movie with Spike Lee?

Michael: I'd already been writing. I started writing not long after I started acting, I just never finished anything. By the time I was thirty, I literally had a huge stack of stuff—halves of screenplays, pieces of plays, just a whole lot of unfinished junk.

Steve: Not unlike Christopher.

Michael: Yes. I used to move once a year, and I would bring the whole big stack of shit with me. And one day I realized, "You're more in love with the idea of being a writer. You don't really have anything to say." So I threw it all away, all of it. Threw it all in the garbage. Somehow, it cleared my head.

Steve: That's what Christopher does! In Season Two. Is that where that came from?

Michael: I might have mentioned it to the writers, yes. Or maybe it was just one of those weird things of life imitating art. Or the other way around.

Anyway, I started working on *Summer of Sam* with Victor Colicchio because he had the original idea for that screenplay. I realized, "I understand what we can say through this story." That changed everything.

Victor wrote the first draft of the story of *Summer of Sam*. It was about this kid who gets beat up by people in the neighborhood who think he's the Son of Sam killer. There's so much paranoia in these neighborhoods, anybody who's different was under suspicion.

The same thing happened in Mount Vernon, to my mother's cousin. He was attacked by people he knew, who he grew up with, who for some bizarre reason suspected him of being the killer at some point. After reading his draft I said, "I'm obsessed with this story because this happened in my family," and it happened a couple of times in New York. I said I wanted to work on the script with him. We started writing together.

We didn't want to make it a movie about the hunt for the serial killer. We wanted to make it about the paranoia that happened in these neighborhoods, specifically this neighborhood in the Bronx where my friend grew up. The idea was to really get into the characters themselves, not just in their relationship to the killer, but in questioning their own morality. In the Bronx, the seventies was the beginning of the sexual liberation movement.

A lot of people who grew up very Catholic and very traditional Italian-American were now going to discos and taking Quaaludes and there's sexual freedom and women's liberation and divorce and abortion, which before then was really not very common at all among Italian-Americans in New York.

So the story was an opportunity to explore one's nature in the face of one's beliefs.

After I shot the first season of *The Sopranos*, *Summer of Sam* was coming out. I invited David to the premiere, and that's when I wrote that spec script for *The Sopranos*, between Season One and Season Two, addressing those same issues, because I was very curious. All right, these guys are Catholic. They go to church. They have their kids baptized. They send their kids to Catholic schools. They pray. Their wives pray. How do these guys reconcile what they do

Tony Sirico greets me in his own inimitable way at a surprise party for my birthday at Ciel Rouge, a bar my wife and I owned in Chelsea when the show began. The Ciel Rouge parties were infamous: sometimes we'd lock the doors at 4:00 A.M. and party on 'til dawn. —Michael

Courtesy of Michael Imperioli

Jamie-Lynn Sigler, Tony, and Edie Falco at the 2004 Emmys—the first time *The Sopranos* won the Emmy for Outstanding Drama Series (and the first time ever that any cable series won).

Courtesy of Steve Schirripa

ACADEMY OF TELEVISION ARTS & SCIENCES
2005 - 2006 PRIMETIME EMMY AWARDS

Honors

MICHAEL IMPERIOLI

NOMINATED FOR

OUTSTANDING SUPPORTING ACTOR IN A DRAMA SERIES

THE SOPRANOS

HBO

Dick Askin
Chairman and CEO

It took a while for *The Sopranos* to gain the respect of the TV world, so I was very proud when the Academy awarded me the Emmy in Season Five. By the end of the show, *The Sopranos* had garnered 112 Emmy nominations, and 21 wins. —Michael
Courtesy of Michael Imperioli

Me with Steven Van Zandt on the set of the episode "To Save Us All from Satan's Power" in Season Three. Bobby Bacala was forced to play Santa. He wasn't very happy about that. Or very good at it, either. —Steve
Courtesy of Steve Schirripa

Robert Iler with Kathrine Narducci at Spago in Beverly Hills. It became another *Sopranos* tradition—after the SAG awards, we'd always party at Spago.

Courtesy of Steve Schirripa

Me with Jim Gandolfini and Tony, singing karaoke at a party at producer Brad Gray's house. Our song: "I Got You Babe." —Steve

Courtesy of Steve Schirripa

Johnny Ventimiglia and Lorraine Bracco, always the life of the party.
—Steve
Courtesy of Steve Schirripa

Me and Dominic Chianese at the Kentucky Derby in 2001. I predicted the winner, Monarchos, a 13-to-1 shot, live on the TV broadcast before the race. When he won, I cleaned up—and word circulated around the racing world that I knew what I was doing, which I certainly did not. —Michael
Courtesy of Michael Imperioli

Me with the great Allen Coulter, along with Dominic and David Proval, during the shooting of the episode "Full Leather Jacket." Allen directed some of the most haunting episodes of *The Sopranos*, including the groundbreaking episode "College," which terrified the suits at HBO; David's portrayal of Richie Aprile just terrified everybody.
Courtesy of Steve Schirripa

The Sopranos
August 27, 2001
David Chase, Robin Green, Mitch Burgess, Terry Winter, Larry Konner

S406 - Outline - Second Draft

1. Pork Store - Paulie drives through shit on his arrival at Pork Store. Figures it's dog shit...a debate. Sil points out pizza. Paulie goes berserk. Lil Paulie arrives, P throws keys at him....drive it away, get it detailed, new tire.

2. Sop house - C and Furio. "When you gonna settle down?" He mentions his neighbor. He says neighbor no good, anyway because she's a divorcee and has kids. She brings up Billy Joel.

3. Brian's office - T stops in to sign paper. Brain compliments T's suit. Brian a clothes horse. They chat. "You like to dress?" T gives him #.

4. Dr. Mascara's - C raves about Furio to hygienist. Hygienist has family mob connection, gets "it', seems interested in Furio.

5. Pork Store - days later. Tony arrives (with Furio driving?), guy babbling. T humors him, gives him $, takes him to Sat. "Give him a sandwich."

6. Sop house - Night - C tell T F should be married. T agrees but... C hits on idea of hygienist. He poo poos it. C suggests Gloria. T jumps back onto hygienist.

7. Pork Store - sunny day - Espressos and reflectors. Guy comes back. Babbling. "How do I contact Andrew Loog Oldham? I wrote "She's a Rainbow." Paulie, Chris Ralphie. "Keep walking." Ralphie tosses him a $20.

8. Brian in office - on phone but distracted by #.

9. Pork Store - later - T and others coming out, see him squatting between cars. Chase. They get him. Paulie wants to kill him. Restrained. Sil says it's an illness. He runs away like a beaten dog.

10. Matt's house - Party. Beer, bullshit. AJ and friends get into AJ's "mob" dad. AJ proud, ashamed, confused, etc. Already has gf Meredith. Talk of Bing. Great idea.

The outline of an episode I wrote, originally called "Nirvana," which aired as "Everybody Hurts." One story line, included in this outline, was about a mentally ill homeless guy obsessed with Andrew Loog Oldham, producer/manager for the Rolling Stones in the sixties. That story line would be dropped—but the outline shows how much detail we'd work out before a writer even started on a script.
—Michael
Courtesy of Michael Imperioli

My good buddy Johnny V., me, and my wife, Victoria, on the way to the Eckle Awards party in 2004, a *Sopranos* family pre-Emmy ritual. The tongue-in-cheek awards were given to actors on the show for crazy things like Best Acting with a Telephone (and then they'd show a clip of Jim smashing a telephone to pieces). It was always a great time. —Michael

Courtesy of Michael Imperioli

Me and the love of my life, my wife, Laura, at the 2007 Emmy Awards. —Steve

Courtesy of Steve Schirripa

With Jim during the first episode we worked together. He makes fun of my weight in the scene we shot that day; I wasn't that much bigger than him, so they put me in a gigantic fat suit that costume designer Juliet Polcsa made from a T-shirt and a lot of cotton stuffing. —Steve
Courtesy of Steve Schirripa

A test shot of me in the second fat suit they had me wear. This one wasn't quite as huge as the first. —Steve
Courtesy of Steve Schirripa

Home Box Office
Cordially invites you and a guest
to the New York premiere of

The Sopranos

Episodes 1 & 2

Thursday, January 7, 1999
7:00 p.m. State Theatre
1540 Broadway
(Broadway and 45th Street)
New York City

Buffet Supper following at
John's Pizzeria
260 West 44th Street
(between Broadway and 8th Avenue)

This invitation is nontransferable

Combining drama and comic irony, "The Sopranos" looks at
the everyday life of modern-day mob boss Tony Soprano,
who's a loving husband and father. When the responsibilities of family
and "family" take their toll, he's plunged into a mid-life crisis.
What's a mob boss to do when business isn't what
it used to be, and life closes in on him?

The first-season premiere party invitation for an unknown TV show, with the after-party held at a local pizza joint.
Courtesy of Michael Imperioli

By the third season, our premieres were huge events, held at Radio City Music Hall. It was crazy; everybody and his brother wanted a ticket.
Courtesy of Michael Imperioli

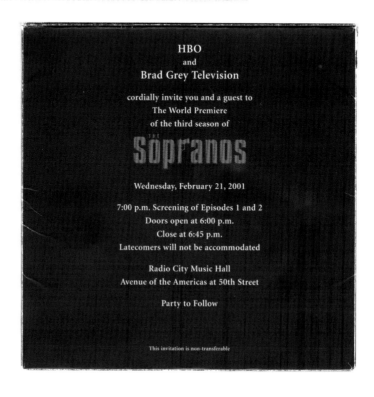

HBO
and
Brad Grey Television

cordially invite you and a guest to
The World Premiere
of the third season of

Sopranos

Wednesday, February 21, 2001

7:00 p.m. Screening of Episodes 1 and 2
Doors open at 6:00 p.m.
Close at 6:45 p.m.
Latecomers will not be accommodated

Radio City Music Hall
Avenue of the Americas at 50th Street

Party to Follow

This invitation is non-transferable

with what they believe? That's what that was about. It's similar to what we talked about in "From Where to Eternity"—those questions about morality and how they live their lives.

Steve: That's what a lot of *The Sopranos* is about too. From the very first show, when Carmela tells Tony, "You're going to hell," that's very much in there. It's in the movie we did together, too. *The Hungry Ghosts*. But I mean, that's a whole different story altogether.

Michael: *The Hungry Ghosts* was written right before I became a Buddhist, right when I started reading some Buddhist stuff. That question of, why are we here, is there something more, is there something higher, all those things were definitely part of what I wanted to serve as an artist.

Steve: When you asked me about doing it, I jumped at the chance. First of all, I liked the script because the role was an incredible one for me. It was the first time I was one of the leads.

Michael: Well, the part was written for you.

Steve: I didn't know if it was written for me.

Michael: I'm telling you it was. I would know.

Steve: This is the first time. I don't think you've ever told me that before.

Michael: What do you mean? Like I had twenty guys in mind and you were the twentieth? No. In fact, most of those parts were written for the people who played them. Believe it or not though, that script started as a little thing years before—I had the idea to write this character who was the host of a children's show. His name was Uncle Frank, and it was a kids' show with a puppet, like Mr. Rogers or something like that. Then when I started writing *The Hungry Ghosts*, I revisited the idea of this TV show but made it a radio thing that was inspired by Joe Franklin and a little bit of Joey Reynolds. And it became your character, the late-night talk show host, where your radio show is *Up All Night with Uncle Frank*. When you write for somebody, you're trying to play to their strengths. It wasn't about you, I mean, Frank is a completely different person, but I was trying to play to your strengths as an actor.

The initial seed for that movie, by the way, was you and Aunjanue Ellis, who played Nadia, on a train. I don't know why. The two of you were on a train for some reason, and how you guys get there was what I had to figure out.

Steve: I'm gonna brag and say that was one of my favorite performances ever. For all you've done, the movies, directing, acting, writing, *The Sopranos*, all that, what's your favorite performance you ever did?

Michael: My favorite performance of mine is a movie that got released in 2019, called *Cabaret Maxime*. I was also a producer on it. We shot it in Lisbon. That has me, John Ventimiglia, Sharon Angela, David Proval, and Arthur Nascarella. You were supposed to do it, but you were doing *Blue Bloods*, you couldn't get off. The director is Bruno de Almeida, a Portuguese filmmaker; Johnny and I have been in several of his films. I love that movie. It's kind of a gangster noir movie.

Steve: You were fantastic in it. I'm not just saying that. I saw it, I was at the screening, and I liked the movie very much, I really did. *Sopranos* fans should check it out. I think they'd really like it. You're actually an interesting guy, my friend. A little weird for my tastes. But interesting, I gotta admit. Lemme ask you two more things. I read your novel. I really liked it a lot.

Michael: Thanks. That's the thing I'm most proud of. *The Perfume Burned His Eyes* was published in 2018. It's a coming-of-age story set in New York in the seventies and Lou Reed is one of the characters. I'm working on adapting it for film right now. A kind of cult following of the book has amassed over the last year. I've also done a lot of live readings of it where I'll read sections and play different roles from it in clubs in New York and L.A. I did it in Europe, where the book was published in French and Italian. The French edition was maybe the best-selling of all.

Steve: What else are you writing?

Michael: I have a story in another book that just came out, *The Nicotine Chronicles*. It's an anthology of short stories edited by Lee Child, who created the *Jack Reacher* series. They all deal with nicotine or tobacco. This is my first short story being published, and it's a magical realist allegory about colonialism.

Steve: I didn't understand one fucking thing you just said.

Michael: It's very *Twilight Zone*–y, set in the Caribbean.

Steve: Why didn't you say that in the first place?

Michael: I kinda did.

Steve: Listen, seriously, this was all really interesting. Now I don't even wanna get into what a jerk you were with me the day we met.

Michael: You won't let that go, will you?

Steve: Never mind. Maybe we'll get into that again later in the book. I'll let you end this chapter on a nice note.

Michael: You're really a sweetheart.

Steve: Okay. Let's get back to *The Sopranos*. Where were we?

Michael: We're up to Season Three.

Steve: Right. Great season. Just when you thought the show couldn't get any bigger, it did.

SIX

Season Three

All in the Family

BY SEASON THREE, The Sopranos was a phenomenon the likes of which TV had never seen. We were mobbed wherever we went. (No pun intended.) The season focused a lot on Tony's kids, Meadow and A. J., both coming into their own in different ways, so we talked some more to the two wonderful young actors who portrayed them, Jamie-Lynn Sigler and Robert Iler. It featured the short but incredibly emotional story arc of Jackie Aprile Jr., so we have to talk about that. And of course it featured two of the most memorable episodes ever, "Employee of the Month," which may have been the most painful to watch, and the first Sopranos episode Steve Buscemi directed, "Pine Barrens." But before we get to any of that, we gotta talk about the crisis that the casting directors, Georgianne Walken and Sheila Jaffe, were facing.

Not enough Italians. —Steve

Georgianne: There was a point in time where we had literally run out of people to bring in for certain things. That's when I started hitting up you guys and your families.

Michael: You read through all the Italians.

Steve: There was not enough guineas. You guys asked me if my father was alive, my real father. I said no, he had passed away. You were looking for Bacala Sr. But then you wound up with Burt Young, who was so good.

Michael: He was perfect. He's so believable. You completely buy that his character is someone very ill. Burt Young is a very honest actor. Whatever he does, you believe every minute.

Sheila: We were lucky, we got a lot of people we really liked, always. It was also great that Steve Buscemi wound up on the show. For us that was special, because that's how we got the job, by working with him.

Steve: Because like you said before, he gave you your first big break, casting his movie *Trees Lounge.*

Georgianne: Yes, without him, we wouldn't have gotten the job at all. It was wonderful. What goes around comes around.

Steve: But you were on the hunt for more guineas. Fat Italians like me, skinny ones like Michael, whatever you could get your hands on. And that led to the open call in New Jersey. Thousands of people showed up, right? Tell us about that.

Georgianne: We got overrun by people, literally, and we got closed down by the police. Henry Bronchtein, one of the producers, was there, and he was having a hemorrhage because there were so many people. Guys showed up in costume, with toy guns, and they were doing scenes out on the street.

Michael: Some of them were dressed like *Guys and Dolls,* too. They were wearing pinstripes and white ties. I'm not kidding.

Georgianne: We had a guy show up with six pizzas as a pizza deliveryman just so he could get in the auditorium. Nobody had ordered pizza and we were all looking at each other.

Michael: They cast Denise Borino-Quinn from that open call, who played Ginny Sack, right? She was one of the only people who got a real speaking part out of the open call.

Georgianne: Right.

Steve: But you got a lot of extras out of it too, right? A lot of those people wound up in scenes?

Georgianne: We had more than five thousand pictures, and we would go through them to find extras. It blew my mind away. That was one of the most successful open calls ever, because sometimes an open call can only have one person show up.

Sheila: At that point *Sopranos* was a phenomenon. People were crazy for it.

THE CHARACTER *of Meadow Soprano, to me, encapsulates everything about how* The Sopranos *begins to change in Season Three. In the first season we see Tony's fears of losing control of the family—or both families, really—symbolized by the ducks flying away from him. That's what leads to his panic attacks. In this season, those fears become manifest; as Meadow moves off to college, she also moves out from under Tony's thumb, increasingly defying him and questioning his authority. In "College," in Season One, she asks him flat out if he's in the Mafia; by Season Three, she has come to terms with it, and with him. All of this—the strength and vulnerability of Meadow, the power and powerlessness of the men in her life, and ultimately the devastation she feels at the death of Jackie Jr.—all of it is indelibly etched in our memories because of the powerful, raw, brave, emotional performance of Jamie-Lynn Sigler.*
—Michael

Steve: You talked earlier about how you came from musical theater, that all this TV stuff was new to you. Was it strange for you?

Jamie-Lynn: Oh yes. Literally, up until *The Sopranos* started, I had never been on a film set. On my first day of work on the pilot, I thought my stand-in was somebody who was also up for the part—I thought they were still deciding who was going to be Meadow. I was so confused.

Steve: What was it like when you first showed up?

Jamie-Lynn: I was living on Long Island with my family. I was a sophomore going into my junior year of high school. I remember showing up to the table read. There's kind of a blessing when you're that young: You don't want to show that you don't know what you're doing. You're nervous, but you fake it till you make it. At least that was my personality. Fortunately, you guys were all so warm and giving, but I sat at that table looking at the caliber of actors and how great everyone was and thinking, "Wow, this is something big in my life right now."

Michael: And then as time went on, with Jim and Edie playing your mom and dad, did you feel a parental vibe from them? Did that kind of feeling eventually blossom between you guys?

Jamie-Lynn: I think so, especially with Jim. I was somebody that was difficult to get close to and that was my fault. I was holding on to a lot of things for a long time. Jim was someone who saw through that, and in his own particular nice, special way, he would always pry and ask, and he became somebody that I eventually did open up to about a lot of things privately. Yes, he definitely felt like another father figure in a way of just somebody that I knew I could count on and who would be there, but was never aggressive about it, or pushy. It was just kind of like, "I got you if you need me."

There was a time in the maybe fourth or fifth season where I was dealing with my divorce privately and my diagnosis of MS and a lot of stuff that I wasn't talking to people about, and he really stepped up.

Michael: You were diagnosed with MS when you were twenty, early on in *The Sopranos,* but you didn't talk about it publicly for a long time. But Jim was a big help to you?

Jamie-Lynn: He sent his acting coach, Susan Aston, to work with me, just to make sure that I was taken care of. Little things like that, that he really just stepped up in amazing ways.

Steve: He wasn't faking it. He really gave a shit.

Jamie-Lynn: Totally.

Michael: What would you say is one of your fondest memories of the whole experience?

Jamie-Lynn: That's a good question. I particularly loved when we would have scenes with everybody, when I could get to work with all you guys.

Steve: That's the one thing people don't realize. Even though we're all on the show together, you don't see everybody. Sometimes I didn't see Michael or whoever for a month. I don't think me and you ever had a scene together just the two of us.

Jamie-Lynn: No. But whenever it's a funeral scene or a dinner scene, I really loved getting to work with all you guys, because we would see each other at events and the table reads, but getting to connect and work with you guys—the best of the best, still, in my opinion— meant a lot to me.

I also loved the quiet scenes I did with Jim and Edie, because I looked up to them so much as actors and they gave me so much encouragement. After they would air, Edie would always call me after a particular episode if she liked what I did, just to tell me how proud she was of me. Those types of things just meant a lot.

Steve: Is there one scene that sticks out in your mind?

Jamie-Lynn: The most powerful scene I ever did—it was directed by John Patterson, rest in peace, who I loved so much, I know we all did—when I face off with Jim and I call him Mr. Mob Boss. It was a magnetic feel that I had never felt before as an actress of like, "We're doing something really cool."

Michael: Incredible scene. From the "No Show" episode. You confront Tony like you never did before, and he gets furious. The honesty the two of you bring to that scene is enormous.

Jamie-Lynn: James leaned into my ear and said, "You hate this man, you're furious at this man." It was a really powerful moment. Those moments you strive for as an actor where they feel really real, and you're shaking afterward. That was one of my favorite scenes I ever got to do.

Michael: You told me earlier this morning that you just watched the first season of *The Sopranos* for the first time these last couple of weeks.

Jamie-Lynn: Yes, as a young girl, self-conscious, I just didn't want to watch myself. I'm also really grateful that I waited 'til now because I wouldn't have gotten it as a seventeen-, eighteen-, nineteen-, twenty-year-old girl. I'm watching it now as a thirty-nine-year-old woman and really appreciating it. I looked at my husband the other day, I'm sitting there watching, thinking, "Holy shit, I got to be a part of this. This is so cool, I'm so proud." Especially watching the pilot. I thought my part was so small, but when I watched it, I was feeling, "Wow I had a significant role in this." I'm so glad that this much time has passed. I am the age now that Edie was playing Carmela.

Michael: That's so bizarre.

Steve: I hear what you're saying. I hate to watch myself. There are a few actors on the show that probably watched themselves on a loop all day long.

Jamie-Lynn: Sirico?

Steve: I won't mention any names.

Michael: Looking back, how do you feel about Meadow and who she was as a person? Do you see similarities between Jamie and Meadow, and differences as well?

Jamie-Lynn: I very much was like that young girl that wanted to have the adult conversations and wanted to act like I knew every-thing, because I just so badly wanted the respect and to tell it like it is. Still to this day, I don't like anyone to give me a pussyfoot answer. I want the real. I can handle it. I'm very similar to Meadow in that way.

The way she affected her parents was pretty significant and I can see it now being a mother. My kid's best day is my best day and his worst day is my worst day. I understand that. The dilemma that she caused to both of them as their child and who she was, I under-stand more now. It was probably better that I didn't understand it then and was just living like a true teenager.

Michael: One of the most fun things for me was watching you and Robert growing up together, both your characters, Meadow and A. J., and the two of you as actors. It was so clear that you two had a very real friendship.

Jamie-Lynn: Rob and I are best friends, and have been since the show. Robert was the old pro when we started. He had been on a bunch of film sets before, so he was the one that's schooling me. He was the one that was telling me, "This is what 'check the gate' means." Theater, that's home to me. I don't even think about how many people are out there. That's my favorite thing to do. It's still a dream I don't want to give up on.

Steve: Robert's four years younger than you? So, you're the big sister for real?

Jamie-Lynn: Yes, but invariably, he's very protective of me. I can guarantee that a week just never goes by without him checking up on me and how I'm doing. Aida was in town a couple of weeks ago, and he came over with her. I cooked them dinner, and she is as kooky and amazing as ever.

ROBERT AND *Jamie have started doing a podcast together called* Pajama Pants. *I got to be on it a little while ago, and I had a ball. We had so much to ask Robert Iler about, but we had to start there. —Steve*

Steve: Jamie-Lynn is like your sister in real life.

Robert: She is like my sister in real life.

Michael: Tell us about the podcast.

Robert: I moved to L.A. six months ago to start the podcast with Jamie-Lynn. It was around the time when we had the twenty-year anniversary, and we were sitting in the hotel room afterward. It was just me and her, we're in pajama pants, and we're saying, "We need to do this." We're smoking a joint and we're saying, "This stupid shit we're talking about now in this conversation, we want to keep it going." I was living in Vegas and I said, "Well, if you want to start a podcast with me, I'll move to L.A.," and she said, "Of course."

Steve: So that's how it started.

Robert: Yes. *Pajama Pants,* we're doing it on YouTube. We have it wherever you get podcasts. Me and Jamie's relationship is—80 percent of it was *Sopranos,* so *Sopranos* does come up, but also, we've talked about going to the bathroom, losing our virginity. It's everything.

Steve: So you lived in Vegas at one point, right? I lived there a long time.

Robert: I lived in Vegas for a little over a year when I was twenty-five, and then I moved back to New York. That's when I got sober. Then, I'm back to Vegas, and when I got there I realized, "Oh, being sober, this place is not for me."

Steve: We still think of you like a kid. You're thirty-five, a grown goddamn man.

Michael: How old were you when we did the pilot?

Robert: I was twelve.

Michael: Did you study acting? Did you have a teacher? Or was it all instinctual? I'm not just saying this because you're here and because you're my friend, but your acting is phenomenal. Even in the pilot. Simple, honest, in the moment. You're so relaxed. You're so natural. What was that process for you?

Robert: Thank you. Obviously, it means a lot coming from you. I never studied acting. And I never thought that I was good, but I did feel toward the end—not that I got good, but I was able to at least hold my own. Obviously, it was from being around Jim and Edie, people like you guys, and just watching. A lot of times people ask, "Oh, what did Jim teach you?" Jim never came to me and tried to put me under his arm and be like, "Here's what you got to do." But when you're around him and Edie doing scenes, you pick up stuff, you see how they do it, and you think, "Oh, this is how you do it."

Steve: Sirico, did he have anything to say to you? Tony usually has advice. He usually gives fatherly advice out, wanted or unwanted.

Robert: Yes! He came to my confirmation in the double-breasted pinstripe suit, he gave me a kiss on the cheek and a card with cash in it, and he says, "You ever have any problems, you call Uncle Tony."

Steve: There was an episode when they asked you to shave your eyebrows. Do you remember that? And you were gonna do it, right?

Robert: At first I said, "Okay," and then Jim said, "Listen, there's horror stories of people who shave their eyebrows when they were drunk, and they never grew back." He was very much like that. Whenever there was anything that made an actor uncomfortable or whatever, Jim said something. He always watched out for you.

Steve: For sure.

Robert: So they had some really famous movie makeup person come in. If we have to shoot at, let's say, six in the morning, I would have to get there at four to do the two hours of makeup, so I would sit in the chair and fall asleep. Then, you open your eyes and you wake up and there's the mirror right in front of you, and you have no eyebrows.

One thing I remember about doing that show was Carmela is going, "Oh my God!" and realizes right away what happened. But Tony looks at me and he just goes, "What's weird about you?" [*laughs*] He can't even figure out that the eyebrows are gone. It was a weird thing. That was the vibe I got from people walking around set all day, and you go to get lunch somewhere and you would see people looking at you super strange, and you didn't remember that you had no eyebrows, so you're thinking, "Why is this person looking at me?"

Steve: You always loved to play poker even while the show was going on, right?

Robert: I played at some underground spots in New York. We had three days off, and I would get in the car, go to Atlantic City, or

Mohegan Sun, or wherever. I could sit there for twelve hours, play poker, go to sleep, wake up, and all I wanted to do was play poker.

Steve: That's how you made your living.

Robert: Yes, I have in the past. Now I'm not really playing enough at all to make a living. Also, I was drinking a lot back in the day, so I would make money playing poker, and then I would go lose it. I would always play poker sober, then after I would be betting on sports, or roulette, trying to make it out of the casino.

Steve: How long have you been sober now?

Robert: Sober seven years. Hard-core drugs, it's also seven years. I was taking Xanax every day. It took me a long time to get off the Xanax, and I had to go see a specialist. That's probably five years without the Xanax.

Steve: Good for you. Now, the show ended 2007. You were in your early twenties, and out in the clubs every night, right?

Robert: Every night, yes.

Steve: Were you dating any famous broads there? Who was big back then? Paris Hilton, Lindsay Lohan, were you dating any of them?

Robert: They were all big back then. I went for regular chicks. I definitely have hooked up with some girls who people know. But I was more about not having to work hard and dating regular chicks, because if you're dating Paris Hilton, Lindsay Lohan, you're working. There's guys trying to date her, nonstop, every day, and trying to be the next pick, and sending flowers, and all that. I never was a work-too-hard-at-a-relationship guy. I'm more, "Oh, if it's going to work, it's going to work." When you try and date those kinds of girls, that's not really how it goes.

Michael: In the scene where you vandalize the swimming pool, Lady Gaga was an extra. Stefani Germanotta, before she was Lady Gaga, she was fifteen years old and she was trying to be an actress. Did you ever see Lady Gaga again after?

Robert: We have some mutual friends in New York. I actually saw her around three months ago at a friend's birthday party out here in L.A.

Steve: So after *The Sopranos,* you basically stopped acting. Why did you just stop?

Robert: After *Sopranos,* I told my manager that I wanted six months off to go play poker, hang out with my friends, and just do whatever. Then he kept calling. "It's been a year. It's been two years," and I said, "I don't want to." The only thing I really have done since *Sopranos* was when I got a call to do jury duty, and I didn't want to go to jury duty. I called my manager and he said, "Well, I can get you a job and it'll get you out of doing jury duty." I said, "All right, fine." He called me and I did it to get out of jury duty. I did an episode of *Law & Order.*

Michael: That's very funny.

Steve: But you must have got a lot of offers after *The Sopranos.*

Robert: I got a great offer for one movie, and then a bunch of shows. I still get calls randomly to do shows. I don't know, it's not that I get anxiety about it; I just get the feeling of, it's like you play for the Yankees and now people are saying, "Hey, do you want to go do this thing?" You don't know if it's going to be good.

I feel that with *Sopranos,* you just knew every episode was going to be great, every scene was going to be great, every person you were acting with was going to be great. I was extremely spoiled. We were a family. The writing was amazing. There's a part of me that's,

"If you do something else, you're going to mess it up." I look back on *The Sopranos,* and I go, "It was perfect."

———————

Michael: So, Steve, this is the season you became a regular. If people don't know, "regular" means that you'll get paid for every episode they shoot, rather than just the ones you appear in. So you don't know how many you're going to be in, you might shoot two, you might shoot three, but you're going to get paid for the whole season.

Steve: Everything changes. Now you got front credits. If you say you are a series regular, it sets a precedent for the rest of your career. It's a big deal.

Michael: Because originally, when you were hired, it was just for one episode.

Steve: Just the one. Did not know if there would be another episode. That's why my agent originally had said, "Don't take it. They're not paying your way, they're giving you crappy money."

Michael: Bad advice.

Steve: Yes, bad advice. He's no longer my agent. After commission, I don't even think I broke even. But I invested in myself. The rest of that season they had me back, but I had to pay my own way. I'm living in Las Vegas, flying back and forth to New York on my own dime, putting myself up in hotels, everything. It cost me $24,000 and I was paid $22,000.

I used to supplement my income in those early days, before I was making any money. HBO would send us out to the call centers. Where they were calling people to get them to try to sign up for HBO. I did it, Johnny V did it, Federico did it. You would go to the call centers, there was this very hardworking sales team, and as an incentive to them you would go and they would take Polaroid pictures with you and you'd have a little party. It was easy money, and fun to do. I got $3,500 for an appearance. I probably did twenty or thirty of those.

Michael: But like you said to me earlier—you hung in there.

Steve: When I finally got the chance to become a series regular, they offered me a third of the money that I was making in Las Vegas. I mean nothing. I have to move back to New York, and I got a role in a Nick Turturro pilot, which I was going to take, and now I had to choose between the pilot and *The Sopranos*. I get a call from David Chase. David says, "Listen. I gotta tell you, you got the chance to be on one of the greatest shows in TV history." I said, "David, they're not offering me enough money, man. I can't do it for this money. I have a wife and two kids."

He says, "Listen. We want you on the show, we'd love to have you." I said, "I need help. I can't go for this money." It was a long weekend, man. I was on pins and needles, and they came through with enough money. That's how I did it. It's just one of those things, you make a decision, you go left, you go right. Your whole life could change.

Michael: So Season Three was your big breakout season.

Steve: Not right away. HBO moved my family and me back to New York from Las Vegas. I was in the second episode a little, the third one a little. I wasn't in the first. I wasn't in the fourth. It was weird to me. I'm saying, "What the hell did I move here for? I could have commuted." I was frustrated. I had a couple of lines in each episode. I really didn't do a whole lot. I'm going, "What the fuck? They made me a series regular to not use me."

Michael: You don't know. Is it going to get bigger? Is it going to stay the same? Are they going to kill you off? Who knows? It's very uncertain.

Steve: Absolutely. That's why as soon as I started making some money, I paid my house off. I figured if all else goes bad, I'll just move back to Vegas, and at least I have somewhere to live.

Michael: So you weren't in the first episode, but if you remember, the first two, we shot them out of sequence. They premiered them together.

Steve: Right. So the funeral parlor scene, that's the first scene I shot for that season.

Michael: Bacala looks sharp in that scene, I have to say. He looked good. That was a nice suit.

Steve: Nice suit. He's got the new belly, it's not as big as the old belly. They gave me the new fat suit. A better fat suit.

Michael: So that's the real perk of becoming a series regular. We talked about the money, the credits, all that, but it's really about the fat suit.

Steve: Look, I'll do whatever the show needs. You know that. But yeah, I was happy for the suit.

Michael: But really, more for the work.

Steve: Absolutely. And they gave me some great scenes in this season. I'm forever grateful to David for that.

Michael: This was the season we started the whole Il Cortile tradition. Whenever anyone got killed off. It started with John Fiore, who played Gigi, the guy who died on the toilet from a heart attack, right? You started that.

Steve: I lived upstairs from Il Cortile, the restaurant on Mulberry Street. It was my home base. I was friends with the owners. John Fiore, who played Gigi, he got killed off. He got that call from David Chase. He said he was pleading for his life, like he was actually getting killed. David told him he'd never sacrifice the master plan for a character, no matter how much he liked him. That day after we shot it, I said, "Come on, I'll take you out to dinner," and before you know it, a bunch of us were going, Jim came, Joey Pants, and a couple of the others, and we wound up at Il Cortile. And that became a tradition. If you were getting killed off, we took you to Il Cortile for dinner. That's a dinner you don't want to be the guest of honor at.

Michael: Il Cortile got to be the home base for a lot of us. I still hang out there. I love Il Cortile, superb Italian food.

Steve: But then we had to stop it because the press caught wind of it.

Michael: Right, the press was trying to get information from the people who worked there about who was getting taken out to dinner, meaning who was going to be whacked. And they were trying to get copies of the scripts. Security got very tight around the story lines. So that's when we had to stop the big send-offs at Il Cortile.

ONE OF *the characters who shows up in Season Three is Patsy Parisi, the twin brother of Philly Parisi, who was killed at the end of Season Two. Dan Grimaldi, who played both roles, told us how that came about.*
—*Steve*

Steve: You came on Season Two?

Dan: Season Two, Episode One, yes. Philly was the first new character introduced after it became a hit. He was written in.

Michael: At that time there was just Philly, there was no Patsy?

Dan: Yes, no Patsy. You guys were in Italy and David came back and they were watching the rushes, he and Allen. After it was over, Allen called me up at home and he said, "Danny, I want you to know this." He said, "David was sitting in the room and he just threw his head back and he said, 'Who is this guy? I like him. Why do I kill him? I don't want him dead.'" Allen said, "It doesn't mean anything, except that I think you should know that." When I got off the phone, I was angry, and my oldest son said, "Dad, what are you angry about?" I said, "Well, I like the praise. It's good to be praised. But I need a job. I want to work."

Then there was talk that I might go back. And they wrote Patsy in in the last episode of Season Two. Just a quick scene where he brings in a fur coat. That was January, and then I had to wait until August to find out if they were bringing him back for the next season.

Steve: Wow. That's a long wait.

Dan: I went to Europe and I told my younger son, "James, if anybody calls from *The Sopranos,* no matter what time it is, no matter where I am, find me." He called me in France and he said, "Dad, you're going back."

Steve: What a great call.

Michael: Here's what happened. Terry talked to David about it. He said, "David, you can bring him back as a twin, but you only get one of those for the whole series."

Dan: So I was lucky on so many levels.

SO LET'S *get into the episodes. I'll be honest, the first episode of Season Three wasn't my favorite. Michael, either. Too much FBI stuff. They spent half the show going over the details of how they're gonna plant a bug in Tony's basement. After the long break between seasons, I think people wanted to see more about the family, about Tony's crews, all of that.*

But one thing Michael and I both loved was the Paulie Walnuts scene right at the top. There's a whole lot of Tony Sirico in that. —*Steve*

Michael: There's that great Paulie Walnuts monologue about cleanliness and germs. How if you tie your shoelaces you have to wash your hands again. Because the tips of the shoelaces are wet from going to a public bathroom. "And even if the ends are dry, bacteria and virus migrate from the sole up." I love that whole thing.

Steve: Paulie is a germophobe. It's a very funny speech: "Men's toilets are a sewer. You ever look at a ladies' john? You can eat maple walnut ice cream off the toilet."

Michael: It's also a great example of what we've been talking about, the specifics the writers bring to every moment. Any writer could say, "The floor is clean enough to eat off of." It's the maple walnut ice cream that makes that line land so well.

Steve: It's great writing—but also, this is how Tony really feels in real life.

Michael: Absolutely. One of the first people I ever saw with hand sanitizer in his pocket. This was a while ago, twenty years ago. Was not a popular thing then, but he had it.

Steve: Remember the anthrax scare? After 9/11?

Michael: Yes, somebody was mailing anthrax to newscasters in 30 Rockefeller Center, the NBC headquarters in New York City. Tony was convinced that he was next. He's seeing they're targeting famous people, and he's thinking, "I'm next." I guess in his own mind, he thinks if you really want to bring down Western civilization, you first go after Brian Williams, and Tony Sirico is next on the list. What he did was, he had his assistant take his mail from the mailbox with rubber gloves, he brings it in the house, and they put the mail in the microwave for a few seconds—because somehow he figured the microwaves would neutralize the anthrax and make it not poisonous. But what actually happened is the mail went on fire and burnt up in the microwave.

Steve: And the West Nile, that was another one. He was absolutely convinced he had the West Nile virus, remember?

Michael: We were shooting the scene where Christopher gets made, in Season Three, which was shot in a basement of a house somewhere in North Jersey.

Steve: It was one of the first scenes I did with all of the guys. It was summertime. It was hot.

Michael: It was early evening before the sunset, and Tony Sirico and I were in the front yard of this house just hanging around waiting for the scene. At the time, the West Nile virus was an issue. A couple of people had it. Not many. Tony Sirico got bit by a mosquito and starts screaming, "Motherfucker! Oh my God! I got bit!" He's screaming. I'm going, "What? What?" It sounded like he got bit by a snake or something. He was panicking.

He goes, "I got bit! I got bit!" I go, "You got bit by what?" He says: "A fucking mosquito!" I said, "Tony. It's summertime. There's mosquitoes. We're in New Jersey." "Oh my God, the fucking West Nile!" I said, "Calm down. You're not going to get the West Nile. You got bit by a mosquito, relax."

Steve: A lot of people would say he's a hypochondriac. Exactly like Paulie Walnuts.

Michael: Exactly. The next morning he calls me up. He says, "Mikey, I got it." I said, "You got what? What are you talking about?" "The West Niles." He called it the West Niles. I'm saying, "The West Niles? What are you talking about?" He said, "I got the symptoms. They said, you can't sleep. You're irritated and you're disoriented.

And, Mikey, I'm very disoriented this morning!"

ONE OF *the most shocking things about Season Three, of course, is the death of Livia. Nancy Marchand passed away between Season Two and Season Three. We knew she was sick, but she wanted to keep working as long as she possibly could. David Chase honored her wishes, and origi-nally, he was going to have her, in Season Three, testify in court against Tony, about the stolen airline tickets he'd given her at the end of the previous season.*

When Nancy died, David obviously had to change that, but he wanted to create some closure—he didn't want her to just disappear. She was too important and powerful a character. So here's what happened: In between Seasons Two and Three, the movie Gladiator *came out. Oliver Reed died during the shooting of that film, but they needed one more scene from him. So they took some snippets of dialogue and a body dou-ble, and digitally inserted Reed's face and were able to create a scene with Oliver Reed after he was dead. David said, "Well, maybe we could do one more scene with Nancy Marchand." —Michael*

Steve: The scene with Tony and Livia. You could tell it was weird for Jim, acting with a different actress. I just could tell that Jim was a little out of sorts here in this scene. Working with somebody different, then probably the whole idea that Nancy passed away. It had to be hard for him.

Michael: The scene was written after she died. Some of the stuff, they got a body double, and then they used some dialogue and maybe some scenes that have been on the cutting room floor or already used. It wasn't quite CGI, actually; it was called a digital composite, which in 2000 was more common. We had no visual effects person on *The Sopranos* at the time, we had to hire somebody for that. You could see in the last two shots of Nancy, her hair is different than it is in the rest of the shots because they probably used some shots of her from different episodes.

Steve: It took them two weeks to do that. And cost maybe $250,000, I heard.

Michael: It's such a complicated scene—they're trying to give Tony some closure, he's trying to make up with her. And it ends on such a sour note—they're fighting over what she might have said to the feds, and she's giving him crap, and finally he says, "For a year, I didn't speak to you. Maybe I should have kept it that way."

Steve: So really, after all that, there's no closure after all.

Michael: Again, very David Chase. Never sewing things up nice and neatly.

Steve: Then we gotta talk about the scene at the Soprano house. The gathering after the funeral, they call that the repast. I don't know if we've mentioned, but we should say, that's on the stage. They built a whole Soprano house onstage. Silvercup Studios. Very rarely did we go back to the Soprano house, only for outdoor stuff. Backyard stuff a couple of times a year. After that first season of the pilot, they built that huge Soprano house on the stage itself.

Michael: This was one of the funniest moments I've ever had on a set anywhere, which is odd because it's after a funeral. It was one of the rare scenes where all of us were there. When they played that music for the first time, which is "If I Loved You" from *Carousel,* in that high schmaltzy voice, we all lost it, everybody. We couldn't stop laughing. The British call that "corpsing," when you can't stop laughing while you're shooting or onstage.

We couldn't do the scene. So they tried to do the scene without the music, but we just couldn't stop laughing, because sometimes once it starts, you don't have control over it, it takes a while just to get it out of your system. You'll take a break, then go, "Okay, ready? Action," and it just comes back because you're connecting the beginning of the scene to that laughter. It took us a long time to get through this. It was very hard. It was just too funny. But it's a memory I really treasure.

WE HAVE a million stories about Nancy Marchand. She was one of a kind. A wonderful actress and a wonderful person. It's hard to pick one story that encapsulates who she was—but I like what my buddy John Ventimiglia told us. It reminds me of her generosity of spirit, her dry wit, and the wry smile that stays with us, like the Cheshire cat's, long after she's gone. —Michael

John Ventimiglia: We had this scene in her hospital room. And in between takes, she's reading a newspaper. She's quiet. I don't want to bother her. She's Nancy Marchand! In those days you could smoke on the set, so I just wait and I'm smoking a cigarette, and she goes, "Oh, this is a very interesting story." She starts describing to me the obituary of somebody that was a member of an acrobat family, who had just died, at ninetysomething. She goes, "Oh, and the family were known for these acrobatic skills." And then, when I got up and walked around, finally I looked at the newspaper. There was no obituary. She was just making it up at that time to entertain me. She just was doing it for my benefit in some way. That really touched me, the fact that she would do that. That was Nancy.

ONE OF the most endearing moments in Season Three is when Jackie Aprile reappears in a flashback. We talked to Michael Rispoli about what it was like to return to the set after two years. He talked about how he had changed in his approach to the character, and how we had changed as well. —Michael

Michael Imperioli: First off, I have to say, what a powerful performance you gave in that episode. In the first season you had to play Jackie as sick, and dying obviously, but here, we see him so vibrant and alive. What were the choices you were making when you came back?

Michael Rispoli: It's exactly what you said: In Season One, I started sick, and then I was going to die, but here, I am completely alive. I am running things, and I am in control of things. That was powerful in that sense. I wanted to make sure my energy was completely different than it was before. I am confident in what I am doing and everything because they had spoken about, "Oh, he was a great leader," and "Oh, if Jackie were here, he'd know what to do" kind of thing. You have to show that when you come back.

Steve: So what was it like to come back, Michael? Was it different? How was it different?

Michael Rispoli: I'll tell you this really quick story. They were over at Silvercup Studios, and I had to go in for the table read. When I had done that in the first season, you go in, sit around, read the script, it was a little bit informal.

This time, I go in, and there's two security guards. Last time, it was just a guy by the phone bank, and now two years later, two security guards and they ask, "What's your name?" "Mike Rispoli, I'm here to do the table read." "Sign right here, ID, go down this hallway, make your first right, make your first left, stage thirty-two." I said, "Okay."

Now I had to take a leak, so I am walking down a long hallway, and there is my right that I was supposed to take, but the bathroom is on the left. I go toward the bathroom, and I hear from down the hallway—no idea I am being looked at—"I said, take a *right*." He's making sure I don't go wandering up into the offices or something. I said, "Hey, I got to take a leak; is that all right with you?" [*chuckles*]

Then you had to sign out the scripts. They needed to keep them hidden because there were so many people trying to get a lead on what the story line was. When I went in, they had the scripts, and I had to sign. Then we read the script, and I'm getting ready to go, I'm going to take my script, I go to put it in my bag and they go, "You got to turn that in." I said, "How can I turn it in? I have to learn my stuff." "No. No scripts leave the building."

Michael Imperioli: They did get very protective. They had to. Because the press was going nuts.

Michael Rispoli: Absolutely. No one was being a jerk or anything. It was just more formal. I'll tell you another thing. The first thing I had to shoot was down in Asbury Park, and I had to do something in a diner. We did the scene and I ad-libbed something. In the first season, I don't want to say I was ad-libbing a lot of stuff, but there was more discussion about like, "Oh yes, try that," or "Can I try this?" "Yes, give it a shot, let's see." But now this is a big business. The show is an iconic show. I threw a line in there, and Jimmy looks at me when we're done, he smiles, he goes, "They're not going to let you keep that." I said, "Why? It's a great fucking line," and he goes, "Yes, it is, but they ain't going to let you keep it." Sure enough, the script supervisor came up to me, and he goes, "You can't ad-lib anything, just stay to the script."

My difference from the first season, which felt a little bit loose because they were still putting it together, but now they're a finely tuned machine. But it wasn't a lack of warmth or anything—there was still that warm feeling.

THE WRITERS *Mitch Burgess and Robin Green told us something we never knew about the episode in Season Three where Ralphie Cifaretto, played* *by Joey Pantoliano, kills the stripper—another one of the most contro-versial episodes of the series—that brought back a kind of odd memory for me as well. —Michael*

Steve: That episode, for all the killings in the series, that one hit people hard.

Robin: That murder was pretty awful. But here's the story. We were in the writers' room and the idea is that Ralphie does something horrible: he kills a dog.

Mitch: We were trying to make Ralphie bad and to act it out so you could see him be bad, because we wanted to really make him evil.

Michael: Cross-the-line bad, to compare him to Tony, to make him that much worse.

Mitch: Yes. We were trying to think of what Ralphie could do to re-ally be bad. I said, "Well, he should kill one of the strippers' dogs." David says, "He can't do that."

Robin: Can't kill his dog, people will go crazy.

Steve: So then you said, you could kill the stripper.

Robin: Let him kill the stripper.

Mitch: Seriously, that would turn this whole thing, if he kills the dog.

Michael: Tell me about it! That episode, where Christopher is stoned and accidentally kills Adriana's dog, I caught more flack for that than any of the people I killed in the whole series.

Robin: You caught so much flack for killing the dog.

Michael: The scene was, Christopher is high on heroin and wakes up from his drug-induced stupor and the dog, Cosette, is underneath his butt and the dog is suffocated and dead. I was always amazed at how fans would be, yes, Christopher killed sixteen people. Nobody is really complaining about any of that or batting an eyelash, but you sit on one dog and people will never forgive you for that.

Steve: Funny.

Michael: I always found that fascinating. No animals were hurt in the filming of *The Sopranos*. The dog was not real, but the dog's tongue—which when the dog is revealed to be dead, the tongue is hanging out—the tongue was made out of prosciutto by the prop master.

Steve: Prosciutto?

Michael: Yes.

Steve: That is absolutely hysterical.

JASON MINTER *became David Chase's assistant around this time, and got insight into something few of us got to watch—David Chase's approach to the editing process. —Steve*

Steve: What was that like, being in the edit room with David? He would tell you the changes he wanted, and then you had to keep track?

Jason: I had to rapidly take notes while we watched episodes. I learned later on to record what he said because I just couldn't keep up a lot of the time. There was a learning curve. I remember misordering an episode so that it made absolutely no sense. It was the first or second show that I edited with him. He looked at me, he said, "It's all fucked up."

Michael: What do you mean mis-ordered?

Jason: Let's say, it was Tony coming out to get the newspaper, but in reality, at that point it was supposed to be a scene at the Bada Bing. I ordered the scenes wrong, they were in the wrong sequence, and it just made no sense; it was ridiculous, and he was angry.

Steve: That's a giant fuckup.

Jason: It was. Yes. And that's just one cut.

Michael: We should explain that in this sense a "cut" is a rough version of the whole show. When you reedit, that's called the next "cut."

Jason: And sometimes we would do ten cuts a show. We could watch them over and over again in his office. Pull all the black curtains across—I don't know if you guys remember those—and we'd just sit there in the dark, just he and I, watching shows over and over.

Michael: Was it drastically recut, like you'd change orders of scenes, and propose new scenes and all that kind of thing?

Jason: Sometimes we would reshoot scenes entirely. We'd get the director's cut in initially; we'd watch that together. He might give me a couple of notes during that first screening, but he'd need to think about it a bit. Then we sit down a couple days later and we really get into it and he would make massive changes. Sometimes he would pull scenes out of one episode and put them in another episode. There were no limits.

Steve: When a director directs the episode, he has the first cut. He hands it in to David and you. Does it ever stay intact?

Jason: No, never. Alan Taylor, the director, who's obviously incredibly talented and directed some of the best episodes of *The Sopranos*, I remember he had this beautiful shot of a diner in Jersey City, and then a cut to another beautiful shot, and David just threw them out.

It was script-first to him. Alan was really upset, like, "Why did you get rid of these shots?" David did things like that constantly. He knew exactly what he wanted. David never doubted himself when it came to cutting those shows. It was pretty amazing to watch.

Michael: But you were saying, for him it was always all about the story first.

Jason: Always. Only about story and script. Of course, acting and the performances, those were important, but story came first for sure.

Steve: But were there some performances that he was just really happy with?

Jason: Some scenes, I think he loved them. I'll never forget the scene when Tony is falling for Melfi and he's watching *Prince of Tides*. Do you guys remember that? He's watching Nick Nolte talk to Barbra Streisand, and Tony's really getting into it and he has this goofy look on his face. David just erupted with laughter. He said, "He couldn't fucking do better. It couldn't be better. It's impossible for this to be better." There were many moments like that. David loves to laugh. He has a wonderful sense of humor.

He and I share an immature love for bathroom humor. There's a little bit of that in *Sopranos*. Remember when Adriana had irritable bowel syndrome, there was a scene where she actually had toilet paper attached to her shoe and she was walking around? That got cut for whatever reason. Denise, David's wife, despises bathroom humor. Often, she would sit in on these shows and we were cutting them together and she just had no patience for any sort of bodily function humor. It was funny hearing them going back and forth about it.

"EMPLOYEE OF *the Month*," *the episode in which Dr. Melfi gets raped, was perhaps the most controversial episode; certainly memorable, indel-*

ibly painful. Earlier, David Chase talked about the whole zeitgeist of The Sopranos—*how he didn't always want to tie everything up neatly at the end of an episode, because that's not how the world works. That's very much a part of what this episode is about. The audience is rooting for Melfi to tell Tony about what happened, and for him to exact revenge. If all you want to see is big Tony Soprano take that guy's head and bang it against the wall like a cantaloupe, you're not going to get that. The point of this episode is that Melfi, despite pain and suffering, made her moral ethical choice. That's more real, that's more honorable—and that's much more difficult.*

Robin Green and Mitch Burgess won the Emmy for the script of "Employee of the Month." We talked to them about how this episode evolved. —*Michael*

Steve: What's the background behind "Employee of the Month"?

Robin: David had this idea that Melfi gets raped and that Tony exacts revenge, or she has to decide whether or not to tell him.

Mitch: David didn't know what to do, whether Tony would find out or not.

Robin: It was my idea that she doesn't tell him, that he doesn't find out. I said it's more interesting. The problem with that was, as it turned out, it was an unusual show because then it was Melfi's show, it was Melfi's story, not Jim's story. That, to me, when all is said and done, it was a different show than *The Sopranos* in a way.

Michael: It's a good episode and very effective.

Robin: It was horrible, though.

Michael: A very, very rough scene.

Robin: The night of that rape she got injured, actually.

Michael: She did, she hurt her shoulder.

Robin: It was a physical scene. I didn't know it would be that horrible, frankly.

Mitch: Lorraine, she just knocked it out of the park.

Steve: It's one of the roughest scenes in the whole series, if not the worst.

Mitch: We did a lot of research on it. They had this hospital down in the Village and we went to a rape crisis center. A lot of what was done came because of researching that.

ONE OF *the things Michael and I were both struck by in "Employee of the Month" was how much you wanted Melfi to tell Tony what happened. How much you wanted him to take revenge for her.* —*Steve*

Michael: People were really frustrated by this episode.

Steve: Certain shows you know at the end of it it's going to be wrapped up in a nice tight bow. They're going to get the bad guy, they're going to get the killer, there's going to be revenge. That's frustrated a lot of the *Soprano* audience, that David didn't always wrap things up. That scene in her office, after the rape, she's walking with the cane, she's really, really banged up. In the office, Tony says, "What's the other guy look like?" He still thinks it's a car accident.

Michael: Yes, and the audience is led to believe that maybe it's going to come out. She looks beat up; she's going to tell Tony this is what happened. But that's not where we go with it.

Steve: No, but the audience is rooting for Tony to kill this guy. Tony also says, "*Jesus,* what's the other guy look like?" Which, that's actually the guy's first name.

Michael: I didn't realize that. Very good point.

Steve: And then to add insult to injury—literally—she goes to the store and she sees his picture, and he's the employee of the month.

Michael: Such a great detail. It's an excellent choice on the writers' part. Really effective.

Steve: There's that amazing dream sequence, where the dog, big head, massive shoulders, tears the rapist to shreds. The dog I think is Tony. And Melfi tells her therapist, "No feeling has ever been so sweet as to see that pig beg and plead and scream for his life." I like when she calls him "employee-of-the-month cocksucker." Lorraine says it so eloquently, "cocksucker." Not like me and you, she says it very eloquently.

Michael: There's that certain satisfaction knowing, "I could have that asshole squashed like a bug if I wanted." It sets up the expectation that she's gonna tell Tony, and he's gonna take revenge.

Steve: But then there's the end of the episode. Tony's in Melfi's office. She breaks down. He consoles her, "What's the matter? Is there something you want to say to me? You want to say something?" The audience at home, at this point, they're just screaming to the TV. "Tell him! Tell him!"

Michael: He's very tender with her and concerned and caring.

Steve: Tony says, "I was thinking about your behavior therapy idea. Maybe you have a point. If they can help me, I should go there." She says, "No." She doesn't want to tell him, but she doesn't want him to leave. She needs him, she wants him in her life.

Michael: And it ends on her saying "no." It's a quiet ending, and quiet music starts. That's "Fisherman's Daughter" by Daniel Lanois, who also did the closing song of the episode "Big Girls Don't

Cry," when Christopher's going to quit writing and he dumps it all in the garbage. That's Daniel Lanois's "White Mustang," and this is another song by him. It's really quiet. Fits the mood really well. A terrific choice, a fantastic song.

BUT OF *course, none of us could imagine what it was like for Lorraine Bracco to live through the creation of this indelible episode. We asked her to walk us through the making of "Employee of the Month."*
—Michael

Lorraine: David called me in and said, "We want to do this episode where Dr. Melfi gets raped." And I said, "I'm the only nice person in this fucking series. Why are you going to hurt me?" And Robin Green wrote it. It apparently happened to a friend of hers. She was raped in a garage, and that's what they wanted to do. And I was like, "Oh my God, I just can't believe it."

So, there were a couple of guys up for the role of the rapist. And one of the guys was a smaller-sized man, and I said to David, "I'm not going down easy. It's just not in me to go down easy. I cannot do that. And this actor," I said, "I will hurt. So you have to get a bigger guy than me." Because I'm not a little girl. I'm five eight and a half. I'm strong.

So they hired this actor who was really a fireman. He was much bigger and stronger than me. And it was very hard. When the actors are doing their scenes, and you have a crew there, and when the director calls "cut" and all of a sudden no one's talking and they're whispering, you know you're getting some kind of very deep, dark, emotional response. Because usually once the director calls "cut," it's very loud, when everyone's talking and trying to put everything back into order for the next shot. So that was very telling to me.

I sat down, and next to me was the actor, the fireman who played the rapist, and he was crying. I said, "Come on. You're all right, you're all right." And he goes, "Lorraine, I save people. I don't hurt people." So I knew that we were doing something right.

Michael: Well you were, clearly. So you realize that you're evoking this very strong, emotional response in the crew. You saw this response from the actor you're playing opposite. Were you yourself also having that kind of deep, emotional response to the moment?

Lorraine: Yes. It's a horrible thing, it's a horrible violation. As you do a little research, you realize that being raped is not about sex. It's about power.

Michael: How were you able to bring yourself to that dark place? Was it the physicality of the moment that brought you there? Or was it the sense of violation? What contributed to that?

Lorraine: It was all of those things. Listen, it's a very convoluted, disgusting, horrible thing for any person, man, woman, or child, to go through. It is scarring.

Steve: Do people react in dealing with you, afterward, as though they were talking to Melfi? Where they are sympathetic and say, "I'm sorry you had to go through this"?

Lorraine: Oh, sure. People were very, very upset. My father was totally horrified. I didn't let my kids see it until much, much later. They were too young for that. But my parents. I called them the week before it aired and I said, "Listen, you might not want to watch this. Dr. Melfi gets raped. It is very harsh."

Steve: Did you watch it with them or did you talk to them after they watched it?

Lorraine: Both. I told them, "Listen, it's a TV show. I wasn't hurt. I wasn't raped." They understood the words, but seeing it was devastating to them. So if it was devastating to them, I knew a lot of parents, a lot of people, would find it really hard. I even found it hard to watch.

Steve: Have you watched it since back in the day?

Lorraine: No. It's too hard.

THE FIFTH *episode of the season, "Another Toothpick," was Steve's first real emotional scene. Not just in* The Sopranos, *but in his career. I asked him what the scene was like and how he approached it. —Michael*

Steve: This was by far the most I've ever done. After Season Two, my first season, I got a big movie, a Warner Bros. movie. *See Spot Run.* That was a big role in a real movie. I got paid real money. I got my feet wet there. The more you do, the better you are, more confidence. But I was looking for an acting coach. Somebody recommended a guy to me, Richard Scanlon. I went to a couple of his classes. I didn't like that, so I worked with him one-on-one. He was a big help to me. I know you weren't supposed to show the script to anyone, but I would get the script, go to his apartment, break it down with him, and then study my lines or work with him, maybe two or three times in the episode.

We made a backstory for Bacala. That was the first time I learned all that stuff. I made a backstory about how he got into the business. How he inherited Junior from his father. And we started building the character. He was a tremendous help to me.

Michael: Interesting. Now break down the scene for me. The big, emotional scene, after Bobby's father, played by Burt Young, does the hit, and then dies in the car crash. You're on the couch in Junior's apartment, and telling him how you had to go to Staten Island to identify the body, and he still had bits of glass in his hair. It's a very raw moment. It was the second scene in the episode, but it was the first one you shot, yes?

Steve: Right. I was very intimidated and scared. How am I going to cry? Some people could cry at the drop of a hat. Molly Ringwald on *Secret Life,* when she had to cry, she cried three, four, five, six times, go back and have a soda. Come back, laugh. Come back, cry. I couldn't do that. It wasn't so easy for me. So I talked to the director, Jack Bender, after the read-through, and I said I never cried on camera before. And he said to me, "Listen, don't worry. We'll do line-by-line if we have to. I'll get cue cards, whatever it takes, I will help you." When you hear that, that the guy is on your side, it's a wonderful thing. Jack Bender, I didn't know him from anywhere, but he said he'd help me, and he really did.

Michael: So how did you prepare yourself for that day?

Steve: I was living in Little Italy. I was all by myself. I watched some sad movies.

Michael: Which movies?

Steve: *Philadelphia* is a horribly sad movie with Tom Hanks. *Beaches* always kills me. I watched that. It was about cancer and it's very sad. I also watched *Bang the Drum Slowly,* one of my favorite movies. I try not to watch sad movies anymore, but for this I needed it.

I was locked up in my apartment. I literally only came out to work. The shades were drawn and I'm going, "Why the fuck did I get myself into this?" I got myself into such a funk, which I needed to do, but you question, "Why am I doing this again?"

Michael: Were you listening to sad music too?

Steve: Yes. Very much so. Back then I had a Walkman. I never took the headset off.

Michael: It worked for you. You did an amazing job in that scene. In all the emotional scenes they gave to Bobby after that.

Steve: Thanks. It was hard but it got me to that place that I needed to get. It took me a while. I've done it numerous times since. I guess it gets easier, I don't know, but at that point, I was very concerned about it, but we got there and I think it came out pretty good.

Michael: It sure did.

Steve: Michael you have one scene in Season Three that stands out for me. It's after Jackie Jr. shoots up the card game, and you find out that Tony's going to let him get away with it. That scene where you confront Tony, walk me through that. What was that like, doing a scene like that with Jim?

Michael: Part of it was, Tony was a father figure to Christopher, for better and for worse, and all that comes with it: discipline, rebellion, resentment. What's interesting is, Jim and I were a lot closer in age than our characters were. Jim and I were only four or five years apart, so he was not a father figure to me, he was a friend and a colleague. But Tony was a father figure to Christopher.

In that scene, when Christopher finds out that Tony's not on board with taking revenge, he's like a teenager getting angry at his father, and the father is laying down the law. Christopher is kind of saying, "Bullshit. You're a fucking hypocrite. You're protecting this kid because you made some oath to his father, and I'm just some disposable guy to do your bidding. It's okay for you to put *me* in harm's way but not *him*." That breaks Christopher's heart. He tells Tony, "I loved you." Tony says, "I'm the boss. I decide. You don't love me? That breaks my heart but too bad. You don't got to love me. But you got to respect me."

Steve: So how do you prepare for a scene like that? How do you get so amped up?

Michael: Christopher was a character who really wore his emotions on his sleeve. He was not a guy who played his cards close to his vest. When he was angry, he was angry. When he was frustrated, he was frustrated. I said earlier that I based Christopher on a guy that I knew who behaved like that. He was on the periphery of the mob in New York and went to Hollywood to escape it all. This guy would be so emotional at times. I'd watch him and it would be so extreme, it was bizarre. I thought that might really work for Christopher.

Steve: But Tony is always trying to calm him down. How does that work into it?

Michael: Christopher often existed on a very high emotional level. Tony gives him a lot to play off of, constantly reining him in, constantly putting him in his place, constantly trying to assuage his anger. For me, as an actor, as long as the stakes are high—like they are in this scene—you can let loose, especially a character like this who's so on the edge of sanity, in a lot of ways. Then, you just trust. You trust the words. You trust Jim. Jim was such a great actor and such a generous actor. We trusted each other a lot and so whatever I bring to that scene is going to be matched by him. He's going to give it back to me and it will make my performance better. His presence and his anger feed mine.

There are things that he does. He was a big guy. He had big hands. Physically imposing. He was a very tactile actor. He used that both for intimidating us or calming us down. He used that physicality. He used his hands. Getting close. If he's grabbing you, you respond in the moment, and then it becomes organic and becomes real.

Steve: That's the thing about Jim. He never phoned anything in.

Michael: Never. I'm sure there were days when he had a cold, or he felt shitty, or he hurt his knee, or he was up all night, or who the hell knows, maybe he's going through difficult times personally. Yet when it was time to dig in, he always did.

SEASON THREE *was when Michael wrote his second episode. Once again, he has to navigate some really powerful moments. —Steve*

Steve: Tell me about "The Telltale Moozadell."

Michael: This is the second out of five episodes that I wrote. The title comes from Edgar Allan Poe's "The Tell-Tale Heart." We talk about how Jackie Jr. is doing a paper on Edgar Allan Poe. When I was in high school, I think I was in tenth grade. I had a really good English teacher, Mrs. German. We had to read a short story and she wanted us to kind of bring it to life. I chose "The Tell-Tale Heart." I love Edgar Allan Poe. "The Tell-Tale Heart" is told from the first person; it's like a confessional monologue, really, and I acted it out.

Steve: How old were you?

Michael: Around fourteen. My teacher said to me, "You should do theater." I didn't want to do theater—there were theater kids in my school, and they weren't people that I particularly felt a kinship to. She said, "No, no, I think you really need to."

Steve: So you wrote some great scenes between Tony and Gloria in this episode. Also Tony's getting along better with Carmela.

Michael: Right, but Carmela is doing better partially because Tony's getting laid regularly with his new and exciting goomar, and that puts him in a better mood. It's very weird because he broke up with Irina, he was miserable, and that made his relationship with Carmela bad. Now his relationship with Carmela is good, yet he's having this very torrid and passionate affair. It's very fucked up. That was really interesting to write.

Steve: Okay, but we gotta talk about the real issue in this episode. We're in the Aprile kitchen. Ralphie shows Jackie Jr. how to make pasta and sauce. Is that your recipe? You put butter in your sauce?

Michael: I heard Francis Coppola mention that once.

Steve: Really?

Michael: Francis Coppola's a good cook. A lot of people finish pasta with a little bit of butter. But that's not the key—tossing the pasta, that last step, that's essential. The pasta's just about cooked, it's a little al dente, you drain it and then you toss it with the sauce while the sauce is still cooking. This way the pasta absorbs the sauce. If you go to an Italian restaurant, and they serve you a pasta with clean noodles and the sauce just sitting on top, that means they don't know what the fuck they're doing. They shouldn't be in business. That's one of the biggest sins in the world. It's American bullshit. Cultural appropriation.

Steve: That's also what they do because it's pre-cooked pasta. They have it laying around.

Michael: Yes, that's crap, is what that is.

Steve: Good that we cleared that up.

Michael: Some things are essential.

THE LOVE *affair between Tony and Gloria, of course, goes south pretty fast. Their stormy affair becomes one of the most powerful subplots of this season. We asked Annabella Sciorra, who played Gloria, about some of the intense scenes the two actors had together. —Steve*

Steve: I gotta ask you about the scene where Jim chokes you. Jim had huge hands. When he was choking you, you got this little head in a giant hand. Jim has choked me in a scene.

Michael: Me too. I guess he's choked the three of us.

Steve: Annabella, what was that like for you?

Annabella: I never got hurt. It was so safe. He was really good about that. I learned a lot from him. When you're shooting something like that and your adrenaline's going, you just want to go, "I'll do it, I'll do it."

Michael: Those things you have to work out very carefully, because yes, your adrenaline flows and you're always feeling, "I want it to be real, I want it to be great." It's so easy to get really hurt doing stuff like that. But Jim was really careful.

Annabella: He was. He even stopped that scene. We had been going at it for a long time. It was one of those long, long Friday nights. It was three or four in the morning. I was on the floor and he was coming toward me to pick me up off the floor and twist my arm and everything. He said, "Do you want me to stop? Should we just pick this up on Monday?" and I said, "No, no, I want to keep going," but he was right.

Steve: Was everything you did, was it all in the script?

Annabella: The only thing I did do that wasn't in the script was I spit at him. I knew what she wanted at that point and I knew why she was taunting him and I just kept going, and I kept going, and then

I spit at him. Then they cut and Jim said, "Did you just spit at me?" I said, "Yes, I did. I'm really sorry."

Steve: You didn't tell him you were going to spit, did you?

Annabella: No, but I didn't plan it. Then we had to cover it from the other side. So I had to spit at him again. [*laughs*]

STUNT COORDINATOR *Pete Bucossi walked us through one of the great moments in that scene.* —*Steve*

Steve: In that fight scene, it really looks like Tony picks up Gloria by the neck and throws her to the ground. It's so believable. How did you do that?

Pete: That was improvised. There was something else in the script. But Jim said, "Why don't I just grab her like this by the neck and just pick her up, and slam her down on the ground?" So we got a stunt double, who's a very good match for Annabella. And we did a lot of rehearsal.

So, Jim's got those big paws. And he puts one big paw under her throat. But realistically, she's grabbing ahold of his arm and taking a ride on his arm. She's not getting any pressure on her throat area. It's not like she's getting choked. And luckily our actress and our double were very light in stature, so that worked very well. And then there was a rug there. We put a small one-inch pad underneath that rug, so he could throw her on the ground. But Jimmy came up with that.

OKAY, LET'S *get to the main event. The "Pine Barrens" episode, a lot of people feel, was not only the best episode in the series, but one of the best hours of television ever. The performances that Tony Sirico and Michael gave have to rank up there with the funniest of all time. Even Lorraine Bracco—when we asked her what her favorite Sopranos episode was— she didn't name any of the great ones she was in. She said her favorite was "Pine Barrens."*

The episode took twelve days to shoot, which was a record at the time. Up until then we were shooting nine or ten days, which was still a lot for a TV show. Later, as the series went on, we'd sometimes take seventeen days. But this was a good one. And they really took their time.

In the episode, Christopher and Paulie go to dump a body in the woods—only the body's not dead, the victim gets away, and the two of them get lost and almost freeze to death. If you haven't seen it, put the fucking book down and go watch. What the hell is wrong with you?

Okay, now that I got that off my chest, let's talk the people who were really responsible for this gem. Beginning with the writer, Terry Winter.
—Steve

Michael: Terry, the "Pine Barrens," where did that story come from?

Terry: That was Tim Van Patten, who was one of our main directors on the show. Todd Kessler and I were sitting in the writers' room alone, and Timmy wandered in one day and sat with us and he said, "What are you guys doing?" I said, "We're just kicking around story ideas." Tim said, "Oh, I had a dream that I thought could be a story, but it's really stupid." I said, "Well, it can't be any stupider than what we're talking about. What is it?" He said, "Well, I had a dream that Paulie and Christopher took this guy into the woods, and then they got lost."

I said, "That's fucking great. Go knock on David's door, go pitch him the story." He said, "'No, no, I don't want to do that." I said, "If you don't, I'm going to do it." I knock on David's door, I go,

"You got to hear this story." I tell him the idea. By this point, we were pretty deep into Season Two. David went, "Oh my God, we've got to do that! But there's really no room for it in Season Two. Let's do that next year." I said, "Great. Timmy, we're going to do this story."

Michael: And then you wound up writing it, and they brought in Steve Buscemi to direct. It was his first episode.

Terry: It's funny, people think, "Oh, they've hired Steve Buscemi because it was like *Fargo*." That had nothing to do with it. First of all, it was written to take place in the fall. I never envisioned snow involved in this.

We hire our directors in TV well in advance of what we're shooting. You have the schedule that's done, nine months in advance, and you slot people in. All we knew was that episode eleven, whatever that ended up being, Steve Buscemi was going to direct it, and just sheer coincidence episode eleven ended up being "Pine Barrens" and that's how I met Steve.

We found our locations—it was December 1999, up in Harriman State Park—and we said, "All right. Great, as long as it doesn't snow, we'll be fine." And then we went away for the holiday break and came back and there was a blizzard of epic proportions. If you remember, Michael, the first day in the woods, as you guys were marching Valery the Russian soldier out into it, it was just the last snowflakes of that blizzard that were falling. He's catching some on his tongue. I did a quick rewrite to accommodate the fact that we're in the snow and David said, "Well, this isn't going to work. They'll just follow their footsteps." I assured David I could get lost with a trail of breadcrumbs. Literally, if you took me a block away from my house and spun me around, I'd have to call my wife to come get me, I have the worst sense of direction. Let's assume Paulie and Christopher do too. Nobody's going to question this and I don't think anybody did, but that's how that whole thing came about.

Steve: Everybody always asks, what happened to the Russian? Didn't you put the Russian in another episode, or were going to put him back in somewhere?

Terry: What's funny, I always have a thing about TV shows where a character you've never seen before appears in an episode and has huge prominence, but you've never heard of or seen this guy before or since. Knowing we were going to do "Pine Barrens," I said to David, "Can we get this actor and just pop them into an episode one or two episodes early, when they go to see Valery's boss Slava? We just have this guy, give him a line of dialogue, so when you see him again in episode eleven, you're, 'Oh, that's the guy who was sweeping the floor.'" So that's what we did. That made me feel good. You've at least established him; he didn't come out of thin air and now he's Slava's best friend.

Then afterward I kept pitching, because people were freaking out, "What happened? What happened?" I had pitched David on the idea—two years later, Christopher goes to see Slava and he walks in and the guy is sweeping the floor again and they meet eyes, and Christopher's like, "Holy shit. He knows me." Then Valery, the Russian guy, turns around and half the back of his head is gone. He's clearly brain-damaged. He doesn't remember anything, and Christopher thinks, "Oh my God. The guy is completely a vegetable." He just sweeps the floor but he keeps looking at Christopher like, *I know, I just can't communicate.* David was on board with it, or so I thought. And I made a fatal error. I said, "Oh, man, the audience is going to love this." He went, "That's the worst reason in the world to do it." He goes, "Fuck it, we're not doing it."

Steve: That certainly sounds like David all right.

BY THE *way, how we wound up in Harriman State Park is a story unto itself. —Steve*

Michael: We were supposed to shoot it at South Mountain Reservation in Essex County. Late in the game, we had to find a new location. The reason we had to switch at the last minute, the county officials in Essex County banned us because they felt we were giving Italian-Americans a bad name.

Steve: I hate that. That's that same bullshit we hear all the time. There's one of these scumbag officials that nixed us and was very vocal about the whole stereotype stuff. Guess what? He got convicted of bribery and of stealing money. He was very vocal about not having us shoot there because we gave Italians a bad name, and this piece of shit was stealing money. There you go. There you have it.

Michael: There you go. If you're against *The Sopranos*, you're probably crooked. That's the lesson.

AS TERRY *said, it was just by chance that Steve Buscemi directed this episode. It was one of the great coincidences of the entire series. He was an incredible director to work with, and his careful eye, his keen cinematographic abilities, and his quirky sense of storytelling were the perfect fit for this perfectly unusual hour of television. —Michael*

Michael: Tell us about coming on board as a director for *The Sopranos*.

Steve Buscemi: I guess David was interested in having me direct in the first season, but I wasn't available. And of course, when I finally watched the first season, [casting director] Sheila Jaffe and I, we would call each other every Monday and just rave about the show, we would just talk for like an hour just about how great it was. But at that time, then I was directing a film and I had some other stuff, and so I really wasn't available.

Michael: Had you directed TV by then or only features?

Steve Buscemi: I directed one episode of *Homicide: Life on the Street*. And I did direct a couple of episodes of *Oz*. That's when I first worked with Edie.

Michael: And how did you wind up doing the "Pine Barrens" episode?

Steve Buscemi: That was the greatest gift that fell into my lap. Tim Van Patten was the one who came up with the genesis of that story. Then, of course, Terry Winter came and just ran with it. Then it fell to me, it was my turn to direct. I wonder, what would Tim have done with that episode, or some of the other directors, John Patterson and Alan Coulter, because these guys I just loved. I just felt so incredibly lucky that I was the one to get it.

Michael: All those guys you mentioned are phenomenal. The one thing you have over them, and I'm going to be really honest about this, you out of everyone were the best to deal with, for me as an actor. I'm sure it's because you're a terrific actor and you deeply understand the process. You were constantly giving me notes and ideas for approaching the character that I didn't think of. By Season Three I had done a lot of episodes as this guy, and you get into a pattern, you get into a mindset, you know what to do. But you were able to shift me and inspire me to make choices that I wouldn't have. You really know how to do that.

Steve Buscemi: Well good. Thank you.

Steve Schirripa: It was a lot of fun when we shot that. We stayed at West Point, remember that?

Michael: It was actually on the grounds of West Point. You had to go through the gate. It's a beautiful hotel.

Steve Schirripa: Sirico couldn't sleep because the pillows were too hard. He sent the production assistant back to Brooklyn, two hours away, to get his pillows off his bed.

Michael: That story's totally true.

Steve Schirripa: Then we went out that night. I was driving and I had you, Michael, Jim, somebody else. We went to this bar.

Steve Buscemi: Yes, there were a lot of cadets from West Point. I partied harder than anybody.

Michael: I played guitar with the band, playing "Free Bird." I was using some shitty acoustic guitar, my hand started bleeding, but I wouldn't stop playing, the blood was flying off my hand.

Steve Schirripa: We stayed out later than we should have. Steve, you were singing with the band. You were singing "I Wanna Be Sedated." I said, "I got to go. I got to get up early." I left Michael and Jim there. You went home, you had to direct. The next morning was ugly. Sirico didn't come out with us, and he was torturing us.

Michael: He was torturing us because we were all hungover.

Steve Schirripa: Yes. Very, very hungover.

Steve Buscemi: Steve, I got to ask you a question because people ask me this. They hear the story about the scene where Tony goes over to Junior's house because he's going to go pick up the guys in the woods, then you come in and you're dressed like Elmer Fudd and Tony Soprano starts laughing. You wanted to surprise him. Do you remember what you did that really made him laugh so hard?

Steve Schirripa: Jim had said to me, he saw the Elmer Fudd outfit the day before. He said, "You're going to have to make me laugh." So when I came in, I didn't tell you, I didn't tell anyone. I turned the corner, with a big giant dildo strapped onto my crotch! Big rubbery three-footer. And Jim started cracking up. You could almost see Dominic cracking a smile too. I figured, let me not ask you because I don't know what you would say, yes or no. Seven in the morning, we shot that. That's what he's laughing at, this big three-foot Italian-bread-looking dildo.

Michael: Where did that come from?

Steve Schirripa: I asked the prop guy for something, and then I was looking around the prop truck and I saw all these dildos hanging.

Michael: They had it on the prop truck.

Steve Schirripa: They had all shapes and sizes. I picked out this giant one.

Michael: Always prepared.

Steve Buscemi: You never know when you might need it.

Michael: Now it's in the Museum of TV and Radio. It's in the *Sopranos* section. They have that there with Steve's Elmer Fudd outfit.

Steve Schirripa: Funny. The humor in the episode is terrific.

Steve Buscemi: Yes, but the thing is, Michael, you and Tony were so great together and you never played it for laughs. You never let on that you thought this was funny.

Michael: But it was freezing.

Steve Schirripa: It was so cold I could barely speak. When we get there at night with a flashlight, it was nine degrees out. But Sirico was the coldest, of course. He was talking to the four of us like we weren't there. "You know how cold it was? You know how I was freezing?" I said, "I was right next to you. You don't remember that?"

Michael: There was so much snow. It's fucking hard to run in the snow.

Steve Buscemi: Now, some of those scenes, we did shoot on the soundstage.

Michael: The scenes in the van.

Steve Schirripa: Really? I had no idea. I am flabbergasted by that. You guys were freezing, so you had to play that. It looked so real, so natural to me.

Michael: The exterior was shot in the woods. But we shot the van's interior on the soundstage. Tony, right when he gets in, and he's freezing, it's very believable.

Steve Schirripa: I did not know that you guys were faking the cold.

Michael: We had to, constantly. It's a lot of work to play cold, actually.

Steve Schirripa: I would have been sweating.

Michael: You've got to really commit to it. They even added the cold breath coming out of our mouth digitally, in post-production; CGI.

Steve Schirripa: Steve, the scene with me and Tony in the car was also shot on the soundstage, but that's a whole different thing. Because we didn't have to play it that we were freezing.

Steve Buscemi: Yes. That scene was almost cut out. It kept getting moved on the schedule. There was talk about cutting it, like, "We don't have time to do this," and I thought, "Oh, man, I don't want to lose that." We had to scramble. When you look at that scene, it looks like you guys are driving.

Steve Schirripa: It was the scene where I tell Tony the joke. "Two guys go hunting. They come to a fork in the road. Sign says, 'Bear Left.' So they went home." I loved doing that scene. They were rocking the SUV. It looks very much like we're on the highway.

Steve Buscemi: Phil Abraham did such an amazing job, the cinematographer. He drew up the episode. That's what I really depended on. Michael, you said my approach to directing is through the acting. I sometimes have trouble visualizing how we're going to do it, but Phil Abraham was just amazing. Do you remember he had a cast on his leg?

Michael: That's right.

Steve Buscemi: He had broken his leg or something and he's trudging through the snow.

Steve Schirripa: There's the scene where Valery, the Russian, he runs off. Paulie and Christopher are talking, he's gone. They think they got him, but then you see that shot from overhead. Is Valery in the tree at that point?

Steve Buscemi: That was really a mistake on my part. It wasn't meant to be a POV of Valery, watching this.

Steve Schirripa: No? Okay. But because of that shot, a lot of people think that the Russian survived. He's a Russian Green Beret, maybe he climbed up the tree.

Steve Buscemi: I think it kind of works as that and I talked about it with David Chase. He says, "Yes, that shot you did from overhead. It makes people think that." I said, "I know, but you're the one who kept it in the show." He goes, "I know, it was a good shot." We were running out of time and I needed some kind of wide shot to show that you guys were lost or something and that was, I guess I could blame it on Phil Abraham.

Michael: It's good.

Steve Schirripa: I don't think there's anything to blame. Maybe the guy did climb the tree. This guy was just incredible.

Steve Buscemi: Maybe he did. Yes.

SPEAKING OF *Phil Abraham, he did remind us of something else about this episode—the great Paulie Walnuts tumble. —Michael*

Phil Abraham: "Pine Barrens" was a really memorable show. Just in terms of having scouted it with no snow and then showing up and there's snow. That was just crazy. There was that scene, we were there in the morning, and we were figuring out one of the first things we were going to do because we were worried about leaving tracks in the snow, and we were talking with the stunt guys about the moment when Paulie tumbles down the hill and he loses his shoe. There were a lot of conversations about how we can do this, because now the rocks were covered with snow and we couldn't see them, and there was no way to do it safely. It was going back and forth. Where were we going to stage it? What were we going to do? Jimmy Leavey, our teamster captain, said, "What the fuck are you guys talking about?" He goes, "You do it like this." He goes up to the edge and he tumbles down the cliff through the rocks and he stands up. He goes, "There, like that. What's so hard about that?"

Michael: So then the stunt double had to follow suit, of course. But Jimmy Leavey was hard-core. He was a marine. He was a martial artist. He was a dangerous guy, yes.

Steve: Yes, he wasn't fucking around, Jimmy Leavey.

AND AS *if there wasn't enough going on in the "Pine Barrens" episode, there's also a key moment in the Gloria-Tony affair—a moment that led to the long-standing drama on the Internet of Just Who Threw the Steak. Here's the story. Gloria got pissed off at Tony and threw a steak at him as he was leaving. That's based on Terry Winter, the writer, saying that a girl-friend once threw a steak at him. It became a big deal—Annabella Sciorra, who played Gloria, got a lot of feedback from female fans saying, "When you threw that steak, and hit Tony with it, you threw it for all womankind."*

So who actually hit Tony with the steak? We went to the sources— Annabella Sciorra and Steve Buscemi—to try to get to the meat of the matter. —Steve

Steve: So Gloria gets pissed off at Tony and throws the steak at him as he's leaving. How many times did you throw the steak at Jim?

Annabella: Everybody likes to claim credit for that. Jeff Marchetti, the prop guy, gave me a prop steak and it was basically, like, a wet sponge that looked like a steak. I thought, "This isn't going to work." Sure enough, when you threw it, it just dropped straight down. So then I threw the actual steak. I threw it a bunch of times. I have a pretty good arm, but then they had to do a close-up and everybody wanted to throw the steak. Steve [Buscemi] took a shot at it. Jeff might have taken a shot at it. [*laughs*] That was fun.

STEVE BUSCEMI, *gently, begs to differ. —Michael*

Steve: I think the steak that was used that smacked him in the back of the head was the one that I threw. I can totally be wrong because everybody had their shot. She did, the props guy, and finally I went, "Give me that." And then I threw it. I think that's the take that was used.

BUT OF course, we can't get through an episode like this without Michael saying something to piss me off. It started out perfectly normal. We were

*talking about our favorite lines in the show. And then—well, you'll see.
—Steve*

Steve: So many funny lines in this episode. I like when they're talking on the phone to Tony about the Russian, and he's asking, "Is there any way the package could have survived?" You hear this all the time on wiretaps, like mob guys go, "The package," like the FBI is listening and they don't know what they're talking about.

Michael: Right. Like it's so hard to figure out what they mean.

Steve: A friend of mine worked on a wiretap thing. He told me they were calling coke like each gram was a pair of pants: "Yes. The guy wanted a pair of pants. I dropped a pair of pants off at his house." "He wanted two pairs of pants." "Listen, bring over three and a half pairs of pants."

Michael: At some point we have to talk about the malaprops that are sprinkled throughout the show. Like: "It's like an albacore around my neck." "Going to a psychiatrist, there's no stigmata to that." But this episode has to be the funniest one of all. Tony says, "The guy you're looking for is some kind of ex-commando or some shit. He's with the interior ministry. He killed sixteen Chechen rebels single-handedly."

Steve: Right. And Paulie, not the brightest guy, tells Christopher, "You're not going to believe this. Guy was an interior decorator. He killed sixteen Czechoslovakians."

Michael: And Christopher says, "Interior decorator? His house looks like shit." I mean, what Terry Winter did with this script, it was just incredible. My favorite line, Christopher is starving, he says, "We should've stopped at Roy Rogers," and Paulie says, "I should've fucked Dale Evans, and I didn't."

Steve: I guess we have to explain that joke for all the young people who have discovered *The Sopranos*, they might not get it, they know Roy Rogers as a food chain, but the real Roy Rogers was a movie star cowboy. And Dale Evans, his wife, starred in the movies with him.

Michael: One more thing I wanted to mention about this season. Do you remember the scene when Ralphie has to apologize to Tony Soprano in Vesuvio? Paulie and Christopher are watching. Tony refuses to get up. It's very humiliating. Tony pretends he doesn't know why Ralphie is there and what he's talking about, and really makes Ralphie bow and scrape. Wanna know what that was inspired by? David Chase was reading a book about the Civil War. Apparently, when Robert E. Lee surrendered to Ulysses S. Grant, Grant made sure Lee was humiliated in the process. It wasn't enough just to surrender; it was done in a very humiliating fashion. And that's what that scene was inspired by.

Steve: Made him grovel.

Michael: Made him grovel. Like you do with me about your first day on set. Like how you make me apologize.

Steve: [*laughs*] But you haven't.

Michael: But we're not going to go into that today.

Steve: But the thing is, you've never apologized.

Michael: Because I don't feel one is necessary. That's the problem.

Steve: That is the problem. That's it in a fucking nutshell.

Michael: Anyway, I wanna go back to that scene when you walk in with all the hunting gear. Were you an outdoors guy? Were you a hunter? Have you done that?

Steve: No. I would never kill anything.

Michael: I went hunting once when I was a kid, my uncle took me hunting. We were in some fields, we had shotguns, and we were trying to shoot rabbits. You don't see the rabbits because it's high grass. You see the grass moving. We kept missing the rabbits, so we started just shooting birds in the sky. It was ridiculous with the shotgun shooting birds. They were just exploding. I never wanted to do it again after that, it was not my thing.

Steve: I would feel so terrible if I went, killed the deer, and I saw it laying there. I would feel terrible, especially for sport. If people do it, and they eat the food, that's different.

Michael: If you're starving, maybe.

Steve: It's survival. Me, personally, it's not my thing to kill a rabbit. I won't kill, it's not my thing. Fishing is one thing.

Michael: Why is fishing one thing? Fishing is okay?

Steve: Fishing is okay.

Michael: Why?

Steve: People eat the fish.

Michael: Fish don't have feelings?

Steve: I don't know if they do.

Michael: Sure they do. Of course they do, what do you mean? They're alive.

Steve: Fish cry? When they're swimming, two of them, and a hook comes out, and gets one of them, the other one is crying?

Michael: When you see a fish on the hook, that fish don't look so happy to be on that fucking hook. They're struggling with their last breath to get off it and get back in the water. You don't think they suffer when they're hanging on the hook?

Steve: I don't know if they suffer.

Michael: Look at dolphins, what about dolphins? Dolphins are smarter than humans, you know that, right?

Steve: They're not smarter than me.

Michael: They communicate telepathically and they're smarter than human beings.

Steve: I don't think a dolphin is smart. I'll take an IQ test.

Michael: You know what else is smarter than humans, they say? Squids. Their DNA is unlike anything else on the planet. They think squids might have come from like a meteor from outer space, their frozen genetic material was on a meteor, and landed here.

Steve: What are you doing? Are you doing this to fucking drive me crazy? Do you hear yourself? Octopus from outer space, do you hear what you're saying?

Michael: Squid is unlike any DNA on the planet, and they think it may have come here in frozen form from an asteroid, direct from outer space and into our oceans.

Steve: I'm going to say publicly I am smarter than a dolphin. I'm certainly smarter than a squid.

Michael: Would you be willing to go up against a dolphin in an IQ test?

Steve: Yes, I would.

Michael: Well the squid from outer space is real. So is the Jersey Devil. From the Pine Barrens.

Steve: Now, what the fuck.

Michael: Okay, I'm going to give you a little history about the Pine Barrens. Now, the Pine Barrens is a wooded area in South Jersey. There's a lot of folklore about the Pine Barrens.

It's a very haunted place. There's the ghost of Captain Kidd. There's a rumor that there's a treasure of Captain Kidd that's buried in the Pine Barrens. And many other ghosts. And then there's the legendary Jersey Devil. The Jersey Devil has the body of a kangaroo, with the head of a horse, the wings of a bat, hooves, a forked tail, and this bloodcurdling scream.

They still have not found him, but apparently, the Jersey Devil is still alive and living in the Pine Barrens.

Steve: Do you believe in the Jersey Devil?

Michael: A hundred percent.

Steve: I know that you haven't been drinking in months, you don't smoke weed. What's going on? Is there something wrong?

Michael: The Jersey Devil is a real thing. This farmer had a picture of it. So many people have seen this Jersey Devil.

Steve: I don't believe any of it. It's so ridiculous. I don't believe that, I don't believe the octopus story.

Michael: You're a real skeptic.

Steve: This is nonsense. I don't know what's going on with you. There's something wrong.

Michael: You don't want to open your mind to the possibility that there's more things in heaven and earth than meets the eye.

Steve: There's something not right with you. No one's ever asked me about the Jersey bullshit Devil.

Michael: They will now, now that we've brought it up. We let the cat out of the bag. And we're gonna start working on the Steve-versus-the-dolphin IQ test. I really want to do that. We're going to have to do it in a tank because the dolphin can't survive outside.

Steve: Think about what you're saying. You're saying that me—I'm a college graduate. I'm not the smartest guy in the world by any means, but I'm smarter than a dolphin.

Michael: I'm not saying just you. Anybody goes against that dolphin, they're going to lose, including you.

Steve: The squid. You're telling me a squid from outer space is smarter than me. Listen to what you're saying.

Michael: It's going to be harder to get the squid to do the test than it would the dolphin. Let's try with the dolphin first.

Steve: There's something going on with you, I don't know what it is. Must be that California air.

So Jersey bullshit Devil aside, Season Three is, to a lot of people, the pinnacle of what The Sopranos *achieved. The emotion, the humor, the violence, the acting, the writing—nobody had ever seen anything like it before. And nobody knew if we could ever top it.*

Turns out they were gonna have to wait more than a year to find out. It was the first time David took so long between seasons—but famously, not the last. —Steve

SEVEN

Inside the Writers' Room

TV IS, ESSENTIALLY, A WRITER'S MEDIUM. Even on shows where the writer isn't the showrunner in charge, the words are central, and on The Sopranos, *the words commanded ultimate respect. As we've discussed, actors who questioned the writing, or said "My character wouldn't say this," usually didn't stick around long. Steve likes to say, the writers created Bobby Bacala, so who is he to tell them what Bobby would and wouldn't do? I think that's a sensible approach, and was certainly a healthy approach on* The Sopranos.

As we've pointed out, I was lucky enough to write five episodes of the series, and one of the most fascinating parts of the process was the collaboration with the other great writers on the show, as well as David Chase. More than most shows, it was considered crucial to keep a level of consistency in the tone of the language, the integrity of the characters, the level of the dialogue.

Another thing I mentioned earlier, which I picked up early on in my time in the writers' room, has served me well all my career as a writer: the attention to detail that went into each script. If the script says, "A guy delivers a pizza," and notes that he's wearing a Brazil soccer jersey, on the day of the shoot you'd better damn well have a Brazil soccer jersey handy. And this affected me as an actor: you become so involved in the material that every choice you make, even if you're not aware of it, springs from this specificity.

I truly don't think there's ever been a collection of writers, all working at the top of their game, as we witnessed in the writers' room at The Sopranos, *and so Steve and I thought it was important to take a moment to dig deep into what makes these geniuses tick. We started off with the outstanding husband-and-wife team of Robin Green and Mitch Burgess. After a successful run at* Northern Exposure—*where they worked with David Chase—they were involved in writing twenty-two episodes of* The Sopranos, *winning Emmys for two of them. They were, without a doubt, one of the mainstays of the writing room.* —Michael

Steve: How did you two meet?

Mitch: I went to the University of Iowa. I wasn't a very good student, but I wrote a paper for this rhetoric class. The guy said I had talent, and he said, "You should go to the writers' workshop." I went over there, and Robin was my teacher. I was an undergraduate, and she was a teaching fellow.

Michael: Did you get an A?

Mitch: Yes. Many of them.

Robin: I didn't touch him 'til the end of the term, he already had his A.

Steve: You were writers at *Party of Five* before *The Sopranos,* correct?

Robin: It wasn't a good match. We thought they wanted us to fix the show. But they actually liked the show the way it was. Also, *Party of Five* was kind of an earnest show for us. We were used to something a little more subversive.

Michael: Right, *Party of Five* was more standard fare, a more typical teen drama. But explain what you mean by "subversive."

Mitch: More layered. There's more texture with the characters and more dimensions.

Robin: More complicated. A little more subtext. Subtext is very important. People lying all the time, saying one thing and meaning another.

Steve: David had already done the pilot for *Sopranos* while you're working on *Party of Five*?

Robin: David had shot the pilot. We were in bed one night, it was August, and David called and asked us, "If the show goes, would you like to come write on it? You'd have to live in New York." It was like, "That's a no-brainer."

Mitch: We really loved the script of the show, and when we saw the pilot, it was just amazing.

Steve: We all know it takes forever for HBO to pick up the pilot. Months and months you were all waiting. What happened?

Robin: We were in a meeting at *Party of Five*. We were in there with Amy Lippman and Chris Keyser, getting notes on a script they weren't happy with. It was the day before Christmas vacation. We're sitting there, we're miserable. The assistant pokes her head in the door and says, "There's a phone call for you from a Tommy Soprano."

Michael: Yes. That's when we got the go-ahead. Tommy was the character's name at the time.

Robin: Amy and Chris raised their eyebrows like, "You know somebody like that?" They could tell from the name that it was some kind of gangster or something, Tommy Soprano. We just knew at that point that we were saved because we knew exactly that's what David would say. What it meant was that the show had been picked up and we were saved.

Steve: Michael has described it some, but tell me about the writers' room. Where exactly was that, what was that like?

Mitch: It's a conference room with whiteboards on the wall. It's not even very big.

Steve: And say that first season, how did it work?

Robin: David had an arc for the season and he knew it would be about Tony and Livia and Uncle Junior. We would come up with stories.

Michael: Earlier, when we talked about the "College" episode, you talked about how you would "beat out" the stories. Can you explain that a little bit more?

Mitch: The beats are the scenes that tell the arc of the story. In *The Sopranos*, there would be an A story, a B story, a C story, most of the time. The A story would be, what, eighteen beats?

Robin: It would be a lot because they wouldn't have commercials. They had the whole hour.

Michael: Right, so the A story would have maybe eighteen beats, twelve for the B story, and maybe six for the C. It wouldn't always be exactly that way, depending on the story, but generally they stuck to that.

Robin: A beat is really a scene. It's a necessary scene to tell the story. It's not shoe leather. It's not "he went here and he went there." It's the scenes necessary to tell the story, and pictures, and dialogue. You stay very close to that outline.

Mitch: Yes, very much. You never write a script without a beat sheet, which is all the beats written out and explained.

Steve: So the writers' room, did you hate it, did you love it?

Michael: All of the above.

Robin: We laughed our heads off.

Michael: It's good but it's rough.

Robin: It was more uptight the first year, because nobody was hired. Essentially there was a lot of competition.

Michael: You mean you were all still basically freelance. You were competing for a permanent job.

Mitch: Yes. So it was pretty intense. It's hard and it's tough.

Michael: You mentioned no commercials. That was one of the things that made *The Sopranos* different, that made HBO shows different. Because in network TV, the structure is around the commercial breaks. You need the cliffhangers to keep people sticking around through the commercials. But *The Sopranos* didn't have to stick to that. So can you talk about how that affected the writing of the shows, that you didn't have to build to those cliffhangers?

Robin: Network TV now has five acts, because you have a teaser, then you have your four acts. *The Sopranos* in its shape was more like a movie structure. A three-act structure. You had the first-third setup, the second third things got to a crisis point, and then you have the resolution. That's the three-act structure.

Mitch: *The Sopranos* didn't have actual act breaks. That's an outline you work with, but there's no act breaks. You just have the scenes melded.

Robin: It's more just a feeling in the pit of your stomach. Really, we didn't work in any kind of formulated way either. We just kind of felt our way through. You beat out the stories separately, the A, B, and C. The one big story, and then there'll be two or three little ones. Then I used to print them all out on paper and I would cut the paper with scissors. Then on the table, I would rearrange the strips of paper to meld them into one script.

Steve: Literally, you cut and paste them together.

Robin: Yes.

Michael: I learned so much from you guys, so much about writing. Especially in the tone meetings. Can you talk about those a little bit?

Mitch: The tone meetings, you get all the people, the heads of the departments, the director's there, David's there, the writer who was going to be on the set, everyone.

Michael: The heads of the departments would be props, locations, wardrobe, sound, the script supervisor, camera, hair and makeup, and so on.

Robin: You go through it scene by scene and say what the tone of the scene is. For example, is this meant to be funny? It's not necessarily there on the page. The writer would explain to the director what his intention was, what our intentions were.

Michael: Another thing I learned from you, Robin, was to make every line count. We've talked a lot about the specificity of the scripts. Do you have a line or a moment that stands out, a very specific line?

Robin: My favorite scene or line in the whole thing that we wrote is Irina, his Russian mistress, saying to him, "I love my new pony boots, Tony." The only way that I can say it is that when you become the person, you enter the body of Irina and experience what she is experiencing, on whatever level. Whatever comes on the page is the result of that.

Mitch: It was very rigorous to do that, too. It took a long time to write those scripts, longer than most.

Robin: It's just caring about every word and every feeling as much as possible.

Mitch: Then you write your dirty draft, and then you drill down some more, and then you drill down some more. About a third pass through it, you're really there with the characters, face-to-face.

Steve: After the script was done, you didn't get a ton of notes from the network, like you were talking about with *Party of Five*?

Mitch: *The Sopranos* was unique in the sense that HBO just took the show. They didn't mess with David. We didn't have a phone call on speakerphone with them giving us ideas and suggestions on a script like you do in most shows. What they got is what they got. And they were very happy to get it. It was amazing to work like that. As compared to a network show, where they're going to be calling you up, seven people on a speakerphone, everybody's got to say something about the script, and you're just going nuts.

Robin: The way we worked on *The Sopranos,* that was pure joy.

Steve: Let me ask you one last question. About being a married couple working together. Some of the married couples who read this are gonna say, "Wouldn't that be great, if we could work together?" A lot will say, "I could never do that. We would kill each other in a week." How did you guys make it work? You're so successful working together. Why is that?

Mitch: Well, in this business, it's better because otherwise you wouldn't see your spouse. The hours of television production, you go in and start working, and you didn't come up until the end of the season, and you never see anybody.

Robin: And we had to watch the set, even at night. David went home, and had dinner with his wife at eight o'clock every night.

Mitch: He had regular hours.

Steve: But would you guys actually write together, or does one write a draft and give it to the other?

Mitch: We write together, nose to nose.

Robin: Thigh to thigh.

Mitch: Whoever has the best lines gets it in. There's very few arguments about what's the best.

Robin: No, never.

Mitch: There's no disagreement.

ANOTHER OF *the incredible writers on* The Sopranos *was Terry Winter. Among the twenty-five episodes he wrote were some of my favorites. As we said, he wrote "Pine Barrens," which was a huge fan favorite. He wound up winning two Emmys for writing, and two more as an executive producer of the show.*

(We should probably take a second to explain, since a lot of people ask us all the time: writers would usually be the "producer on set" and work with the director to help make sure the script was shot as intended. At some point, some of their titles would be elevated to "executive producer" or "co-executive producer" as kind of an indication of seniority. So when you see a writer with those titles, it's kind of like they've become a made man in the writers' room.)

He also was one of the creators of Boardwalk Empire *and* Vinyl, *and wrote* The Wolf of Wall Street *for Scorsese. An amazingly talented guy. And funny as the day is long. —Steve*

Steve: You started out as an attorney, but somehow you morphed into this incredible executive producer and writer. How'd that happen?

Terry: I grew up in Brooklyn, it was a very blue-collar area. The idea of being a TV writer or a screenwriter was just so off my radar. If I would've told my friends, "I want to be a screenwriter," they would've beat the shit out of me. They would've thrown me in the creek, in Gerritsen Beach. It sounded so ridiculous. Anyway, I'd push back those fleeting thoughts I had about it. I wanted to make money, and the two jobs I knew that made money were doctor and lawyer. So I ended up going to law school. Slogged my way through.

Finally I got a job in a big Manhattan firm and literally within two days, I realized I had made a grave, grave error. It just wasn't me. I finally got to the point where I said, "All right, forget about the money and the diploma written in Latin and everything else. What do you want to do when you wake up in the morning?" The deep dark secret was, I wanted to be a writer.

Like everybody I knew, I watched a billion hours of TV as a kid. *Abbott and Costello, The Honeymooners,* the Bowery Boys, and all the classic Warner Bros. gangster films. Plus, I worked in a neighborhood where I rubbed elbows with a lot of guys, including Tony Sirico, in real life, who at that time was known as Junior Sirico.

Steve: You knew him?

Terry: I knew of him. I actually worked in a butcher shop owned by Paul Castellano. I also worked at a card game run by Roy DeMeo, which if you read the book *Murder Machine,* that's the DeMeo crew. That was my neighborhood. I was never involved with any of these guys, but the osmosis of how they thought, how they talked, how they acted, it seeped into me.

Steve: You go to law school, you get the degree, you're at a big law firm, and you just pack up and move to L.A.?

Terry: Showed up like a country bumpkin, did not know anything. Rented a car and checked into this fleabag hotel on MacArthur Park. I took a job as a paralegal. I actually took my law degree off my résumé because I just wanted a nine-to-five job and people would see my law degree and say I was overqualified. I got a job at

Unocal, the oil company, where they didn't know I was actually a lawyer. I was home by five thirty and I started writing sitcom specs.

Michael: For those who don't know, in this case a spec is a sample script of an existing TV show. You use it kind of as an audition. The spec scripts that you wrote, Terry, were they original, or were they scripts for shows that already existed?

Terry: Generally the wisdom is, or was at least, that you needed to write for shows that were on the air. I ended up writing a *Doogie Howser* script, a *Frasier, Mad About You, Seinfeld, Cheers, Home Improvement.*

Steve: And these weren't getting produced or anything, you were just doing this to basically learn to write?

Terry: I always make this analogy: it's like kids who grow up and they want to be engineers, they take radios apart and put them back together again. I did that with stories. I would take six or eight episodes of *Home Improvement,* watch what happened, write down each scene, and I have a blueprint. I'd go, "Oh, okay, this is how they tell a *Home Improvement* story. There's a cold open, in the first scene the problem is introduced, the problem gets exacerbated right before the commercial. You come back from the commercial, he talks to the guy over the backyard fence, gets some advice, then uses that advice to solve the problem. That's a *Home Improvement* blueprint."

Steve: So did you get an agent?

Terry: The Hollywood conundrum is, okay, you got to get an agent. You can't get a job without an agent and you can't get an agent without a job, so how the fuck does anybody ever do anything? It's like nobody knows.

Steve: So what did you do?

Terry: I created a phony agency. First, I called a million agents and I couldn't get anybody. In frustration, I went down to the Writers Guild and they happened to have a list of agents who would take unsolicited scripts. And what happened was a complete stroke of luck. On this list is the name of a guy that sat five seats away from me during law school. The name's Doug. I called Doug, who I haven't spoken to in years. He's a real estate agent in Long Island.

I said, "What are you doing? Are you an agent now?" He goes, "No, I'm a real estate lawyer, but I had a client who wrote a book on real estate and I used my fee to get bonded as an agent. I don't know anything about being an agent." I said, "Well, you sound perfect. You're my agent now." He goes, "What do you mean?" I say, "I'm in Hollywood. I'm trying to write. I need to send my scripts in from an agent, so you're my guy." I created an agency out here with a mailbox, a phone mail system, an address, a letterhead, and I paid for everything.

I took a day off from my paralegal job and I hit every sitcom in Los Angeles. Back in the day, you could do this. I'd pull up to the Warner Bros. lot with a baseball hat and go, "Yes, I'm the messenger from this agency. I got to drop off these scripts." A couple of weeks in, I get a call from the executive producer of *Fresh Prince of Bel-Air*. It's a woman named Winifred Hervey Stallworth. She calls the "agency." She says, "Hey, Doug. It's Winifred Hervey, I read Terry Winter's scripts. I think he's really talented. We might like to have him in to pitch." I call Doug in New York and it's Friday and it's already late, he's gone for the day. I say, "Shit, I got to wait until Monday now." Then I thought, "You know, he doesn't know anything about being an agent. I'll just call and say I'm him." I call her up and go, "Hi, it's Doug. I'm the agent." I have no idea what agents say or do. I just wing it. She says, "Oh yes, Terry's so talented." I go, "Oh, he's the most talented writer I've ever read. That's for sure."

Michael: So that's how you get your foot in the door. Amazing. That's a good lesson for people who want to know how writers get started in Hollywood. Look at how far you went. Look at the sacrifice. That's what it takes. So what happened next? You started writing, and you met Frank Renzulli at a writers' workshop?

Terry: Yes, Frankie, of course, is one of the great writers and hands-down one of the funniest people, easily. Literally, when you say somebody's so funny they almost made you pee your pants, that's Frankie. Just an incredibly funny guy.

A couple years later, my agent sends me the pilot of *The Sopranos*. I call Frankie. Frankie says, "Yes, I'm meeting this guy, David Chase." I said, "You got to get me in there."

Michael: Now, you met David in Season Two, right? If I remember, only a few writers had been carried over from Season One, and the doors were open to some new writers.

Terry: The only ones who survived were Frankie, Robin Green, and Mitch Burgess. That's it. The funny thing is, as Frankie was writing on Season One, he would tell me about the writers' room and we'd riff and pitch. I pitched him stories and he pitched them to David. He'd write scenes and send them to me and I'd edit them. I'd add some lines. I was writing on the show a little, even though I wasn't! In the meantime, I was writing what became my first feature, a movie called *Brooklyn Rules*. It's a movie about me and my two best friends growing up in New York, it had some mob component stuff. I thought, "Oh, this would be a great sample for David." David reads and hates it. I'm thinking, "Oh my God, really?" I thought I just shot myself in the foot.

But Season Two comes along and David's ready to hire more

people. Frankie said to David, "Look, I know you don't like that script. You got to trust me on this guy. I know he can write the show." David said, "All right, you're vouching for the guy. I'll meet him."

Steve: So what was it like when you got to *The Sopranos*?

Terry: First thing, literally on day one, Tony Sirico comes up to me. The first thing he ever said to me was, "You're the new writer. Let me tell you something. You ever write the script where I die, first I die, then you die." I was like, "Okay." He goes, "I'm telling you, don't fucking think about killing me." Every once in a while, we would type up a phony script page that had Paulie dying and leave it around. He got wise to that after a while.

Michael: Do you remember any story lines that never became scripts? Ideas that never made it to the show?

Terry: There were very few. I can maybe count on one hand the stories that didn't go. I used to like to say that we used even our scraps of story ideas; we ended up making soup out of everything. We had a storyboard on one of the walls in the writers' room, where there were just notions that we wanted to remember. By the end, we had checked off almost every little obscure thing we wanted to get to, like "Bear in New Jersey." Boom! That was a whole episode. Just things we wanted to do.

There was one episode during the sequence of episodes where Tony was in the hospital, where we wanted to do a script about the privilege of rich people in hospitals, that at a fancy hospital in New York, there's a floor that the average person doesn't know about, but if you're a celebrity or you're a rich person, that's where you go. There's rooms where the family can stay, and Tony pulls some strings to get that special treatment. We might've actually had a script that was written. But by that point we just felt like we'd been in that hospital so long, let's not do it.

There was another script that was about the home life of the female FBI agent, who was flipping Adriana. We got to spend time with her at home; maybe Tony had an affair with her or something like that. That never really got any traction.

I had pitched an episode where a young kid breaks into Tony's house and Tony is the only one there and he catches the kid and doesn't know what to do. The idea was, the whole thing takes place entirely in the house, it's just Tony and this kid. And he ends up killing him rather than let them go. Obviously, we never did that one either.

Michael, you were involved in a story line about a mentally ill guy outside the pork store?

Michael: Yes, who is obsessed with Andrew Loog Oldham, the Rolling Stones producer. There was also one other one that we never did. I remember seeing it on the whiteboard—"A rat and nobody cares." There was a rat who got out of prison and nobody gave a shit anymore. One of the guys says, "We got to get this guy," but nobody cared at this point.

Terry: That's the thing too. It sort of goes back to the Sammy Gravano thing. He's out and he's saying, "Okay, here's my address, I'm in Arizona. If anybody wants to come get me, here I am." You got to really have a very serious grudge to go to Arizona and confront that guy, so unless it's very personal, what you'll say is, "Oh, somebody should do that. Not me, I'm not getting involved." The thing that people don't realize is that it's not even so much that you're putting your own life in danger going to confront a rat or to bring honor to the family, it's a murder rap. You don't put yourself in a situation theoretically where you could get put away the rest of your life on a murder rap because you're avenging some code of honor that doesn't directly affect you. It's not as casual as it seems in TV or in the movies. The whole gun-happy trigger-finger thing is not as accurate as we like to depict it in our business.

Michael: Very true. I have to say that I think *The Sopranos* was more accurate to mob reality than most TV or film.

———————

Steve: You know, I didn't bring it up, but I remember the first time I met Terry Winter.

Michael: When was that?

Steve: When I auditioned for the show, there was, I don't know, a hundred people in the hallway at Silvercup. It was a long hallway. I said to one guy, "Hey, where's the sign-in sheet?" Guy says, "Down there." The guy that I talked to happened to be Terry Winter. I didn't know him from Adam. I went all the way to the end, signed in, sat in my chair, working on the stuff. Now, when I go in to read, I'm looking around, there's about fifteen people in the room, including the guy that I asked where's the sign-in sheet.

Michael: Terry was a producer-writer by then.

Steve: I didn't know that. I'm going, "What do you do, you audition and then they let you stay here?" I had no idea.

Michael: You didn't know what was going on.

Steve: I didn't know what was going on. I said, "What the fuck is this? After auditioning, you stay and you judge the other people?" I mean, I didn't know but he *was* auditioning for this. He had to audition for this role. He played a patient in Melfi's office. He did a great job.

Michael: Wait, he had to audition for the role even though he was already on the staff as a writer-producer?

Steve: Absolutely.

Michael: I did not know that.

Steve: So here's something I don't know. While we're talking about writing, Michael, let me ask you. David Chase is only credited as a writer occasionally on the show. But he was involved in every script, wasn't he?

Michael: Yes. He pretty much always did a pass. A pass is a rewrite. He was always the final authority on every script.

Steve: You write an episode. You got to turn it in by X amount of days. David reads it. All the writers read it. How does that work?

Michael: Yes, you usually get about three weeks to write the first draft. Then all the writers read it. You'd get notes. Then you do another draft, you do two or three drafts. Then David would always add his touch to it. Sometimes more, sometimes less. Why that's important on a show like this, is that David's the auteur of this show. He's the creator. He's the person who makes this vision unified. There's consistency through all the episodes. They don't do that as much on network television.

Steve: They don't have the time.

Michael: They don't have the time, but also they're not as committed to one unified vision like on a film. It was important that David always contributed and had his imprint on the episodes.

ONE OF *the well-known alumni from the writers' room is Matt Weiner, who of course went on to create one of the other great iconic TV dramas,* Mad Men. *He's been nominated for twenty-six Emmy awards and won nine of them. Matt came on late in the series but quickly became an essential part of the team, writing twelve episodes of* The Sopranos—

with some of our most memorable episodes among them—and producing or exec-producing thirty-four episodes. I have to say that, along with David Chase, I consider Matt Weiner to be one of the great influencers in television in the twenty-first century. —Michael

Steve: You came in Season Five, right?

Matt: Yeah. Season Four was on the air. That was in 2002. I got there in November, and I was given the rest of the season on VHS. And I went home and watched them all in one night. The first one I saw was Ralphie getting killed. I was laughing my ass off, by the way.

Steve: Now, you had been working in TV. Was it your dream to get on this show?

Matt: I worked in half-hour comedy. I was on *Andy Richter Controls the Universe,* and before that I was on *Becker.* My joke was that everyone said, "What was it like? The difference between your previous job and *The Sopranos*?" And I said, "It was exactly the same. I sat in a room with a bunch of writers talking about *The Sopranos* all day." Everything was measured by that show. When I got to *The Sopranos,* Michael Patrick King, who I knew, was right next door at *Sex and the City.* I would occasionally go over there for an infusion of nontoxic blood. They were laughing, whatever. They were like, "How's it going?" I said, "Oh, we're shooting an old man in the face today," stuff like that.

Steve: Had you written any drama?

Matt: I wrote the *Mad Men* pilot right around the same time *The Sopranos* came on. I'd been working on it for a couple of years.

Steve: So you wrote the *Mad Men* pilot early on. This is years before it went on the air, obviously. What happened with it? Did your agent get it to David?

Matt: *Mad Men* was submitted to HBO about five times, I'm not exaggerating. No one looked at it. HBO was not interested in it. And finally my manager at the time got it to David's agent and said, "You have to read this." And all of a sudden I got a call from David Chase! I had so much I wanted to ask him about. Because he was already an inspiration, honestly. I am the same age now that he was when *The Sopranos* hit. So the idea that no matter how long I've worked, eventually I might be able to express myself the way he could, that was an inspiration. He'd been successful on TV forever—he was kind of a wunderkind actually—but that show happened to him at an age that was hopeful for people who were sort of struggling in the trenches. And then I talked to him on the phone, and the incredible thing was, all he wanted to do was talk about the *Mad Men* pilot.

He said a lot of very complimentary things about the *Mad Men* pilot. And ironically, by the way, he was very interested in how old I was. I know he didn't ask me, because I don't think that's legal, but he wanted adults on that show. I was thirty-seven. He did not want twenty-five-year-olds on the show, which is very unusual for TV to begin with.

Michael: The first episode you wrote for *The Sopranos* was "Rat Pack." A very key episode. The second one of Season Five. It's the first time we meet Steve Buscemi's character, Tony B.

Matt: Steve had been introduced, you see him on the news on TV briefly in the very first episode of the season—which hadn't been written yet, by the way. It was very exciting—I don't even have to tell you—the first time you typed "Tony." And it was terrifying, also. And all the writers went off on vacation after we broke the stories, but the new people, we had to do our script over the Christmas vacation.

Michael: We've explained this, when you say "break the stories," you mean break them down into beats, into an outline of the various scenes.

Matt: Yes. It's probably part of my success that I'm a good mimic, but I wasn't going to open every scene with, "Oh, there he is!" or say, "Forget about it," or whatever else it is. I knew that. I also didn't know shit about the Mafia other than what I'd seen in the movies, but David said, "Don't worry about it, because that's not why you're here." But I had watched him breaking the story. It was so intuitive, the way he worked, and, honestly, I almost got fired a month into it anyway, not because of the writing, but because I was talking too much in the writers' room. But by the end it was better. Was I okay?

Michael: [*Laughs*] You were fine. I was in the writers' room with you on Season Five. You were fine. I just think the writers' room is a very hard place to be sometimes. On one specific day we had come in—you, me, Terry, and David—and the morning was really kind of slow. And we were just talking, we were reading the paper, and then all of a sudden David gets up and starts writing on the board. Fills the whole board. And we're going, "This is great! Wow, whoa, yeah!" And then an hour later, he goes, "This fucking sucks," and he erases a whole morning's worth of work. Just erased the whole thing. And then all of us are just sitting there, including David, thinking, "What the fuck are we doing?" And that's a typical day in the writers' room.

Matt: And it's obviously very different than a half-hour-comedy writers' room where honestly, it's usually like, at the time when I was in it, half Jewish, half Irish, and just a lot of people complaining, and there's always somebody buying a house and always somebody getting divorced and there's always crap going on and a lot of jokes and a lot of stuff that has nothing to do with it, but it's a lot of talking. And I get there and David is just lying on the couch in pain. But then eventually David would get so sick that he would just get up and throw things up on the board.

Michael: We'd sit there for a couple of hours, maybe talk about stories, maybe not. Then he'd spit out all this stuff on the board in very, very minute detail. That's the thing about David that always knocked me out.

Steve: So I guess it could get pretty tense in there sometimes. I can't even imagine it. So were you told to stop talking?

Matt: No. David never told you anything. But I called a friend of mine who was a pro. He said, "You better stop talking. You're there to write. There's nothing you can say that that man doesn't already know. Come up with a story on your own. Pitch the whole story out." Because for David, in the end, it was all about the draft.

Michael: That's absolutely right. It's all about the writing. So tell us what happened when you finally turned in your first draft, for "Rat Pack."

Matt: I got a phone call three weeks after I turned it in. I was just on ice in New York, all by myself. It was a dark time, it was January. I was at a movie theater watching *The Hours*. It was on Third Avenue, that movie theater that's underground. I got the call, which I missed because I was underground. I come out and there's a message. David says, "I read the script. Sounds like our people. Characters sound like the people. Story's all fucked up, but we'll talk about that. You'll come in." I played it a million times. I still have it somewhere.

Michael: That's actually a big compliment. Coming from David.

Matt: It was huge. And so I went in to get my notes on the draft. As I was walking in, you remember that long hallway at Silvercup that you could barely fit two people? I walked by this guy. I said, "How'd it go?" And he said, "I got fired."

Steve: Uh-oh.

Matt: I walked in with rubber legs and I sat down, and David gave me his notes. He did it in front of Robin and Mitch and Terry. I wrote down everything he said. But it was very complimentary.

Michael: But that was three weeks from start to finish, right? I mean, three weeks from the time you broke the story until the time you handed it in? That's a pretty tall order.

Matt: Michael, you may not even know this, but they had given me two first drafts that had not been touched by David because I was like, "When I go off to write, I'm measuring it against the show. Can I see some first drafts?" Terry gave me "Another Toothpick" and "Telltale Moozadell." That's yours, right?

Michael: Yes.

Matt: I had both of those first drafts to see, okay, if I can get it this good, I can probably keep my job. Because it's very hard.

Michael: But there's a lot of rewriting. You have to get used to that. It's part of the process.

Matt: I have to explain this to you guys. There are so many things in my scripts, whether they had David's name on them as well or not—people come up and pat me on the back and they're saying, "What a great line." And you're like, "I didn't write that." My challenge was—and I tried to explain this when I had my own show—to *not* say, "Well, you're just going to change it anyway." To just say, "First of all, I'm going to make your life easier. And one day I'm going to write a script that you're not even going to feel like rewriting. You're not even going to know what's yours and what's not." It did get there.

Michael: You have to accept the collaborative aspect of the show. You're collaborating with people who inspire you. And you might be inspiring something as well. Even though your thing gets changed, you're inspiring a thought.

Matt: I used to say to Terry, "Is it good?" And Terry used to say, "No, but it will be."

ANOTHER OF *the alums of the writers' room who went on to great things was Todd Kessler, who later created the award-winning series* Damages. *He was only on* The Sopranos *for two seasons but wrote some of the most memorable episodes, including "D-Girl," as well as "Funhouse," which he cowrote with David Chase. He told us about how his time on the show started, and how it ended. And how, as for many of us, his relationship with David was . . . complicated. —Michael*

Michael: You were in touch with David while you were working on another show, *Providence,* which was on NBC for many years, correct?

Todd: Yes. And then sometime during the editing of the first season of *The Sopranos,* I got a call from David, asking, would I want to come in and maybe meet to write for the show in Season Two?

Michael: And so you left *Providence?*

Todd: That's a very good question. I actually had a month left on my contract. And that show became a huge hit. And so when I came to meet with David, we talked about an episode for me to write. And he said, "Okay, you have three weeks." And I said, "Well, I'm under contract for another month at NBC." And he said, "Okay, you have two choices. You can either go to them and ask them to let you out of your contract, which they probably won't do. Or you can write it. And most likely they'll never find out." And he said, "Go outside.

You have ten minutes to think about it and come back in and tell me what you want to do."

Steve: That's what he said? Literally?

Todd: Yeah. I'm twenty-five years old. And I go out in the parking lot and I'm shaking. And I call the people at *Providence,* and I called my brothers in New York. No one's answering. And so I go back in to see David and he said, "Which one is it?" And I said, "I'm going to go to my boss and ask him to let me out of my contract." And he basically said, "Good luck." And I drove from Santa Monica to the Van Nuys Airport, which is where our offices were. And I talked to my boss and he says, "Go, go, just go. If that's where your heart is, go," and he let me out.

And so in the first episode that I wrote, "D-Girl"—Michael, you'll remember this scene—there's a moment where Tony says to Christopher, at Anthony Jr.'s confirmation, "Go outside, you have ten minutes to think about whether you're in or you're out." And he goes out and sits outside and thinks, "What? Am I going back into the family or not?" And that was directly from my experience with what David made me do.

Michael: Oh, I didn't know that. That's really cool.

Todd: And David never said anything to me about it. I don't know whether he realized it or not, but he probably did. He's a super-smart guy, but I used that thing that he did to me, that Tony then would do to Christopher.

Steve: You wrote the episode "Funhouse," where you kill off Big Pussy. How did that come about?

Todd: "Funhouse" was the second-season finale that David and I wrote together, and we wrote together in a way I had never done before. It was my slot to write the finale. And Nancy was in failing health and we weren't sure whether she was going to be able to act in the episode. So I went to David and said, so much of the show is about David and his relationship with his mother that if he wanted to write the episode, that was fine with me. I could understand that. Because it may be her last episode in the series. And David said that he really appreciated it, and that he did want to write it.

But then a week or two later, he called me and said that he wasn't going to be able to write it alone. So would I write it with him? And of course I said yes. And then he said, "All right, do you want to take the first half or the second half?" And in the first half of that episode, there's a lot that's pretty subjective—Tony has food poisoning, and he has the talking fish and a lot of stuff like that—and I felt that would be better for David to take. So I took the second half, which ended up being an amazing experience to write, including the scene where Pussy gets killed on the boat.

We had a week to write the whole episode and I ended up writing that scene on Thanksgiving morning, from probably two in the morning to seven in the morning. And then a little bit later that day, I went to Thanksgiving with my family. And I will never forget, my oldest brother took me aside at some point and he asks, "Are you okay?" And I said, "What do you mean?" He says, "It kind of looks like your eyes are sunken into your head. What is going on?" It was super emotional to write, the killing of Pussy. And I didn't want to tell him what it was. I said, "I'm fine, I just had to write this intense scene. But it was a really rewarding experience." And then David and I were both nominated for an Emmy for writing that episode.

Steve: But then, a little after that, for whatever reason, David decided not to pick up your contract. That must have been horrible.

Todd: I remember the day when David basically said to me, "You know what, I think it will be best if you're just not here." And I was just devastated. I mean, the show is my entire life. I was very young. I started writing on the show when I was twenty-six. And I put everything I had into writing on the show, being on set, being in editing, being in casting, the whole thing. Ultimately I guess something just didn't fully click as we got further into our relationship, me and David.

I got also very close to Jim. He became one of my dearest friends in life as we worked on the show. Jim called me up after he finished work that day. He knew what had happened, and he said, "I'm taking you out." We went to Pastis. We were sitting at the table, and these two women came up to us to talk to Jim. Jim introduced me and he said, "This is Todd. He was one of the writers on the show. He just got fired today." I shrunk, I was so embarrassed.

But they didn't care. And we talked a little bit, they laughed, and then Jim said to me—and it was really one of those moments that will forever stick with me of Jim—he said: "You do not shrink. You have nothing to hang your head about. I just did to you what an actor did to me when I got fired from my first play. You hold your head high and know that you did great work."

Michael: But nobody was safe. It didn't matter if you were an actor who could get whacked or a writer. Our fate dangled by a thread.

Todd: But all of those things that I've gone on to create, all the pressures that the person running the show is under—I understand all that now. It's never easy to part ways with people, it's never easy to fire someone. And when I look back, getting fired was something that was really painful but formative. Those experiences in life, and how you move forward.

Steve: You get fired, you think it's the worst thing in the world. But you went on to create an incredible show and a huge success. You pulled yourself off the mat and you got back out there punching and things worked out. Some people define themselves by getting fired. Some people curl up and can't go on. That didn't happen to you. Thank goodness.

IN THE *end, these talented people were nominated for twenty-one Emmys, won six of them, and wrote a million great lines. Everybody's got their favorites. Here's my top ten best* Sopranos *quotes. If you disagree, go write your own book. —Steve*

10. *Uncle Junior: "You steer the ship the best way you know. Sometimes it's smooth. Sometimes you hit the rocks. In the meantime you find your pleasures where you can."*

9. *Carmela Soprano: "More is lost by indecision than by the wrong decision."*

8. *Christopher Moltisanti: "Other people's definitions of you, sometimes they're more about making themselves feel better. You gotta define yourself."*

7. *Janice Soprano: "For every twenty wrongs a child does, ignore nineteen."*

6. *Dr. Jennifer Melfi: "People only see what you allow them to see."*

5. *Bobby Baccalieri: "Quasimodo predicted all this."*

4. *Tony Soprano: "What's the point? You go to Italy, you lift some weights, you watch a movie. It's all a series of distractions until you die."*

3. *Silvio Dante: "You're only as good as your last envelope."*

2. *Tony Soprano: "Cunnilingus and psychiatry brought us to this."*

1. *Christopher Moltisanti: "The Emerald Piper. That's our hell. It's an Irish bar where it's St. Patrick's Day every day forever."*

EIGHT

Season Four

Paint It Black

IT'S TOO BAD THAT LEONARD COHEN'S "You Want It Darker" wasn't around for Season Four of The Sopranos, *or I'm sure David Chase would have worked it in somewhere. The show definitely takes a darker turn in this season—not that there weren't many dark moments to get us here, but as we pass the halfway point of the historic run of* The Sopranos, *there is an unmistakable feeling of dread, of decay, of impending doom. Fans waited fourteen months for new episodes after Season Three ended, and these did not disappoint. Certainly the stakes are higher: Tony has built his empire, but the threats to his power, from without and within, are becoming more insistent and more constant. Junior is threatened with lawsuits, Tony's goomar has committed suicide, his marriage is falling apart, Christopher has a drug problem, and the evils of Ralphie—presented as the devil incarnate—are coming to fruition. In one of the episodes I wrote, there is the image of a crumbling ceiling in a dream sequence—a nod, in a way, to the crumbling of Tony's world. The beginning of the end. Or as another songwriter of Leonard Cohen's generation, Paul Simon, sang on his first solo album: "Everything put together sooner or later falls apart."* —Michael

Michael: So things are getting pretty heavy for Tony Soprano in Season Four.

Steve: I don't know how Tony does it. I get aggravated when I got to go to the dry cleaner and the post office in the same day. This guy has got eighty problems a day, literally. From his daughter, Meadow, who wants to run off to Europe. That's a whole big megillah there, right? Then you've got the problem with New York and Johnny Sack, who is a troublemaker. He wants to whack Carmine. Ralphie with the whole mole-on-Ginny's-ass thing that started all that crap. Carmela and Tony. Also, Paulie doesn't shut his mouth. These are whackable offenses, what Paulie's doing from prison. I got to tell you, I couldn't wait for those scripts to get FedExed to my apartment. The security around the scripts had gotten really tight but the regulars were still getting the scripts. Only the regulars. I looked forward to reading them because I was such a fan. The descriptions were so good, the scripts were so heavy and so funny.

You know what I remember? Tony Sirico at the read-throughs. He had a lot of good moments in the second half of Season Four. If Tony had a good episode, he would always go, to the writers, "Thank you for the episode! Thank you!" Like it was written just to make him happy.

Michael: That's Tony. And I'll say another thing about Tony and the scripts: by the time we got to the set, he would have already memorized every bit. Weeks before we got there.

Steve: Soon as he got the script, he learned it.

Michael: He called it "locking it in." That was what he did.

Steve: Which you could do, because there weren't a lot of changes by the time you got to the set. It wasn't a sitcom, where they change the lines every single day. It's funny on Monday; by Thursday they've thrown it out and gotten a whole new script. If you gave Tony a change, he couldn't do it.

Michael: That's because he wouldn't just learn the lines, he learned every single gesture. He practiced in the mirror, something I could never even dream of doing. That's not my thing.

Steve: That's hard to believe, with your ego, that you don't look at the mirror constantly.

Michael: I'm not vain, Steve.

Steve: I find it hard to believe that you don't walk around with a mirror.

Michael: I have a big ego but I'm not vain. You're mistaking ego for vanity. They're two different things. Sometimes they go together, but not always.

Steve: But really, Michael, we have to talk more about Tony Sirico. We have so many stories about him. Season Four is a big season for him. All of a sudden a lot of plotlines revolve around him.

Michael: There's his whole resentment of Tony not contacting him in prison, and the question of whether he's going to go over to work for Johnny Sack.

Steve: And Silvio thinks Tony's spying for Johnny, and all that. So that's all pretty serious, but also there's a whole fight with Tony over the Pie-O-My painting, which is really funny. And the stuff with his mother being snubbed at the nursing home, which gives him a chance to be really emotional.

Michael: And sympathetic. So he really gets to play a wide range of emotions here.

Steve: And yet he's not really around for the first six episodes. I don't know if people know, it was because he was in a car accident.

Michael: He was in a taxi going uptown from Marylou's, which was a restaurant and bar on Ninth Street between Fifth and Sixth. I used to live across the street. It was a big showbiz hangout, especially in its heyday, in the nineties. Tony was on his way from there and he was coming to meet either us or Jim at a bar uptown when the cab crashed.

Steve: After the accident he had to have surgery. That's why they shot all those scenes, from that one room in the jail, after he was better. They always shot the whole season before it aired, so they could plug him into all those episodes.

Michael: I love that the first line the writers gave him, when he got out of prison, was "Whattaya hear, whattaya say!" That was a famous Jimmy Cagney line, he says it in *Angels with Dirty Faces*.

Steve: He's a huge Jimmy Cagney fan, Tony. Huge. That's how that got into the script.

Michael: That happened a lot. As the writers got to know the actors, they started to tailor the material to them, play to their strengths, bring pieces of their life into the characters.

Steve: You could never say a bad word about James Cagney around Tony. When you talk about hero worship, man, people have no idea how big a fan Tony Sirico is. One time, we were in Detroit doing one of these "Conversations with the Sopranos" shows. At the end we would take questions from the audience. So I told the owner of the club to ask Tony a question about James Cagney, and little did I know, the guy stands up, in front of nine hundred people, and he says, "Tony, my uncle was friends with James Cagney. He told me that Cagney used to be a cross-dresser." Sirico jumps up and yells, "Shut your fucking mouth!" On the stage!

Michael: In the middle of the show. Yes, I remember that.

Steve: He went off the deep end. I almost fell off the stool. I was laughing so hard.

Michael: You don't say anything about Cagney in front of Tony Sirico.

Steve: In a lot of scenes, you see Tony standing with his hands in front of him, kind of pinching his fingers together. Is that a Cagney thing?

Michael: No. It's a jail thing. It's so you always have your hands at the ready, in front of you, in case you need to defend yourself or attack. You don't want your hands behind your back or in your pockets where you can't use them quickly. That's what he told me, at least.

Steve: We have so many Tony stories. We could do a whole book just on Tony. Once he told us that back when he started out, he was like a doorman or a bouncer at a club in the Village near Sheridan Square and he knew Jimi Hendrix.

Michael: Jimi lived in the Village. He had a studio on Eighth Street, called Electric Lady. He used to go to Tony's club, and Tony said he would give Jimi a wedgie. Which is really bizarre. The image of Paulie Walnuts and Jimi Hendrix together.

Steve: But Tony, when he started on the show, was fifty-five years old. He was living with his mother. He was sleeping on a cot in his mother's living room, and he had been—well, we can say, because he's been open about it—he was the most authentic, right?

Michael: Yes. He went to jail because he was robbing nightclubs. First, he would bring a bunch of guys and start fights and bother people, so the owners would pay him off. If they didn't, then he would go a step further.

Steve: And he was involved with organized crime figures back as a young guy.

Michael: I think he drove for a couple of people. He did some time in prison. But you're right, he never made any bones about who he was. I've heard him say on a lot of projects, a director might try to tell him, "Well, the character is like this or like this," and he would say, "What you see is what you get." That's what he'd say about himself and about his acting style or acting ability: "What you see is what you get."

Steve: He was also a ladies' man, apparently. He was a good-looking guy in his day, in great shape.

Michael: There was a porno magazine in the 1970s called *Viva*. It was for women. And he was a cover star in one of them. He's wearing what looks like a Freddie Mercury outfit.

Steve: But you could not touch his hair.

Michael: He would do his own hair at home. Before he came to the set. It would take him hours.

Steve: Tons of hair spray. And it was only Aqua Net. That was the only kind he would use. He would do it on the set, too, sometimes. This is after he came back from the barber, like we talked about, to get his hair dyed black and then get the silver wings put in on the sides.

Michael: He would spray a cloud of hair spray and then let it fall. He would not spray directly on the hair. He had those professional-grade cans of Aqua Net which were meant for beauty parlors. They were gigantic.

Steve: And the Binaca, too. The breath spray. Did he ever do this to you? You're in a scene with him, and he'd go, "Hold on, hold on, hold on," and he would pull out the little bottle of Binaca. "Open your mouth." And he'd give you a big shpritz. Or he'd say, "You gotta take the stink off," and he'd hit you with a big spray of cologne, Obsession for Men, and you would smell like Tony Sirico for the rest of the day.

Michael: But like you said, no matter what, Tony was the real deal.

Steve: Tony would always say, "I'll never play a rat."

Michael: I'll tell you something else Tony wouldn't play. It's an interesting story—it's one of the only times an actor influenced a change in the script and it wasn't even their lines.

Steve: I don't think I know this story.

Michael: It's the scene where the bordello owner is talking about Makazian, the corrupt cop played by John Heard. In the original script, it said, "Makazian didn't like Paulie. He thought Paulie was a bully." Tony Sirico read that and was horrified, and very angry, that Paulie was labeled a bully. And he went to either Frank Renzulli, who wrote that episode, or David Chase, and said, "Paulie's not a bully. I don't like this. I'm really against it." So they took it into consideration, thought about it, and said, "How about psycho?" and Tony Sirico said, "Fine."

Steve: He'd rather be called a psycho than a bully? That's Tony Sirico. They threw the mold away when they made him. I love him. He's one of a kind.

SO LET'S *talk about the episodes. Starting with the first one. In Season Four, one of the scenes I get asked the most about that I was in was the famous Nostradamus-Quasimodo scene between Tony and Bobby, from the first episode of Season Four. It's almost like an Abbott and Costello routine:*

Bobby: Mom really went downhill after the World Trade Center. You know Quasimodo predicted all this.

Tony: Who did what?

Bobby: All these problems—the Middle East, the end of the world.

Tony: Nostradamus. Quasimodo's the Hunchback of Notre Dame.

Bobby: Oh right. Notre Damus.

Tony: Nostradamus, and Notre Dame. Two different things completely.

Bobby: It's interesting though, they'd be so similar, isn't it? And I always thought okay, Hunchback of Notre Dame. You also got your quarterback and halfback of Notre Dame.

Tony: One's a fucking cathedral.

Bobby: Obviously. I know, I'm just saying. It's interesting, the coincidence. What, you're gonna tell me you never pondered that? The back thing with Notre Dame?

Tony: No!

It was a scene I could really sink my teeth into. And not just because I had to keep eating steak through the whole thing. —Steve

Michael: You had a lot of fun doing that scene, I could tell.

Steve: I had an acting coach in the East Village on St. Mark's. I would go to his place to run lines. He would read Tony's part. We did it a thousand times. I was at his place in the afternoon, and then a few hours later, I was actually doing it in a diner, a real diner in Jersey. I wanted it to look real so I was eating the steaks, and I kept eating them. I was in the rhythm. They had six rib eyes, and I ate them.

Michael: You ate six rib eyes that day?

Steve: Six of them. I didn't eat another steak for many months after that. We did a lot of takes. Many, many hours. You know, different angles, the camera behind us, the camera in front of us, a single on me, single on Jim, a two-shot. There's that side angle, when I'm looking to the left, to Jim, they're getting him the other way. So maybe thirty takes. And I'm eating the whole time.

Michael: But by the way, even though they're still referencing your weight, this is the moment they lost the fat suit, right? Because maybe by this point, they thought it was a little over-the-top.

Steve: Yes, by this season they eliminated it completely.

Michael: Also because Bobby had more serious stuff. You were becoming more of an important character, they didn't need the sight gag. They wanted to make him more real, more down-to-earth.

Steve: Yes, I think that's right. But the Quasimodo scene, I was happy that they gave it to me. I heard a rumor that Sirico was supposed to do it, but Tony wasn't feeling well. They turned it over to Bobby.

Michael: What's funniest is that you play it completely straight. There's no hint that Bobby thinks this is in the least bit funny.

Steve: With the comedy you got to play it straight all the time. Obviously, you want to get the right pacing, and then when you're doing the scene, you'll know when it's the right way. But also, after a take, you could go, "Let's go right back and do it again." I like to get into that rhythm.

Michael: Because when they cut, then they have to reset the camera, and people's energy drops.

Steve: If you have a note, something you want to say about the way I played the scene, then give me the note. If not, let's go right back.

Michael: But that's what was wonderful about *The Sopranos*. It was always very actor-oriented. When you had a heavy scene, the crew was behind you. They wanted you to do a good job. They read the script, so they know that this is a big scene. You're learning your fiancé is in the FBI or so-and-so died, so the stakes are really high. It's a big dramatic scene or a big moment and the crew was behind you. They wanted it to be a good scene and you could feel them with you. I felt that very often.

Steve: And if you ever said, "Give me another take. I could do better," you would get it. Absolutely. It wasn't moving on, moving on, moving on. They gave you plenty of time.

One more thing about the first episode. At the end, Christopher has pictures of his dad in the navy. Who is that in the pictures?

Michael: That's my brother, John, who actually posed for that picture. He came into Silvercup and he put on the sailor suit and they took a photo of him.

Steve: And the other photo? The baby photo?

Michael: The other photo of the baby with the blueberry pie on his face and the young man, that's my father and me when I was baby. But I wanna bring up one more thing about this episode as well—this is the first time you see Bobby's kids. His son, Bobby Jr., and his daughter, Sophia.

Steve: There were two actresses who played my daughter, two Sophias. The first one was Lexie Sperduto. She's now about thirty years old and she's married with a baby. Terrific girl. My daughter actually keeps in touch with her.

Michael: Is she still an actress?

Steve: No, I don't believe so. She got a master's in nutrition. Works with pregnant women. Good, good person. Miryam Coppersmith, the other actress to play Sophia, she came on later.

Michael: And Bobby Jr., played by Angelo Massagli, he became a lawyer.

THE EPISODE *I wrote, "Christopher," the third one in this season, was pretty complicated—and complicated more by the fact that it was intended in part for Tony Sirico, who as we said was out of commission. Tony's character had been set up, earlier, as the protector of Italian culture—back in Season Two, he's the one who gets furious in a Starbucks-type café because of the cultural appropriation ("How did we miss out on this shit? Espresso, cappuccino—we invented this shit and all these cocksuckers are getting rich off of it. It's not just the money— it's a pride thing"). Without Tony around, we had to make Silvio the one who was angry that protesters were trying to disrupt the Columbus Day parade.*

But what I loved about writing this episode was one of the things I love about all the episodes—the whipsawing between humor and pathos, comedy and drama, farce and tragedy. The Columbus Day theme is played somewhat comically—but it's in juxtaposition to the death of Bobby's wife, Karen, the split-up of Ralph and Janice, hints of the beginnings of the relationship between Janice and Bobby. A lot to pack into fifty-four minutes. —Michael

Steve: So, Michael, how did this work? How much of this episode was you bringing the ideas, and how much came to you from David?

Michael: Before we go off individually to write a draft, we do a macro thing of what the whole arc of the season is. Then you divide it up, and you look at each episode, and as I mentioned, each episode usually has three story lines, an, A, B, and C story line. The only episode where I brought a ton of stuff out of nowhere was the first one, "From Where to Eternity," because a lot of it was from a spec script that I wrote. When you are breaking stories in the writers' room, it's David and the writing staff jamming on ideas and then making an outline.

Steve: So for the people reading this who don't know, when it says, "Story by Michael Imperioli and Maria Laurino, teleplay by Michael Imperioli," what does that mean?

Michael: Those distinctions are created by the Writers Guild. Maria Laurino had written a bestselling memoir called *Were You Always an Italian?*, about the ethnic identity of Italians, and she came up with a story line involving Italian-American identity politics. But then it turns out she wasn't going to write the script. Whoever actually writes the script gets the teleplay credit. If you did both, if there's no one that needs to be credited for the story outside of you, you get just a "written by" credit.

It was a hard episode to write, because part of me never really 100 percent believed that these guys would care that much about Columbus. But when I got into it, I did find it hilarious that our gang would be so passionate and be the ones standing up for this political-cultural-social cause.

It was interesting also, though, because of all the anger about *The Sopranos* from Italian-American groups that thought the show was bad for the image of Italians. In a lot of ways this episode was David's way of sticking it to them. Because this was his baby, *The Sopranos*, and we all took a lot of heat from these various Italian-American anti-defamation people about negative portrayals and stereotypes.

Steve: Which, by the way, that was all bullshit.

Michael: For one thing, a lot of them never watched the show.

Steve: I got that all the time. "I think your show stinks." "Well do you watch it?" "I would never watch that show." "Well then how the fuck do you know what you're talking about?"

Michael: For the most part, *The Sopranos* is very beloved among Italian-Americans. Overwhelmingly. And most people who watch it understand that not all Italians are gangsters. They know that.

Steve: To say we're portraying all Italian-Americans as being in the mob is just pure ignorance.

Michael: But it started almost as soon as the show went on the air. Back in the first season, a group called the National Ethnic Coalition of Organizations was trying to get us thrown off the air. I found a quote from the chairman, Bill Fugazy, who said, "The media constantly makes Italians look like boobs or mobsters, and *The Sopranos* does put Italians in very bad light."

Steve: Billy Fugazy, he was a big swinging dick in New York City back then.

Michael: What? Swinging dick?

Steve: You don't know what a swinging dick is? It's a powerful guy.

Michael: I've actually never heard that used.

Steve: Hanging with me, you learn something every day. But yeah, he was a big deal in New York, and he criticized us constantly for portraying Italians in a bad light—and then guess what? He declares bankruptcy, he gets sued, he owes millions of dollars, and winds up getting convicted for perjury.

Michael: So who's portraying Italians in a bad light?

Steve: Meanwhile we have the most positive images of Italians ever on television—Melfi is a doctor, her husband is a doctor, Carmela's parents, all these positive images of Italians you never saw before.

Michael: Let alone that they should be celebrating the fact that one of the most successful shows in television history—but more than that, one of the greatest pieces of art in the medium of television—was written and created and acted and produced by a team of dedicated, incredibly talented Italian-Americans.

Steve: And this guy Fugazy—that's where the word comes from by the way.

Michael: I know. For people who don't know, "fugazi" is Italian slang for something that's totally fake.

Steve: And this guy is committing perjury and complaining about us. And then later, we're a huge hit, he tries to suck up to us. We were at Elaine's one night—myself, Federico, a couple other guys—having dinner. And he sent us a bottle of wine. And we refused it. And then Federico sent him a bottle of wine. Then we sent them another. Like, keep your own fucking wine, buddy. We don't need it.

Michael: After this episode aired, Dominic and Lorraine were supposed to march in the Columbus Day Parade in New York City. And they were both banned from marching in the parade, despite having received an invitation to participate from Mayor Michael Bloomberg. And Bloomberg was so pissed off, he bailed on the parade and took them out to lunch. It was the first time the mayor of New York didn't march in the Columbus Day Parade.

Steve: You know what I think? I used to be a regular on *Imus*. I went on his radio show on a Monday morning one time. He said, "I read a lot of complaints about the violence on your show." I made reference to, "They're a bunch of losers sitting in their mother's basement, talking in chat rooms about whether the show is good or not, and complaining about violence." When I got out of the studio, I got numerous messages from the guy at HBO that was in charge of the social media. I called him. I said, "Pete, what's up?" He said, "Did you say something?" I went, "Yes." He said, "Well, they're fucking killing you online."

Michael: In the chat rooms.

Steve: He said, "Don't say a word, let me handle it." He wrote an apology.

Michael: To all the people in their mother's basement. [*laughs*]

Steve: It went away, but they were killing me. They were saying, "Your fifteen minutes are up. You're a fucking loser. You're a horrible actor. You'll never work again." It was brutal. But you know what? The thing is that you can't make everyone happy.

Michael: No. You can't make everyone happy, but you've got to be willing to stay true to your thing and not censor yourself and still be creative and still push the envelope. David did that.

Steve: It's just like you said early on in the podcast, Michael. A lot of people were giving their opinions, and you said, "This ain't Burger King. You can't have it your way."

Michael: Exactly.

Steve: But getting back to the episode—Joey Pants, Joe Pantoliano, he won the Emmy this season, it said for this episode and the one later, "Whoever Did This." He was good in both of them. But he really pissed me off in this one.

Michael: Why? What happened?

Steve: It was the beginning scene, the opening scene of the "Christopher" episode. We're all in front of Satriale's, at a long table, on a cold day.

Michael: Which, by the way, we keep forgetting to mention, Satriale's was one of the few locations that didn't really exist.

Steve: No, there was no pork store there.

Michael: For the pilot, they filmed at a real pork store. But once the show got picked up, they found an empty storefront in Kearny and turned it into a pork store.

Steve: They tore it down after the series ended. People were pissed off, like they were destroying a landmark.

Michael: They were, in a way. Anyway, what happened with Joey Pants?

Steve: So we're all in front of Satriale's. That's where Bobby reads the paper about what's going on with the Columbus Day thing. I kept stumbling on a line. When I learned the line, I knew it was going to fuck me up. One of the few times, knock on wood, and Joey Pants kept laughing at me. Remember?

Michael: Yes. It wasn't cool.

Steve: You had Bobby Funaro in the scene, who played Eugene, and you had Dan Grimaldi, you could see in their eyes they were trying to help me, because that's who I was delivering the line to. They were rooting for me.

Michael: I was rooting for you.

Steve: Yes. Everyone, they all were, except Joey. I love him, but he could be a dick at times.

Michael: Ball-breaker.

Steve: He was being a dick and I got up and I tried to chase him.

Michael: You got mad at him. You blew up.

Steve: I started motherfucking him. That's for sure. In front of everybody, I was calling him a motherfucker, and he was just laughing. I threw something at him. David said to me later on, "I know you and Joey don't get along." I went, "No, no, we get along. It was just an isolated incident and I was very frustrated with myself and he made it ten times worse. I would never do that to someone."

Michael: That was funny, but you had some of your most serious moments in this episode. When Bobby and Janice are talking about Karen, his wife, who died in the car crash, those scenes are incredibly moving.

Steve: You gave me great stuff to do. Talk about writing that scene for Bobby. How did you write those scenes?

Michael: For me it was getting into who Bobby was. They talk about Bobby—Bobby never had a goomar. Bobby was a faithful husband. He really, really loved his wife. She's irreplaceable to him. So you come at it from that angle. Bobby is overwhelmed with emotion after her death. Overwhelmed with guilt because she was dead on the highway, and he was stuck in the traffic behind the accident beeping his horn, aggravated, a little bit mad at Karen because she was making him go to the store. I had to imagine that that kind of guilt really affects a guy like Bacala.

But also, Steve, I knew you really well by this time, and as a writer, you do try to play to people's strengths, and give them something they're really going to ace, rather than something they're going to rub up against. And you went all in on it. It was beautiful, what you did with Bobby's grief. With scenes like that you can go as far as you want with the emotion, because the stakes don't get any higher. And you rose to the occasion, my friend, without a doubt.

Steve: We shot this one, with Karen dying and Bobby going to the funeral, and another tough one, back-to-back. So there were a number of emotional scenes. I had a breakdown and cried in this one, at the coffin in front of all those people, and then another one at the kitchen table. I got myself into such a funk. Tim Van Patten, he directed it, he was very sympathetic, very understanding. That was good, as opposed to another director yelling and screaming. It was all quiet. Everybody was very respectful. You got the crew and what, fifty extras or a hundred extras. It's not an easy thing to do but they were all so supportive. I'll never forget that.

Michael: It's not easy to create that atmosphere.

Steve: No it's not. You know what else I think about? The poor girl who played Karen. Her name is Christine Pedi. She thought that she was in for a long haul, but she only wound up doing two episodes. She came to the read-through for this one but no one told her that she was getting killed and she hadn't seen the script.

Michael: Oh boy. That's rough.

Steve: The people that were day players didn't get a script. She didn't know. Kristin Bernstein, who was our assistant director back then, realized that no one had told her, she took Christine outside and said, "I just want to let you know that in this one you're going to be in a coffin."

Michael: Yes, that's a shocker. And the way you play in that scene, at the coffin, was really remarkable. I want to ask you: Bobby goes through all the stages of grief in this and the next few episodes—denial, at first; anger at Janice; the bargaining, like I should have been there, I wish I could trade my life for hers. Depression, the scenes where you're lying in bed, you can't get up, and then acceptance when Bobby finally eats the ziti, the last ziti Karen left in the freezer. Tell me how you got there.

Steve: I worked really, really hard at it. I like to think I became a better actor in Season Four. Season Two, my first season, I cringe at some of those scenes, I'll be honest. It's amazing they stuck with me, because you could see I was a green banana. I guess David must have seen something in me.

But also Aida. Aida was terrific. You know, Janice is such a big manipulator as a character. And Aida couldn't have been nicer. You know, if you're working against an actress who is not giving you what you need, or distracting you, you could prepare all you want and it won't matter. But she was great. She's in the moment every moment.

Michael: One other scene I really liked with you and her is when Bobby's getting angry at Janice at the food court. That's the first time we see Bobby really get pissed off. In that moment, I felt a little bit of Steve Schirripa coming through, the angry Steve coming through Bobby.

Steve: I'm an angry guy, Michael? Me?

Michael: It was good because Bobby is a gangster. He's not just this nice emotional sweetheart of a guy. When it comes down to it, if he's got to do shit, he'll do it. You see his anger. He's not going to take shit, he's going to call her out for being insensitive. It's a nice color to see from Bacala in that moment.

Steve: That's easy, Michael. Angry is no problem for Steve Schirripa. I could go zero to sixty in three seconds. Not a problem. That's one emotion I have no problem with. It's not like crying. I could get angry right now if I had to.

Michael: So you didn't have to listen to angry mood music?

Steve: No, no angry music, no angry movies. Angry is the easy one.

Michael: There is nothing surprising in that statement.

Steve: One more thing. As we go to black at the end of the episode, we hear Frankie Valli singing the line, from the song "Dawn," he sings, "Girl we can't change the places where we were born." That's one of those perfect lines that matches the episode, and everything you were writing about in the episode. Is that something you came up with?

Michael: I wish I could take credit for that. But no, Martin Bruestle, the producer who came up with lots of the music, he came up with that. David and Martin together. But you're right, it's so perfect, because the episode is all about how our identity is tied up with our heritage, where we came from. And the song speaks directly to that.

Steve: You wrote another episode for Season Four, "Everybody Hurts." This is the first time you wrote one that Steve Buscemi directed. Take me behind the scenes of that.

Michael: It was fun because Steve Buscemi, myself, and Johnny Ventimiglia were friends together before *The Sopranos*, so it was a collaboration with the three of us and there was a lot of hilarious stuff. Buscemi has a really good sense of humor. He's very funny as an actor and as a writer-director. Johnny V had a big story line in this one, where he's clearly attracted to his new hostess and winds up loaning money to her brother, and the whole thing goes south and he goes home and overdoses on alcohol and pills. So he has to play some very intense emotions, and he plays them incredibly well. But he also has a lot of funny moments, and he's an excellent comedic actor. He can really be funny and be physical and very specific physically.

Steve: Tell people what you mean by "specific."

Michael: He does little things, at little moments, that say a lot. For example, there's that moment in Season Four when he's putting black pepper on one of his customers' meals, and he does this one last little flourish and slaps the pepper grinder, firmly but gently and with a bit of swagger. Little things like that—he makes something out of nothing all the time, constantly. So really, the pleasure of writing this episode was doing a collaboration with the three of us.

Steve: One of the most famous lines from the show also comes in this season: "A don doesn't wear shorts." There's a story about how that came about.

Michael: Carmine says it to Tony. It disturbs Tony because it means that somebody's blabbing about him. It's pretty obvious it's Johnny Sack, who was invited to Tony's house. He's bitching to Carmine that Tony is wearing shorts.

But the story goes like this: Gandolfini got a call in the middle of the night on his cell phone, it was an unknown number. He answers the phone, "Hello," and the guy on the other line says, "Hello," and then nobody's talking. The guy doesn't identify himself. Guy finally says, "Listen, you're a great actor, we like what you're doing, but you got to know one thing: a don never wears shorts." And click, the guy hung up. That was it. Jim never knew who he was, he doesn't know how the person got his number. Jim told the writers and it made its way into the script.

Steve: And we never found out who called.

Michael: Never found out. But it's a true story.

Steve: Do you remember what Jim's reaction was?

Michael: I think Jim was disturbed by it. Who knows who made the call—but the invasion of privacy is definitely disturbing.

ANIMALS PLAY *a big part in* The Sopranos, *obviously, from the ducks in the first episode to the bear that haunts Carmela's backyard after Tony moves out. None is more prominent than Pie-O-My, the horse that steals Tony's heart. The writers Robin Green and Mitch Burgess tell us more.* —Michael

Robin: "Pie-O-My" was a great episode. That one, we had traveled the night before 9/11. We were in a plane from New York to L.A. My stockbroker at the time had horses out there at Santa Anita.

Mitch: We were going out for the Emmys anyway, which got canceled.

Steve: Because the Emmys were supposed to be a couple days after 9/11.

Robin: We're driving, it's dawn in Los Angeles, and we researched the horse part at the track. We saw the goats there!

Mitch: The horses needed friends. They couldn't just be racers, they needed buddies, so they have goats for them.

Robin: That scene where Tony's there and the goat comes, and the goat has devil eyes. It was so lucky, but we couldn't have done that if we hadn't gone there and seen the goat in the first place. That's part of the process. That's part of the rigor, isn't it? If you're going to write about horses, you better know what you're talking about.

Mitch: Pure luck.

LIKE WE *said earlier, Tony Sirico was missing in action for the first six episodes of this season, but when he came back, he came back with a bang. Right from the start, you could see that David and the writers were gonna focus more on him. But I think my favorite moment was the first scene when he comes back. —Steve*

Steve: We already talked about his first line, "Whattaya hear, what-taya say," the Cagney line. But there's another funny line in that first scene. Paulie hears the song "Nancy (with the Laughing Face)," the Frank Sinatra song. And he says, "That's my song."

Michael: That song was actually written by Phil Silvers, who played Sergeant Bilko. He wrote it for his daughter Nancy. Everybody thinks it was about Frank Sinatra's daughter. It's actually about Phil Silvers's daughter, who's also named Nancy.

Steve: Anyway, Paulie says, "That's my song." Bobby Baccalieri says, "Why the fuck is that his song?" It's never explained. I always wondered about that, even though it was my line. Do you know what that was about? Did the writers talk about that?

Michael: I think it's just to be funny, it's like at the end of Season Three when Uncle Junior sings that song "Core 'ngrato." David just used that to talk about sentimentality and pop music basically. He's using it in that scene to say, "Hey, I have a bunch of these gangsters crying at this song that really means nothing to them. They're not really connected to Italy, to Italian music. They're just connecting to sentimentality." I think that's what he's doing in this scene with Paulie and the Frank Sinatra song. It's like, it's his song but who knows why? He doesn't have kids, he's not married. Why is he so moved by a song about a young girl, a song about a "tomboy in lace"? Is it about a girl from the past? It's just funny that he's so touched by this specific song and nobody knows why.

Steve: And that sets up a scene later in this same episode. Tony hears the Chi-Lites song "Oh Girl," and he starts crying. You never see this happen, but Tony starts crying over a song.

THERE'S A *scene in Episode Seven that epitomizes James Gandolfini— he always had our backs. All of us. Peter Riegert, who played Assembly- man Zellman, told us when he discovered what we all knew. —Michael*

Michael: There's the episode where Tony finds out that Zellman is sleeping with his old girlfriend, and Tony gets drunk and decides to beat him up. What was it like playing that scene with Jim?

Peter: As you guys know, nobody except you regulars got the script in advance. So I show up at the read and find out what I was going to be doing. The scene was Tony beating the living shit out of me with a belt, but in the scene description, it's written that he pulls my un- derwear off. We did this whole table read and I was not happy about that.

Michael: Nobody would want to do that.

Steve: It was that he pulled your underwear down and spanked your ass?

Peter: It was. I was going to be naked. As far as I'm concerned, I would have liked a heads-up on that. David, who's always been nice, and I couldn't say more complimentary things for what he created, but that one really caught me off guard.

After the table read, I was just sitting there by myself. James came over, he said, "How are you with this?" I said, "I'm not happy about this, man. I don't think you have to humiliate an actor in order to humiliate a character, and I'm a little upset."

He called David over and he explained what I was feeling. David said, "Well, that's the way I wrote the scene." I said, "David, I think I can act the shit out of this part and I promise you, the audience will be horrified by what they see, but you don't have to humiliate me for me to get this across." David said, "Well, okay," and he left.

I didn't know whether I was going to get fired or not, but Jimmy said to me, "Whatever you decide to do, I promise you I will have your back." I said, "Okay." I knew that I was not going to take my underwear off, and Jimmy wasn't going to rip them off either. Then the director, John Patterson, very sweet guy. He tried to convince me, and I said, "John, I can't do it."

We went and got ready to do the scene. I went up to the prop guy and I said, "What kind of belt are you using?" He said, "You know, a Styrofoam belt." I took my shirt off. I said, "Would you hit me with it?" He said, "What?" I said, "I want to know how it feels, hit me with that belt." I couldn't feel anything. I kept saying, "Harder, harder," and I didn't feel a thing.

Now I knew how I could win this scene. I told Jimmy, "Listen, this belt is Styrofoam, I had the prop guy whack me with it, I didn't feel nothing. You can whale away on me." So you know what he did? He went to the prop guy and said, "Hit me with that belt." Because he wanted to prove to himself that I wasn't making this up.

Steve: So that's how you had him humiliate you, without taking your underwear off. Smart.

Peter: We finished around three thirty in the morning. I went out and there was a car going to take me back to my place. Jimmy was standing next to me. I just said, "Thanks for a great night." It was really terrific and he was very complimentary.

I said to him, "Do you know the word 'mensch'?" He said, "Yes, I think I know what it means." I said, "It means 'human.'" That's what it really means. It's as great a compliment as you can give. I said, "You are a mensch," because he really did something. The thing was, at that table read, I didn't realize that Jim recognized, on my face, that there was an actor in trouble. And he made it so it was my choice. And I know this was not the only time that he did so.

Steve: No, he was that guy, for sure.

One of the biggest plots of Season Four involves Furio and Carmela. There's an unspoken attraction between the two of them—nothing is ever said, they never even kiss, but you can see it in their faces every time they're in a scene together. I think Federico Castelluccio, who played Furio, did an amazing job in this season. What a lot of people don't know is that Federico is an incredible painter. And one famous painting that he did grew out of a scene in Season Four. —Steve

Steve: Federico, there's a scene later on in Season Four where you're talking to your uncle. Now, was that shot in Italy?

Federico: That was actually there, yeah. We went back. What was interesting about it is that they were looking for actors, they didn't want to keep going through the same Rolodex. Georgianne Walken used to call me from time to time and say, "Hey, Federico, you know anybody that might fit this role?" And so I went back into my old neighborhood in Paterson and there were some interesting characters there. I brought three people to the table, and the one that auditioned for my uncle Maurizio in Italy, his name was Nino DelDuca. Really interesting character. He was a poet, a Neapolitan poet. He met David Chase that day when we went to the audition. And he says, [*Italian accent*] "I have to tell you, I am not an actor." And David Chase goes, "But you are. You did a phenomenal job." And he got hired right on the spot. He worked with me on the Neapolitan as well, that scene in Italy where Furio confesses to him that he's in love with the boss's wife. And he goes, "Out of all the stupid things I did in my life, I never fucked the boss's wife." It's a great scene.

Steve: Now, he passed away, yes?

Federico: Unfortunately, but it was the highlight of his life. We went to Italy together and it was just a great thing. His family, his daughter and his son-in-law, couldn't stop talking about it. They were so happy to see their father on the show.

Steve: Now, we know you're a painter, a phenomenal painter, but one famous painting you did, of Tony and Carmela, that came out of this trip, right?

Federico: Yes. It's after Piero della Francesca's fifteenth-century painting of the Duke and Duchess of Urbino. After I went to Italy, I took a couple of weeks and went up north to visit the Uffizi Gallery in Florence. And, you know, there were certain paintings that I've seen in art history books my entire life. And there was this one painting that I saw that reminded me of James Gandolfini and Edie Falco. I'll tell you why. It's because they're two separate panels and there was a line that separates them, and they're looking at each other, but kind of looking past each other, a kind of a thousand-yard stare. And my character obviously sort of splits them up in the fourth season. And so to me, it was an interesting kind of take. It was just a fleeting thought—I said, I'd love to do a painting of James Gandolfini and Edie Falco and call it *The Duke and Duchess of North Caldwell*. I'm sure I never would have gotten to do the painting, but when I got on the plane to go back to Jersey, I get a call from *TV Guide* magazine and they wanted me to do a painting of the entire cast.

Steve: But you never did that one.

Federico: My style of realism, it would take a long time. And they only had a couple of weeks' lead time. So I said, "Listen, I've got an idea. Because since, you know, there's a lot of Shakespearean plot twists in the show, and it's a very classical show, what do you think of this painting of Jim and Edie? It would combine classical art and art history with pop culture." And they loved the idea. *TV Guide* came to my studio while I was painting it. And then they featured the painting in the magazine.

Steve: It turned out great, really. But you should have done one with Bobby and Janice. That would have been kind of nice. Right?

Michael: The Duke and Duchess of Bacala.

ANOTHER FASCINATING *character central to Season Four is Svetlana, the one-legged Russian played by Alla Kliouka. She first appears briefly at the end of Season Two but did such an outstanding job that her character was expanded in this season. —Michael*

Steve: There were scenes, I could swear, I thought you really had one leg.

Michael: When you were walking, did they ever CGI anything?

Alla: No. That was a special connection between me and the person who was behind the camera. What we did to help me move more comfortably, we had a girdle that they made a loop in in the back, and I put my leg into it behind me so I could relax and just move around. Then that was a kind of dance with the camera, so that the way the camera moved, he would turn the right way so they would not see my leg. We never did anything tricky. Only one time they used a double who had one leg, when Janice stole my leg. I hopped in the hallway and I cursed her in Russian, and the part when I hopped, that was the double.

Michael: What was your way into playing her? How did you approach that character specifically?

Alla: I have enough—what do you call it? Life experience?—to stay tough. Because growing up, both my parents were deaf, and to grow up in an environment when you speak in sign language, and when people look at you, you are handicapped, because they're treating you like you are not normal. It's no different—you have no leg, or you have no way to say anything—and they feel sorry for you, or they feel they don't want to talk to you.

But that actually gives me a lot of balls to go forward and just prove that I could do what I wanted to do. When I started school, nobody believed that I would be an actress. And I just said, "Fine, I'm just going to go on and try it."

Michael: It's also what Tony Soprano found attractive in Svetlana: someone who came from a lot of hardship, who was not self-pitying, and yet was still very motivated and driven. She found *him* to be self-pitying and too complicated. "You Americans lie on couches and bitch to your psychiatrists," you tell him.

Alla: My favorite line is when we're talking about the situation of how American people are always complaining about everything, and I said, "That's the whole purpose for people like me, to inspire people like you." I use that all the time.

AS STEVE *mentioned earlier, Joe Pantoliano, who we all know as Joey Pants, won the Primetime Emmy Award for outstanding supporting actor in a drama series for his work on Season Four. Technically he won it for two episodes—but it's his work on Episode Nine, "Whoever Did This," that I think won him the award. The central plotline—Tony suspecting that Ralphie set the fire that killed Pie-O-My—brings their strained relationship to a head and leads to some of the most electrifying scenes of the season. There's so much to unpack in this episode: the terrific acting, the incredibly high stakes, and—as usual when Robin Green and Mitch Burgess are writing—the palpable tension interlaced with some of the best humor of the season. —Michael*

Steve: I can't say enough about Joey Pants in this episode. First, the grief he shows in the beginning, after his son is messing around with a friend and gets hit in the chest with an arrow.

Michael: As we've talked about, Ralph has been set up as the incarnation of pure evil. After he kills Tracee, the stripper at the Bada Bing, there's a scene in Season Four where Silvio goes, "He killed that girl for—what was it again?" He doesn't even remember because there wasn't really much of a reason! Ralph is just a purely evil guy.

Steve: The most evil character. Of all these bad guys, Ralphie is top of the list. And he was set up as a sexual deviant, too. That was you, wasn't it? You wrote Ralphie getting rammed by Janice with a dildo? You put that in earlier, right? And it comes back in this episode?

Michael: Yes. When we first introduce it, it's a little weird, but it's not really disturbing yet, but it sets you up for what came later, when Valentina says he's really into pain, he wants a cheese grater on his balls or something like that. It progresses in that little bit of time. It's just another way to make the audience uncomfortable with Ralph. But now his kid gets really wounded, horribly wounded, and Ralph is probably thinking that this is the result of his own sins. The sins of the father coming to fruition on the son. He probably feels guilty.

Steve: He does. And he puts up a $20,000 scholarship in the name of Jackie Jr., who he had killed, of course. He puts up the scholarship, thinking the money cures all. It's what some people do with the Catholic Church. They could be sinners all their life, but when it comes down the home stretch, they make donations and they go to church and they think that's going to eradicate everything that they did the last fifty years.

Michael: To Joe Pantoliano's credit, this episode is incredible. The depth of emotion he shows in the early scenes.

Steve: You feel bad for Ralphie at the beginning.

Michael: Everyone can relate. God forbid your kid is hurt like that. Many of us have kids. You feel bad for Ralphie, absolutely. That's Joe as an actor. Not everyone could have pulled that off. Ralphie's a jokester, he's very outspoken. Very smart. Very evil. So to make him sympathetic, and make it believable, that's great acting.

Steve: It almost makes you feel bad for the motherfucker, as evil as he is.

Michael: Sympathy for the devil, literally!

Steve: So let's talk about that. In the middle of that scene with Father Phil, they start quoting lines from "Sympathy for the Devil," the Rolling Stones song. It's hysterical. Where did that come from?

Michael: David's a huge Rolling Stones fan. We have used some of their music on the show. As a matter of fact, there was one story line I wrote that we never made. We talked about it earlier: It was about a mentally ill homeless guy who was living behind the pork store and he was obsessed with Andrew Loog Oldham, who was a manager of the Stones for a while in the sixties.

Anyway, Ralph says to Father Phil, "Please allow me to introduce myself," and "Pleased to meet you," and Father Phil says, "Were you there when Jesus Christ had his moment of doubt and pain?" All lines from the song. But they're just saying them as dialogue. The characters aren't aware that they're quoting the song. So it's almost like David is breaking the fourth wall here. I love that he's doing that, almost allowing some very weird supernatural infusion. David was always willing to do that kind of thing because, you know, people might say, "You can't have him speaking lyrics of the Stones song. It doesn't make sense." It does make sense. It's just as crazy as anything else that's going on.

Steve: Your character, Christopher, didn't he then quote a Bruce Springsteen song?

Michael: Yes. He shows up late and he says, "The highway's jammed with broken heroes on a last chance power drive," from "Born to Run." But that is deliberate. Christopher's saying that deliberately.

Steve: It's especially funny because Stevie Van Zandt is sitting right there.

Michael: Absolutely. But that was different because Christopher is intentionally quoting the song. With Ralph and Father Phil, they're not aware of the Rolling Stones song. It adds this other level of how you perceive this character. It's like, "Oh, wow. Are they really saying that he's evil incarnate?"

Steve: But talk about evil incarnate, we gotta talk about the big fight scene. Again, Joey Pants is incredible in that. He puts up a hell of a fight with Tony. He's so much smaller than Tony, so to see him matching Tony blow for blow, you get that it's coming from this incredible fury. The fight goes on and on. Swinging the pots and pans, smashing Ralphie into the glasses, Ralphie blasts Tony in the face with bug spray, then Tony chokes him with his bare hands—it's endless.

Michael: Yes, it's a great fight, man. You believe that he's dangerous, you believe that he's completely ruthless and unhinged. His performance is exceptional. It also shows the warped values these guys have—Tony is more upset about Ralphie killing the horse than he was about killing the stripper.

Steve: Kind of like how the fans were more upset about you killing the dog than all the people Christopher whacked.

Michael: Good point.

Steve: Now, you have a lot of really good scenes in this episode too.

Michael: Robin and Mitch wrote "Whoever Did This." They wrote terrific stuff for Tony and Christopher. After the murder, in Ralph's house, he needs to get rid of the body, so he calls Christopher, who's high on heroin. I really, really liked that episode.

Steve: That's the thing with Robin and Mitch. They already have this fantastic scene, they have to get rid of the body, but then they add that Christopher is stoned, so it takes it to a whole other level.

Michael: I loved playing this scene. They're in the house, they're dealing with the body and they have to wait for nightfall. It's a long, weird stretch of time with these two guys doing something really sinister, really crazy, and really dangerous. And the fact that Christopher shows up high and Tony is forced to deal with it because he desperately needs Christopher's help, well that's just icing on the cake. It's the kind of twist and spin on something that's uniquely *Sopranos*.

Steve: And all the little details too. We always talk about it. They're in the middle of this big thing, and then Tony's eating peanut butter from the jar with a knife. And then the surprise when Ralphie's wig comes off. It's all these little nuances that make the show full and layered and what it is. Somebody else, it would have been: Tony goes in, he kills Ralph. There would have been nobody taking the wig off. You wouldn't have been sitting there so long.

Michael: I find those scenes really fun to play, because it immediately takes you away from just playing the scene of "All right, I'm there, I got to cut up the body." I got this big obstacle because I'm really high, and I don't want my boss to know that I'm high and I have to deal with this body, so now instead of one thing, it's three things that you're playing as an actor. You go back and forth between focusing your attention on those different things.

WE ASKED *Robin and Mitch about writing that episode. They told us some things that we didn't know—and revealed that there's something about it even* they *don't know. —Michael*

Robin: That scene where we kill Ralphie was a big scene for us because I don't think we'd ever really killed anybody that way. You couldn't just write, "He throttles him." We had to actually act it out. We wrote in this office downstairs in our apartment. We choreographed it.

Mitch: It was choreographed like a dance routine, so the director knew how to do it.

Robin: I put my hands around his neck to choke him, and we did all that stuff.

Mitch: That was completely choreographed.

Steve: You didn't just write, "They fight, Tony kills him," you write out exactly how it happens?

Mitch: We wrote it that way, yes. But we didn't write that Tony burned his hand at the end of the scene. It was a practical stove, and he put his hand down on it while it was lit.

Robin: "Practical" meaning it was a real stove. Mitch was on the scene for that one. When Jim puts his hand on the stove, somebody hadn't turned it off, so his hand really was burned. Also David had always wanted to use bug killer in a fight scene, so that became part of the scene, the bug killer sprayed into Tony's face. David, he had that in his pocket, his wish list of scenes, for a long time.

Mitch: I was on set on that show, and I came back after lunch or something. Tim Van Patten, who was directing, said to me, "Joey Pants wants to play it like he didn't kill the horse. You know what I mean?" Tim was worried about it. But you could just let him play it, because he's such a great actor. That's where Joey Pants was coming from, that he didn't do it. It was interesting. His take.

Robin: I think even the viewer gets the feeling it's possible he didn't do it. At that point, it doesn't matter.

Steve: That's how you wrote it, or is this happening after the script is written?

Mitch: No, Joey Pants brought that.

Robin: We didn't know the answer.

Michael: When you wrote it, you left it vague enough you could have played it either way.

Robin: This show is from Tony's point of view, pretty much. So we didn't have to decide about that. He probably did, but it's possible he didn't. [*laughs*]

Michael: Well we know David loves it when things aren't tied up in a nice little bow, so leaving that question open is kind of the perfect way to end it.

LIKE I *said earlier, I thought Michael did an amazing job playing Christopher being totally stoned, which, of course, Michael is always totally*

sober when he plays those scenes. But there is one scene—and he knows
I'm gonna ask about this—that he played totally shit-faced. —Steve

Steve: Tell us about the end of the episode, when you had to throw
Ralphie's body off the cliff.

Michael: We were shooting it in some state park in New Jersey. It
was a Friday night shoot. We got there before the sun went down.
We were going to shoot all night.

We rehearsed the scene, which was basically Jim and I carrying whatever we had, which was supposed to be Ralph's body,
wrapped up in a carpet. Jim and I carry the body from the car, go
to the edge of this cliff, and toss the body way down into the river
at the bottom. They were going to have the one camera down in
a boat on this little river looking up at us. We're going to have a
couple of cameras up on the cliff with us, we're going to light up
the whole forest, a lot of wide shots, a lot of production value. We
rehearsed, everything was good, and they said, "This is going to
take a long time to set up. We got to put lights everywhere, we're
going to put the camera in the boat, we got to wait for the sun to
go down." Jim and I go back to his trailer. We knew we had a long
time, and we were just relaxing. Then he said, "You want a drink?"
I said, "Sure, why not?"

Mitchell Burgess, who wrote that episode, joined us in the trailer
and we started drinking. Jim had a bottle of Wild Turkey that was
not open, not cracked. Well, when they finally set it up and come
get us to shoot, that bottle of Wild Turkey was empty. Jim and I
stumbled out of the trailer, reeking of bourbon, weaving and bob-
bing. They were going, "Whoa, we can't let these guys get to the
edge of the cliff because there might not be a Season Five." We were
that drunk.

They were debating what to do, and before long they show up

with these chains. They shackled them to our ankles, and tied the chains to trees, and covered the chains up with leaves so we could walk to the edge of the cliff and not fall off as we throw the body. And that's exactly what we did. We got right up to the edge, but we were chained to these trees so we wouldn't drunkenly fall to our demise in the river.

Steve: What was it like trying to do that scene drunk?

Michael: I don't really remember very much.

Steve: I'll bet.

Michael: The thing was, we would never drink if you had to drive in a scene or you had to do any fight choreography where someone else is relying on you to have physical control so you're not going to hurt them or anything. But the scene on the cliff, we didn't even have any dialogue, we just walk out, we throw the thing. We weren't really that concerned. We both felt comfortable with it. The producers were not so comfortable though.

ONE OF *my favorite scenes to play, in the entire series, came in Episode Ten of this season: the intervention. There is so much at stake, it is such a serious moment, and then it devolves into such slapstick—it's an incredibly well-constructed moment. And one of the many things I loved about it was that so many of us got to do it together. —Michael*

Michael: The intervention scene is just so ridiculous. The therapist is played by Elias Koteas, who did a play at Studio Dante, the theater that my wife, Victoria, and I had. He's a friend of ours, a really good guy and a great actor. When Christopher sees him, he says, "Yes, I know you. You're the guy who broke into Stew Leonard's that time. You stole all those pork loins." And he's totally deadpan, and goes, "Yeah, but that's not why I'm here today." I had to play Christopher being stunned and trying to figure out what's going on, but I was cracking up inside.

Steve: Paulie is great too. The therapist says, "My name is Dominic. I'm an addict and alcoholic." And Paulie goes, "And a scumbag." [*laughs*] I've seen Tony Sirico say that before in real life.

Sometimes I'm so sorry I don't get to play a scene. This is one of them. That scene is so serious and so funny. Tell us more about it.

Michael: It was hilarious to have all of those characters and actors there for something that's very intimate. Often when it was all of us like that, it would be a funeral, a wedding, a party, or some event at the house. Jim, Edie, Drea, Tony, Stevie, they were all there. Marianne Leone Cooper, who plays my mother.

Steve: You think it's gonna be serious, but then it gets crazy. Christopher calls his mother a fucking whore. He starts calling everybody out on their shit.

Michael: Dominic, the therapist, says, "We're supposed to be nonjudgmental," which is the last thing these guys can be, right? What's *The Sopranos* if not everybody judging everybody else? It's pretty fucking funny. We broke up laughing a lot during that scene.

Steve: A lot of funny scenes in this season. Then there's the thing when Paulie kills the old lady. He's stealing the money, she catches him.

Michael: David Chase has told the story that Tony didn't want to kill the old lady.

Steve: Yes, Tony was very worried about this. He thought the audience would hate him killing an old woman. The way it played out, it was actually a funny scene. He's looking for the money under the bed, and she says, "You were always a bad kid." Like he's eight years old. She's screaming. I know Tony was very worried that the audience would turn on him there.

Michael: This is actually one of those rare times that David compromised a little bit.

Steve: Tony went to David and said he didn't want to kill her. They're going to hate Paulie. In the script, he strangles her. But Tony said, at least let me kill her with the pillow. Smothering her I guess is a little softer than strangling her.

BUT FROM *the ridiculous to the sublime: the last episode of the season, "Whitecaps," is, for me, the greatest hour of* The Sopranos, *and perhaps the greatest hour of television ever. The arc of this episode—from the twilight-bathed romantic shots of Tony and Carmela by the sea in the beginning, to the furious battle between them at the end, this episode plays as a master class in how to create dramatic television. We've talked about "Pine Barrens" as a fan favorite; I think it's hilarious, and it's very entertaining. But in this episode, the writing and the acting just hit another level completely. So honest and real. Like looking into the window of someone's home and watching a relationship disintegrate. —Michael*

Michael: The two of them, Jim and Edie, are just incredible. It's the longest of all the episodes; seventy-five minutes, almost like a little movie. It's set up so well: what's been going on between the two of them, his affairs, she just reaches her breaking point with all that. She's turned a blind eye, she's dealt with it, and finally, she's just ready to explode.

Steve: But it all starts out so nice, they're gonna buy this vacation house by the shore, it's all so happy.

Michael: That's one of the brilliant things about this episode: it begins with the two of them so loving, so you see how strong the relationship has been. If it's just breaking up a rotten marriage it wouldn't be so painful, but it's almost as though they want you to see how much love there was there, so it's more painful when it falls apart.

Steve: And then the big scene when he comes home. Carmela got the call from Irina, she's drunk and she tells Carmela she's sleeping with him, and says he also had sex with Svetlana. And he comes home and his things are flying out the window. When she confronts him, he has no idea what's coming. He denies it and then he's kind of glib about it. She is hyperventilating, sobbing. Gasping for air. This is as real as it gets. This is an acting lesson going on, and they just let her go. They weren't stopping and going here. This was just an incredible, real performance. And it just went on and on.

Michael: It's all the energy that's built up for four seasons, all about to be unleashed. And it's all coming after she fell in love with Furio, coming off of the emotion of that loss, then just being battered by Irina calling the house and revealing that Tony had an affair with her cousin. Carmela is just done. And Edie Falco communicates all of it with absolute perfection.

Steve: But then Tony finally explodes. He tells her, "You knew the deal. You knew my father, you knew my past, you knew Dickie Moltisanti," who was Christopher's father. "You knew what you were getting yourself into." And then that moment that he punches the wall. That's a very real moment. Do you think this is the best scene Edie and Jim did?

Michael: I think it's their best work.

Steve: The writing is incredible as well.

Michael: And yet, as serious as this episode is, it ends on a funny moment.

Steve: That's right. A brilliant moment. The homeowner, the lawyer who won't give Tony the money back for his beach house. And Tony's guys are harassing him, they have the *Stugots* there, and they're blaring the music from the speakers. It's Dean Martin, singing "I Love Paris." Only it's "I Love Vegas."

Michael: A really funny song. Steve, you must love that song.

Steve: Love it.

Michael: The lyrics, if you listen to the whole thing, are terrific: "I love Vegas, like the army loves its manuals. I love Vegas, like Sinatra loves Jack Daniel's."

Steve: The whole scene is just hysterical. But that's what I loved. Doing something so funny at the end of such a serious episode. That's very David Chase, isn't it?

Michael: That's the beauty of the show.

AS I *mentioned, as good as the acting was in this episode, Steve and I both thought the writing was just spectacular. We went back one more time to Robin Green and Mitch Burgess to unlock the process behind this astounding episode. —Michael*

Michael: Talk to us about the climactic scene between Tony and Carmela, the huge fight scene. How did that come about?

Mitch: That script took a while to do. It didn't come out right. The scene you saw, took a long time to get that. It's pretty intense.

Michael: What was the hardest part about it? Did you start smaller and then keep building and building?

Mitch: I thought we should escalate that, when he puts his hand through the wall. Our biggest contribution was the violence of it.

Robin: She was terrified that he was going to hit her.

Mitch: I said, "I think Tony should put his hand through it," because it is really violent when he does it.

Robin: There's another part of it later up in the bedroom, where he slammed Edie against the jamb of the door, and actually hurt her even though she had padding on.

Michael: Early in the scene Tony says: "You said I'm going to hell, nice thing to say to somebody heading into an MRI," recalling a moment from the first season, the big fight they have when he's getting an MRI and they suddenly started confronting each other about all sorts of stuff, and she says, "What's different between you and me is, you're going to hell when you die." That was a powerful scene and it's brilliant that you call back to it here.

Tony walks away after he says that and she feels bad about it, and she starts the scene apologetically, so you think that there's going to be some kind of reconciliation, and then you built it. You're saying the idea was not only to build it, but then to go one more layer and have it become that violent at the end?

Robin: Yes. Like with the Furio stuff when she says, "And he listens to me." Then when Tony finds out that they didn't even have sex, and he starts laughing at her, she really gives it back to him.

Mitch: It's a tough scene to watch.

Michael: We talked about the ending, that very funny scene where they're torturing Sapinsly, the lawyer who is selling the house to Tony, by playing the loud music off the boat. The Dean Martin music. It's such an unusual choice, such an offbeat choice for such an intense show. Whose idea is that and how does that beat happen? Most TV shows that are that intense would end on a quiet or serious moment, not something that funny.

Robin: There was none of that. David never went for the big emotional moment, no hugging, no "Are you okay?" It just reminded us so much of the necessities of network TV, where you have to be very heavy-handed and make a point. Really, there was an avoidance of that. So it evolved very naturally. That would be David. He edited all the shows. He had the final edit.

Steve: Let me ask you one more thing about that show. I think I heard you tell a story about shooting one long scene. John Patterson was the director. He was a pleasure to work with.

Robin: There was a long scene at the end with Tony and Mr. Sapinsly. It was very late at night, we have been filming all week. It's three in the morning on a Friday night. This is the final shot.

Mitch: It had been a long week.

Robin: A long week, and you're away from home, it's Friday night. We were ready to go home, and Jim was having a hard time getting through the speech. He would flub it, and then we would have to reset, relight, touch up the makeup. All that you go through with everything.

Mitch: The crew was exhausted by this part of the evening.

Robin: Now we're on take three. Another hour has gone by, and Jim nails it. John Patterson yells out, "Bingo"—and ruins the scene.

Michael: And you can't just cut around it.

Robin: No you can't, it's not professional, it would be cheating.

Michael: Whenever you cut around something like that it's obvious, it kinda ruins the scene. The edit isn't being made for the sake of the scene, it's like a Band-Aid.

Robin: Right. So he ruined it for Jim. Jim comes over, goes to the back of John Patterson's chair, takes John's head in his big hands and bends over and gives him this big kiss on the top of the head [*laughs*]. It was so wonderfully out of control and outrageous and joyous.

AT THE *end of Season Four, Jim Gandolfini got into a big contract dispute with HBO. It got pretty ugly. But we stood with Jim. Nobody went to the press, nobody said a bad word about anybody. At the end of it, he made out okay, but here's what you need to know. This wasn't an easy moment for any of us—there was another yearlong hiatus after this season, and none of us would have a paycheck coming in. But here's what Jim did. He called all the series regulars into his trailer—there were sixteen of us—and gave us each a check for $33,333. He said, "Thanks for sticking by me." He was incredibly generous. And not just then. Years later, we found out all sorts of things he did behind the scenes. He paid off people's doctor bills. He paid off mortgages. Often anonymously. None of us knew anything about it.*

Gestures like that really meant a lot to us. It wasn't about how much money or anything like that—it was what it symbolized. It told us that Jim wanted us to know that he cared. He was acknowledging our hard work and our contributions. He was generous with his money, it's true— but more important, he was generous in his praise. When I think back on it, that's what meant the most to me. —Steve

NINE

Bada Bing Back Room
with Steve Schirripa

I KNOW SOMETHING NOT TOO MANY people know about Steve. Behind that gruff exterior, he's—well, he's pretty gruff. And behind that, he's still pretty gruff. But behind that, he's one of the kindest guys I know.

And one of the most interesting. He and I both grew up in the world of New York Italians, but we could not have taken more different paths to wind up in this place together. I've loved hearing his stories over the years, and I've really been looking forward to getting him to share those stories here. —Michael

Michael: You grew up in Bensonhurst, right?

Steve: Yes.

Michael: Was there a visible presence of the mob when you grew up?

Steve: Absolutely. In the sixties and the seventies, Bensonhurst was a huge mob enclave. Huge! That Bath Avenue gang. I grew up right off of Bath Avenue. They were everywhere. You didn't necessarily know they were wiseguys, especially when you were younger.

Michael: No, they didn't wear badges.

Steve: No, but there would be a guy on my little league team whose uncle was a wiseguy, and another kid's dad, and this kid Jimmy's uncle, and then you open up the paper, you go, "Holy shit. I had no idea Jimmy's uncle murdered three people." Some of them knew my father. I lived around the corner from my grandmother, where my father grew up. The butcher downstairs, he was mobbed up—just a lot of people. My neighbor across the street did twenty-five years for killing somebody and I knew them. Patty Boxcars, he was one of the local mobsters.

Michael: Patty Boxcars. Was that referring to the railroad or to the dice?

Steve: The dice. Patty Boxcars, his son, Petey. There were all these guys; you knew them, you respected them, and as long as you stay out of their way, nobody is bothering you. Guys that I grew up with, some of them became pharmacists, doctors, cops, plumbers, and some of them became mob guys. One guy did twenty-five years, guys that I played ball with every day. Why? Why does one guy go right, one guy goes left? I don't know. You see the lifestyle, they got money, cars, the Cadillac.

Michael: Power, respect, fear.

Steve: That's for sure. But it is not an easy gig. Nowadays, they usually wind up dead or in jail. I also think that's why so many guys have become informants. Mikey Scars, you know that name, he was a big informer, he wound up in witness protection. I went to elementary school with him. I played softball with him up until I was nineteen years old. He was a guy from the neighborhood, a good guy.

Look, everybody in the neighborhood had a piece of the action one way or another. I used to sell stuff. Did you use to sell hot stuff when you were younger?

Michael: No, but my grandfather used to do it a lot. The thing when they had Members Only jackets. All of a sudden, all the guys in the family had them. The same color, the same thing.

Steve: I sold little purses, pen and pencil sets. I would get them for two dollars, sell them for four dollars, five dollars. A guy would front me. I didn't steal the stuff, but there was always stuff around. Knockoff perfumes, leisure suits. Cushioned toilet seats, that was a big one. What did I make? Twenty-five dollars, fifty dollars? Whatever. That was a lot of money. People love the idea that they're buying something hot.

Michael: So you knew all these mob guys, you sold some stuff for them, but your father was not a wiseguy.

Steve: No, he was a small-time wannabe wiseguy. And he was a bookmaker. He went away a couple of times.

Michael: What was your relationship with him? When you were a kid, was he around a lot?

Steve: No, he was in and out. He left my mother with five kids and we were on welfare. The power was getting shut off, I had holes in my shoes.

Michael: I'm sorry to hear that. There's something else I want to ask you about your childhood. A lot of *Sopranos* story lines involve Tony's goomar, the girlfriends on the side. From what I understand, you have some insight into the world of goomars, not personally but growing up.

Steve: Absolutely. My father had a goomar, and he had two kids with the goomar. They're out there somewhere with the same last name as me.

Michael: That's heavy.

Steve: Yes, it's heavy. He had a goomar for, I guess, forever.

Michael: You're half Jewish. What's your mother's maiden name?

Steve: Lorraine Bernstein.

Michael: So you could have been Steve Bernstein just as easily? Did you have a bar mitzvah and all that stuff?

Steve: No, I was raised Catholic, but I had a whole Jewish side of the family, so I'm very in tune with that whole world. I had all kinds of uncles and aunts.

My mom didn't really work. She wasn't well. It was terrible, the way we lived—the food stamps and the government-cheese shit, waiting in line for all that stuff.

Michael: You were a big basketball player. Is that what you went to college to do? To play basketball?

Steve: I played for a year at John Jay, I was a criminal justice major. I was thinking about going that route maybe. But I really didn't know. Then I transferred to Brooklyn College. I was a phys ed major.

Michael: What was the thing you told me, that you almost went to Israel to play?

Steve: After college, I tried out for an Israeli team. I was eligible because my mother was Jewish. I had a tryout in Long Island and I made the team. But they wanted me to work on the kibbutz, and that didn't sound so hot.

Michael: That was a deal-breaker, the kibbutz?

Steve: Yes, I didn't want to work on a kibbutz. What am I going to do? Fucking dig up turnips?

Michael: Pick avocados.

Steve: I don't know what they do in a kibbutz, but it didn't sound that great.

Michael: What did you do?

Steve: I did promise my mother that I would graduate and I wanted the degree for her. I had gone to Vegas the summer before, I worked, met some people, and as soon as I graduated school, I was gone. I hopped in my car and drove to Vegas.

Michael: Did you go to Vegas to work in the casinos?

Steve: No, I never wanted to be in the casino business. I worked at a pizza place. But once I got into Paul Anka's club as a bouncer, I said, "I like that maître d' thing. You wear the tux. You're the guy. People are asking you for favors." I got off on that. I could do favors for people. I'm okay with that. I wound up getting that eventually.

Michael: So how did you go from being maître d', bouncer, to entertainment director at the Riviera Hotel running the Comedy Club? Didn't you create the Riviera Comedy Club?

Steve: I got the job on a fluke. A guy that I was friendly with, Israeli guy named Dov Odents, was the vice president of the Riviera. There was a job opening, he came and found me. Just one of those people you meet along the way that changes your life, right? They hired me to start their comedy club. There was a stack of chairs and there was an odd-shaped room, and they said, "Hey, make us a show room." We started this comedy club and for about six months it was doing nothing. And then suddenly it just took off and the thing started to make some money and I was the boss.

Then they gave me two more show rooms. Now I had fifty-four employees under me, I'm running the three rooms, I'm making $200, $300, $400 a night every night. I worked six days a week for nine years. I didn't want to take a day off. I had the money stacked up.

Michael: Literally?

Steve: Seriously, I had the money stacked up in a safe, in my garage. Then I built this huge house.

Michael: Who were your favorite comics as people to work with that you liked? I won't ask who you hate most because there's probably a long list.

Steve: I got to know a lot of the guys. My favorite comic of all was Rodney Dangerfield.

Michael: He was one of the greats.

Steve: He was opening a comedy club and I was helping him, so we became friends. And I took Laura, before we were married, to go see him at the MGM. We went backstage after the show, and he's in his bathrobe. And he had these giant balls. My wife-to-be was sitting across from him. The balls hung low on Rodney Dangerfield.

Michael: What? He had his robe open?

Steve: Open. He didn't give a shit. His balls were hanging down. He had no underwear on. Swear to God. His balls were swinging like a grandfather clock.

Michael: Somehow that doesn't surprise me about Rodney.

Steve: Nothing should ever surprise you about Rodney. But really, what a great guy.

Michael: You're getting pretty successful by this time. You became the entertainment director of the whole Riviera Hotel.

Steve: I was booking big acts in the big room, the Beach Boys, Dion, the Osmond Brothers, oldies shows. Big comedians upstairs, a thousand-seat room, Drew Carey, Ray Romano, Kevin James, George

Lopez, Denis Leary, David Spade, Rob Schneider. We also had Rich Little, David Brenner.

Then I started booking the lounge. We had three acts every day, it was around a $2 million budget. I had jazz on Monday nights, that was a huge hit. I booked a lot of jazz acts, Chick Corea, Maynard Ferguson, Michael Franks, John Pizzarelli. We had a lot going on.

Michael: There has to be one moment, one exact moment, when you went from putting other people on the stage to going up there yourself and deciding that's what you wanted to do. Do you remember when that happened?

Steve: I do. There was a comic, Bruce Baum, who put me in one of his sketches. I did that, and got the bug right there.

Michael: That was your first acting gig? With Bruce Baum, doing a sketch?

Steve: It was for a thing called *The Sunday Comics* on Fox. I played a guy with a tuxedo on the golf course.

Michael: On TV?

Steve: Early nineties, yes. I flew out there to L.A. on the weekend and we shot it. I had never read a script before. I knew nothing about nothing. But I got a little rush. Then they had a casting person at Fox that was doing these shows, who hired me for a couple more of them. They were little five-minute sketches, film pieces. Then a couple more for Bruce Baum. I did another one, I had a fight with a duck. Funny. Quite a bit of people saw them when they first aired and that got me started.

Michael: How long was it between that and *Casino*?

Steve: A few years. I sat in on the production meetings for *Casino* because they shot it there in the Riviera. I got to read for the casting director somehow, Ellen Lewis, who's one of the biggest casting directors. She does all of Scorsese's movies. She liked what she saw and sent me to meet Scorsese and De Niro.

Michael: What was that like? Were you nervous?

Steve: I wasn't nervous. They were nice. De Niro did most of the talking. He was respectful and polite. They had me read for the role of the maître d', and I didn't do great. I could have done better. They gave that role to someone else, and then they gave me a role in that scene with Pesci. I was a glorified extra. Frank Vincent was in the scene. Frank helped me get my SAG card. I didn't do anything for a while, and then Ray Favero, who was a casting director in Vegas who I am indebted to for my life, he was a huge help. If something came into Vegas, he would have me audition.

I did *Fear and Loathing in Las Vegas*. He brought me in for *Chicago Hope*. He also helped me when I finally got the *Sopranos* audition, he came up to my office. I would lock the door and we would go over the scene over and over and over.

Michael: You talked about how when you came onto *The Sopranos*, at first you were just hired for an episode. When did you learn you were coming back?

Steve: I was hired for one episode, but I wound up doing six episodes in Season Two. On the last day of shooting that season, I ran into David Chase on the street outside of Silvercup. I'm going this way, he's going that way, I stick out my hand, I say, "Mr. Chase, Hi. My name's Steve Schirripa. I play Bobby Baccalieri." He goes, "I know who you are." I said, "I just wanted to thank you for having me," and he says, "You did great. We'll have you back. We'll see Bobby again." Which made me feel great.

Michael: You knew mob guys growing up. When you were on *The Sopranos*, did any of them approach you? Anybody come up to you and offer you advice?

Steve: Yeah, this one time, I'm living on Mulberry Street. This is Season Three. There's still wiseguys left in the neighborhood. I'm bringing my laundry down on a Monday morning, and there's one of the neighborhood guys. He goes, "Steve. Hey, buddy, how are you doing?" I said, "How are you doing, pal?" He said, "You know I love the show, right? But anyone who has ever whacked anyone knows that's not how you do it."

I went, "Okay, listen, I got to get going. I'll be talking to you." Here I am with my dirty dry-cleaning and he's telling me that you don't whack a guy that way.

Michael: You know that happened to me one time, in Rao's. I was with Tony Sirico and Vinny Pastore early on after Season One. We were together at a table, and a guy came over, who was a captain in one of the Five Families. He knew Tony, and he said, "I can show you the real way, how to garrote a guy." That piano-wire thing. He could show me the real way how that's done.

Steve: Those things did happen.

Michael: After *The Sopranos* you got a lot of work. But it was tricky, wasn't it?

Steve: Let's be honest. Before *The Sopranos*, I had no career. I'm a big overweight guy, my voice is not exactly beautiful. Without *The Sopranos* I would not be here talking to you, but when *The Sopranos* ended, casting people want to put you in a box. You have a vowel at the end of your name and when there's a movie that they call every Italian-American in the country for, that's what you get called for.

Michael: They want to stereotype you.

Steve: Let's not kid ourselves, I'm not going to play an English professor. But certainly, people want to typecast you. Fortunately, I managed to get away from that. I was very lucky to be on a show, *Secret Life of the American Teenager,* where I just play the suburban dad, Leo Boykewich, and that was for five years, 110 episodes. Now, on *Blue Bloods,* yes, I play an Italian-American, but I play a detective. I got away from that mob thing and that was a conscious effort to do that. Not that I wouldn't do it again if it was something great.

Michael: But you've been in a lot of excellent movies and TV shows. What did you try out for that you didn't get?

Steve: Once I got onto *Sopranos,* Ellen Lewis, who cast me for *Casino,* was casting *Gigli.*

Michael: *Gigli.* She cast a lot of big names. Ben Affleck and Jennifer Lopez wind up starring in that.

Steve: I say to myself, I've been on *The Sopranos* a couple of years, I know what I'm doing. I was excited to show her what I learned, because when I auditioned for her earlier, I was a green banana. Now, I'm living in Little Italy and it's a humid day in June. I say, "Fuck it, I'm too early. I won't take a cab, I'll hop on the train."

I'm wearing a gray shirt, I'm sweating like a farm animal. I walk down the subway and it's hot as hell. I get off the train, it's still five blocks away. By the time I get to her office, I am soaked. Embarrassingly soaked. Like, Albert Brooks in the movie *Broadcast News.* I go to the bathroom, I'm trying to dry off with towels, it is a disaster. Then I go on tape. Of course, it's not any good. The worst audition in the history of auditions. Ellen could not have been more polite about it, of course. Didn't say a word about how bad I screwed up. But I hope they burned that tape.

Michael: *Gigli* is known as one of the worst movies ever made.

Steve: Well I didn't get the part in the worst movie ever made.

Michael: You were in the very last *Columbo*, right?

Steve: Yeah, just by chance, the very last scene of the very last *Columbo*.

Michael: And in the middle of all this you started writing the "Goomba" books. We talked about *The Goomba's Guide to Life*, and then there was *The Goomba's Book of Love*.

Steve: And then *The Goomba Diet*. The promo line they used was, "Is the air freshener in your car a slice of provolone?"

Michael: *The Goomba Diet*. Were there a few that you proposed and got rejected, like *The Goomba's Guide to S & M Sex*, that kind of thing?

Steve: No. Never got that one.

Michael: But then you got into fiction. *Nicky Deuce*. About a teenage kid who goes to Brooklyn to live with his uncle and starts getting mixed up with the mob. Where did you come up with the idea for that?

Steve: I literally had a dream about this. I dreamt the premise for this book.

Michael: It was a dream?

Steve: I swear. I dreamt about this and the next morning I called my publisher. She set me up with Beverly Horowitz at Random House, who I love to death. I told her my idea and she had some suggestions and basically I sold it in the room. That was great. It got made into a movie but it took me seven years to make that. We went through nine scripts. That was one of the best things I accomplished, getting that movie made.

Michael: And the final book was *Big Daddy's Rules*. That's about raising teenagers. You have two wonderful girls.

Steve: The loves of my life. My wife and my daughters.

Michael: I remember talking to you about *Big Daddy's Rules*. You said, "On TV, it's always like, the father's the dummy. Homer Simpson, *Married with Children*, the wife is always the smart one and the father's the dummy." You wanted to really get rid of that stereotype, because fathers are not always dummies.

Steve: That's what the book was. It was a comedic look at raising kids. My two daughters, knock on wood, me and my wife raised two terrific kids. I don't think everything's so complicated. Sometimes it is what it is. I don't like when you see the kids disrespect the parents. That doesn't fly with me.

Michael: Meadow and A. J. are very disrespectful to their parents.

Steve: They're both very rude, spoiled, entitled kids. Both of the Soprano kids, very much so. Meadow, in seasons later on, she grows up to be a respectful woman, but terrible the way she treats her mother. I won't put up with that for ten seconds. That kind of shit just pisses me off.

Michael: As long as we're going through the list Things That Piss Off Steve Schirripa, we might as well talk about the T-shirts.

Steve: So one day I get this *Talking Sopranos* shirt in the mail, and what does it say? "*Talking Sopranos* with Michael Imperioli and Steve Schirripa."

Michael: All right. Those are our names.

Steve: I did not approve this shirt, Michael.

Michael: What's the problem?

Jim with his wife, Deborah, at a beach party at Breezy Point in 2007, a few weeks after the finale aired. Somehow word leaked out about the party, and hundreds of people showed up. (And by the way—yes, Tony Sirico is the kind of guy who shows up to a beach party in a suit jacket. They broke the mold when they made Tony.) —Steve
Courtesy of Steve Schirripa

My first draft of my second Sopranos script, "The Telltale Moozadell." I did a lot of my writing downstairs at our bar, Ciel Rouge, in the early hours of the morning (and I still do my first drafts longhand).
—Michael
Courtesy of Michael Imperioli

(15) INT. PIZZERIA

Cop enters and puts exhibit A (pizza remnants and box) on the counter. Guiseppe an older Italian man speaks with an accent, may be a bit senile, is immediately warned off the intimidating look of the cop.

COP
Did you make this pizza?

Who? Guiseppe

COP
Did you make this pizza? This is your store on the box (indicates box)

Johnny V., Stevie, and me. —Michael
Courtesy of Steve Schirripa

At the Yankees party after the ticker-tape parade down the Canyon of Heroes, celebrating their 2000 World Series win. That's Robin Green second from left; Tony, Jamie-Lynn, and Lorraine are on the right. Members of the *Sopranos* cast were invited to ride in their own floats in the parade. My car was right in front of Derek Jeter's; Stevie Van Zandt and Tony Sirico were in the car behind. It's an honor we'll never forget. —Michael

Courtesy of Michael Imperioli

With Dominic. A lot of my scenes on the show were with him; just as Bobby was protective of Uncle Junior, that's how I felt about Dominic. He is really like a beloved uncle to me. —Steve
Courtesy of Steve Schirripa

With Burt Young, who I think is one of the most underrated actors ever. Burt played Bobby's father in one episode, "Another Toothpick." When Bobby Senior died at the end of the episode, it was the first time I had to cry on camera. —Steve
Courtesy of Steve Schirripa

Terry Winter and his wife, Rachel. After writing or co-writing twenty-five episodes of *The Sopranos,* he went on to create *Boardwalk Empire* and wrote the screenplay for Martin Scorsese's *The Wolf of Wall Street,* for which he was nominated for an Academy Award. Rachel Winter was nominated for an Academy Award for Best Picture for producing the 2013 film *Dallas Buyer's Club.*
Courtesy of Steve Schirripa

With Robin Green, the night she and her husband and writing partner, Mitchell Burgess, won one of their three Emmys.
Courtesy of Steve Schirripa

With my wife, Victoria, at the Emmys. —Michael
Courtesy of Steve Schirripa

Steve, me, Johnny V., and our good friend Nick Sandow (on the far right) with a couple of our idols: Seymour Cassel and Peter Falk, who appeared in the films of the great John Cassavetes. I consider John one of the greatest directors in cinema history; his work was very influential on a number of the folks who wound up on *The Sopranos*, and it continues to inspire. —Michael
Jeff Kravitz/Getty Images

Here's to good friends: with Dominic and Jim. —Steve
Courtesy of Steve Schirripa

To watch the series finale, we all flew to the Hard Rock Casino in Hollywood, Florida. Ten thousand people showed up to greet us on the red carpet. A few minutes after this shot was taken, we went into a small room to watch the finale—and for the first time, we all saw the now-infamous cut to black.
Courtesy of Steve Schirripa

Steve,

I hoped I'd be back to say goodbye, but post intervened. I think we did something special. I'm so glad you were a part of it.

Love,
David

This is a note David Chase wrote when it was all over. It's one of my most cherished mementos; Michael and I—and everyone else—truly believe we did something very special. —Steve
Courtesy of Steve Schirripa

Me, Michael, and Steven—let the party begin. —Steve
Courtesy of Steve Schirripa

Me and Jim in front of his apartment in Tribeca a couple of years after the show ended, waiting for Tony Sirico to show up.
Courtesy of Jose Perez

Jim at Yankee Stadium in September 2002, with my daughters Bria and Ciara. Jim, me, Johnny V., Lorraine, and Tony threw out the first pitch; Jamie-Lynn sang the national anthem; and we all watched the game from Steinbrenner's box. A great, great day. —Steve
Courtesy of Steve Schirripa

With Jim at the premiere of Steve's film *Nicky Deuce* in Los Angeles on May 20, 2013. It was the last night we were all together. Jim died a month later. Rest in peace, our dear friend.
Tommaso Boddi/Getty Images

Michael, Vinny Pastore, and I took our *Conversations with the Sopranos* stage show to Australia in 2019—and could not believe that the show was still such a worldwide phenomenon twelve years after it went off the air. We played to packed houses all across Australia; this was after our final show, in Melbourne, when we sold out the 2,900-seat Palais Theatre. —Steve
Courtesy of Michelle Cop

We launched the podcast *Talking Sopranos* on April 6 2020, just as COVID hit. We considered canceling it before it even began, but the fans asked us to keep it going—so we did. We had to do it remotely for a long time, but were happy to finally get to do it face-to-face starting in April of 2021.
Courtesy of Michael Imperioli and Steve Schirripa

Steve: Okay. I'm supposed to be your partner, but everything we do, in the last twenty years, everything we've done together, your name is first and I'm the second banana. This is not right.

Michael: It's alphabetical, Steve. Both first name and last name. M before S, I before S.

Steve: You're giving me the bullshit.

Michael: No, I'm not. Abbott and Costello, Lewis and Martin, Kramden and Norton, Lennon and McCartney. It's all alphabetical.

Steve: McCartney's still not happy about that, believe me.

Michael: You think he bears a grudge, because his name was second in the partnership?

Steve: I think he absolutely bears a grudge, like I'm bearing. Why? Because you won an Emmy Award? You were nominated for a couple of Golden Globes? You wrote five episodes? You've been throwing this in my face for years.

Michael: You got a problem with these things. I don't really give a shit.

Steve: You know exactly what you're doing. You're pulling the strings from behind.

Michael: I'm not pulling any strings.

Steve: The next batch I better get approval or we're through.

Michael: Duly noted. Let's move on. Listen, I've known you for twenty years, we have worked together many times, we have traveled the globe together, we're doing a podcast together, now a book, you are one of my best friends, but I have absolutely no idea what your philosophy is. What's your philosophy of life, my friend?

Steve: All I want to do is have a couple of drinks, a good sandwich, a few laughs, and take care of my girls. That's all.

Michael: But what about the big picture? Like, what do you think happens when we die?

Steve: I don't know. I was raised Catholic. My mother was Jewish. My kids are baptized. I don't really know. As you get older, I hope it's what it's supposed to be.

Michael: You don't ask for much. That's good.

Steve: Did I ever tell you what I want on my tombstone? "It was all bullshit."

Michael: "It was all bullshit." We'll all stand at your funeral and see that.

Steve: I don't want a funeral service. I want to be cremated. Make sure this happens.

Michael: How do you know I'm going to be there? I might go before you.

Steve: Listen, I doubt that. I told my wife, "You know who I like and as the days go by, there's less and less. Have a party if you want, and then we're going to make my death testimonial, and I'm going to let people know what I think about them."

Michael: You're going to make a video, a living will kind of thing?

Steve: Yes, and you're going to introduce it.

Michael: What is in the video?

Steve: I have some things to say about a lot of people. Let's stop the bullshit. I'm taking the gloves off. I'm going to tell you what I really think about you.

Michael: You already have a list?

Steve: I'm making notes. I got a list of these motherfuckers a mile long.

Michael: There's your title. *Steve Schirripa Motherfucks the World.* Maybe you should do it while you're alive. This way, you can benefit from it. It might work as a series.

Steve: There you go, I like the title, *Steve Schirripa Motherfucks the World,* not bad.

TEN

Season Five

Hellos and Goodbyes

WHEN YOU TALK ABOUT SEASON FIVE of The Sopranos, *you gotta talk about Steve Buscemi.*

The season starts with a bunch of the old-time gangsters getting out of prison. The characters of Feech La Manna and Phil Leotardo, played by veteran actors Robert Loggia and Frank Vincent, brought up a whole bunch of new story lines and new conflicts for the Soprano family. They were terrific. But I gotta say, it was Buscemi, who came on as Tony's cousin Tony Blundetto, who really electrified things. —Steve

Steve Schirripa: So let's talk about how you wound up in the show. David Chase, I know, said he thought he could never get you. He thought it was ridiculous to even think that you would direct it, let alone act in it.

Steve Buscemi: I don't know why. Equally, I thought I wouldn't be right for the show because before that, I never played a wiseguy. I've played a lot of bad guys, but I'd never played a wiseguy or a mob guy. I'm only Italian on my dad's side; my mom is Irish, English, Dutch. I have blue eyes, I'm pale, I didn't think I fit in that role.

Steve Schirripa: Are you saying you're not a fat, sweaty, greasy Italian guy, is that what you mean? [*laughs*]

Steve Buscemi: In my heart I am.

Steve Schirripa: You're a Wonder Bread wop, Steve.

Steve Buscemi: [*laughs*] Yes.

Steve Schirripa: Steve, when they asked you to direct, back in Season Three with the "Pine Barrens," did they also ask you to be on the show then as an actor?

Steve Buscemi: No, not at all.

Steve Schirripa: In Season Five, you came on as Tony Blundetto. You didn't have to read, right? Did you read?

Steve Buscemi: No.

Steve Schirripa: You're one of the few that didn't have to audition.

Michael: Tony B. was a very interesting character. He was very specific; he had a lot going on. The whole massage therapy thing, the idea of whether one of these guys could go straight, could live a normal life.

Steve Buscemi: I was excited to play this character who was not only a new mob guy coming on the scene, he actually had a history with Chrissy and with Tony; he grew up with them. He went away and he could have been one of them, except for that one job where Tony didn't show up because he had a panic attack and Tony B. got arrested and took the fall. So I had such wonderful background information.

Michael: What I really appreciated about Tony B., he went away, it was hard, and now he was trying to get it all together.

Steve Buscemi: You're right. And the key to that character for me was the fact that he was an ex-convict. The second movie I directed was *Animal Factory*, a prison movie that was written by Eddie Bunker. He's such a great writer and knows that world. Danny Trejo was in it. They talked to me a lot about how you acclimate yourself in prison, how you survive.

Michael: Both of them had served time in San Quentin, right? Danny Trejo had been in prison several times?

Steve Buscemi: Yes. And Eddie Bunker I met doing *Reservoir Dogs*, he played Mister Blue. Eddie Bunker had spent twenty years in San Quentin and became a writer in prison. So it was them two. They told me what the mindset of the ex-con is. What it's like when you get out and why so many of them return. That it really can be this self-destructive streak and they can't adjust to the normal world.

And even though they're wanting to get out of prison, there's something that they miss, because maybe in prison they were somebody, they had a reputation. And now you're out in the real world and you're kind of back to nothing. So I just always remembered that for Tony B.

Michael: So given that background, that understanding, how did that help you create the emotions and the colors that you were bringing to that character?

Steve Buscemi: I should say first that Matt Weiner wrote the episode where Tony B. appears, and so I had a lot of talks with him about the character. I gave him my ideas and he gave me his. And as an actor you use what you have to go on in the script; you try to create a backstory—although in this case there already was a backstory, of Tony B. being Tony Soprano's cousin, and what happened in the past.

My first day on set, the scene when Tony B. appears at Vesuvio's, and he's got the white jacket, and he just feels out of place. I used what was available to me in that real situation, that I was nervous about being an actor on the show.

Steve Schirripa: You were nervous? Really? With all your background, you were nervous?

Steve Buscemi: I was very nervous and I thought, "Tony B., he's got to be nervous coming back, and seeing all these people. It's overwhelming." And it was overwhelming to me to be in a scene with almost every character in the show, and they're welcoming me back. The cast themselves, they were very friendly and very welcoming, but I was still really, really nervous, because I didn't feel a part of the group yet.

Michael: That's very interesting. Because Tony B. does show all of that, there's a kind of vulnerability to the character. You feel for the guy. You want him to succeed. But he does seem out of place. Even the white suit didn't seem to fit quite right.

Steve Buscemi: Yeah, it was ridiculous.

Steve: But what was that like for you? I mean, a lot of actors come onto the show, a lot of new actors, we've been talking about, showed up in Season Five, but you're one of the only ones who's really on the inside, you're in the back room at the Bing, you're with all the other characters, Paulie Walnuts, Christopher, Tony, everybody. And all those characters have become such cultural icons by now. What was that like?

Steve Buscemi: The real nervousness came, as I said before, on the first episode that I directed. That was a surreal experience, stepping into this world that I had only known from watching it on TV. And even though I knew some of the actors, my first scene, directing a scene that had Jimmy Gandolfini in it—I had to keep reminding myself that he's a regular guy. He's not the guy that he's playing. It was just a little bit nerve-racking.

Then the more I directed them, and I got to know the cast, that feeling was a little bit less. But still, knowing that I was now going to be on camera and be a character, when all these characters are so well developed—to be a new character on that show was a little bit intimidating.

Michael: Sure, because when you're the director you have a certain amount of control and you have to give that up when you step on the other side of the camera. That had to be an unusual moment.

Steve Buscemi: It was unusual, but it was also exciting. It helped that everybody was just so supportive, and they were glad to have me acting on the show. And everybody's so talented. That was also a little bit of a concern for me. I said, "Oh my God, they're so good at what they do. And they've been doing this for five seasons. I'm the new guy, still trying to figure out who this guy is." Which was fine, because, like I said, all of that I could use. All of my nervousness and self-doubt, all of that I could incorporate into the character. Because it just felt like that's what Tony B. would be feeling, even though he could mask it and be quick with the barbs, and if somebody busted his chops, he'd dish it right back.

Michael: Is there one particular moment you can remember, where you felt that what Tony B. was feeling was a reflection of what you were feeling in that sense?

Steve Buscemi: There was a scene in Vesuvio, the restaurant, where Tony B. just takes a moment—he's just by himself, and he's having a drink, and he just sighs. You could just tell, he just needs this moment. And you can tell how stressed out he feels. Even though everybody's being so welcoming and warm, they want him to have a good time, and Tony gives him that great toast, but he still is just feeling, "Oh my God, this is too much for me." A part of him wanting to just crawl back to the safety of his jail cell.

Michael: You've been in so many excellent movies with so many terrific directors—Tim Burton, the Coen brothers, Tarantino— Schirripa and I have talked a lot about how *The Sopranos* was in a lot of ways more like a movie than a TV show. How was acting on *The Sopranos* similar to all the film work you've done? How was it different?

Steve Buscemi: It felt like we were making a film, like a long-playing movie. It did not feel like a typical TV show. And that's not to say that there weren't a lot of great shows before *The Sopranos,* but *The Sopranos* just felt like they were breaking the rules of what television could be. And that also was reflected through the directors. My favorite directors are the ones that I worked with on that show. Tim Van Patten, John Patterson, Allen Coulter, they were all great. What's amazing is that they all had their different styles, but they were all on the same page of the vision that David Chase had for the show, and they're able to execute it in their own way.

Michael: What did you feel distinguished each of their styles?

Steve Buscemi: That's hard. I noticed with Allen Coulter when I watched the shows that he directed, and then when I was with him on set, he would set up certain shots that would frame a scene really well.

Tim Van Patten was so great with actors. He has a great way about being on set and figuring things out and being able to adapt. Whatever came his way, he was able to figure it out in a calm manner and relay that to the actors. And sometimes Tim didn't say much. I always loved the episodes that he did on *The Sopranos.*

And then John Patterson was so smart about how to shoot a scene. Sometimes when I was directing, if I was sort of stumped, I would think, "Well, what would John do? How would he approach this? What would be most important to him?"

Michael: Well I said before, you were my favorite director.

Steve Buscemi: Thank you. A lot of directing is finding solutions for the challenges that you have. Some of it just kind of happens, and the actors come on, and you just see it. But I always had a lot of help from the DPs, Phil Abraham and Alik Sakharov. The directors of photography. They were both amazing.

Michael: You were one of the actors who had a lot of scenes with Jim Gandolfini. A lot of very intense scenes. What was that dynamic like?

Steve Buscemi: Jimmy was fascinating to work with because he gets so internal. He was so committed to that character, and for him to go to the places that he needed to go to, it took time. And he went there. Sometimes he resisted it, as a person, and that was understandable. Because he had to go to those dark places to really feel it.

So for example—you remember that the episode where Polly Bergen plays the mistress of Tony's dad who Tony runs into at the cemetery, and she's playing him, because he's helping her out, then she does this thing at her apartment? She sings the "Happy Birthday" song.

Steve Schirripa: Yes.

Steve Buscemi: With that scene, Jimmy, he's sitting on the couch thinking, "This was my dad's girlfriend? This is why I never saw him, because he was with her?" You see all these things just happening on his face, with no dialogue. It was just amazing.

Michael: That was "In Camelot," which you directed. What was it like for you when you were playing opposite him?

Steve Buscemi: It really felt like I was in that world. When I was acting in a scene with him, I felt that it made me better, because I felt as though Jimmy *was* Tony Soprano. It put me on my toes a little bit more. Just knowing that he would give a thousand percent every take, and really be listening to you, and be looking at you. And not to take away anything from any of the other actors, because everybody has their own process. But Jimmy had this internal thing going on that just drew you into him. And so that was thrilling, to work with an actor like that, to feel like you're getting this attention from this other actor. And you better be giving it all right back.

Steve Schirripa: You were originally going to be on the show as an actor for two years, right?

Steve Buscemi: Yes. They hired me for two seasons, and I thought I would do two seasons, so I was really shocked and disappointed that I only made it through one season.

Steve Schirripa: How did you find out? Did you get the call from David?

Steve Buscemi: The thing on the show was you didn't want to get a call from David, right? One day I get a call, he leaves a voicemail. I'm thinking, "Oh, I guess this is it," so I call him back. It was on a Sunday. He says, "Hey, you want to have lunch tomorrow?" I went, "Oh, yes, sure." We agreed to meet. Now I had that whole night to think, "Is this it?" Then I went, "Don't go to that place where you think you're going to get killed. Maybe he's got another project for you. Maybe he wants to talk to you about the next season and how your character's going to develop." Then I was like, "That's what it is."

I go to the lunch and of course, first thing he says is, "I'm sorry. We got to kill you." [*chuckles*] Then he says, "The reason I wanted to have lunch with you is because the last person I told, I told over the phone, and he got upset that I didn't tell him in person."

Steve Schirripa: I got it in person also. Even yourself, you've done a gazillion projects and worked with the biggest actors and directors and you get that call from David and it even had you thinking. Keeping you up at night. You don't want that call.

Steve Buscemi: I didn't want to leave this show. I was having so much fun.

Michael: A lot of laughs and a lot of just great people.

Steve Schirripa: A lot of parties, a lot of premieres, a lot of finales. All the award shows and red carpets. It was a hell of a thing to be a part of, that's for sure.

FINALLY! I'VE *been waiting the whole book for this one. I've already said how much Dominic Chianese meant to me over the years—we spent a lot of time together, and he really became a close friend. He also played one of my favorite characters on* The Sopranos*—Michael's favorite, too.*

Dominic has the distinction of being the only actor who crossed over from the Godfather *movies to* The Sopranos. *Technically Tony Sirico did too, but Dominic was the only one with a speaking role, in* The Godfather Part II. *So he's kind of mob-movie royalty in that way.*

I love Uncle Junior for a lot of reasons, but one of them is that he says whatever he's thinking. He doesn't hold back. Some people say that I might be that way. A little bit. I don't know. I'm just saying.

But it's not just the writing—sure, he had some great lines. (Everybody has their favorite Uncle Junior quote. Like, "Federal marshals are so far up my ass I can taste Brylcreem.") But it was the way he delivered them—that deadpan look, and spitting out the words like they were olive pits—that's what made it so great.

That, and just his amazing acting ability. Season Five was a real tour de force for Dominic. He had to display so many emotions—elation, despair, rage, confusion, depression—as Junior sank deeper and deeper into Alzheimer's. I actually still get teary a little bit, just watching those shows. Dominic is just that good. —Steve

Steve: Dominic, you grew up in the Bronx. How did you get into acting? You were a singer first, and then a bricklayer?

Dominic: That's right. One day I was on a bricklayer bus and I decided to ask my father, who was the foreman, if I could get off the bus. The bus was heading over the George Washington Bridge to New Jersey. We were actually going to Clifton, New Jersey. Now, that's a very important part of this whole story, because there was a little baby born who lived in Clifton at that time. He must have been four or five years old. His name was David Chase, and he was living in the same places where we were going to work.

Anyway, he let me off the bus, and I went and got a job with the Gilbert and Sullivan repertory company. Musical operetta was my first start, and that's what I wanted to do. I wanted to be a musical comedy singer and actor.

Michael: Was that in Manhattan?

Dominic: Yes. It was down at 351 East Seventy-Fourth Street, right off First Avenue. That's called the Jan Hus church. They were an organization, the American Savoyards, with ties to the D'Oyly Carte company here in England.

Michael: Savoyards are performers of Gilbert and Sullivan. D'Oyly was a famous one.

Dominic: Yes, and the director, Dorothy Raedler, asked me if I had ever done some Gilbert and Sullivan before, so I said I understudied the Duke of Plaza-Toro. I still had my Bronx accent, so I said "dook," and she said to me, "You mean the *'Dyook'*?" I looked at her, and I said, "Yes, that's what I just said." She laughed, thank God, and she thought that I was a kind of diamond in the rough. She took me into the company and I'm eternally grateful for that wonderful woman.

Michael: How did you make your way from Gilbert and Sullivan into dramatic acting in the theater world? What was your path?

Dominic: I realized that once I left Gilbert and Sullivan, I had to learn the technique of acting. I started to read Stanislavski books and that got me interested. Stanislavski was very clear that acting took a technique, like any other art or craft. My father was a brick-layer; he taught me how to lay brick. Bricklaying is a craft. You have to handle things right; you have to do the process first. You can't lay a brick without the cement, that kind of thing.

I realized I had to go to school. I got into Brooklyn College. I met two wonderful teachers there. Bernie Barrow, he was Mr. Ryan on *Ryan's Hope,* the soap opera; he was my mentor. And Wilson Lehr. Both of these fellows gave me some college jobs to do. Then I went to the HB Studios, the great acting studio, and met with Walt Wit-cover there, a great teacher. I took his class and he assigned me a scene from a play—I'm with a young woman, I'm about to murder her, and she gets so frightened that she knocked over the set in the classroom. I thought I had done a good job, I said, "Wow, my anger must be really believable."

There was a hush and all the students were there, about seven-teen students, and Walt Witcover said, "Dominic, I want you to go home and do the scene again, but I want to tell you something. I didn't believe a word you said." I said, "What is this? I don't under-stand it. I shouted at that girl, man. She got so scared," but he said, "You are a good faker. You can fake it. You could scream and yell." And I was very good at that. I went back to the next class with my tail between my legs because I knew he was right.

My turn came up again to do a scene and Walt said, "Dominic, I'm going to do a little exercise for you." He says, "Sit down on a chair and relax. Now, I want you to think about something that's very dear to your heart." I sat on the chair and I was thinking about my grandfather. Walt said to me, "Can you describe what you're thinking about?"

I said, "Yes, Walt. I'm thinking about my grandfather." "What was his name?" I said, "Dominic." "What did he do for a living?" "He was a stonemason like my father. He was a very strong man, knew how to cut stone, and very large hands, strong hands." Walt said, "Really, can you describe the hands?" He said, "Just describe the hands. Talk about your grandfather." I said, "Okay. My grandfather," and all of a sudden I started to cry, and I didn't stop.

He said, "Keep talking, Dominic, keep talking." I talked about my father's hands, and I cried for about a minute and a half. There was a stunned silence in the classroom. Walt said, "Dominic," he said, "that's acting." Then I realized what he meant that acting is really an inside thing. It comes from the inside; you can't fake it.

Michael: That's an amazing story, Dominic. That might be the best acting lesson I've ever heard. Anyone reading this book, if you want to be an actor—listen to what Dominic just said. That's just beautiful.

Steve: Dominic, there are so many things I want to ask you about, about your career. But during this time, is this when you are MC'ing at Folk City in the Village?

Dominic: Not yet. I didn't start that 'til a couple of years later. I started that in '65.

Steve: When you were there, was Bob Dylan there?

Dominic: Dylan had already become famous. He would drop in once in a while. Yes, he did come in one night. Folk City, it's a tiny little stage with one microphone, but I had asked the owner, Mike Porco, if he needed an emcee because I was very good in front of an audience. "How much you want?" he said. I said, "I'll take a hundred dollars a week, I'll come every night." He said, "I'll give you ninety." I said, "All right." I started introducing, believe it or not, the greatest folk singers, guitar players, musicians, blues players, in America at the time. You name them—John Lee Hooker, Pete Seeger. I met all these people.

And I learned a lot about relaxing in front of an audience. Because the more you get out of yourself, the more you know what you're doing, the better off you are. We all know that self-consciousness is anathema to an actor. I learned a lot about that too.

Steve: Now, you did a lot of stage acting, but then of course years later you wind up in *Godfather Part II,* which kind of launches your career in the movies.

Dominic: I'm very thankful for that. Of course, by the time *Sopranos* came along, I was sixty-eight years old and it was great because then I could make what my grandfather always told me was the truth—money. [*laughs*]

Michael: What was your way in for Uncle Junior? How did you approach that character?

Dominic: There was a scene where I was driving a car. David said something to me: "Come on, Dominic. Give me something, give me an attitude." I went right back to an uncle of mine, whom I loved. He was a boxer, and he would drive the car like it was boxing. David said, "That's it, that's it." I used a lot of my family intuitively, it was my father, it was all my uncles, I had a lot of uncles. Uncle Junior was everybody. He was a neighborhood.

Steve: What was your neighborhood like, Dominic? Growing up in the Bronx.

Dominic: My dad used to take me around the Bronx and point out the butcher and the baker. He said, "That's Giovanni. He's the guy that makes the bread." I said, "Yes, I know him." He said, "There's the Father from the church. There's Mr. Caputo, who lives upstairs." I said, "Who are the guys with the hats, Papa?" "Those are racketeers," he said. [*laughs*] They would always be in a pastry shop. They would all be there drinking coffee, well dressed. I knew how they walked and how they talked, and how they could become friendly, and how they'd tease each other and all that stuff. You just absorbed that.

Steve: You and me had a lot of scenes. We had so much fun together, on the set laughing and laughing, and we really had a good time. I would tell you stories about Vegas and you would tell me stories about your days as an emcee in the Village, and we would crack each other up. But also you really helped me a lot. As an actor. We had fun, but also I learned a lot from you.

Dominic: You had to play this very heavy fat guy and that wasn't easy because that's a real character. Didn't they put a pillow in your stomach or something to make you really heavy?

Steve: Yes. You used to tell me, "Use your stomach. Use your belly."

Dominic: That was a wonderful character. Bobby Bacala is a great character.

Michael: Dominic, tell us about working with Jim Gandolfini.

Dominic: There was no sense that we were acting. I went in and he's Tony Soprano to me. You didn't have to use anything as an actor, except just to stay with him in a room. That was really uncanny because we really liked each other. At one point Jim said to David, "He's my uncle." Working with Jim was just like talking to a nephew. He's supposed to be my nephew and I believed it 100 percent. When I acted with him, I was playing my real-life uncles.

Michael: Now, you're still singing professionally. And you're so good. Does your acting training help with your singing?

Dominic: Absolutely. It's about the words. Learning the words. Sinatra was a good actor. He used to study the lyrics before he worked on a song. Because he appreciated it. If you don't love words, don't be an actor. A lot of the singers today, they sing the music. You can't sing the music. You have to sing the lyrics, make them count. I would tell them, "What are you singing about?" It's very important.

Michael: Just like an actor approaches the script. You could see that in your singing. Like that time you sang the Neapolitan song, "Core 'ngrato."

Dominic: I knew exactly what it meant. I had the words translated. I knew some Neapolitan, my family was Neapolitan, but if there's a word I didn't know, I would find out what that word meant.

Steve: We talk about this business, how hard it can be. You were sixty-two years old. You didn't have any money to speak of. You get the job, your whole life changes. Is that correct?

Dominic: Yes. That's right. I was sixty-two years old. I was making myself sausage and peppers and living in a ten-by-seventeen room. It had no furniture. The bed was outside in the hall. I was down and out. That was the winter of 1993. We had seventeen storms that winter. For eleven months, I hardly left the house. I used to say thank God, beneath my house, even though I didn't have any money, there was a Neapolitan restaurant. Not just an Italian restaurant, a Neapolitan Italian restaurant, and somehow it reminded me of my grandfather. I was comfortable. I was waiting for something to happen.

All of a sudden, I get a call, "Your social security kicked in." I said, "Oh wow." "Would you like to get it?" I said, "Yes, I'll take it." That's the first time I had some money coming in, because I never collected unemployment. That was because some of my kids were on welfare and I didn't want to. It was my own way of doing things. I wouldn't take money from the city because they were helping my children in Brooklyn.

Grandpa was right. Money is truth. It sounds very depressing, but it's not. Because all's well that ends well.

Steve: Michael, I can't tell you how much I loved talking with Dominic.

Michael: Me too. I'd love to go hear him sing.

Steve: He sang at his own bachelor party when he got married.

Michael: When was that?

Steve: That was 2003. He was seventy-two years old, believe it or not. He married a wonderful woman, Jane. A lot of the cast came. You were out of town. I said to him, "Dominic, what do you want? Do you want us to get some girls, strippers? What do you want at the bachelor party?" All he wanted to do was sing. We got some Italian musicians and he sang all night. You know, he's been singing in nursing homes for years and years.

Michael: He also does nightclubs and bars.

Steve: I opened for him in Vegas one time.

Michael: Really? Bobby and Junior together again.

Steve: I would do anything for that man. I was so lucky to do so many scenes with him. He was such an integral part of the show.

SO AS *Steve said earlier, there was another long break between Season Four and Season Five. More than a year. It was tough for a lot of the cast—you're under contract, so you're limited in what you can do. And you know it's possible that after that year you might get back to the show and get bumped off in the first episode. But Steve and I were fortunate enough to wind up in a movie together during that break. We bust each other's balls a lot on the podcast, but I love hanging out with the guy. We spent a lot of time together on* High Roller. *—Michael*

Michael: *High Roller*, the story of Stu Ungar, the famous poker champion, has become a cult favorite, especially among gamblers. Do you remember how we wound up together on that?

Steve: So Ray Favero, my buddy in Vegas, the casting director, he gave me the script. He said, "I'll send it to you. See if you can give it to Michael Imperioli. I think he's perfect for it." It was Season Three. I still didn't know you that well. You know, when I met you, you were a little aloof.

Michael: Really? You've never mentioned that.

Steve: Until you get to know someone, you can be a little distant. But we got to know each other, and we went out one night. You just said, "Let's go out."

Michael: That was the beginning of a thousand nights.

Steve: So I knocked on your trailer door and I handed it to you. You liked it. Long story short, I winded up playing your friend. So we shot some scenes. I was out of the movie earlier. You were there the whole way.

Michael: Also, remember when we ate in that café in Columbia, Tennessee? The local specialty was called Rooster Fries. We said, "What are Rooster Fries?" she said, "Deep-fried rooster testicles." She said, "You have to have them if you're here. Unless you're not man enough." So we tried them. They were like fried calamari but gamey. [*chuckles*] Then after we wrapped, we went to Nashville. We rented a limo and went to a bar.

Steve: We spent a week in Nashville one night.

Michael: Wherever I go out with you, there's always someone you know. Whatever state you're in, probably whatever country, there's always someone that you worked with in Vegas, a cocktail waitress that you once had a thing with, or whatever. So we go into this bar. It's one in the morning in Nashville and I said, "What are the odds you know somebody in this place?" As soon as the words came out of my mouth, this woman runs over, "Steve!" It was Rich Little's ex-wife.

Steve: Yes. She was a showgirl. Big, tall blonde. Now she's a country singer. That was really funny. We stayed out very late and we went to an after-hours place. It got very ugly there.

We went to an after-hours club until five in the morning, and then we had a nine A.M. call. You could do that, Michael. I couldn't.

Michael: Did you regret it?

Steve: I regret it to this day.

Michael: Then I went to Vegas and shot the rest of the movie. I was living at the Hard Rock Hotel for a month, and I went pretty insane. Playing a gambler, shooting fifteen hours a day. Then I would get home from work at three in the morning, go have a drink, and sit at the blackjack table until who knows when. I wasn't sleeping. Then I go back to work. It was nuts. There's rock music 24/7. You don't know what time it is. I'm playing a gambler so I felt like gambling. I pushed it to the limit.

Steve: You really fell into the Stu Ungar character.

Michael: "Fell" is exactly what I did. Fell hard.

WHEN WE *finally did return to shoot Season Five, the level of fame that* The Sopranos *brought to all of us had reached epic proportions. Everybody in the world was coming around. Sometimes it became a little overwhelming—but sometimes it would lead to the most incredible experiences of our lives. —Michael*

Steve: Tell about the time Muhammad Ali came to the set, Michael.

Michael: One day, my manager calls me and says, "Muhammad Ali wants to take you to lunch," which was one of the weirdest things anybody's ever said to me on the phone. I said, "What are you talking about?" She goes, "His publicist called me. Muhammad Ali is a big fan of yours and *The Sopranos*." I said, "If he's a fan of the show, why doesn't he come and have lunch on the set?" They make these arrangements.

I go to Silvercup Studios and I'm waiting. This van pulls up and out comes Muhammad Ali with his daughter, Rasheda, and he gives me a big hug. He wasn't talking a lot at that point of his life, but he was really sweet and kind, and had a big presence. On the set, you build these walls within the big soundstage for various rooms, and Jim Gandolfini is in the hospital room, doing the scenes where he's in a coma. It's between takes and he's taking a nap in this hospital bed, so he can't see us walking into the stage.

The crew sees me walking in with Muhammad Ali, and this hush comes over the whole studio. I was telling people to be quiet just because I wanted to surprise Jim. It's like this ripple effect as people see us walking into the hospital room set. Jim is in the hospital gown, and he's turned away from the door. Everyone was waiting to see what was going to happen.

I tap Jim on the shoulder. He turns around and looks up, and sees Muhammad Ali, and he just says, "Holy shit!"

The whole crew—there's sixty, seventy people—erupt in applause. People are crying. The applause goes on. I've never seen anything like this. Basically, everybody stopped working for a couple of hours and Ali took pictures with everyone on the crew, signing autographs. It was very emotional. He stayed for lunch and we hung out for the afternoon. He was just beautiful. I never really saw a celebrity affect people that much. The degree of respect and admiration people had for him was incredible. It was really, really special and so cool. I'll never forget it.

Steve: Nobody is bigger than Muhammad Ali. But all sorts of celebrities used to stop by.

Michael: Jon Bon Jovi came to lunch, one time, just to visit the set. And Vinny Pastore said to him, "We already got one Italian rock star from New Jersey, Jon. You're not going to get on the show." Referring to Steve Van Zandt, of course. But Jon's always been a good friend of ours and actually is a very good actor as well.

Steve: Even the Brits got into the act.

Michael: We had a visit one day from Ricky Gervais, who is a big *Sopranos* fan. He'd just started working with HBO on *Extras* at the time. They knew that I was a big fan of the British *The Office*, and a big fan of Ricky's. He came and he just was obsessed with the show. He watched us shoot and looked at all the sets and was like a kid in a candy store. He really loved being there. We became friends and stay in touch. It was always fun when those guys would drop by. A welcome diversion.

THE FIRST *shots of every season of* The Sopranos *set the tone for the rest of the season, and Season Five is a perfect case in point. The opening images are among the most haunting we've seen: They are echoes of what we've seen before, but things have changed. The driveway and the yard are a mess; no one is there to pick up the Newark* Star-Ledger. *The pool is closed. It is autumn in New Jersey, and you sense that it's the autumn of Tony's reign. There is a feeling of loneliness, of abandonment, of loss.*

This is also reflected, for me, in the absence of the women in Tony's life during the first few episodes. Livia is gone, Carmela is gone, Melfi is gone. The strong women characters are, as we've talked about, one of the backbones of The Sopranos, *one of the things that sets it apart: without them the show, and Tony's life, feel off-kilter.*

Season Five is also about how difficult it is to be the guy at the top. Tony's ultimately alone, and by the end of the season, it's clearly every man for himself.

But as difficult as it was for Tony to have all these new mobsters arriving and causing chaos, for us, it was a little bit of a homecoming week, to have the actors playing those characters show up. —Michael

Michael: So the new guys coming out of prison, the new actors showing up on the set, we knew a lot of those guys.

Steve: We talked about Steve Buscemi and how he was already a part of this—he'd been directing since Season Three. Also everyone knew Frank Vincent.

Michael: I had worked with Frank several times; a lot of people knew him. Not many of us knew Robert Loggia—we knew his work, of course, he was in so many terrific movies—but it was interesting to see these characters, how these guys come out of prison.

Steve: In the first scene I had with Robert Loggia it's the one where we have dinner with Junior and Tony. We're at Junior's house, and Bobby is doing the cooking and he makes chicken cacciatore with rice. It's seven o'clock in the morning and I'm going, "This is fantastic. I got the green light to eat chicken cacciatore at seven o'clock in the morning!" We ate chicken all day long, me and Jim. It was great at seven A.M. Then, by one o'clock, we're still eating chicken. It was like, "What the fuck am I doing here?" We ate so much chicken, I think I heard Jim clucking.

Michael: You were a Method actor when it came to eating in the scene. You didn't hold anything back.

Steve: They always had great food on the set. We made sure it was from a good Italian restaurant. The prop people were in charge of that. They didn't just whip it up in the back. This came from legit, really good restaurants in Queens, in the neighborhood. Or if you were in a restaurant shooting, you would get the food from that restaurant. And the catering and also craft services. Every day there was mozzarella, provolone, soppressata. Every single day, there was Italian stuff on the set. They fed us well.

Michael: But Robert had some trouble with his lines, didn't he?

Steve: Robert had a very difficult time with his lines. Sometimes he would paraphrase.

Michael: Which is a big no-no.

Steve: We've talked about how you got to stick to the script, stick to the script, stick to the script. I'm not saying he wasn't prepared, but he had a tough time. But that shows you what it was like on the set of *The Sopranos:* We all showed the utmost respect for Robert. Especially Jim.

Michael: Robert was about seventy-four by then.

Steve: Yes. A scene that was scheduled for four hours took eight hours. It was off the charts. He's trying to tell the story about beating up a guy in prison, where he says, "Then I hit him, bam, right in the fucking coconut"—only he's making up lines, saying, "Then I hit him in the snot locker," stuff like that. He was having a rough time. But you know what happened? Jim sent his dialogue coach Susan to work with him that night at the hotel. Jim couldn't have been more encouraging. You know, Michael, how some people would have gone, "Get him out of here, get someone else." The stars of a lot of shows would not be so patient.

Michael: And then Robert winds up turning in an excellent, very funny performance over those first couple of episodes.

Steve: And how about Frank Vincent showing up? That was great to see him.

Michael: He had auditioned in the beginning for Uncle Junior. I think he auditioned for Paulie Walnuts, too.

Steve: Frank was very well-known from *Goodfellas* and a bunch of other work.

Michael: After *Goodfellas* he did *Casino*, he did Spike Lee's *Jungle Fever*, where he played the father of Annabella Sciorra and myself, and he did a lot of indie movies, so when he came onto *The Sopranos*, he was a natural fit. He's from New Jersey, he knew most of us, and he did an excellent job.

Steve: For four seasons he had to watch everyone he knows, on this show that I'm sure he felt he deserved to be on, and he wasn't there. But then he finally got his chance. He delivered above and beyond.

Michael: He was an amazing villain. Really good and very authentic. A guy I know—he's not a wiseguy, but he runs card games for the mob—always felt that Frank Vincent was one of the most authentic actors to play a wiseguy. They always felt he really nailed it somehow.

Steve: You know who else the real wiseguys thought was very authentic? Johnny Sack. Vince Curatola.

Michael: Vince did a great job this season. You know, they were gonna kill Johnny Sack off at one point, but Vince was doing such an amazing job, they felt they had to keep him in, so they wrote this whole story line for him. He becomes another one of these fascinating, powerful villainous characters throughout this season.

Steve: I've spoken to people over the years, real wiseguys, who believed Johnny Sack was the real deal. Some wiseguys would go, "I don't know if I'm buying everybody, but I believe Johnny Sack every step of the way."

Michael: Anyway, there were some really funny moments in these first few episodes. I like the whole *Prince of Tides* thing.

Steve: Tony and the girlfriend Valentina are watching that movie, the Barbra Streisand movie.

Michael: There's an interesting parallel with *The Prince of Tides*. Nick Nolte is dealing with the trauma of childhood, his abusive father, a manipulative mother, he has an affair with a psychiatrist. An interesting connection with Tony Soprano.

Steve: I heard that Barbra Streisand is very, very difficult in terms of allowing her stuff to be used. Do you know if there was some connection with her and the show?

Michael: I know she's friends with Lorraine. We were once at some event, Barbra Streisand was there, and she lit up when she saw Lorraine. They were hanging out together that night.

Steve: Another funny moment is the whole Larry David thing. You've got Uncle Junior watching *Curb Your Enthusiasm*. He mistakes Larry David and Jeff Garlin for himself and Bobby. I guess it's the beginning of the idea that maybe Junior really is losing it, in a way.

Michael: That was hilarious.

Steve: Jeff Garlin worked for me in Vegas one time. He opened for Denis Leary. He gets mistaken for me constantly and vice versa. I like Jeff. Larry, I met a few times. He's not far off from who he is on that show. Nothing bad, just a true genius there, for sure.

Michael: You played a lot of scenes with Dominic this season where Junior is clearly going downhill, but you can't tell if it's really dementia or if he's faking it. It was brilliant and really complex. What were those scenes like between the two of you?

Steve: First of all, as I've said, Dominic became a mentor to me without even knowing it. We spent a lot of hours talking, just talking in between takes. He was a believer in using whatever you had for your character. It rubbed off on me.

Bobby loved Junior like a father. He expressed it numerous times and I felt that way about Dominic. I found myself playing the Bobby role in real life with him.

Michael: How so?

Steve: When we were leaving a restaurant, making sure he had a ride. Or if he drove, helping him into his car. Stuff like that. Just making sure that he was okay.

Michael: Really? When you would go out with Dominic, it was a little like you were protective of him the way Bobby would be?

Steve: A thousand percent. Michael, don't you think that happens somewhat with all of us, with our characters? Like with Jim? He wasn't the boss of us, but just like Tony was our leader on camera, Jim was the leader off camera, no?

Michael: You're right. But as you know it wasn't always easy for him. He had a hard time being so famous, and so easily recognizable wherever he went. I think the pressure of having people expect, and want, to meet Tony Soprano—that became a burden as time went on.

Steve: But he really was a leader in so many ways. He helped people get raises at the end, especially those last nine episodes of Season

Six. He went to bat for people. I'll tell you one story. This just illustrates what I'm saying. They came out with a *Sopranos* slot machine. Me and Jim went out to Vegas to promote it right after the show ended. We cut the ribbon on the slot machine at this big convention, and that night, we had a little meet-and-greet with this big group of people.

I was getting paid good money. I don't know what Jim got paid. But he wasn't really into it so much. He wasn't rude, he was just floating around, not really engaging with people. We were standing in front of a step-and-repeat and I was playing host.

Michael: We should explain that a "step-and-repeat" is those banners you see at awards shows, the big backgrounds that the publicity photos are taken in front of. They're called that because one celebrity steps up and gets their picture taken, and the next one comes and they repeat the process.

Steve: Right, so we're there, and Jim's not into it, and I'm playing host. "Hi, Jim, this is Mr. Smith," "Hey, Jim, we've got to take this picture," like that. I was doing a lot of that all night. I was working it.

Then the next day at breakfast, it's me, him, and Roger Haber, our lawyer. Jim goes, "Hey, man, I just want to apologize about last night. You were doing all the fucking work." I said, "No." He said, "Roger, give him ten thousand dollars." I said, "No, I'm fine, I got paid good money. I'm good." "No, Roger, give him ten thousand dollars." Roger said, "Take the money." I went, "All right. Thank you." He gave me $10,000.

Michael: That was Jim.

Steve: That was the week I went off the rails, by the way.

Michael: You hurt yourself, huh? You almost didn't come back from that one.

Steve: In addition to the slots, I also had a show at the HBO Comedy Festival that week. It was called *Steve Schirripa's Va-Va-Voom Spectacular.* I had showgirls and comics and magicians and stuff like that. And then the night with Jim, and I had an appearance at the Hard Rock, so about six nights in a row I'm up until five, six, seven in the morning. When I wasn't working I was drinking. I was about fifty at the time, it knocked the shit out of me. I came home, I didn't drink for a month.

Michael: It could get rough out there, that's for sure. One more thing we have to talk about in these first couple of episodes, by the way—the death of Carmine. Having a heart attack while he's eating the egg salad.

Steve: I wish you didn't bring that up. I couldn't stop thinking about him dying with egg salad in his mouth, which just scarred me for life.

Michael: You never want to eat egg salad again.

A lot of people think eggs are really significant. Adriana offers to make Christopher eggs after she admits she's working for the FBI. Ralph offers to make Tony eggs just before Tony kills him. Valentina's making eggs for Tony just before her kimono catches fire.

Steve: Oh come on. That's just more of that bullshit conspiracy theory that you like.

Michael: I'm just saying, people think this.

Steve: Some people are idiots.

I GOT *Michael on this one. I asked Ilene Landress, the executive producer, about the eggs. She backed me up. —Steve*

Steve: So, Ilene, Michael and I disagree about this. I say the eggs in the show are just eggs. Where did this all come from?

Ilene: Some writer, way after we finished this show, talked about the eggs. That every time we killed the character, they were eating eggs first. And nobody was conscious in the writers' room about that. But if you look back, it's like Ralphie was making eggs. The guy at the golf club was eating an egg salad sandwich when he keeled over. But I mean, the thing about eggs—it's just common stuff. What do you eat at a country club? It's a tuna sandwich, it's an egg sandwich. It's just what the old guy would have been eating. Or if Ralphie's cooking, it's the middle of the day or the morning, whatever, that's what he would have been doing. It's very specific.

Steve: That's what I'm saying. It's just always these specific things in the script.

Ilene: One image could be of Tony Soprano sitting on the couch, eating a bowl of ice cream, because that's what he'd do. Things that people do in real life. You go to the refrigerator, you grab a piece of turkey and cheese. It's like the orange juice. Because when we were growing up, you just went to the store and it was one kind of orange juice. But now, you went to the supermarket, all of a sudden you're staring at the orange juice section and it's not just orange juice. There's orange juice with no pulp. There's orange juice with some pulp, with lots of pulp. And it's those kinds of little quirky things. Those are the things that were just happening in the world, and just in front of our faces. And that's what went into the script. I've never compared *Sopranos* to *Seinfeld,* but it's the same thing about products. It's not made up out of thin air, it's just stuff that you see every day.

THE DEATH *of Carmine Lupertazzi, in the "Rat Pack" episode, brought up something I didn't know. As we talked about earlier, Matt Weiner, who went on to create* Mad Men, *had just come on board as a writer. He told us the secret behind Carmine's casket. —Steve*

Matt: That was my first episode, Carmine's funeral. One of many. And I got to see the casket that had been used in every episode of the show.

Steve: Really? They always used the same casket?

Matt: Yes. We had that on *Mad Men* too. We had a mattress, because you couldn't buy an old mattress, so we had a mattress made that cost $2,000 with a fake antique ticking on it. And every time you saw somebody change sheets in *Mad Men,* we would take this mattress out, just like how they would use that casket on *Sopranos.* We owned one casket. Let's change the color maybe for this episode.

Speaking of the "Rat Pack" episode, by the way—I remember one great line David added to the script. He was laughing out loud when he was giving me notes about the scene where Steve Buscemi, Tony B., was giving massages in the back of the pork store. And then David added that line, "This is a place of business, not a Jack LaLanne."

WHEN WE *talked earlier about all the new actors who showed up in Season Five, we left out my absolute favorite. I've been a fan of Frankie Valli since forever. Nobody epitomizes New Jersey Italians for me like Frankie. I love his music, and I love the guy, and I love that he showed up to play Rusty in Episode Four. —Steve*

Steve: We were all so happy when you showed up on *The Sopranos.* How did that happen? You came on in Season Five, but you read for David Chase early on, is that correct?

Frankie: Yeah. I did read for David. And the part that I read, at the time, he felt that it wasn't the right part for me.

Michael: Do you remember the character you first auditioned for? Or was it more just a general audition?

Frankie: It was a character that did a lot of profanities. Paulie Herman ended up with it.

Michael: Oh, Beansie.

Frankie: Beansie, yes. David said, "This part is just not right for you." I guess he was also trying to protect who I was to my fans and didn't want anybody to get turned off. It was heavy and using the name of the Lord in vain and all that stuff. But he said that he would write me in at some point. And I thought he was just blowing me off, to be very honest with you.

Steve: Really. You thought, he's just saying that to be nice.

Frankie: Yeah, and not 'til a couple of years later when they called me, and he said that he had a part that was specifically written for me. And that's how it came about. It's probably one of the highlights of my life, because it's something that I always wanted to do.

Michael: Now, you hadn't done a lot of acting before that. You'd been in one or two TV shows, movies, so what made you decide to do *The Sopranos*? Was that your idea to go in and audition for it, initially? Or did he call you? How did that happen?

Frankie: No, it was my idea. I wanted to do it. I loved the show. It was about New Jersey. It's the background that I grew up in, in Newark. And the area that I hung out in and grew up with, there was a lot of organized crime. And I knew that this guy was a boss here, and that guy was a boss there, so I saw a lot of it, and a lot of poolroom activity and social club activity where these guys were around, whether they be bookmakers or capos of various different crime families.

Steve: And when you were a young singer, you were singing in the clubs, some of those clubs must've been owned by those guys.

Frankie: Yeah, most of the clubs in those days were somehow connected to wiseguys. They either had money in the clubs, or they owned them outright. So, I worked for these guys, and I got to know all of them.

Michael: So when you were creating the character of Rusty, did you lean on some of your knowledge of those guys? Did you pattern him after them? Where did that come from?

Frankie: Actually, I thought about the different guys and the different bookmakers and different bosses that were in the area I grew up in. One of the episodes I did, the one that you wrote, Michael, was probably the best one of all of them that I did, because you gave me some space to establish the character. And that's very important.

Michael: One of the things I saw you doing was creating a quiet sense of power. A guy who could convey anger without ever raising his voice. As opposed to, say, Robert Loggia, who came on at around the same time, he was going full guns blazing all the time. But I thought Rusty had a kind of quiet power, which you portrayed so beautifully.

Frankie: There were a lot of guys that were in organized crime and that's how I saw them. They kept themselves very contained. That didn't mean that they couldn't erupt at any point.

Steve: But it's like we were always waiting for you to erupt. Like when you're talking about, "We should take down Johnny Sack. Everybody in Brooklyn would cheer us." You made that character very frightening.

Frankie: Well, when you had to be really serious about something, that's how I pictured it to be. You could do that where you get very excited—"We should take out Johnny!"—you could do that kind of flavor, but I didn't feel that kind of flavor. It wasn't necessary or right for the part.

Steve: So you have been on the stage thousands and thousands of times. You've been in front of audiences for all your life. How much did your experience on the stage as a performer make you feel comfortable in front of the cameras? Did that translate or was it very different?

Frankie: It was different in a way, but it did translate. One of the things I learned is that when you're performing, you have to have the people that are watching your performance believe that you are in charge. And that's very, very important. If you go out onstage and you look frightened, it's going to affect the audience. Or something goes wrong, a musician hits a wrong note, you have to continue and go on as though nothing happened. You can blow off steam when the show is over, but while you're doing the show, you don't interrupt what you're supposed to be doing.

Michael: And that's exactly what Rusty conveys. He conveys confidence. He conveys that he is in control.

Frankie: Exactly. Because Rusty would not have been a boss if it was any different than that. Rusty was a capo. He was a captain in the family. He didn't become a captain because he was just a loudmouth.

Steve: Just like you're the captain of the ship when you're out there on the stage, with the Four Seasons. You're the one who was in charge, and you had that in your life, and that's what you brought to Rusty.

Frankie: Exactly.

Steve: So I gotta ask you both—Michael, you wrote that episode where Rusty has lunch at the Four Seasons. I thought that was hysterical. Was that something you all talked about?

Michael: Yes, when we were planning out the episode, it was always that we were gonna do the scene at the Four Seasons. As an homage to Frankie and the group.

Steve: Frankie what did you think of that when you found out?

Frankie: I thought that was terrific. And the scene was written so incredibly.

Steve: Everybody talks about on *The Sopranos*, "You never know when your character is going to get whacked." How did you find out that Rusty was going to get whacked? Did David come find you?

Frankie: I finally found out when I was doing the episode.

Steve: You didn't know ahead of time?

Frankie: I did not know ahead of time. I had a feeling it was coming, because these things have to move along.

Steve: How did you feel when you found out? Were you upset or did you say, "Well, that's how it goes. It's *The Sopranos*"?

Frankie: Well, that's how it goes. But in a way, I was sad. I enjoyed so much the part of doing it, of having the opportunity. And David and everybody who was involved with that show were really terrific to me.

Michael: I want to ask about the use of your music in *The Sopranos*. Because David used it a lot. And one of the most poignant for me was another episode I wrote, the one where all the Italians are upset that the people are protesting Christopher Columbus, back in Season Four. Do you happen to remember that episode?

Frankie: Yes, I do.

Michael: So it became a conversation about Italian heritage, stereotypes, and the theme that runs all through *The Sopranos*, "Is your life predestined by where you were born? Can you escape your past? Are you bound to your past?" And when it goes to black, they come up with you singing the line, "Girl, we can't change the places where we were born." Were you aware that they used that there? And what did you think about that?

Frankie: To start off, I was impressed that they used as much of my music in *Sopranos* as they did. But David Chase was a big fan. He grew up in New Jersey. He was around the same elements that I grew up in, and he knew what he was doing when he was writing about gangsters. As far as that line goes—it makes sense to me. Because you *can't* change the places where you were born. And there's a part of your life, no matter what your successes are, your failures are, that will follow you all through your life. Sometimes in a good way and sometimes not in a good way. You can't live and dwell in the past either—but you came from where you came and you shouldn't be ashamed of that.

Steve: Do you have a favorite memory of the show?

Frankie: All of my memories are good, except the day that I was finally wiped out. It was kind of sad, because I would have loved to have been able to do it right until the end of it. And Gandolfini was probably one of the greatest actors I've ever worked with.

FRANKIE RAN *into an old friend on the set of* The Sopranos—*who shared a similar understanding of going from music idol to* Sopranos *star.*
—*Michael*

Steve Schirripa: What was it like for you when Frankie Valli showed up?

Steven Van Zandt: I was a big fan. I met Frankie very early on. I did a year with a group called the Dovells on what was called the oldies circuit. And part of it was playing Vegas, so we got to open for the Four Seasons. When David Chase brought up getting Frankie Valli I was like, "We got to find a way to do this." He was a big, big, big hero for me growing up. I always used to call him the Frank Sinatra of our generation and I meant that. He has that sort of class but he was part of a connection between the past and the future.

Michael: Frankie told us that being a performer, performing on-stage thousands of times, helped him in the transition to acting. You had that same experience—did that help you in any way?

Steven Van Zandt: Every singer is an actor, whether they know it or not, whether they're conscious of it or not. Every song is a script, every song is a movie, and you are selling that to the audience. You're the one convincing the audience that what you're telling them actually happened, is the truth, whether it's true or not, whether it happened or not, whether you wrote it or not. That's why Sinatra was known for being the great interpreter of songs, even though he never wrote anything, it was because he was a good actor.

And Frankie was also a good actor. So it went naturally, because that's part of the job. You're becoming the character of that song. Our pop world, the music world, appears to be the most autobiographical of all the art forms, but it's really a perception thing. It's not really true, but it seems to be true.

Every singer that's singing a song, you figure, "They lived that in life." And it's very often not true, but that's an essential part of the craft. So I think every singer has the potential to be a screen actor.

Michael: So is that the connection between singing and acting, the connection that you brought to those scenes, to that role?

Steven Van Zandt: Yeah. You got to be that guy. You got to find that guy inside you and then become him.

THE MIDDLE *section of Season Five—beginning with the fifth episode, "Irregular Around the Margins"—takes a very different turn. The first four episodes focused a great deal on the new characters, but now the season shifts into creating frightening conflicts between the older established ones. It's the first episode of the season written by Robin and Mitch, and it brings back their signature style of mixing great drama with dark humor. The developing conflict—Tony seemingly disrespecting Christopher by what appears to everyone to be a dalliance with Adriana, and Christopher's violent reaction, are both the culmination of the tensions between them to this point and a portent of what's to come later. —Michael*

Steve: This episode is when the real tension between Christopher and Tony erupts. Your big scene, when you come in, shooting up the bar. These are emotions Christopher has never shown with Tony before, the fury and the rage. He has dishonored you, because you think he had a thing with Adriana. You're screaming at him, you're shooting the place up. What were those scenes like for you to play?

Michael: When the stakes are that high and it's life and death, it's always fun to push yourself to a certain extreme. Jim and I were really good friends by then and enjoyed being together, enjoyed working together. Those things are gold for an actor. Plus the different states of mind, drinking, or especially doing heroin, playing those scenes, it was really fun.

Steve: How about those scenes where it was just you and Buscemi, the two of you up at the farm? You're very intimate there. You're really bonding. Where were those shot? How long were you there? It was really just the two of you for a while, right?

Michael: That was on a farm upstate. I don't think it was far from where we did the "Pine Barrens." That was Mike Figgis's episode, the only one he directed, and I really enjoyed working with him. Mike Figgis is a great filmmaker, and he was very cool. He also used to play in a band with Bryan Ferry, right before Roxy Music.

Steve: When you do a little breakout like that, where it's just you and one other actor and the director, it doesn't mean a small crew went with you, right? It's still the whole megillah?

Michael: Right. The whole big crew. It's exciting playing those scenes because there's a certain intimacy that you can create. But it is also fun because the whole crew was on location. Most of the time people lived at home—you'd either go to Silvercup in Queens to shoot or you'd go to North Jersey and shoot, and you go home at night. This was like a class trip, we all went upstate, we moved into hotels, and we stayed for a week.

Steve: I can imagine what that was like.

Michael: One night we had a big karaoke party at the hotel. I sang onstage with Ginger, who was our first team production assistant, doing "Wild Thing." [*laughs*] I'll tell you a very scary story. I've never told this. Maybe it's not appropriate.

Steve: Tell me. Then we'll decide.

Michael: So there was a cop that we met in upstate New York. I'm not going to say which town. He was saying, "We'll look after you," and he took us out one night, me and one of the guys on the crew. We went to a bar, and we were drinking a lot. He was drinking too, and he was driving.

Steve: Was he in a cop uniform?

Michael: No. He was going to drive me back to my hotel, and he said, "We got to stop at my house to meet my wife." Now, it's three in the morning. We go to his house and he has a giant-screen TV and he puts on a porno movie, and he starts laughing! "Look at that," he says. I mean, the thing was huge.

Steve: "The thing was huge." I'm gonna assume you mean the TV set.

Michael: [*laughs*] Very funny. Yeah, the TV set. Anyway, then he wakes up his wife. His wife comes out of the bedroom, holding a baby. The giant porno movie is playing. He starts laughing. He goes, "Look who's here, honey!" And the porno's running, his wife is shocked to see me, the baby starts crying. I am drunk and very uncomfortable.

Then we go outside. and he takes his gun out and he tries to hand it to me! He goes, "Take the gun." I say, "I don't want your gun." He goes, "Take it, take it. Don't be afraid."

Steve: Wow.

Michael: Then he starts shooting the gun in the air in his backyard! [*laughs*]

Steve: Was he really bombed?

Michael: Shit-faced.

Steve: So what happened?

Michael: Then he drove me to the hotel.

Steve: You never saw him after that?

Michael: No, and I don't think I went out the rest of that trip. [*laughs*]

Steve: But that can happen. Remember when we got hijacked in Philly, at the NBA All-Star Game?

Michael: Yes, we got kidnapped by a limo driver.

Steve: The guy was what? Ex-wrestler? Six-foot-seven, six-foot-eight guy. Took us to eat in some real hole-in-the-wall, and then he started driving again and wouldn't shut up. He kept saying, "What kind of girls do you like, big boy? What kind of girls do you like?" All sorts of weird stuff like that. And then he said, "I got to make a stop." And he took us to his house. He was scary, right?

Michael: Yes. He wanted to introduce us to his family.

Steve: Yes. His wife came out to the car. She was nervous and shaking. We didn't get out of the car, though. Same thing, late at night. Crazy.

Michael: Yes. Dangerous being a Soprano.

Steve: Very dangerous.

THE LAST episode I wrote for The Sopranos was the eighth episode of Season Five, "Marco Polo." It's an absolute gift to be handed an episode like this one—there's so much to work with. There was Steve Buscemi's character acting on his jealousy of Tony Soprano and doing a hit for the New York mob. The whole tension of whether Tony will come to Carmela's dad's party. The business of Carmela's mom being embarrassed by Tony's behavior, which gave me the opportunity to write about the whole Northern Italy–Southern Italy rivalry. And then, of course, I got to figure out how to get Tony and Carmela back into bed. It was always great to get a chance to write for this show, but like I said, this one was really a gift. —Michael

Steve: I gotta start with this—"Phil treats nickels like manhole covers." I've always loved that. I always heard it as he throws nickels around like manhole covers. Where did you get it?

Michael: In 1997, I was living in a weird triplex apartment. It was very small, but it was actually three little levels on the East Side, by Fifty-Fourth and Park Avenue. My middle child was just born and it turned out that the building was infested with mice. There was a restaurant on the ground floor that was filthy, and all of a sudden, we realized our apartment was infested. There were holes in the walls. If we left a piece of fruit out, the mice, by the morning, would have eaten it. We were trying to get the super to patch the holes, and we decided we had to move. It was horrible.

We got this lawyer, Stephen Erlitz, from Sheepshead Bay, and we took the landlord to court because they wouldn't let us out of the lease. So in court, Stephen put on this amazing performance. I'll never forget it. I had a bunch of Polaroids that I took of mice on traps and stuff. He had them in his hand and he was shuffling them in front of himself. We were trying to negotiate but the landlord wasn't budging. Steve was this little short guy but he was yelling and screaming, and one point he's yelling at the landlord for being so cheap, and he goes, "You people treat nickels like manhole covers!" I'll never forget it and it just stuck in my head and I was waiting to use it for a long long time. This episode, I finally got the chance.

Steve: It means you're a cheap fuck. They used to say that about a guy that I knew, throws nickels around like manhole covers. It's the same thing, like "He's got alligator arms." Or "He's got long pockets and short arms." Anyway, it's an amazing episode. There's so much going on.

Michael: A lot going on.

Steve: Another episode I'm not in, by the way. It's the third one of yours that you kept me out of. You could have put me in.

Michael: No, I couldn't.

Steve: It's very obvious, years later, that you didn't care for what I was doing and you didn't want to put me in it. I could have been by the pool.

Michael: It was a family-only party.

Steve: I'm part of the family. I'm married to the sister.

Michael: Janice wasn't at the party.

Steve: Admit it. You didn't like me. Also Bruce Kirby, who played Dr. Fegoli, you didn't like him. Bruce is the father of Bruno Kirby. I'm a huge fan of his work, Bruno Kirby. But Bruce, the father, you didn't like.

Michael: It wasn't me. It was John Patterson, who directed this episode. He could not stand Bruce Kirby. They're both dead so I don't have a problem saying this now, but John kept referring to Bruce Kirby as The Great Caruso. I don't know why. That was a hard role to cast, actually. It was very hard to find somebody to play that role of this pretentious Italian guy who looks down on the working-class Italian-Americans. At one point, I tried to convince David to let Dominic play Dr. Fegoli, wearing maybe a goatee and a beret, darkening his beard and disguising himself, and David was really into that at one point. Then we realized, this is just not going to work.

Steve: So you went with Bruce Kirby. I thought he did a good job, actually. I really hated the character, so I guess it worked.

Michael: The name Fegoli, by the way, was from the guy who delivered me. He was our family pediatrician in Mount Vernon. He grew up with my grandfather.

Steve: That whole thing with the Beretta, when Tony buys Carmela's father the shotgun and then Dr. Fegoli puts him down for it. Where'd that all that come from?

Michael: I had to go to the Beretta showroom, which was on Sixty-Fourth Street and Madison Avenue. It looks like a jewelry store from the outside—they have these incredible, beautifully crafted guns, mostly shotguns and hunting rifles.

Steve: I used to have a Beretta handgun in Vegas.

Michael: They're based in Brescia, Italy, in the north. Those were some amazing firearms.

Steve: Then Bruce Kirby, Fegoli, puts it down.

Michael: He says, "The best pieces, they don't import." That came from my grandfather who said that about wine from Italy: "The best stuff they don't send over here." I heard him say that many times.

Steve: And then you used that for the Beretta.

Michael: You're always pulling things from your life, wherever you find them.

Steve: How did you figure out how to get Carmela and Tony back together?

Michael: Those are some my favorite scenes that I've written for the show. First there's that moment when she gets him a beer when he's grilling, she's seeing him in a different light and she's thinking, "Look at this guy, he goes out of his way for my father. My father loves him, and he knows that." Tony buys him this very extravagant gift. He shows up, he's bringing the sausage because Hugh loves it. Carmela defends Tony to her mother.

Steve: For one day they're back to the way it used to be. The backyard's back in action.

Michael: We're seeing Tony, sincerely, trying to win back Carmela's affection. And she's reminded of the respect that she does have for him and who he is as a person. And then of course the pool scene, I enjoyed that scene immensely, the sensuality of being in a pool and it's late at night and the air is cold outside but the water's warm, and suddenly they're alone. That intimacy that happens between them—it's a scene that I'm really fond of.

Steve: How did Edie deal with you having them throw her in the pool?

Michael: You know Edie. She was game for anything. She's somebody who really always got into the spirit of whatever you were doing.

THE TENSION builds and builds through the end of Season Five, between my character and Janice and Tony—Bobby kind of gets caught in the middle of that sibling rivalry, and it all blows up. Those were some really amazing scenes to play with them. —Steve

Michael: Steve, what stands out in your memory about those scenes?

Steve: There was a moment where Tony keeps telling Bobby he's got to control his wife, and knowing Bobby's personality, obviously, he's not going to control her. Who controlled her? Ralphie and Richie Aprile couldn't control her, certainly Bobby can't.

Michael: No. Tony can't either.

Steve: Exactly.

Michael: But then Bobby stands up to Janice. It's the most powerful we've seen him. You really had to get in her face.

Steve: There's a whole speech where I said, "This was a nice house. Peaceful. There wasn't all this yelling and tension." He gives her an ultimatum. "If you don't go to those anger management classes this ain't gonna work out."

Michael: You are very real in those scenes. Very real. Were you thinking about your own childhood when you were preparing for that? You've talked about what your house was like growing up. Did that help you here?

Steve: Absolutely. I just let it all out, right there. I could totally relate to what Bobby was saying. I'll tell you, Aida was great to play that scene with. She was always so in-the-moment.

Michael: It was one of her best scenes, too. When she says, "It was easy for you growing up, in my house it was dog-eat-dog"—I feel for both of you in that scene.

Steve: But then later in that episode, Tony can't stand to see her being calm, and he goads her. Talks about "blowing roadies" and everything. This is the scene Aida talked about earlier—when she and Jim got really angry at each other, and I got caught in the middle of their fight, just like Bobby got caught in between Janice and Tony.

Michael: Life imitating art.

THE STRANGEST *part of the season for me—no big surprise, and I'm not alone in this—is "The Test Dream." A lot of people ask what that was all supposed to mean. Here's my answer: all I can say is, that's a very good question. —Steve*

Steve: I don't know what any of these dreams mean. I really don't. But I enjoy them tremendously. I'm not that deep a thinker anyway, but I try not to delve into it. David has said that sometimes he doesn't even know what they mean. Do you think every beat means something, Michael?

Michael: Not necessarily. It was a really cool, ballsy experiment to basically have twenty minutes, a third of the episode, just be a dream, which is a real big risk, it's a gamble and an exciting choice. It's delving into his psyche. The classic dream, the test dream, is that you're unprepared for the test. Tony is unprepared for whatever task is now at hand for him. It really connects to the finale of the season, which is Tony realizing that being number one is isolating and you're going to make unpopular decisions, and ultimately, you're all alone. Is he man enough to be in that position? Is he prepared enough? Does he have what it takes? As a husband, as a father, as a mob boss? I think that's what it's about. It's about regret, and it's about fear.

Steve: When the bullets melt in the dream, a lot of people think that it means that the task he's not prepared for is that he's gotta kill Tony B.

Michael: Yes, that's the most obvious.

Steve: But so many weird moments in the dream. Who knows what they mean.

Michael: When Tony is in bed with Carmine, that's really funny.

Steve: Jim jumps out of bed and he's crawling on the floor. Incredible moment. When David Chase said that Jim might complain about stuff but he always did it—that was one of those moments. Crawling on the floor horrified, and of all people Carmine is in bed with no shirt on.

Michael: You show up in the dream. You were dressed like a member of the Frankenstein mob.

Steve: I was running down an alleyway numerous times. We shot that in Williamsburg, late at night. I'm with a group of people chasing Tony with a torch in my hand, and with the lederhosen.

Michael: Were these your own lederhosen or they had to give you?

Steve: They had to buy some for me.

Michael: You're not a lederhosen kind of guy?

Steve: No.

BUT LIKE *I said, I couldn't really make heads or tails out of the "Test Dream" episode, so we went right to the source—the guy who wrote it with David Chase, Matthew Weiner. —Steve*

Michael: Can you go into, a little bit, how you approach the dream sequence? How was that tackled?

Matt: It's an interesting thing because it actually came out of a very concrete problem, which is that Tony and Carmela were separated and they had to be brought back together. That was what we felt was going to happen. And you don't just make that happen. They had a lot of shit between them. And there were some things that David had made jokes about. There was a line in "Rat Pack" when Tony was talking to Silvio, and Silvio says, "How do you enjoy living alone?" When Tony was living at the mother's house. And Tony says, "I get up whenever I want to, I fuck whoever I want, I do whatever." And Silvio goes, "So, what's the difference from before?" And he goes, "I don't know. It's a mindset."

Michael: So that genesis of the idea of reuniting Tony and Carmela goes all the way back to your first episode, "Rat Pack." That's interesting. Then later, you started on the "Test Dream" episode.

Matt: And we talked about this dream as having some rules because I like Buñuel, David likes Buñuel. David Lynch is a huge part of the show. There was a picture of Federico Fellini over the whiteboard in the writers' room. I mean, the dream language is important.

It probably starts with "Isabella." Isn't that the first one where the entire episode is like in another world?

Michael: Right, we find out at the end of that episode that none of it really happened, like it was all in Tony's imagination or something. It's never really clear—it's very surreal.

Matt: So just seeing that on TV and seeing it executed is like a really great foreign movie. American movies do it too. We talked about Hitchcock and about how you could make things feel like dreams, but then there was a logic that was superimposed on it, so we decided that everything had to happen in an order. That you couldn't just throw them around. And then it became this mood of us talking about our dreams and saying things like, "What is going to bring Tony back home?" From what I remember, it was a series of events. A lot of it was just really intuitive and about my own loneliness at that time. And then David had things that he wanted. He wanted to see some of these people. He wanted this to be like Tony's coming to a crossroads in his life. And so everything worked up to that. And one scene was added after the dream was done— David added this thing with the coach at the end, which really kind of clarified it.

Michael: Where he's back in high school, and the coach is saying how he's not prepared. The question, of course, is what he's not prepared for—that brings us back to the conflicts in his real life. And then he wakes up. What about the phone call between Tony and Carmela, at the end, after Tony wakes up?

Matt: I didn't write that part. David did. And it's one of the most awesome things I've ever seen in my life. I saw it on the page. And then when—I will start to cry if I think about that—that phone call between Tony and Carmela, that reconciliation phone call that had been earned by Tony going through hell in that dream and seeing what his life would be. It's part *Christmas Carol*, you know? All the ghosts are coming to visit. There's a lot of *It's a Wonderful Life*. There's a lot of the alternate-universe clichés, if you want to say, but they're done so specifically to Tony, the way our dreams are.

And then they have this conversation, and Carmela's in bed and he's in bed, and he keeps saying, "Is it light where you are?" I get emotional about it because—it's the Jim thing. It's about that man's access to his vulnerability. It's really hard thinking about it.

THERE ARE *so many moments when Jim triggered deep emotions in people on the set, and deeper emotions now when we think back on them. But clearly, the emotional peak of this season for me—and for many viewers, obviously—was the murder of Adriana.*

It was enormously emotional for me, as well. Drea and I became very close friends very quickly, and had the utmost respect and trust for each other. I can't imagine having done this with anyone else. When I think back on the relationship between Christopher and Adriana, it seems very powerful and very real to me. Christopher truly loved Adriana and really wanted to make things work with her; he just couldn't bring himself to get past the fact that she had been informing for the feds. It just struck at the heart of values that had been ingrained in him all his life. And as for Adriana, I think she had unconditional love for him in return. Some call her an enabler, or say she was in denial, but she always came from a place of pure love.

So I was feeling the impact of this moment right along with all the fans. I don't think I've ever seen the kind of reaction to the death of a character that I witnessed after this episode. —Michael

Steve: Talk about the scene when Adriana tells Christopher she's been working with the FBI. The level of emotion between you and Drea De Matteo, when you start choking her, it was frightening for the audience. You told me that it was your favorite scene to play. I was surprised to hear you say that.

Michael: I've talked about what it's like to play scenes when the stakes are high, and that's a scene where the stakes could not be higher. At that point, Christopher realizes life will never, ever be the same again. That no matter what's going to happen, whether they're going to run off into the sunset to witness protection, or she's going to get whacked, or they're going to go to jail, whatever it is, from then on, life is going to be different. The stakes are so high that as an actor, the scene will hold whatever you want to bring it. It's almost impossible to do too much in a scene like that.

It's always hard to do those scenes where you get violent, because you've got to be very careful. You don't want to hurt the person, and especially, obviously, somebody I care about. At that point, Drea and I were really good friends, so it was even more difficult. It was a long scene; it took us eight hours to shoot, and there's a lot of beats, so all those little shifts of emotion have to be played and worked out, but you also have to learn the physical choreography of the violence very precisely.

Steve: Did Christopher really think about scramming with her?

Michael: Yes, he did. But then he does have that moment when he sees the family and that guy with the mullet at the 7-Eleven and he realizes he can't live that life, that normal life. It always reminded me of the end of *Goodfellas* where Henry Hill, who's narrating the movie, says that being a gangster was like being a movie star with muscle, and now, "I'm an average nobody. I get to live the rest of my life like a schnook." And how that was a downer for him. He survived, but you get the sense life is not as good being a regular schnook, and that's what Christopher's weighing at that point. Then there is a scene when Christopher goes to Tony and tells him in the basement about Adriana, but that wasn't in the episode.

Steve: You shot that scene but they didn't use it?

Michael: Drea spoke to David and said, "You should cut that scene, it ruins the surprise." Because in the next scene Tony calls her and says, "Hey, Christopher tried to kill himself," which could have really happened if you think about it. Christopher was using drugs, maybe he took a bunch of pills. So when Silvio goes to pick up Adriana, maybe the audience can believe that he's going to bring her to the hospital because Christopher tried to kill himself. There's great tension when Syl is driving her, because the audience doesn't know. They suspect, but they don't know. And Adriana is going through the same thing—the realization comes over her little by little, just as it comes over the audience in the same way. But if that scene stays in, then the audience knows that Tony's lying. It takes away that suspense.

Steve: We never see that scene, do we?

Michael: We see it in a flashback. In Season Six, they use the scene we shot.

Steve: Now, her death, this was probably the most horrifying death for the audience.

Michael: You don't see it on camera.

Steve: But people were horrified by that and it was a very sad moment. Why didn't we see the murder? It's the only murder that you don't see on camera. Was this a conscious decision that it would just be too painful to see her murdered?

Michael: Oh, yes. People still write to me to this day—to this day!—and say that Adriana was done wrong by Christopher, by Tony, by Silvio, by the writers.

Steve: You heard it everywhere. Everywhere. People forget, in those days, everybody hung on every episode. Every Monday, all the morning TV shows, all the radio shows, they would dissect everything that happened. So when this happened you couldn't turn your head and not hear people talking about how horrified they were. It was like that every week. I remember even when Bobby died, there was a full-page article in the *New York Post,* "Bye Bye Bacala."

Michael: It was intense. A lot of people thought she shouldn't have been killed off.

Steve: I don't think it was necessary, but there were also theories, of course, conspiracy theories out there.

Michael: That he didn't kill her?

Steve: That he let her go.

Michael: Of course that doesn't make any sense. Although there is a moment, in Season Six, where Carmela sees Adriana in Paris, and for a half second you think, "Wait, maybe she's not really dead," but that's a dream.

Steve: But once again, it's the twelfth episode of the season that packs the biggest punch. Not to take anything away from the season finale, but nothing could touch this one.

Michael: As I said, I think the finale is about Tony realizing that being the boss means being alone. By the end of the season, that moment when he's just reached a deal with Johnny Sack, and then he sees the feds coming and takes off running—you kind of get a sense it's every man for himself. That moment has one of the best uses of song in the whole series, by the way. Van Morrison's "Glad Tidings." It's just so ironic—Tony's rival from the New York gang is being arrested, and Tony's running away while Van Morrison is singing, "We'll send you glad tidings from New York." It's just brilliant.

THE LAST *episode of Season Five aired on June 6 of 2004. Remember at that time HBO was still only available in about a third of the homes that broadcast TV reached—and still, eleven million people watched the finale. Even though it was up against the Tony Awards and Game One of the NBA Finals. But it was not clear, at that moment, after Tony dodged the feds with a run through the snow, how much more running there would be to do. —Michael*

ELEVEN

Bada Bing Jukebox

Behind the Music

When I was doing *The Sopranos*, I liked putting music together
with the film; that was my favorite part of it.
—*David Chase*

MUSIC SCHOLARS CAN ARGUE LONG INTO *the night about the influence
of music on movies and how and when it changed, but most of them
agree—and I agree with them—that the turning point comes in 1967,
when Mike Nichols infuses* The Graduate *with the music of Simon and
Garfunkel. It's not that pop music never appeared in movies, certainly;
think of all those Elvis movies, for example. And of course* A Hard
Day's Night *preceded* The Graduate *by a good three years. But the
use of pop music as a kind of Greek chorus, to underscore and illumi-
nate the emotions and drama of what's happening on-screen, changed
forever when—as Nichols has told the story—he had been listening
to the album* Sounds of Silence *in the shower, and said to himself one
morning, "Schmuck! This is your soundtrack!"*

*Over the course of the next several years, the use of prerecorded pop
music exploded in movies. The music and the film quickly became inex-
tricably intertwined (for example, you can't think about* Easy Rider

without hearing "Born to Be Wild"). I don't think anyone used music better than Martin Scorsese did in 1973 with Mean Streets—*that first moment, when Harvey Keitel is lying in bed and you hear the driving, opening drumbeats of "Be My Baby," announces loud and clear that this is not your father's gangster film. Or your mother's idea of a soundtrack.*

But it's fascinating to me that this music revolution, by and large, didn't make it to television for another twenty-five years. Sure, there were the soundtrack songs, like the theme song from Welcome Back Kotter *and such, but infusing drama with popular music, sometimes to reflect the tension and emotion of a scene, sometimes to undercut it with humor or irony, was not the norm on TV like it is today. The occasional show would dabble in it—*Miami Vice *springs to mind, for example—but for the most part, it just wasn't done on a large and effective scale.*

Until David Chase decided to do it.

Music became such an important part of his series Northern Exposure—*and much more so with* The Sopranos—*that it was almost like another cast member. So we decided to take a few moments in this book to talk just about the music: how it was used, how this all came about, and—just to start a huge argument online, which I know is gonna happen once I say this—what the best music moments of* The Sopranos *are.*

The man who had the most influence on the music, besides David Chase, was our producer Martin Bruestle. Martin gave us the story behind the story of all that marvelous music. —Michael

Michael: Martin, what was your involvement in the music for *The Sopranos*?

Martin: When we first started *The Sopranos*, we did the pilot and we didn't have a composer. We tracked the entire episode with licensed music, meaning you have to clear the publishing and the master for the song. David predominantly selected the pilot music but we worked on it together, and we had a little bit of time between the pilot and when the series took off. And David was convinced that he wanted to use a large amount of licensed music.

Now, we're talking about money that had never been spent on a television series before. *Miami Vice* and *Northern Exposure* had used music, but the sad thing about *Northern Exposure* is, we spent five years working on that show in picking all the music with Josh Brand—but for the rest of its lifetime, in perpetuity, they have stripped out all of the licensed music on *Northern Exposure* and re-placed it with cheap library music.

Steve: Thank God that didn't happen with *The Sopranos*.

Martin: It didn't because for *The Sopranos*, they cleared it forever. David had me call the music clearance people and say, if we use this many songs, for example if we use twelve master recordings in an episode, how much is our music license going to be? David just went to HBO and said, "This is what I want to do."

Michael: Did you usually pick the music before you edited the scenes, or did it come after?

Martin: When David edited the episodes, he didn't want any added music in the beginning process of editing, because what he really felt it did was interrupt him in telling the story. It was like a Band-Aid. So you want to watch them clean with no music. I usually would have to wait five or six passes until I started interjecting music ideas in this show. He felt it would mask the problems in the scene if you put the song in too early.

Michael: So the thinking was that the song would dictate how to edit and complete the scene and present the scene, rather than the scene being complete on its own and then have the music be an added color to it.

Martin: Exactly.

Michael: How did you find this music? What would be the process of finding the right song for each episode?

Martin: It's a lot of needle-dropping. I'm dating myself, but when you would drop the stylus on a record—

Michael: Right, that's where the term came from, when you're editing a movie or TV show, you would call each piece of music a "needle-drop."

Martin: I would get thousands of CDs sent to me once the show got established because publishers and record companies want that money. So a lot of stuff got sent to me. But here's a rule I set for myself: Record companies would send producers like me CDs of "focus tracks." The record companies push ten tracks every month. I would just, basically, ignore those because then you're just part of the funnel of the mass media of music and what's being fed to all the outlets, whatever they are.

Steve: But you always found really interesting music. Different stuff.

Martin: I've loved music my whole life. I can't sing at all; I'm a horrible singer. But I discovered that if you play rock and roll or Wagner against a cartoon, you can create twenty different scenes, just by playing something different.

David had found a song by the Tindersticks called "Tiny Tears" and we used it when Tony was depressed in the "Isabella" episode. It was Tony sitting on the toilet, and then walking to take his Prozac, and then going to take a shower. Before we added the music, it was a ten-second scene. We put the song in and it became a two-minute moment. David stretched it out and used the Tindersticks songs very effectively.

Michael: But how did using the licensed music differ from using a composer?

Martin: What we looked at was, what is the environment where these characters exist? Where would music naturally exist in their lives? A. J.'s bedroom, the Bada Bing strip club, obviously, had wall-to-wall music. Somebody driving in their car. We'd look at all the natural spots where music could exist just organically within their lives and not adding it just where it would feel like a producer's just dropping a hit song at the end of a scene.

Michael: But there were two levels of that—the music that, as you say, was working as an underscore, like the Tindersticks song, and then the music that appears to actually be playing in their world. That was very different.

Martin: Yes. And that was a lot of fun. A lot of fun also was mixing with David. David's very sound savvy. So when we mixed the show, we would use a lot of treatment—like if you were in the Bada Bing back room, we would play an AC/DC song or a Metallica song, but we smashed the hell out of it so all you hear is the low end coming through the wall. I hate it when you watch something and they play a song and then the actors start talking and they dip the sound down in order to be able to hear the actor. You're so conscious of the process of mixing.

You always do little tricks like using the musical bridge on a song or an instrumental portion over the dialogue, which is the primary focus. With David, you always have to be aware of the dialogue. You can't fight the dialogue because we're telling a story and as a writer, he works from a writer's perspective of the words.

Steve: You guys spent a lot of money on the music, didn't you? No show ever probably spent that much.

Martin: We spent a lot of money. We used one song to introduce the character of Jackie Jr.—I think we spent $100,000 total on that song.

Michael: That was "Rock and Roll" by Led Zeppelin. I think it's the first time that anyone used Led Zeppelin on TV.

Martin: It is. We got great things. Ric Ocasek from the Cars called me and loved the music. Jerry Vale wanted me to have his music on the show, Martha Davis from the Motels sent me a CD of their greatest hits and said, "Great fucking show." David was a musician before he was a TV writer and because of his musician's sensibility, of somebody who's a musician and into music, he has a certain mindset or a certain thought process.

There was definitely a connection between the music industry and our show, and music people wanting to be a part of it. Once the show took off, they wanted their music to be included. We used a lot of people who had never licensed for music before. Warner Bros. told me that a Fleetwood Mac song, "Rhiannon," that we used in a scene that you were in, Michael, where you're talking about the acid being poured on somebody's face—do you remember that?

Michael: Yes. In the pizza parlor.

Martin: All five members of Fleetwood Mac cleared that song in two hours.

Michael: Wow. There are different prices for different songs and different artists, right? The more famous the song, the more famous the artist, the more you're going to pay? That's how it works?

Martin: Yes. Generally, back in the day, we would spend anywhere from $15,000 to $50,000 per song for its initial broadcast, and then you had to double that for DVD and then add 27 percent of that on for auxiliary future markets. We spent a lot of money. It was very expensive. But going back to the reason for not having a composer, I think it's one of the things that keeps this show fresh. Because other than our main title song, "Woke Up This Morning," it's a clean slate on every episode. Since you don't have an underscore that laces throughout the thing, every episode is a chance to have a different tone or a different feeling.

Michael: David originally wanted the show to start with a different song every week but HBO thought that would be too confusing. He heard "Woke Up This Morning" on his car radio in Santa Monica one day and fell in love with it. A lucky accident. He told me once that he thought the lyrics—"Woke up this mornin', got yourself a gun," "got a blue moon in your eyes"—really spoke to a mobster with depression.

Steve: Was there anyone who turned you down, that didn't want their music associated?

Martin: Prince. This was in Season Four.

Steve: Ah, him and Michael had a beef.

Michael: Prince was very religious; maybe that's why he didn't want to license his stuff to us. I had a similar problem with *Summer of Sam*. I wrote the script with Victor Colicchio, and the main character was a big Hendrix fan. We wanted to use his music but the Hendrix estate would not license his songs because the movie had a lot of violence in it. They didn't want to associate Jimi Hendrix's legacy with so much violence. So the character in *Summer of Sam* became a Pete Townshend fan instead, and we got the Who's music.

Steve: Also, in the episode "Second Opinion" in Season Three, Bobby McFerrin didn't want "Don't Worry Be Happy" to come out of the mouth of that Big Mouth Billy Bass, the fish.

Martin: Out of the singing fish, you mean? You are correct. Bobby McFerrin does not license his music to anything rated R and so we basically had five or six days from hearing that to having to replace what the fish sings. I talked to the company that made the fish. The chip which produces the animation on the fish singing the song actually comes from a place in Japan. They sent the information to Japan and we sent a recording of "YMCA" by the Village People, for the fish, and sent it to Japan. They put it on a chip, they sent it back to the place, they put it into the singing fish and sent four of them exclusively to the *Sopranos* set. Three backups and one original.

Steve: That's amazing attention to detail. You could have just dubbed it over. But you actually had it come out of the fish.

Michael: In general, did the artists want to know what the scene was before they'd clear the music?

Martin: When I clear a song with the music clearance people who actually call the publishers and record companies, I fill out a form and I give, basically, a brief description of the scene that allows them to grant permission. Sometimes certain artists will say, "I want to see the script." Or, "I want to see pages from the scene." For example, we used AC/DC's "Back in Black" with Tony getting a blow job. It's him driving his car and you'd think he's having an anxiety attack, which you've seen before, and then all of a sudden this head pops up and he's getting a blow job from one of the Bada Bing girls as he's driving her home from work. My description for getting permission for the AC/DC song was "Tony gives a co-worker a ride home. The song is playing on the radio."

Steve: A little misrepresentation.

Martin: It's 100 percent the truth. One of the members of AC/DC reacted, "You didn't tell us about the blow job!" I said, "Well, you're in a rock and roll band."

Steve: What about Dylan? Dylan did a song.

Martin: Dylan was a fan of the show. We used "It's Alright Ma (I'm Only Bleeding)" in the episode where A. J. blows up his SUV. Dylan also did a cover of the Dean Martin song "Return to Me."

Steve: Did he do that just for *The Sopranos*?

Martin: He did it just for *The Sopranos*.

Michael: The finale, the "Don't Stop Believin'," that's one of the most famous uses of music in the show, or any show in history for that matter. David talked to us about how he came up with that. Tell us what you remember.

Martin: David selected the song. We wanted something that was appropriate for Tony Soprano. A guy his age, something that would be representative of what he would play on a jukebox.

David was confident that he wanted that song and that doesn't happen very often on a script level, where David will want a song at that stage. We approached Journey and Steve Perry asked the question, "Does anyone get killed in the scene?"

Since nobody was killed, they said yes. Steve Perry granted permission.

Michael: The song makes a very powerful impact in that scene. And David has said, it's one of the few times he did cut the scene specifically to the music.

Martin: When we did the final mix of the show, David had me take the volume down on the song and make it lower in the diner. Make it a more natural sound. Like from little white greasy speakers in the ceiling. But then he brought it back up. He just said, "This is it. The music is doing something here."

We raised the volume and played it more like half underscore, half score. I often wonder if we would have kept it in the greasy white speaker level from up above if it would have ever had the same impact.

Michael: In general, did a song just pop out at you for a scene, or would you go through a lot of songs until you found just the right one?

Martin: Sometimes there were multiple songs. We would get episodes where David would give us a list. There was one episode where Carmela or Meadow is floating in the pool at the end. He sent us a list of twenty songs to put against that scene.

Steve: A lot of work.

Martin: The thing about music is a song can be great independently but then you put it against the film and it becomes a different beast. There's this magic that happens when you put the image of film and music together, both of them working together to create magic. You could try playing opera over Tony Soprano walking down the street and then you could try a Lilith Fair song and it'd be a totally different scene. So we're constantly trying different things.

Also, you look at the whole arc of the episode. I can't remember what it's called in a musical, but at the three-quarter point of a musical you have a piece of music that wakes everyone up because they've been sitting in the theater for two hours.

Michael: The eleven o'clock number. The showstopper.

Martin: We look at moments like that. We need an energy boost in this scene. Or, is there an underlying tone from the actors that's not on the film that we want to amplify? So we find that piece of music that'll boost that up. Boost their anger, boost their solitude, boost their whatever.

Michael: Do you also sometimes look for literal things in the lyrics that reflect what's going on in the scene?

Martin: David as a writer would tend to use words in songs but not in the traditional sense of saying something that literal. He usually would use something that added a commentary or a note to the scene that he wasn't telling you already with what you see on the film. It's like, you don't need to repeat what you're already seeing. You don't want to play "Walk Like a Man" if somebody is walking down the street.

OKAY. HERE *we go. Here are my top ten music moments. Each of these is a terrific song on its own, but each of them also enhances the scene it's played over. Either they set the mood, or they amplify it, or, as Martin said, bring something to the scene that's not already there on film. As I said earlier, the songs sometimes work as a kind of Greek chorus, to comment on what you're seeing—sometimes sincerely, sometimes ironically, sometimes sentimentally, sometimes paradoxically, but always to great effect.*

Steve and I have already talked about a number of marvelous musical moments on the show—like the "It Was a Very Good Year" montage that begins Season Two, and the "Thru and Thru" montage that ends it. And of course "Don't Stop Believin'" from the finale. There are so many songs you could put on this list—for a lot of people, the Italian songs that become Carmela's theme are absolutely essential moments in The Sopranos—*but these are my personal top ten.*

I'm sure, as I said, there'll be plenty of disagreement, both with what I included and what I left out. Send all your hate mail to Steve and tell him to pass it along. I'm sure he'll do exactly what's appropriate. —Michael

10. "Look on Down from the Bridge," Mazzy Star

From "Meadowlands," Season One, Episode Four

The song is played at Jackie's funeral and continues into the end credits. It's a great song by one of my favorite bands. This is a terrific example of using music to set a mood. The scene shifts from the harsh reality of the Sopranos' world—Christopher and Tony snidely commenting on the feds' taking photographs at the funeral—to a surreal, moody slow motion as the music starts, its opening chords played on an organ that sounds like something you might hear at a funeral. As a slow, bittersweet melody accompanies the organ, Tony catches A. J.'s eye and gives him a loving wink; the scene is bathed in not only the warmth of their relationship, but also the warmth of Hope Sandoval's beautiful, haunting voice as the credits start to roll. She sings about looking down from above and asks, "How could I say goodbye"—perfect lyrics for a moment when the Soprano family is sending a beloved friend off to the great beyond.

9. "Mystic Eyes," Them (Van Morrison)

From "Down Neck," Season One, Episode Seven

When young Tony hides in the trunk of his dad's car and follows his dad and Janice to the carnival, this fabulous Van Morrison song provides the soundtrack. The rollicking harmonica riff conveys the excitement of Tony's caper and the joy of Janice's going to the carnival—and when the music abruptly cuts out, it underscores the older Tony's pain as he says, "My heart was broken." It's just one of those magical moments that David created with music, made more magical by one of my favorite Van Morrison tunes.

8. "Gloria," Them (Van Morrison)

From "Pine Barrens," Season Three, Episode Eleven

This song appears during the opening scene, when Gloria Trillo, Tony's latest goomar, arrives at the docks. The opening of this episode is incred-

ibly cinematic, and from the first moment we see Gloria, parking the car, wearing the head scarf, putting on her sunglasses, sporting those boots and that fur coat—the smoking-hot image of a free-spirited Manhattanite, and Annabella Sciorra just nails it. The song has endured as an anthem of pure teenage libido, as Van Morrison speak-sings in a Howlin' Wolf growl, "Watch her come to my house / She knock upon my door / And then she comes to my room / Yeah, and she make me feel all right!"— it's the perfect song to convey the breathless passion that fuels the tryst between Tony and Gloria. And the contrast with Carmela, who is always presented as the suburban housewife, and whose musical tastes, like her clothing, are much more conservative.

Morrison wrote the song when he was just eighteen. It was released in '64, and there have been several famous cover versions. My favorite is Patti Smith's, on the Horses *album, in 1975; much less well-known is a cover version by the Doors, in which Jim Morrison improvises the filthiest, dirtiest lyrics I've ever heard. Go look it up (but be careful— definitely* not safe for work).

7. "Space Invader," the Pretenders
From "House Arrest," Season Two, Episode Eleven

This is kind of an inside joke—the burning, screaming guitar solo that you hear over the scene conveys the power and the danger of the truck that's headed your way, and if you know the title of the song, you get that the garbage truck is literally about to invade the space of the store owner. I like that.

The song is from the excellent first Pretenders album, which also has "Precious," "Stop Your Sobbing," "Brass in Pocket," and "Mystery Achievement." The guitar work that we hear over the scene is by James Honeyman-Scott. He died at twenty-five of a cocaine overdose but was very influential to a number of guitarists who came after him. (The song, by the way, appears once more, in the "Kennedy and Heidi" episode of Season Six, while Tony is in bed with Chris's former mistress.)

6. "It's Alright, Ma (I'm Only Bleeding)," Bob Dylan

From "Made in America," Season Six, Episode Twenty-One

I love all the Bob Dylan music that was used in The Sopranos. *We talked about the episode that included versions of "Return to Me" by Dean Martin and Bob Dylan (which may be the only time in history you could use those two names in the same sentence). Certainly "Gotta Serve Somebody," playing on the radio in Tony's kitchen in the "House Arrest" episode, makes a great commentary on the strange place religion inhabits in Tony and Carmela's lives ("It may be the devil or it may be the Lord, but you're gonna have to serve somebody").*

But my absolute favorite use of Dylan music is in the final episode. Everybody talks about the use of "Don't Stop Believin'," the final song, but the "It's Alright, Ma" sequence often gets overlooked. The scene with A. J. and his girlfriend Rhiannon, parked in his SUV, is a seemingly innocuous one—she's turning him on to the lyrics of Bob Dylan, saying, "It's amazing it was written so long ago, it's like it's about right now"— but the incendiary lyrics of the song, decrying hypocrisy, commercialism, and the war mentality in American culture, tell you something more portentous is coming. And sure enough, the SUV catches fire and A. J. and Rhiannon barely escape with their lives.

David Chase talked earlier about how much he loves this song; Dylan always said this was one of his favorites of his own songs, and it's mine as well. It was the beginning of the period when he sang prophetic songs full of cascading, surrealistic images, and its presence here doesn't just foretell the literal conflagration that follows it, but the greater conflagration to come in the lives of the Sopranos.

5. "Complicated Shadows," Elvis Costello

From "Denial, Anger, Acceptance," Season One, Episode Three

This is actually a twofer. First, the haunting contrast of Meadow singing the Christmas carol "All Through the Night" with the choir, a beautiful,

*stirring rendition of a song of peace, with Tony moved to tears in the au-
dience, cutting back and forth to the murder of Brendan. The murder is
played almost romantically, silently, as Brendan lies in the bathtub and
the blood slowly seeps around him. Junior is right outside the bathroom
watching. He's smiling. Very creepy. Like he's very satisfied with this hit.
So you have those two conflicting images, of Tony watching Meadow
singing and Junior watching Brendan die. And then, as we cut to black,
they have the amazing Elvis Costello song "Complicated Shadows." The
lyrics go so well with the moment:*

> *Well you know your time has come
> And you're sorry for what you've done
> You should've never been playing with a gun
> In those complicated shadows*

*It's just a very cool interplay of the music, and the moods, and the
lyrics. Brilliant.*

4. "Glad Tidings," Van Morrison
From "All Due Respect," Season Five, Episode Thirteen

*I'm including this third Van Morrison song on the list not just because
Steve is such a big Van fan—I am too—but because it brings the season
to such a satisfying conclusion. The song is played several times in the
episode, and each one illustrates a different aspect of what Martin was
talking about. The first time we hear it, Christopher is meeting Silvio,
clandestinely, in a parking lot; the music is clearly playing in Christopher's car. It sounds like it's coming from a cheap car stereo speaker, and
we only hear it when Christopher rolls down the window.*

*The second time is when Tony Blundetto is bringing some groceries
to his hideout; the sudden fade-out of the upbeat music makes us worry
that something sinister is about to happen—and sure enough, Tony So-*

prano comes around the corner bringing anything but glad tidings. He shows up with a shotgun and kills his cousin. The contrast between the two moments, created by the music, makes the murder all the more terrifying.

The final time is at the end of the episode. Tony has just narrowly escaped as the feds come to arrest Johnny Sack; he makes a frightened run through the snow, but Van Morrison's joyous "la-la-la-la" tells us that all of his troubles are over. For now, anyway.

As dark as The Sopranos *can be, you'll notice that David ends several of the seasons on an upbeat note: a family gathering at Vesuvio's, a Christmas postcard scene, and—even though Tony and Carmela are in a panic—the arrest of Johnny Sack portends the possibility of peace among the families. Glad tidings indeed.*

3. "My Lover's Prayer," Otis Redding
From "From Where to Eternity," Season Two, Episode Nine

When I wrote this episode, I originally had a music cue for "Angel Baby," by Rosie and the Originals, as the opening song. David decided on "My Lover's Prayer," and it's a much better choice. We fade in on a tearful Adriana at the hospital bedside of Christopher, and Otis's mournful wail, "This is my lover's prayer / I hope it'll reach out to you, my love," embodies so much—musically and lyrically—of what Adriana is so desperately feeling. I'm in awe of how well David puts music and film together sometimes, and this is one of those times. The song continues with the lines about needing "loving arms to hold you tight," as Gabriella Dante enters and wraps Adriana in her arms; the tenderness of the moment is enhanced, so much, by the song that David chose.

"My Lover's Prayer" appears twice more in the episode: when the gang is hanging out in the hospital while Christopher is in surgery, and, again to great effect, when Tony and Carmela make love—for the first time in the series—in the final scene. Carmela has expressed to Tony her wish

to, possibly, have another child, and so the "lover's prayer" takes on a whole new meaning. All in all, just a brilliant, brilliant choice.

2. "The Dolphins," Fred Neil
From "The Ride," Season Six, Episode Nine

I've never had any question about my two favorite music moments in the show. This is one of them. It comes in the scene where Christopher does heroin at the feast. It's a wonderful montage sequence with a song called "The Dolphins" by Fred Neil. I just love the tone of it, the vibe of the song, and how it matches the energy of the heroin high and Christopher's floating through the feast.

A lot of people don't know Fred Neil. He wrote "Everybody's Talkin'," the song from Midnight Cowboy, *although Harry Nilsson recorded it for the movie. Bob Dylan's first job as a musician was as a backup harmonica player for Fred Neil in Greenwich Village in the early sixties. Fred Neil had an incredibly deep, soulful voice that spoke of mystery and sadness, especially in this song, and it fit the moment so well. David let it play for a long time and gave me a lot of room to try a lot of things in this scene, and I credit Fred Neil for creating that otherworldly space and mood. His languorous guitar strumming, the melancholy bass line, the meandering melody, all contribute to giving the scene the ethereal, dreamy feeling that it has. I gave that scene my all, but there's no question in my mind that Fred Neil's music elevated my performance enormously. When you want to understand what Martin was talking about in terms of using music to add more to the scene than what's on the screen, look no further than this moment.*

1. "You Can't Put Your Arms Around a Memory," Johnny Thunders
From "House Arrest," Season Two, Episode Eleven

His real name was John Anthony Genzale; he was born in Queens and died way too young, when he was just thirty-nine. I'm a huge Johnny

Thunders fan, from when he started with the New York Dolls, and that song is just one of my favorites. The title comes from The Honeymooners; *Johnny got it when he was watching the classic sitcom on Channel 11 late one night in New York: Ralph says to Alice, "You can't put your arms around a memory," and she says, "I can't even put my arms around you." The* Sopranos *episode featuring the song includes a very tender moment with Junior; he's feeling very vulnerable after Catherine Romano, a woman from his past, spots him in the hospital. At first Junior is embarrassed, because of his infirmity and his house arrest, so he puts her off, but finally he relents and calls her. It's such a sweet note to end on: you can almost hear David Chase saying to Junior, "Go ahead, call her, Corrado. Admit that you're lonely. You can't put your arms around a memory."*

Although in truth, it's not the relationship of the music to the episode that moves me so much—in this case it's just the fact that it's Johnny Thunders. That's how much I love the man and his work—to me, just to be on-screen with him, in any capacity, is a privilege and an honor. Until the next life, brother.

TWELVE

Bada Bing Back Room

The Gang's All Here

SO IF EVER THERE WAS AN ensemble show, this was it. On both sides of the camera. Everybody played their part and played it well. The Sopranos wouldn't be The Sopranos without that huge parade of excellent actors, directors, camera people, everybody. So before we go any further, Steve and I wanted to talk to some of those folks. Our big extended family. Starting with some of the talented people behind the scenes.

One of the first things we learned was about the relationship between the way the brilliant Sopranos directors would shoot an episode and the way David Chase would edit them. It led to some interesting conflicts—always resolved, I think, in a way that made the show better. One of those great directors, Jack Bender, who directed four memorable episodes, explained the dynamic to us. —Michael

Michael: Would you guys generally like the way David cut the shows you shot, or would he sometimes change your vision a lot in ways that you might or might not agree with?

Jack: It would depend. A lot of the directors, especially the guys who did it a lot, like Alan Coulter, would complain to me about "the way he cuts them." Because Alan is a director who really designs transitions. The way you walk out of one scene and start another. They're very designed transitions; that's part of his style, and David would frequently just cut them. Eventually, I was told, David would cut with his eyes shut to the rhythm of you guys and your dialogue.

So you'd be watching a crane shot that as a director took a long time to get and was precious and important to you, suddenly, boom, halfway through it would cut off!

Michael: The actors felt that too. Sometimes, as an actor, you're acting when someone else is talking, you're listening, or you're taking a pause, and as an actor, I feel that sometimes your best acting is not the line, it's the reaction to someone else's line before or after, and when that gets cut, sometimes you feel like your performance has suffered. That's not to say anything negative about the editing—David was a genius as an editor—but you would sometimes feel, "Oh, damn, my best stuff is on the cutting room floor."

Jack: No, I know, and I understand that. Many times directorially, for me, what you guys do when you're not talking is absolutely sometimes more important or as important as when you're talking.

Michael: But on the flip side, David would find things in your performance that you didn't know were there. And he wouldn't edit the way network TV was edited—he was always doing whatever worked best.

Jack: Absolutely. When I was doing "Another Toothpick," it was the first scene where Carmela goes to therapy. It starts off with Tony and Dr. Melfi talking, a couple of lines of dialogue, and then Carmela has something to say, and you want the audience to go, "Holy shit, she's here?"

I came up with a shot—I shot it the classic way you guys did, but I wanted to reveal her. I didn't want to do anything tricky. Terence Winter wrote "Another Toothpick," so I was very fortunate to have Terry with me that first episode, and it was a brilliant script. I started on a shot of James, and as Carmela says something and he glances over, I just do a very slow drift over to reveal her profile in the foreground. And the script supervisor—

Michael: Christine Gee.

Jack: Yes, I remember her vividly. She says, "Jack, come here," and Terry Winter, who wrote the episode, is standing there, and it's, "Basically you can't move the camera in therapy. That's the only rule David has. No camera movement in therapy." But David never said a word to me in the tone meeting, where he walked me through the script. There were no rules except don't screw it up.

Terry said, "Look, why don't I call David and ask him." Terry goes to the phone, David says, "Try it." I had already said, "Let's light it; if he throws it out or wants to crucify me, it's fine, he won't use it." But it ended up being in the show.

ANOTHER ONE *of the interesting aspects of* The Sopranos, *that people don't think about much, was the sound. Because we did a lot of locations, it could get very tricky. Again, as we've been talking about, it was like a movie set, only you were making a movie every week. We asked sound man extraordinaire Mathew Price about the experience. —Steve*

Steve: Matt, so how did you wind up on *The Sopranos*?

Matt: I don't know if you guys know this, but the pilot started with a whole different sound team.

Michael: I didn't know that.

Matt: I actually started on day three. On day one, the original sound team got into a big beef with Henry Bronchtein, who was the assistant director on the pilot. Depending on who you ask, they either quit or got fired on day one. So I got the call and I came in on day three. Fortunately, I was available, and it changed my life because it became ten years, and it was the greatest show on TV.

Steve: Do you remember your first day, what it was like?

Matt: I remember one story, within the first week. It's a Henry story. I love Henry. I have so much respect for him. I love him as a director. But Henry and I would have these epic battles on set all the time. So there was a scene when Meadow had snuck out and she's trying to sneak into the house again through the back window and Carmela comes out with the rifle.

Steve: Right. She thinks there's an intruder.

Matt: I had to put radio mics on all the actors because the way they were shooting it, I couldn't get a boom microphone in close enough.

Steve: Just so people know, explain a radio mic.

Matt: You hide a mic on clothing and it transmits from there. You put a little transmitter pack on the actors. They transmit and I receive it at my sound cart and I mix it in with everything else. Anyways, I had to wire four actors. Henry was up my ass to hurry up. I'm saying, "I'm moving as fast as I can." And he's yelling. I said, "You already lost one sound department. I don't think you want to lose another one." That's the first day I remember being on set.

Steve: It's not an easy job. People don't know that the microphone is in your hat, your tie, your jacket. What's the weirdest place you ever hid a microphone on somebody?

Matt: The guys on *Sopranos* were great because they always wore these polo shirts with nice cotton. It was easy to hide the mic in the pocket. They always sounded great. The women were tougher. Drea—Adriana—was wearing these really short skirts, so it was really tough finding ways. Nowadays, the transmitters are very small, but back then they were huge. We had to try to hide it. I did a movie, *Sidewalks of New York,* with Brittany Murphy, rest in peace. She was wearing a towel, and I had to put a transmitter on her and I had to hide it in unmentionable places.

Steve: How about on *The Sopranos*?

Matt: The funny thing is, I wire the guys, I got to run a wire down the leg, put the transmitter on the ankle. With the women, I'm sitting there on my knees, their pants are open, it's a little uncomfortable. Jimmy was tricky because I went down his pants a lot. Jimmy would always be walking around. I'm trying to wire and I'm chasing him around with a microphone and he's talking to everybody.

Michael: What were some of the big challenges of the show for you?

Matt: The biggest challenge for the show was noisy locations.

Michael: McCarter Highway in Newark? Remember that?

Matt: Yes, that's Route 21. Also the exterior of Bada Bing, in Lodi. It's on the highway. They would always do the biggest dialogue scenes at rush hour. You got these semis flying by and it was just so loud. Which is why we never won an Emmy, because it was just so noisy all the time. [*laughs*]

Steve: I used to bust your balls. I called you the Susan Lucci of sound men. She was always nominated for Emmys for *All My Children* and always lost. You got nominated I don't know how many times.

Matt: I got six nominations for *Sopranos* and two for *Maisel*. I finally won for *Maisel*.

Steve: That's fantastic. I'm really proud of you, my friend. I really am.

WE TALKED *a little before to Pete Bucossi, the incredible stunt coordinator. Since violence was such an integral part of the show, and was always so believable, we wanted to know more about how he made all those fights so realistic. —Steve*

Steve: First off, Pete, your claim to fame, you were the guy in the trunk of the car in *Goodfellas*?

Pete: Yeah, I was doubling Billy Batts at the bar when Pesci and De Niro were beating the hell out of him. That was me. And then they throw me in the trunk of the car.

Steve: Billy Batts, played by Frank Vincent, who also of course goes on to *The Sopranos*.

Pete: Yep, that's me. Frank Vincent actually had surgery, on his back I believe, so he really couldn't do a lot. So I picked up the slack.

Steve: Tell me a little bit about the beatings, some of them. How do you make a beating look as realistic as you do?

Pete: The actors play a huge part in it—correctly snapping the head to the punch or throwing the punch correctly in the right spot. But we say, let the cameras do the work.

Steve: What do you mean by that?

Pete: When you're throwing a punch across somebody's face, if you have the camera on almost a side angle, you'd see that the punch missed. So we'd bring the camera around to the back side. So when the hand crosses the face and when the other character snaps his head, all in unison, and then adding in the sound effects, it just plays out. So I always tell actors when they're throwing a punch on another actor, you don't have to get three inches from his nose. You could be ten inches from his nose. Let the cameras do the work.

Steve: Jim was involved in so many fights. He did a lot of the stunts himself, right?

Pete: Yeah. Jimmy did do a lot. We would double Jimmy for some of the driving stuff, some of the wide stuff. Or a lot of times you have doubles just for safety reasons. Because the situation gets a little bit more heated than expected and we think a double should step in. But Jimmy handled most of the stuff. He was always mindful of what he was doing and making sure he wasn't going to hurt anybody.

Steve: Was it ever scary, to do some of those scenes? Were you ever worried? Did anything ever go really wrong?

Pete: You do all this stuff ahead of time, and then when the cameras start rolling and shooting it, it becomes magic. But yes, it gets terrifying at times. I'm always happy when the day ends and nobody has a broken nail on their hands. Somebody said once, "If a stunt goes good, it's good. If it goes bad, it's great." I'm not like that. I don't ever want anything to get out of hand. I don't think we really ever got out of hand on anything that we did on the show.

ALAN TAYLOR *was chosen by David Chase to direct the new movie,* The Many Saints of Newark, *the prequel to* The Sopranos. *None of us knew that Alan, one of the premier directors of the show—he directed nine episodes—nearly got axed after his first. After which he learned a lesson we all learned: never say no to David Chase. —Michael*

Steve: Now, Alan, your first episode was in Season One, "Pax Soprana," right?

Alan: It was. It featured Junior. I came out of film school wanting to be a filmmaker and thinking TV was stupid. They sent me the pilot for *Sopranos* and I thought, "Whoa, whoa, whoa. I've never seen anything like this before." I said, "Yes, I'd love to do one." I did that one episode and it was amazing, but I still thought, "No, I want to be a filmmaker. I want to go write my scripts."

They offered me a second episode that season and I said, "No, I want to go make my movies." That burned my reputation. [*laughs*] I don't think I was invited back for Season Two or Season Three.

Steve: David doesn't like when you say no, I don't think.

Alan: Yes, I learned that! But I guess he got over it. He came around because he gave me another shot in Season Four.

Michael: That was one of my favorite episodes, with the intervention for Christopher. I loved working with you on that.

Alan: Thanks. And then beyond that, into Seasons Five and Six, I felt more and more at home.

Steve: And you're doing the prequel. What's bigger than that? Alan Taylor is directing the *Sopranos* movie, which is quite incredible. It's quite an honor. Let's face it, David had many people to choose from, and he chose you.

Michael: But he could be tough on the directors, right? Very tough.

Alan: It could be terrifying because David Chase was rarely on set, but he is a very strong-willed person who has very strong ideas, so the desire to not screw it up was higher on that show than any show I've ever worked on. There are these tone meetings that, on every other show, you sit down with the writers before you shoot, and you flip through the script, and you make jokes and you talk about what you have in mind. But on *The Sopranos,* it was like a graduate seminar. Tim Van Patten referred to it as defending your life. That's what he called the tone meetings. Defending your life.

EVERYBODY HAS *their Jim Gandolfini stories. Here's one from Phil Abraham, the brilliant* Sopranos *cinematographer.*

When you meet Jim Gandolfini, you think he's the most confident person who ever walked the earth. But Phil gave us a little behind-the-scenes insight into what it was like to have to live up to the high expectations of playing Tony Soprano. —Steve

Steve: You got to know Jim pretty well, right?

Phil: Jim and I had a really very, very close relationship. I think he suffered a little bit of never getting any feedback. I don't know if David ever felt the need to come down and say, "Jim, you're just killing it. It's incredible."

Steve: That didn't happen that much, no.

Phil: It didn't happen. Jim was feeling like it'd be nice to hear that. But I do remember one thing with Jim. Early on, we were shooting a scene with one director—I won't say which director—he said, "Okay. Cut, print. Let's move on." That was still in the first season when we had a lot of different directors come through. There was a different director on every episode. Jim says, "Phil, come here." He pulls me off to the side, behind the stage, to talk to me. He goes, "Listen, I need you to keep an eye on me, because I just tanked that last shot. I wanted to see if this guy knew what he was doing, so I tanked it and he just printed it and moved on." I'm thinking, "Whoa, okay, yes."

Steve: He trusted your judgment.

LET'S MOVE on to the incredible ensemble cast. So many amazing actors. One of the folks we haven't talked to much so far played a really big role for a really short time: Annabella Sciorra, who portrayed Tony's unforgettable goomar Gloria. —Steve

Michael: Annabella, you were tremendous in that role. What was your way into Gloria?

Annabella: I just made a decision to give her the same background as Tony, the same kind of mother. I gave her a physically violent upbringing. There was always this pressure, and she learned how to do things to make herself feel better.

It was also the only character that I've ever played where she used her body and her sexuality to get what she wanted, in the hopes that that would make her feel better. The line that you wrote in, "I pray a little bit and I meditate"—it's like, she tries that and she tries therapy, and she's doing everything she can to make herself feel happy. I always felt Gloria didn't want to be alive. I felt like she didn't know how to stop the pain, and the shame and the guilt, and everything that she was feeling.

Michael: That's interesting. People don't really understand that the words are on the page, those don't change—but what you bring to the character can change what those words mean, who that character is.

Annabella: It was very specific too. David wanted Gloria to dress like Dr. Melfi. I was thinking, "No, no." Juliet, our wonderful costume designer, she says, "Well, we're going to have to show him some suits and some more professional-looking things." I was like, "Okay, but I know that that's not the way in for me."

Then we came across this skirt with the big slit and I go, "Fishnet stockings!" When he came down for the costume fitting and saw that he said, "Oh, okay, yes, I get it." Gloria was professional and appropriate, but it was always just slightly too much.

Steve: I think that's what Tony loved about Gloria. His wife didn't dress like that, and the people in his world didn't dress that way. Very sophisticated.

Michael: It was a combination of the intelligence of someone like Melfi, the passionate sexuality of his younger goomars, and the darkness of Livia. You put all those things together, and it was deadly, like a moth to a flame.

SPEAKING OF *our wonderful costume designer Juliet Polcsa—we can't say enough about what she added to the show. Creating the look of all those men and women was a big part of inventing the world those characters lived in. —Michael*

Michael: What would you say is the mission statement of what you had to do? Was there one overarching theme that you had to kind of keep in mind in terms of what David wanted?

Juliet: What David wanted was reality. He didn't want stereotypes, or preconceived notions of what people thought a mob family was. And much to my surprise, when I started looking into it, and doing research, and finding these stores where these guys shopped at, it was running suits and garish shirts. There was a store in a mall in Jersey called Caché, which isn't there anymore, and I thought, "Oh, my God. This is like Carmela all over the place." And I found a store on Eighteenth Avenue in Bensonhurst called Jack Charles. The owner there was immeasurably helpful as far as what guys should wear.

Steve: In a lot of the scenes with Melfi and Tony, their colors either match or clash. Was that a David thing, a direction, a writer thing, or was that you, or it was a coincidence?

Juliet: Probably a little bit of all of it. Every time we had an episode, we always would have a costume meeting. Every department would meet with the writers and the director, and we'd go through the script and discuss specifics. If it was something that we really wanted to get across, we did that. Sometimes it was intentional, sometimes it was an accident.

Michael: But sometimes when you'd create a costume, it would help us get into the feel of the scene. You were really helpful.

Juliet: Thanks. I tried to do whatever I could. In fact, there was one scene Jim had to do with Annabella where he has to go to Globe Motors and threaten her, and he had to be so angry. I looked at my costume plot, and it didn't have continuity to anything else, it could just be a costume on its own.

Michael: We should say, a "costume plot" is kind of like a spreadsheet where you plan out what everyone wears from scene to scene.

Juliet: Right. I knew all the pieces that Jim hated, all the clothes that made him feel uncomfortable, so I made that costume out of all the things that Jim didn't like because I figured it would make him mad. [*laughs*]

Steve: That's funny. You were helping his performance. Wonderful.

Juliet: Yes, exactly. When I went in to explain to him what I had done, he was great. He was just so appreciative.

SO MANY *excellent actors passed through the front doors at Silvercup Studios. Some of them wound up with big parts, some were only on for one episode, but all of them left their mark. Of all the one-episode characters, I don't think any affected the audience as much as Tracee, the stripper who was killed by Ralphie in Season Three. Ariel Kiley talked about how she created that unforgettable character—and why she quit acting shortly afterward. —Michael*

Michael: Tell us about how you came up with the character for Tracee.

Ariel: It was actually my first acting job ever. I really jumped in the deep end. I did the table read. I was coming from getting my nails done, and once I got those giant pink nails, I was in character. I was next to James, and it was surreal. I had been going around to strip clubs, to do research, and a lot of the erotic dancers were very glazed over. But I thought, "I understand how you have to get that way to continue in that profession, but Tracee's going to be wide open. She's going to be so innocent."

Steve: The episode got a lot of pushback, and rightfully so. People thought it was too violent, with Ralphie killing this innocent young girl. A lot of people got turned off. Did people contact you? Did you get a lot of that?

Ariel: I heard about it a lot. I was proud that she had that much of an impact on people. I really think it's part of the genius of the show and of David Chase that he would expose his own heroes in that way and show that they are, in a lot of ways, ruthless killers. I think that's one of the real, beautiful things about why they chose my interpretation of the character; they let her be lovable. They let her have three dimensions instead of two.

Tracee is basically in a completely dissociated state. That's how I played it. I'm like, "Imagine you grew up on the wrong side of the tracks, and you have nothing. Then you get this opportunity to dance onstage." To her, she's just been cast as Cinderella in Disney World. That's how I imagined it, as though, "Oh my goodness, and there's that big boss of the club. Of course, we're going to be friends, and I made him this bread. I'm going to dance, and all these men love me," but she's totally checked out from the fact that this is a scary, violent world.

Michael: Her story got to people. She's someone who really wants just to be loved and to be accepted. That's why it works. It was important because by this point in the show, David's concern was that the audience was getting too enamored of these gangsters.

They were these lovable guys, and people really liked them. I think David was making a point of saying, "Let's not lose sight of what this world can really be like, let's not forget who is victimized and exploited."

Steve: You really felt bad for Tracee. You played it great.

Ariel: Isn't it nice to see that I'm alive?

Steve: You did a terrific job. What was it like for you, working with Jim?

Ariel: Oh, can I tell you a little story about the question he asked me that changed my life?

Michael: Please do.

Ariel: We were shooting that scene when I walk out, and I'm topless, and I say, "Look at me, what do you think?" He says, "What am I looking at?" Then I say, "My teeth. I got braces."

Steve: Tony says, "What do you want? A parade?" [*laughs*]

Ariel: Between takes on that scene, James kept asking me, "What are you going to do when you're famous?" I don't know if he was just doing that to help me feel confident or what he was doing, but I wasn't going to give him a bullshit answer. I was thinking about it all day.

Later that night, we were shooting the scene where I was dead in the ditch. My face was covered with plaster, fake blood. I'm lying there, and it's cold. It's two A.M. in New Jersey out behind the Satin Dolls club. James is worried about me, and he says, "Hey, does she need a blanket? Are you okay?"

And right there, the answer hit me. What would I do if I was famous? It struck me, the idea of getting to be a famous actress meant I got to be totally myself, and people would love me for it. I said, "James," and he comes over, and he asked, "What?" I said, "I know what I'd do. If I'm famous, I know what I'd do. I just want to be more myself." He looks down at me, and he goes, "You will, but everyone else will change."

I just saw something—it makes me feel a little teary—about how what I wanted, I wasn't going to get it from fame. The right question at the right time from the right person made me really rethink, "Do I love acting? Is this my calling?" I had to admit, "No, I love being a part of *Sopranos*." I have a performer in me, for sure. But that wasn't my calling. Especially in the industry as it was then, it did not feel safe being in show business.

Michael: But you've used those feelings to help others.

Ariel: I've spent a long time teaching yoga and yoga therapy. I've shifted into trauma healing work, which is basically people who have unfinished business from the past. I work with a lot of people who have had experiences, some similar to what Tracee has had.

Michael: How long after *The Sopranos* did you decide to stop acting?

Ariel: After *The Sopranos*, I immediately got the big agents and the big managers. I was in L.A. I was testing for pilots. I was meeting Aaron Spelling. But the quality of the projects I was going out for was embarrassing. I was in the "hot chick" category and the industry itself was humiliating to be in. I was just thinking, "I don't think I can do this," so I quit and went back to school.

Steve: I'm glad that you found out early. I really am. You seem like you're very happy, and you're doing great.

Ariel: Yes, thank you.

ANOTHER CHARACTER *who appeared for a short time but left a lasting impression was Eugene Pontecorvo, the guy who wanted to get out of*

the mob life. It became a heartbreaking role, through the great acting of
Bobby Funaro. —Michael

Michael: So how did you wind up playing Eugene? He wasn't in the
original script, is that right?

Bobby: I auditioned for Ralph Cifaretto, and I was cast. Signed the
contract, everything. Then, when I got to the set, it didn't seem like
the chemistry was working out for me and James. I did my best to
keep going with it, but David didn't think it was the right fit, and
James was telling me the same thing. David came up to me and he
said, "What do you want to do?" I said, "I want to stay on the show,
of course." [*chuckles*]

It was really tough to live with, as an actor. But I had the ability
to say, "Okay, I'm going to keep on going. I'm going to keep on keeping on." I'm happy to share the story because it's a good example of
not quitting. Look how I ended up—I ended up with a really great
episode, and I met a great bunch of friends and everything. That's
how it really happened for me.

Michael: So then they created the role of Eugene specifically for you?

Bobby: Yes, they came up with the character Eugene Pontecorvo. I
asked Terry Winter, "Who is Eugene?" He said, "We'll figure it out,
don't worry about it."

Michael: And you had a good run—you wound up in twenty-four
episodes altogether. As you mentioned, you had a great episode,
"Members Only," at the beginning of Season Six. It's an iconic moment, because we know the show is ending, and your character is
the first to go in this last season.

Bobby: When "Members Only" came around, I read that script and
I said, "Well, this is a really great script that allows me the oppor-

tunity to open up a bit and show the human side of my character." I really identified with Eugene in his plight to try to get out. Because before then, he was just the guy that hit the guy in the head with the Snapple bottle.

Steve: So we've asked this a lot: how did you find out you were getting killed?

Bobby: First, I started hearing rumors. "Hey, Bobby, do you know that you're getting a wife on the show?" "Hey, Bobby, you know you're getting a son?" I'm thinking, "Hey, this is freaking great. I got a wife, I got a son, it's fantastic." But before the season began, David gave me the call and he said, "I got great news for you and I got bad news. What do you want first?" I said, "Give me the good news."

He said, "We wrote the first episode for Season Six. It's a great one and it's going to really show what you can do. Your character wants to get out, and all of a sudden, he can't get out. He kills himself, so you're dead."

Steve: That's David giving you the good news.

Michael: But those scenes are very memorable. It's the death scene that often sticks in people's minds with a lot of characters. They had given him a real life, so his death made a difference to people.

Bobby: That's very true.

WHEN WE *talked to Vinny Pastore, we didn't get around to talking about the life-long friendship between the two actors who played a mob informant and the FBI agent who handles him. It's one of the great behind-the-scenes stories that fans asked us about. We asked Louis Lombardi to fill us in.* —*Steve*

414 | Michael Imperioli & Steve Schirripa

Louis: Guess how long I know Vinny, since I'm fourteen. I knew Jimmy since '94 or '95. Do you know who I know since I'm a baby? Frankie Pellegrino, and he played my boss in *Sopranos*.

Steve: Wow. Look at that. It's pretty amazing. So you and Vinny go way back, and all your scenes were with him, right?

Louis: Me and Vinny—he still lives in City Island, so I live right there. I would drive to his house, sit in his house all day, run the lines over and over. Then we would drive to the set together, run the lines in the car. We rehearsed the heck out of it. You know what? It was great. I love Vinny. I love Vinny like an uncle.

Michael: Let me ask you about the character a little bit. Skip Lipari, the FBI agent. At some point Skip turns and becomes really hard. In the beginning, you're trying to be Big Pussy's buddy, you're both from the neighborhood—not so different from you and Vinny, in a way. At some point, you just get really hard with him. You're just like, "I'm not the one who's selling heroin. This is not a romance, we're not friends."

Louis: Yes. At one point I said, "I'll pull a bullet in this big, fat boar's head."

WE TALKED *earlier about how Tony Sirico gave me and Michael a hard time when we first met him—and then later we became great friends. Turns out we weren't alone. Max Casella, who played Bennie Fazio for twenty-eight episodes, has a classic Tony story.* —Steve

Steve: Max, you came on in Season Three. Did you know when you got the gig you were going to be around, or was it episode by episode?

Max: No, episode by episode. I thought I'd be gone after my first appearance.

Steve: Really?

Max: Yes. I did that first episode, I'm like, "They're not going to call me ever again, I was terrible." I felt like an imposter. You guys were all authentic and I was an imposter. My mother was Italian, my father was Jewish, I grew up in Cambridge, I didn't grow up around Italian-American culture at all. I had no concept of what it meant to be Italian until I moved to Hollywood and everybody put this thing on me

Steve: Because of your last name, you think?

Max: Absolutely, but even that's imposter. I changed my name to my mother's maiden name. My birth name is Maximilian Deitch, my father's name was Deitch. He was Jewish. When I got on with you guys, I was just like, "I'm not worthy man, you guys are the real thing." They obviously see that and they're going to be like, "Get this kid out of here with this bullshit." In fact, Tony Sirico, the first fucking thing he said to me when I met him was like, "Hey, you're not gonna get on this show with that bullshit Brooklyn accent you have."

Michael: The ever-subtle Tony. J to make you feel comfortable on your first day.

Steve: What did you say to him? Did you say, "Fuck you!"?

Max: Of course not. I'm like, "Oh god, he knows. Oh god, he knows. They all know."

Steve: Well you stuck around for twenty-eight episodes, so clearly, they liked what they saw.

WE WERE *lucky to have the terrific director Peter Bogdanovich become part of the* Sopranos *family. In addition to directing a beautiful epi-*

sode, he was a unique member of the cast, playing almost all of his scenes opposite Lorraine Bracco. He was the only one besides Jim who got to appear a lot with Lorraine. —Steve

Michael: You played Dr. Melfi's psychiatrist. A really unusual role. What was your approach to the role? Was there somebody you modeled the character after?

Peter: At some point, I realized that I was doing a version of a good friend of mine, an actor named George Morfogen. He was in *What's Up, Doc?* and played a big part in *Daisy Miller*. He was very much like my character Elliot Kupferberg; very precise and a little bit of a pain in the ass. Very specific. George was one of my closest friends.

Michael: Elliot's not afraid to just be very blunt and honest and call her on her shit. Is that how George was?

Peter: George was very straight, very honest. Slightly like a teacher.

Steve: You're one of the few people that actually worked with Lorraine besides Jim. You guys were beyond fantastic together. Did you enjoy that?

Peter: Oh, she was wonderful. The funny thing about her was, she never did two takes the same way. She'd do one take and they said, "Fine, cut. Let's do another one." Then she'd do it but it'd be completely different. I had to be on my toes, because I couldn't play it the same way; she wasn't playing it the same way so I had to change my attitude. It was a little tricky.

ARTHUR NASCARELLA *played Carlo Gervasi, the mobster who turned informant. He's an interesting guy—Arthur was a marine for eight years and an NYPD cop for twenty-one years. Everybody has a story about their first day on the set. I really like Arthur's. —Steve*

Arthur: On the first day that I got there, I went into the dressing room, and they've got two big white shoes there for me. Inside the shoes, it says, "Big Pussy." Pussy had just wound up in the Hudson River, he's dead already, and I've got to wear his shoes on my first episode. I went, "Why did you leave a fucking black cat in here?"

Steve: But it all worked out for you. You got pretty lucky. You never got whacked. And you had a nice relationship with Jim. Jim loved you, as a person and an actor.

Arthur: We liked each other right away. The first day I ever met him was at the bar in the hotel we stayed in when we were doing "Pie-O-My." I went to the bar for a drink. There was a pool right next to me. On the other side of that pool walks up a man, it's Jimmy Gandolfini. He says, "Hello, how are you?" I said to him, "Let me buy you a drink." He said, "No, let me buy *you* a drink." I looked at him and I says, "Hey, gugutz, let me buy you a drink." He looked at me and says, "That's what my father always calls me, gugutz." That means a "squash" in Italian. He said, "My father always calls me that." That was the beginning of our friendship,

SPEAKING OF *NYPD cops who made the transition to* The Sopranos— *Joe Lisi, who played Dick Barone, the owner of Barone Sanitation, spent twenty-four years as one of New York's finest.* —Steve

Steve: Were you an actor before you became a cop?

Joe: No. But I took my first acting lesson when I was twenty-nine years old. I made my Broadway debut when I was fifty-two years old. There was a time in the eighties and nineties where I was on active duty in the police department and working as an actor as well. As a matter of fact, in 1989, there was a show called *True Blue*, an NBC series. It was about emergency service cops. They hired me to play the precinct commander. The irony of life is that I was a captain in the police department, and I was playing a captain on television. I made more in one day as a captain on television than I made all week as a real cop.

ANGELO MASSAGLI *played my son on the show, Little Bobby Bacala. I'm embarrassed to say that the best lesson he learned about eating on the set, he didn't learn from me. —Steve*

Steve: What's your favorite memory from the show, Ange?

Angelo: One tip that James gave me at a dinner scene was, if you can avoid it, try not to take a bite of food. Because if they catch you in one angle where you're taking a bite, then for continuity, they're going to have you take a bite for the rest of the day. We filmed this thing in the street fair in Jersey City. I had a bag of zeppoles and I made the mistake of taking a bite of one in the first shot of the day, and the shot was good. And so I had to eat zeppoles for the rest of the day. I almost had 150 zeppoles that day. Sick to my stomach, and they're saying, "You have to keep eating."

Steve: Because you had to keep matching the shot! [*laughs*]

Angelo: James was in that scene, too. He looked at me just like, "I told you, it's just a day-one tip. Move your food around, don't eat it unless you have to."

Steve: Nobody ever told me that. Nobody ever gave me that tip.

Michael: Jimmy didn't follow that either. Jimmy was eating all the time in scenes. But he had to. They really wanted him to be eating a lot.

MARIANNE LEONE *was a very special person for me on the* Sopranos *cast. She played my mother, so we had some very meaningful scenes, but even better is the fact that I've known her for more than thirty years. What many people don't know is that she and her husband, the actor Chris Cooper, suffered the most terrible tragedy in their own lives. Their son, Jesse, who was diagnosed at a very young age with cerebral palsy and spastic quadriplegia, died in 2005 at the age of eighteen from SUDEP (sudden unexpected death in epilepsy). Marianne became a dedicated advocate for disabled children.*

None of us knew how she would deal with having to play the scene in which she reacts to the death of Christopher, her TV son. —Michael

Michael: Can I ask you about that day you had to play that scene? What that was like for you?

Marianne: After Jesse died, I worried about if they were going to kill Christopher off, and of course they did. And then I had to do that scene and everybody was incredibly nice to me that day.

Michael: I remember, that was not that long after.

Marianne: No, it was about a year or so after Jesse passed away. I fainted on set that day. Do you remember that?

Michael: Yes, of course, I do.

Marianne: I passed out. I came to, and Arthur, who was one of the cast who was an ex-cop, he had his face really close to me, with his fingers on my neck. He was saying, "Are you on meds? Are you on meds?"

Michael: That would have been Arthur Nascarella, who played Carlo Gervasi. He used to be NYPD. And then people were yelling for the doctor.

Marianne: It was crazy. And there was an extra there, a woman who raised her hand and said, "I'm a dentist." I was sitting afterward with the set doctor, and Jimmy walked by and—it was so sweet of him, I think he wanted to make me feel better—he's teasing me. He goes, "Anything for attention." [*laughs*]

Michael: I remember that.

Steve: I gotta be honest, I don't want to go to a dentist who on her days off, she's an extra on *The Sopranos*. That's just me.

ONE OF *the more subtle relationships on* The Sopranos *was Carmela's interaction with her parents, played by Suzanne Shepherd and Tom Aldredge. Suzanne told us about getting that role and playing opposite Tom.* —Michael

Michael: Originally, they cast another actress to play Carmela's mother. What happened with that?

Suzanne: When they brought me in, David said, "Would you mind if we showed you the other actress who had the part and we fired her? The reason we want you to see it is so you get the blocking and save a lot of time." I said, "No, I don't mind at all." So I saw it. She was a very pretty lady. And then I did it, and I said to James, "Why did they fire that pretty lady?" He said, "Oh, it's the simple reason that she had no edge. You're all edge and she didn't have any." I said, "I don't know what that means." I swear to God, I didn't know what it meant. I still don't know, but I say I do.

Michael: I loved you and Tom together. You two were magic.

Suzanne: My God what a man he was. I hope he rests in peace. Here's what my lifelong memory is: I get out of the car and he'd be walking on the sidewalk outside. And he'd say, "Hi, darling." I love that sound. "Hi, darling." And then we would start hugging. There was a scene where we were in bed together. He took my hand under the blankets. He put his arm around me under the blankets. What a man. And everything that came out of his mouth made me laugh.

WHEN WE *talked to David Chase, he told us the story of how Al Sapienza, who was Mikey Palmice, tried to talk him out of killing off the character. We asked Al for his side of the story.* —Steve

Michael: First off, how did you approach Mikey? Did you base him on someone you knew? What were you trying to do with him?

Al: When I read the script and I realized I'm going to shoot a guy in the eye, I realized, I don't have to play this guy tough. He kills somebody. He shoots someone in the eye. I wanted to make him a little stupid. I wanted him to be a little bit Joe Pesci, a little bit James Caan. I wanted him to be a little funny, a little goofy. He was a little dumb.

Steve: Al, David told us specifically that when he told you that you were getting whacked, you tried every which way to talk him out of it. He told us how you came up with all these sappy story lines. Tell me about that.

Al: David comes up to me in Paterson, New Jersey, and goes, "I didn't envision Mikey Palmice this way, but I love what you're doing with the character," and I was thinking, "I'm in. This is great." I actually moved out of L.A. I thought I was going to be on the show for a while. I moved to New York. And I never told them that to make them feel guilty.

Steve: Same thing could have happened to me when I moved to New York. At first they weren't using me, I thought I was done for.

Al: So David calls me into his office, Episode Seven of the first season. I'm telling you, Steve, I almost started to cry. I knew the show was great. Just like this, he goes, "You know you're getting killed at the end of this season, don't you?" [*laughs*] I'm sitting there, and I'm saying, "David, please." I said, "Let's get a costar for the last five episodes, kill him. Give me a sidekick." He goes, "No, this isn't that kind of show." I'm begging him, I'm literally begging him. He goes, "Why are you so upset?" I said, "It's a great job. It's so well written. I think it's going to be a gigantic hit."

We're not even on the air yet but I knew it was going to be a hit. And there's no work in New York. There's only Dick Wolf and *Law & Order*. I was just so happy to be working in New York City. I die, I'm dead, I'm out of work, I don't get to hang out with you guys a lot anymore. It was tough. Then, the show goes on the air, and it's the biggest show in history. I'm like, "Shit."

I was at a turning point. I could have been completely depressed. I could have got drunk all the time, and I thought, "No, I'm not going to do that. I'm going to look at this as something to build on. I'm going to use this, that I was on *The Sopranos*."

I was happy it went on. But it was tough for me as an individual to pick up from this and get my shit together again because that was a blow, man. The last time I saw Jim, I told him that. He goes, "Al, I never thought of that." I said, "Yes, but it all worked out."

PAUL SCHULZE *played the not-so-saintly Father Phil, who had a thing for Carmela. He had a lot to draw on for that role. For one thing, he and Edie Falco go way back—he was part of the "Purchase Mafia" gang, and he would go on to play opposite her later, in the acclaimed* Nurse Jackie. *But he had more to draw on than their shared history.* —Michael

Michael: You grew up in the church. Your dad was a pastor.

Paul: Yes. There was a church on Eighty-Eighth and Lexington. He was the pastor of that church for twenty-one years. He took that call to New York when I was seven. I would say I was certainly a churchgoer. I was under the yoke of my folks and wanted to not disappoint them. By the time I got to be around fourteen I started to get a little more wild, acting like a tough kid in the neighborhood on the Upper East Side for years and years. And then I auditioned for David Chase and *The Sopranos* to play this tough guy, this Mikey Palmice character.

Steve: You auditioned for Mikey Palmice? Good thing you didn't get it. We talked to Al Sapienza about that. That didn't last too long. What happened with the audition?

Paul: David said, "Oh, Paul, that was great. Thanks a lot." Then he said, "I'm curious if you wouldn't be interested in reading for a part of a priest." Here's somebody who had no idea who I was. But he saw something in me. My father was a very complicated, beautiful pastor but had a lot of demons. The fact that I ended up playing a flawed priest—somehow, David saw this.

Steve: That's incredible.

Paul: Here's another interesting little bit of trivia. I worked on a pretty terrible movie just before *The Sopranos*, but the greatest part was, I worked with Christopher Walken. At the very end of this ridiculous project, Walken said to me, "You should play a priest." And his wife is Georgianne Walken.

Steve: Our terrific casting director.

Paul: So all this stuff comes together.

Steve: Obviously there was attraction between Carmela and Father Phil. Father Phil was a weasel. A sleazy, freeloading guy.

Paul: I don't know who coined it, but everybody on set called me Father Philanderer. It's funny. You guys know how it is—when you play someone who on the surface is certainly unsavory, you still are tasked to find out what you love about this guy. I was often surprised how people thought my guy came off as sleazy. I saw him as a little complicated and definitely trying to navigate between his vows and his human taste.

Michael: Did you ever get fans or people almost treating you like you were a priest from that role?

Paul: Yes, actually. I don't know, maybe I gravitate to it a little bit. Just like my father, I've always been able to convince people that the grace of God is there for them, even though neither he nor I were always so sure it was there for us.

ONE OF *the many reasons the relationship between Carmela and Tony is so fraught is the fact that he always has a goomar on the side. But one of the reasons that all plays so believably is that the women who portray the girlfriends bring such honesty to their roles—roles that in other hands could be simple stereotypes, but in their capable hands become sympathetic, real human beings. We talked to two of them—Oksana Lada, who portrayed Irina, and Leslie Bega, who played Valentina— about the serendipity of landing the roles, and learning to make them real. —Michael*

Steve: Oksana, I can't believe this was your first acting job.

Oksana: Here's my story. I studied to be an engineer in oil and gas production in Ukraine. Going into my second year, I visited New York. I loved the city so much so I decided to drop out of school. I landed in New York City with no money, no English language skills, no nothing, and I stayed here. Acting was something I always wanted to do back in Ukraine. My parents really didn't want me to study acting—understandably so. I decided to run away from them and start my acting career in New York. I was trying to survive as a waitress, doing all these things. There was this small theater in the East Village at that time, La MaMa.

Michael: Sure, it's still there. I was on the lighting crew for a while. I used to hang lights there.

Oksana: It's still there? Wow. I was a dancer, and then I began modeling. How I got into acting—funny enough, my husband at the time, Slava, was on the show, actually. He played one of the Russian guys that scared you so much in the first season. Apparently, the casting director asked him, "Do you know of any Russian actress that speaks Russian?" He said, "Of course I do. My wife." That's how I got into the office of Georgianne Walken.

Steve: What was your first scene?

Oksana: My first scene was in bed with Tony. What I liked about the first season of the show is everybody was still developing their characters. You guys were shooting for so long and there were so many takes. I remember James Gandolfini working on his character. My scene was supposed to start shooting at eight P.M. but it started around three A.M. I was so scared. I'm thinking, "Oh my God, what am I going to do? How am I going to do it?" By the time people got to my scene, everybody was just so exhausted that nobody even cared about how I did it. It's just, "Okay, we're done. We're done. That's it."

Steve: They just wanted to get it in the can.

Oksana: I was thinking, "Oh my God. How did I do? How did I do?" David Chase was really supportive. He was always very encouraging. He said, "Okay, you did good, Oksana. You did great." It was my first job, first experience on a set and working with big actors. I needed it, and he always was there for me.

Michael: Leslie, Valentina is a very specific character. You brought a lot to that part. Tell us, who do you think Valentina was?

Leslie: When I read her, I saw her like an Italian Jessica Rabbit. That's who I saw. David had a completely different vision for her, but when they saw my read David immediately said, "That's who we're going with. That's the direction we're going." I made her have fun, and I think that was the specificity you were talking about.

Steve: Do you remember your first scene?

Leslie: This is hilarious because I was so excited to work with Joey Pants. We walk into the horse stables. I took Joey aside, and I said, "We're walking in together and we've been dating. Do you want to do backstory?" He goes, "Yes, yes, yes, let's do backstory." I said, "How do you think we met? Were we clubbing?" He goes, "Yes, we were bar-hopping. Then we started going out to all-night underground clubs." I said, "Yes, we were getting lit, right?" He goes, "Yes. We were snorting amyl nitrate." I was like, "Amyl nitrate? What's that? Okay, I'm going to go for it. Were we dancing in pink foam coming from the ceiling?" That's why, when you see me and Joey walk in, and we've been having a blast, we've been partying, we've been clubbing, and we just walk in with these big smiles on our face.

Steve: You had a connection with Ralph, but you had a real connection with Tony. You and Jim had these intimate scenes. I know Jim wasn't the most comfortable with that stuff. Did you help each other along or did you make him feel more comfortable?

Leslie: At the end of the day, it's just two people. We had a friendship and we'd hung out before, during the day, or we'd go to dinner. We went to a ball game once. We were friends, so we had a trust. We knew we had to make it hot, and I knew that I wanted it to be like you were spying on someone through a window but you shouldn't be watching this. I felt that would be the truth of the scene.

Steve: One of the best things, the scene in the bar where you smack Jim, it looked like you really smacked him. What did he say to you?

Leslie: Jimmy said, "Hit me." And I hit him.

Michael: Yes, you really did.

Leslie: The whole side of his face was red by the time we got done with all of our takes.

Steve: Did you know what you were going to have to do, that you were going to have all these sex scenes?

Leslie: I knew that there would be some graphic nudity and sex scenes, but I didn't know how much. They kept piling them on. We shot stuff that never made the cut, and I got to say, it was graphic. It was more graphic than what ended up on the show, and that's pretty graphic.

MEADOW HAD *a few boyfriends throughout the series, and they were always played by interesting actors. Jason Cerbone was the first. He was one of those great guys who showed up on the show basically for one season, but people remember him forever. The Sopranos is about living in two worlds—the mob world and the everyday world. Jackie Jr. is the guy with one foot in each world, like there's an angel and a devil on his shoulders, and they're pulling him in different directions. People related to it because we all have those big conflicts in our lives sometimes—and because Jason did such a fantastic job of making you care about that kid. —Steve*

Michael: So, Jason, what are some of your favorite moments from your experience at *The Sopranos*? Which scenes really stand out for you?

Jason: I had a lot of great scenes with Meadow, obviously. But the one scene that always comes to mind was when I go to Vesuvio to see Tony because I feel like he killed Richie. We have this little thing, he tells me to take the sunglasses off, and it's sort of a back-and-forth, just a one-on-one with Jim. For me, that was my first real meaty scene on the show and it just stands out. Working with him was definitely a big deal.

Another scene that I loved was when Tony finds me at the strip club and he throws me in the bathroom and gives me this beating—it was this physical thing, where you're really in it. I ended up getting my head smacked against the tile! But honestly, just the reality of that whole situation and being there with him and that intensity that he had, I loved that. He was amazing.

Steve: When you start this show, nobody knows who you are. Then the season starts, you've got this huge story line. What's the first time someone recognizes you? How does that feel? I mean, boom. All of a sudden, Jason Cerbone is famous on the top show on TV. Tell me about it.

Jason: It happened really quick. One of the first things was when I was in *TV Guide* as one of the new characters. I'm with my grandfather at the supermarket and he's opening the *TV Guide* while we're getting checked out, and he's going to the cashier, "Do you see him? Do you recognize him?" You got family doing that. But shortly thereafter, yes, a lot of people started to notice. I was a short-order cook at our family's restaurant, and I'd be working in the back cooking. We weren't filming then, so I was back in the kitchen. Then I'd bring the food out to the front, and then people would be going, "Isn't that the guy who's on *The Sopranos*?"

JASON PLAYED *the first of Meadow's boyfriends; Will Janowitz played the last one, Finn. I've talked about how, even when I had to play a scene in which Christopher was stoned, I would never get stoned or drunk myself. And most actors feel the same way. Will had a number of scenes where the two of them were smoking pot. And always fake pot, of course.*

Or, almost *always . . . —Michael*

Will: Jamie was super, super nice to me, and we had a lovely time. And there was this one scene where we supposedly just had sex and I'm smoking a joint. And Jamie goes, "You want to rehearse this scene? Come into my trailer." And I said, "Yeah, sure." We rehearse it, and I'm pretending to be stoned, and so is she, and she goes, "You know, Will, you're so good at being stoned. You're better at being stoned than I am." And I go, "Really? I think you're doing a great job." She goes, "I brought a little, if you want to just have it." And I go, "I don't think that's a good idea. I get really in my head." And she goes, "No, no, no, we'll take one drag." And I'm feeling the peer pressure, and I don't want her to do it without me. So she lights up. She takes a puff. I take maybe one puff, two puffs, and knock, knock, knock—"Hey, guys, we're ready for you."

Steve: Oh, no.

Will: The second somebody knocks on the door, I'm full-blown baked out of my head. And they're walking us to set and I'm freaking out and I'm going, "I can't do this. I don't know what I'm going to do." I get on set. It's Tim Van Patten, luckily. And we get down onto a futon in the room that they had placed there, and we're supposed to have a big fight, a lot of dialogue. And we light the fake joint, and the lights are kind of orbing around me and I'm looking around and, oh my God, I'm freaking out. And Jamie's looking at me and she goes, "Are you okay?" And I said, "No, no." I fuck up my lines about four or five times. And Tim Van Patten goes, "Will, you all right?" And I'm like, "I don't know." So what I did was, I got angry at myself, and I kind of mentally broke through. And I just said to myself, "Will, just say the lines angry, just get it out of your system." And we got the scene, but I mean, holy shit. Jamie still laughs about it. She was fine. I was gone.

Lola Glaudini played the unusual part of a dual character—she was FBI agent Deborah Ciccerone, who doubled undercover as Adriana's friend "Danielle." We wondered what it was like to play that two-fold role. —Michael

Michael: Now, you took over for Fairuza Balk, who originally played the part. She appeared in the original airing.

Lola: She did the season finale of Season Three, which aired once, but then we reshot it with me and that's what it is on the DVDs, the reruns, and the streaming.

Steve: For whatever reason, she didn't come back.

Michael: I heard it was that she didn't want to commit to coming back for more shows. She only wanted to do one episode, and then they said, "No, we're going to bring you back," for what came to be seven episodes, and she didn't want to.

Steve: Did you find it hard to play? You were playing an Italian girl from Jersey, and then we also see you as this very buttoned-down FBI agent. Was it hard to go back and forth?

Lola: I didn't find it hard. What I noticed—and I talked to David Chase about this—was that even as an agent, she was still Italian-American, just like Frank Pellegrino and Matt Servitto's characters, even though they were feds. They still peppered their language with Italian phrases and intonations and stuff.

Michael: What was your first day on the set like?

Lola: Every day on the set was really like Christmas Eve to me. I was giddy beforehand and certainly, the first day, I was popping out of my shoes, but also, I kept having to tell myself, "Cool your jets, Glaudini. Cool your jets." My first day was the scene that we shot in your apartment.

Michael: When I come home and you're already there with Adriana and I'm bummed out that you're hanging around.

Lola: Yes. I remember Allen Coulter, the director, who I've worked with a bunch subsequently—he's so charming and Texan and everything—he explained how he was shooting it like a Vermeer. How he was lighting this sequence like a Vermeer. I was really taken by that kind of attention to detail.

Michael: Not something you hear on TV very often, that they want to light a scene like a seventeenth-century Dutch painter.

Lola Everyone was so lovely. The crew was so warm and welcoming. Drea was so awesome. She was like, "I'm so excited to have a friend." Then, Michael, you were sitting off to the side, I just looked at you and [*laughs*] you were reading Kierkegaard.

Michael: Really?

Lola: You had a dog-eared book, reading Kierkegaard, and I remember after my first day going back to my apartment one of my best friends, Didi, who was such a fan of *The Sopranos* along with me, was saying, "What was it like? What was so-and-so like?" I said, "Michael Imperioli was reading Kierkegaard" [*laughs*], and then that was your code name.

AS LOLA *mentioned, she played a lot of scenes with Matt Servitto, who portrayed FBI agent Dwight Harris. Matt told us one of the secret rea-*

sons that the portrayal of FBI agents was so authentic—a secret he thinks maybe even he wasn't supposed to know. —Steve

Matt: The first episode or two, I just didn't think I was going to stick around, so really, I just want to hit the mark, say the lines, and then I'll go home. Once it got extended, David brought me to some FBI guys that ran a training clinic for civilians.

Michael: Like a fantasy camp.

Matt: Yes, like a fantasy camp for the FBI. They put you through small-arms fire, through interrogation techniques, through studying on a stakeout, what things you'll look for. It was really great.

But then these other guys—you guys probably didn't see them, but David would invite people to set, and they'd just be watching the scene, and then they'd sidle up to me and go, "Hey, man, I'm FBI. David invited us. We just want to see. We love what you do. It's great." Then I started picking their brains. They were always coy.

I don't know if David wanted us to know that they were on set, but they were there. And he had relationships with guys at the Bureau who vetted some of the story lines and scripts. Every guy I've ever met from the Bureau that watched the show said, "You guys nailed it. There's things in there that only somebody from the Bureau would know."

Michael: Can you explain or elaborate a little on the relationship between Harris and Tony Soprano? As it went on, it seemed like there were points where there was actual mutual respect, or sympathy.

Matt: There's a couple of things to that. I always describe the relationship as Wile E. Coyote and the sheepdog in Looney Tunes. They both punch the clock. Then the sheepdog chases Wile E. Coyote all day, and then at the end of the episode, they go, "Good night, John. Good night, Bob."

Steve: Did you have a favorite scene?

Matt: There's only one scene on my reel from the show. It's just special to me. It is one of those scenes at the pork store, and I'm, yet again, eating another fucking sandwich. It's just a scene where I tell Tony to watch out, that Phil Leotardo has put a hit on him. It's a small scene, very intimate. He's saying, "Why are you telling me this?" and I say, "It's Christmas." That's it. It's just a small little scene, but Jimmy and I just got it in the first few takes, and the director, Alan Taylor, said, "I'm done. This is beautiful. It's a great little moment." The way he framed it, and the two of us just sitting at a café table, I love that little scene. I went home just thinking, "That was lovely."

STEVEN VAN *Zandt, who played Silvio Dante, calls his wife, Maureen, "the real actor in the family." People who think Maureen got the role of Silvio's wife, Gabriella, just because she's married to Stevie in real life don't know her history. Maureen has a long and storied theater career: She began as a dancer in ballet and on Broadway, trained with acclaimed acting coaches Stella Adler and Herbert Berghof, started her own theater company, and has performed everything from Tennessee Williams to Shakespeare.*

But what we didn't know is how much history she brought to the role of Gabriella. —Michael

Michael: What was your way into the character of Gabriella? Was this world familiar to you?

Maureen: Actually I had grown up in a Mafia family in New Jersey.

Michael: Ah, I did not know that.

Maureen: This was very much my life. And all my life, I tried to work at being the little ballerina and getting rid of the New Jersey accent and not saying "You jerk-off!" and things like that to everybody. And then I get the part and I think I have to go back to that. So I kind of based her on my youngest sister, who was very sort of naive in a way, very New Jersey, with the nails and the hair and the jewelry and all this stuff, but a very sweet and nice kind of version of a New Jersey housewife.

So I based the character a little bit on her and also the women that I grew up around, more of the old-school Mafia wives who didn't really want to run the show. They didn't want to be the boss or take charge of anything. They just wanted to get their nails done and their hair done and have nice clothes and just do that. Just be a support to their husbands. And that's what Gabby was really.

Michael: Accepting that lifestyle for what it is and that's okay with them.

Maureen: Yeah. Accepting it and appreciating the benefits that you get from it and maybe not really looking closely at the really scary things that happen with it.

Steve: I have to ask because we forgot to ask Steven—did Little Richard marry you guys?

Maureen: Yes. We were actually going to get married in Italy and just have nobody there and be very quiet about it. And then the Italian families got really pissed off that we were sneaking off and doing that. So then we ended up having a big wedding, and Steven always thinks, like, "What's the biggest thing I can do here?" And he thought, "I'll get Little Richard to do it. He's a minister."

Michael: Steven called Little Richard his namesake. That's why he became Little Steven. And Little Richard was also his mentor. So that makes sense.

Maureen: Yeah, but I'm like, "Yeah. Okay. Not going to happen." And he did it! Little Richard came up from Georgia with his entourage. This would rival that Livia memorial scene. That's how crazy the whole thing was. And the rap he gave at that ceremony was beyond belief.

Michael: And that's the first wedding Little Richard ever did. After that he did a number of others, but yours was the first.

Steve: And didn't you have Percy Sledge do "When a Man Loves a Woman"?

Maureen: Yes, he did. And we had the orchestra from the *Godfather* movie. They were the band.

Michael: The one that was onstage at the wedding scene in *The Godfather*?

Maureen: Yes.

Michael: That's fantastic.

CARL CAPOTORTO *played Little Paulie. I always wondered what his relationship was to Big Paulie. —Steve*

Steve: Was Little Paulie related to Paulie Walnuts? Or was he a protégé? What is he to you?

Carl: Nothing.

Steve: He wasn't anything?

Carl: He's called his nephew. And I asked David about that once— "Am I related on the mother's side or whatever?" He said, "You know what it probably is? It's probably that he was an old friend of your father who's probably not around anymore, and he's always been like an uncle to you, and you call him Uncle Paulie. It may not be blood."

Steve: What was it like the first time you met Tony Sirico, big Paulie?

Carl: The very first time I met Tony was before I started actually working. I was at Silvercup and they were testing looks, and apparently David had drawn a little sketch of what he wanted from Little Paulie. And he wanted a silver streak in the hair.

Steve: Like Paulie, with the wings, but only one streak.

Carl: And he wanted him dressed like Paulie, especially the running suit look with the white shoes or sneakers and the pinky ring. So they were trying out this look, and I'm walking through the studio with my hair done with the white streak, and the running suit and the white sneakers and the pinky ring, and here comes Tony Sirico, coming in the other direction. And he stopped in the hallway, and he said, "Hey, that's my look!" And I said, "No, I know. You know why? That's because I'm Little Paulie. You're Paulie, and then I'm Little Paulie." And he said, "Oh, you're a mini me?" I said, "Yeah, a mini you." Then it was okay.

CHRIS CALDOVINO *became Phil Leotardo's brother Billy, a key role in the later seasons. But we found out it only happened because of a glitch in the arcane system of clearing names. —Michael*

Michael: How did your character become Phil Leotardo's brother? He didn't start out that way, right?

Chris: I had auditioned for Little Carmine previously, and I wasn't right for it. And then when the Billy Leotardo audition came up— originally the character's name was Billy Siracusa. It wasn't Billy Leotardo. And I was just going to be one of the guys. The day I started working, I was still Billy Siracusa through that whole day. But apparently the producers, for some reason, they couldn't use the name Billy Siracusa. It didn't clear for some reason.

Michael: We should just say, clearing character names means they have to actually do research to see if there's some real people with the same name who may sue because they feel the character is based on them somehow.

Chris: They decided to name me Billy Leotardo because while I was working with Frank Vincent, who played Phil Leotardo, I guess they saw a resemblance or whatever; that sparked that idea. And then my next episode, I was Billy Leotardo. If that didn't happen, I would have maybe done one or two episodes as Billy Siracusa, as a guy in a crew. So that was a stroke of luck.

PEOPLE THINK *appearing on* The Sopranos *is an automatic ticket to the big time. Matt Del Negro, who played Carmela's cousin Brian, admits he was one of those.* —Steve

Steve: So after *The Sopranos*, what happens? Do you get a lot of offers?

Matt: I thought I would. I had visions of me sitting on Letterman's couch. I had a whole different vision of what was going to happen. And I came out to L.A. after that. After all my stuff aired, I thought, "Okay, this is the time. Strike while the iron's hot." And I came out here and it was the busiest it's ever been. Everybody was meeting with me, "Oh, Cousin Brian, we love you." And I was thinking, "Okay, where's my show? I'm just going to sign the next thing." Got nothing. Rifled through money. Went back to New York. Bartended another two years after *Sopranos*.

Michael: That's what people don't realize, that being on the show didn't guarantee anything. But you landed on your feet.

Matt: I was out here for pilot season and I got a *West Wing*, and it was supposed to be a one-and-done, but they brought me back for the rest of that season and that's what moved us out here.

Steve: How many *West Wings* did you do?

Matt: I did around sixteen.

Steve: It just goes to show, like we keep saying, in this business, you gotta never give up.

SPEAKING OF *life after* The Sopranos, *William DeMeo is a perfect example of someone who parlayed that moment into a greater opportunity. He had a small recurring role as Jason Molinaro—a member of the crew you saw hanging around the Bada Bing a lot—but persistence and perseverance turned him into a successful director of several movies and TV shows, including his current project,* Gravesend *on Amazon Prime, which he writes, directs, and stars in. A lot of the listeners to the podcast ask us how they can get into the business; William has some excellent advice for them. —Michael*

Michael: You didn't wait around after *The Sopranos* for things to fall into your lap. You said, "I'm gonna write, I'm gonna produce, I'm gonna create my own opportunities." For people who want to get into the business, what can they learn from your experience? What can you tell them?

William: I would think no matter what it is, even a short film, that you could do yourself, to showcase yourself, if you can even put a little financing together—it's hard today to break in for young actors and filmmakers. The best thing you can do is put something together to showcase yourself, even if it's fifteen minutes. The first film I did was called *One Deadly Road*. It started as a short, and that's how I started, with my first little film. And then I did my movie *Wannabes*. More people believed in me as I had products that I had distribution for.

Steve: So how did you get into the directing? Did you go to film school?

William: My biggest film school was being on the *Sopranos* set. Just watching great directors like Steve Buscemi and Alan Taylor. I always would just be like a fly on the wall. When I talk to extras on sets, I say, "If you wanna be a director, just watch."

WE ALL *remember our first scene with Jim Gandolfini. For Ray Abruzzo, who had a significant role as Little Carmine, it was a moment he'll never forget. —Steve*

Ray: My first big scene was with Jimmy down at the Fontainebleau Hotel in Miami. We had to shoot after the restaurant was closed. I couldn't sleep the night before, I had this nightmare that I say my first line, and Jimmy says, "Well, that's not your line."

So we go to sit down, first rehearsal, we shake hands across the table. Now, this is the scene I auditioned with, so I felt pretty confident because I've done it enough times. I delivered my first line, and Jimmy goes, "That's not your line." They had done a rewrite and never sent me the new pages! He just handed me the sides, I looked at it and said, "Okay, let's go," and then that was it. You know how fortunate I was—I had a lot of one-on-one scenes with Jimmy. That being my introduction was pretty amazing because he's such an easy actor to work with.

Michael: Your role was very significant because you bring ideas to Tony that no one else did. That role was very specific.

Ray: In the early years, Little Carmine wanted to be boss, but then he came to realize being happy might be a little bit more important. In the end, he really learns how to find happiness and tells Tony—in that big scene that Terry Winter wrote at the golf course—how it's not about being boss, it's about being happy, how his wife doesn't want to be the wealthiest widow on Long Island—that resonated with Tony. You see it on Jimmy's face in that scene. You almost see it in that very last scene of the series too, when he's with his family, when they make a reference to remembering the happy moments.

TO FINISH *up going around the horn, we gotta tell one more Jim Gandolfini story. We'll let director Alan Taylor get the last word.* —*Steve*

Michael: Alan, what was your favorite episode to direct?

Alan Taylor: "Kennedy and Heidi" is probably my favorite, partly because I got to do your character's final scene, Michael, but also, we went crazy places. We went to Vegas at the end. That's when Tony has his "I get it" moment. One of the most amazing things for me was that we shot that scene out of order, for once. Because it was in Vegas, that was put at the end of the whole schedule for the last season. The entire series was done, and we flew out to Vegas and stayed at Caesars Palace. All these magical things happened.

Between takes, Jim was playing roulette in Caesars Palace. I came over to give him a note about the scene we were about to do, and he gave me some chips. I put them down on my daughter's birthday and talked to him a bit, and I won $400. It's amazing. I talked to him some more and I put some on my other daughter's birthday, and I won again. Then I went back to work. There was that magical thing, but also, at the very end, we did the last shot of Jim.

He was sitting in a lawn chair by the pool. When we were done, he said, "Do you have it?" I said, "Yes." He said, "Are you sure you have it?" Because this was literally the last shot he was going to have to do as Tony Soprano. I said, "Yes." And he picked me up and threw me into the swimming pool. It was such a great way to end. Of course, David Chase being David Chase, we all went back and he had to do reshoots. He wasn't quite liberated yet, but it was a great way, for me, to finish.

THIRTEEN

Season Six

Cut to Black

BRAD GRAY AT HBO HAD ANNOUNCED *that there would indeed be a Season Six of* The Sopranos, *consisting of only ten episodes (which later became twelve). But a year after the death of Tony Blundetto, with no new episodes in sight, viewers were beginning to wonder if maybe he had taken the rest of the Sopranos with him.*

Part of the long delay was that Jim Gandolfini had had knee surgery. But the other part of it was David making sure he still had good stories to tell. When you're working on what a lot of people are already calling the greatest show of all time, the cultural expectations are enormous: When you're the best, it's not good enough to just be good enough.

People went their own way. I was in Vegas, Michael was running his theater in New York, everybody was kind of scattered. Those of us who were regulars were under contract—we could do a movie or a TV episode, but we couldn't do any regular work like a series. The decision on bringing the show back kept getting pushed back and back and back. So the clock was ticking, and months were passing by, and lot of the actors would call up me and Michael and say, "Have you heard anything? Do you know anything?"—because our lawyer was Jim's lawyer too, so they thought we had an inside track. We all tried to stay in touch—but after a year, year and a half, it gets harder. The filming of Season Six finally started in the spring of 2005, but the episodes would not begin airing until a year later, in March of 2006.

Executive producer Ilene Landress, who had been with the show from the very beginning, told us those were trying times for everyone involved. —*Steve*

Michael: Take me back to that moment, Ilene. What were you all thinking?

Ilene: We did really well up until Season Five. After that, it just became this thing, are we going to do more episodes? Aren't we going to do more episodes? So after Season Five ended, I was like, "Is there a Season Six?" Between Season Five and Season Six, my life was a little bit miserable, because we were supposed to start at a certain time, and then we pushed, and then HBO was asking for more than ten episodes, and to David's credit, he didn't just want to take his idea and just string it along. He wanted to really feel like he had enough story. And then, sadly John Patterson was dying. John, who was very close friends with David, was one of our best directors. So for the writing staff in L.A., it was a depressing time.

Michael: A really hard time. And then you had to worry about losing the crew, as well, because of the long delay.

Ilene: There was a point between Season Five and Six where you wanted to be able to keep people, and our crew really wanted to stick with us, but at the same time they had to work. So there was that thing of calling people up and saying, "Okay, we're pushing. Take other jobs, but then also be available for us." So it's sort of a bummer when you're calling and going, "Yeah, we're going to have another season, but yeah, I can't tell you exactly when."

Steve: But also, for the rest of us, we finish shooting and we're done, but for David he's still working.

Ilene: Right. What you have to realize is, we'd finish shooting the show, and then we'd have to edit the show, and David is really involved in editing. And as time went on, he wanted a little bit of space. Okay, we finished editing. Even though it seems like a long break before it went on the air, it wasn't a long break in terms of the workload for David. I mean, David would finish editing, he'd probably have a month off, while he was hiding out and thinking about what happens next, because David would always want to have some sort of plan before he got in the room with the writers. He'd have some sort of map, some idea of what the arc of the season was going to be. And he'd present the arc, and then in the writers' room they'd come up with the stories.

———

Steve: That was hard for all of us, when John Patterson passed away.

Michael: I loved John Patterson. I miss him a lot. He was a wonderful guy, and a great spirit, and he had an exquisite sense of humor. He was very warm and a lovely man. He was a good friend too. His episodes really are always right on. He did really excellent work with the camera and with the actors, and his interpretation of the script. He was a master.

Steve: He was so well liked among the cast. Really one of the guys. He was funny on the set, too. He used to send the assistant director over, and he would say, "John said bring it down a little. Maybe three-eighths."

Michael: Right. "Could you take it down, maybe thirty-two percent?"

Steve: That was great. He had such an even temper. But you know what? I did see him get aggravated once. He got aggravated with a guy who was a Broadway actor. An older guy, out of his element. He was acting like he was on the stage.

Michael: I know exactly who. I'm not going to say it.

Steve: I'm not knocking the guy at all. He just wasn't getting it.

Michael: No, and John lost patience with him.

Steve: The guy was being too actor-y, too theatrical. John tried. He talked and talked and talked. Then finally, John just flat-out gave him a line reading. He just flat-out said, "Do it like this." It was embarrassing.

Michael: You never want the director to give you a line reading. It's not done.

Steve: I tried to move away. He just lost his patience. In the final cut of the episode, they dubbed the actor's voice. But that was the exception with John, not the rule. He was a prince.

In the shadow of John Patterson's death, the arc of the stories in Season Six—and again, at the time, it could have ended after those first twelve episodes—had a lot to do with death and redemption. Those who think Tony dies at the end of the series point to the beginning of Season Six, a long montage over narration by William Burroughs about what happens to the soul when you die.

The season quickly becomes centered on a long near-death experience for Tony, the likes of which had never before been seen on television. Having Uncle Junior shoot Tony in the very first episode, and spending two more episodes with Tony in a coma, dreaming that he's someone else, was by far the most daring—and controversial—step David Chase had taken.

We talked again with Matthew Weiner, who wrote some of those coma-dream sequences with David, about how they came about, and what they meant. —Michael

Steve: Okay, I've said it before, I'm not the deepest thinker, so walk me through this, Matt. What was that coma dream all about?

Matt: John Patterson, who was a huge part of the show, had passed away and David had lived through that experience with him. They'd known each other forever.

Michael: He kept it very quiet, until the very end. He was only sixty-four. He died of prostate cancer. That was very hard on David.

Matt: David is an existential person and was very close with John. They were friends since grad school. John's passing was a spiritual event for David. I think he wanted to share that. He started creating this hospital thing. Which, remember, we built the hospital set and everything. It was going to go as long as it went, for Tony to be shot by Uncle Junior and to be in there. And then for Tony to be in this other world. He has to be someone else in this other reality. He's going to be this Kevin Finnerty, that was the name they came up with.

Michael: One of you guys told me that that name, "Kevin Finnerty," you picked it because when you say it out loud you hear "infinity," like Tony is teetering on the brink of infinity. That's really cool. But really, the transformation into Kevin Finnerty—Jim becomes this whole other person. The transformation is amazing. I know Jim loved doing it. He was happy to take on the challenge of becoming this Tony Soprano–in–an–alternate–universe.

Matt: I remember Jim coming in and showing us what Kevin Finnerty walked like. That he was a little bit like Alec Baldwin. Not Jim. And he just transformed. It was so exciting, to have that access to that subconscious, or unconscious, process. David was so interested in the intuitive process.

Steve: That wasn't Edie doing the voice on the other end of the phone, by the way. The girl on the line was played by Wendy Hammers. She used to work for me as a comic in Vegas. But anyway—I was going to say, a lot of people didn't like these episodes. Or didn't understand them. But David didn't care.

Matt: It's something I'd never heard before on a television show, but actors say it to each other: if you understand it, the audience understands it. That is not a point of view that I was raised with in the TV business. In network TV it was literally like, "No one's going to get that. Nobody understands that. We just got back from a commercial. You better explain it again." But David had been in that world his whole career and hated it. He hated network TV so much. There are things in *The Sopranos,* if you study the history of TV, that are just fuck-yous to network TV.

Michael: This was unusual, though, even for *The Sopranos.* There's a real Buddhist sense to these scenes, not just because actual literal Buddhists show up.

Matt: David had drawn a lot of this— He doesn't talk about it, and I don't know if I should talk about it, but a lot of Kevin Finnerty's journey to death—I mean, I read *The Snow Leopard.* David had a lot of Buddhism that he understood.

Michael: *The Snow Leopard,* by Peter Matthiessen, is a book about an actual physical journey that's really a spiritual journey, a kind of Zen meditation on reality. On impermanence. So there's a lot of that in the coma dream.

Matt: And then, we were big fans of Buñuel, too. And David was like, "I'm going to express that other world and the audience will get it."

Michael: Anyway it's a brilliant sequence of scenes. The searchlight off in the distance, the whole question of identity, Tony showing up with the briefcase at the end—like, lay down your self and join the afterlife—all of that.

Matt: And then my part of it was him coming out of the dream. And that is a *Twilight Zone*. We're huge fans. David's a huge fan. Terry, obviously. I didn't know *The Honeymooners* like they did. But I knew *The Twilight Zone* as well as David. It was a huge part of my life. And that's all I wanted, was the idea that something in the other world brought him back. David's pass on that script included adding the trees blowing and Meadow's voice.

Michael: Meadow's voice, in the hospital room, he hears that in the dream, coming out of the trees, and it brings him back. Maybe the most powerful image of the whole season.

Steve: Once again, it's all about the family.

———————

Steve: All the stuff from the coma dream episode, that comes up again later, in "The Fleshy Part of the Thigh."

Michael: This season brings up a lot of philosophical points about humanity's search for meaning, going beyond just worldly existence. It's something that's addressed in the season through Tony's coma dream but even more so when he comes out of it. One of the biggest moments that is connected to this theme of the soul and the eternal is Hal Holbrook's character; he plays that scientist who dies in the hospital.

It's actually a very Buddhist concept, where he says, "How we perceive the world is an illusion, and the truth of the matter is: Non-duality is really the ultimate reality, that we're all one in terms of science and physics, not just religious theory or spiritual theory." I think David is making that big point, trying to see some bigger picture here.

Steve: Is David a Buddhist?

Michael: No, but he's interested in it.

Steve: But like I've said, for a lot of fans, this season was a little hard. There are fans who say there should be a killing every episode, or at least a beating. This is not their cup of tea.

Michael: To David's credit, he had a lot of balls to say, "I'm just going to make this as creative and as interesting to me as possible. I'm not worried about giving the fans what they want. If they like what I'm doing, they're going to like the show." It was a big diversion from what they were used to on the show, yet it was consistent with the show because there were always elements of the unconscious and subconscious and the dream life. He just took it really far in this season. I really admire that.

Steve: I'll tell you what. If David would have pandered to the audience, the show would not have lasted as long as it did.

Michael: Would not have been as good.

Steve: But going back to the coma scenes, you had some really nice moments. Christopher's holding Carmela in the hospital. Do you remember what it was like shooting that?

Michael: I remember it really well. Edie and I didn't get a lot of opportunities to work together, so when we did, it was really special. All the emotion there is real. Christopher has this up-and-down thing with Tony up until the end. He loves him. He wants to get close to him. Then he resents him. Then he feels underappreciated. Then he feels appreciated when Tony does something for him. At the end of the day, I think he did love him. It's very complicated. So that moment is very important. Christopher is Carmela's cousin, but they always relate through Tony. But here, they have this touching moment together. I'm very glad I got to do that scene with Edie.

Steve: One of the best things in the whole hospital thing was Carmela's speech to Tony when he's in the coma.

Michael: Yes. It's like a long soliloquy. David wrote that.

Steve: I think Carmela feels guilty, especially when she brings up the time she said, in the first season, "You're going to hell," and she admits it was a horrible thing to say and she'll be judged for it. Edie's performance in this whole thing is just incredible.

Michael: It's very beautiful and really important to have this monologue because this is a guy who's been unfaithful to her for years. He's embarrassed her, he's humiliated her, he's hurt her again and again, he's belittled her. Yet, in this moment, she's forgiving all that, and realizing that she does love him, and that in his own way, he's a good man despite his flaws. Because he's a human being.

Steve: We talked before about David Chase's eulogy at Jim's funeral. This felt a little bit like that to me, to tell you the truth. To see Edie making this speech, and Jim lying there, I couldn't help but think about that.

Michael: Good point, Steve. That's very true. It reminds me of something else at Jim's funeral. Susan Aston, his dialogue coach. They were friends for many, many years. She spoke at the memorial. She said Jim was always very hard on himself, but she always encouraged him to remember that he was a human being like everybody else who has flaws and is doing their best in the face of that. "In order to create, one has to be willing to miss the mark," she said, "and to be willing to be seen as human."

Steve: I remember something else she said, now that you mention it. She said a long time ago they were in a play together, and they were gonna go out onstage and she was nervous, and he said, "Aston, what's the worst that can happen? We suck?"

OF COURSE, *even in a series of episodes dealing with the great questions of the meaning of life, the universe, and everything, some humor is gonna seep through. In the episode "Mayham"—another one of those funny malaprops we mentioned earlier—there's a little subplot of Paulie ripping off some drug dealers and getting kicked in the balls. Only this time, for once, David Chase had nothing to do with it. Matt Weiner filled us in. —Steve*

Matt: In the first draft of "Mayham," Paulie hadn't gotten kicked in the balls. That was a thing where I had added it off the outline and almost lost my job for that because you're not allowed to screw with the outline.

Michael: They had beat out the story, and that wasn't one of the beats.

Matt: And I didn't think David would notice it, but somebody tattled on me.

Michael: I did the same thing once. David was not happy when I did that. He said, "What is this scene? This isn't in the outline."

Matt: Yeah. I said, "We talked about that." He goes, "No we didn't." But it was so good that it ended up in the show.

Steve: That was the third time Paulie got kicked in the nuts, you know.

Michael: Really?

Steve: Yeah, In "Pine Barrens," the Russian kicked him in the balls, and then when he goes to kill Minn, the old lady, she kicks him in the balls. So, Matt, you're carrying on a great tradition. Did Tony give you shit for that?

Matt: Tony was sweet to me because I think Terry told him I was good. And I also had written a bunch of jokes for him. I think the most out-of-line thing that Tony Sirico did was he showed one of my kids his nickel-plated gun that he had in his waistband at catering. I was like, "I didn't know about that." But Tony Sirico—I can't believe that I came in contact with him. He was a joy to write for. That was the first time in my life when I was writing dialogue and I knew that it was going to be better than I wrote it. It was going to surprise me, and it was going to be better.

ANOTHER ONE of the big story lines in Season Six is when we find out that Vito is gay, and he runs away to a town in New Hampshire. It was a new thing on TV, and you gotta give David Chase a lot of credit for that. But watching it now, you gotta wonder about the homophobia—how much the mob guys hate the gay guys. David showed that as well. He never pulled any punches. —Steve

Steve: I don't know if a lot of the *Sopranos* fans out there expected to see a gay character. You see them kissing, you see them in bed. I know it was based on a true story that Joe Gannascoli brought to the writers. Joe, who played Vito. He read the story in a book.

Michael: It's based on a book called *Murder Machine,* about an openly gay member of the Gambino crime family who was allowed to live because he was a good earner.

Steve: That's Tony exactly. Tony didn't care. He just cared that Vito was his biggest earner. But the homophobia comes into play when they bring Finn in, and he tells the crew that Vito was blowing the security guard. It's so twisted because it would have somehow been easier for the guys to handle if he was the one getting a blow job, right? [*chuckles*] Paulie Walnuts was appalled. He's going, "What? Son of a bitch."

Michael: Let's face it, homophobia exists in the world, whether David Chase portrays it or not. It exists not just in the mob, but in a lot of the world. Homosexuality has, thankfully, become an accepted part of our culture, and we've made incredible strides since this show aired, but there's still a lot of homophobia in the world.

Steve: David is just telling it like it is.

Michael: John Costelloe did a terrific job in those episodes. He played the character of Jim, also known as Johnny Cakes, who becomes Vito's lover. John Costelloe was in acting class at Elaine Aiken's back in the eighties, with me, John Ventimiglia, Sharon Angela. Alec Baldwin was there for a while, he was already on Broadway and had done movies, but John Costelloe was the first out of our crew that started working legit. He always stood out as somebody who was very talented. He also was a fireman in real life, and I guess that's why they worked that into the script. Tragically, John wound up taking his own life a couple of years after *The Sopranos*. We miss him a lot. He was a really good guy, and a very good actor.

Steve: "Johnny Cakes" was also the first episode you got to act with the wonderful Julianna Margulies. Her character—they named her Julianna also—almost has an affair with Tony, and then she winds up for a little while with Christopher.

Michael: I think Julianna Margulies is a superb actress. She's somebody I've known for a long time, way before *The Sopranos*. I actually knew her before she was on *ER*. I met her in the early nineties right before that all happened. I always liked her a lot and I always thought she was a phenomenal actress. She just comes onto *The Sopranos* and nails it right from the beginning.

Steve: What was it like working with her?

Michael: I liked that story line for Christopher because she was a little bit out of his element in a way, not the usual type of woman that he's been with in the past. They connected on a certain level that was very intense for Christopher, and having them relapse together, and having that connection, was really powerful.

Steve: Up to this point you did a lot of scenes where you're stoned, but you're mostly on your own. Like at the end of "The Ride." Or you're trying to pretend you're not stoned in front of Tony. So what was it like to take that into a two-person scene and have somebody to play that with?

Michael: It was really cool. It was like we were stepping out into our own little world. Obviously, it was sexual, and then it goes from being sexual to being not sexual. You add the drugs, then the sex falls off and it's just about the drugs. The progression of their relationship happens really fast, and I found it really interesting. Also, her character goes from selling real estate to getting interested in Tony, and then when he rejects her she winds up with Christopher because of her involvement in recovery. It's a brief story line, but I think a really good one. Christopher really fell for her. He was in love with her.

Steve: You see her again at the end of the season. She shows up at Christopher's wake. I thought that was a nice touch.

Michael: One of the listeners to our podcast asked, which guest-star celebrity of the entire run of the show was your favorite to work with? Julianna Margulies was my favorite. The scenes we had together were very intimate and there was something about the chemistry of the characters and what she gave as an actor—I just loved working with her.

BY THIS *time, the efforts by the press to find out details of the plots of upcoming episodes had reached a fever pitch. Jason Minter, David Chase's assistant, is the one who had to deal with it. —Steve*

Steve: Jason, you were privy to a lot of stuff obviously; you knew who was getting killed.

Jason: I did know everything. And yes, there's a lot of responsibility with that, and then there were leaks. There were issues where the *National Enquirer* would find out about Christopher's death, for example. We tried to sleuth that stuff pretty hard-core. We had attorneys from HBO in. I had been a location manager and I knew the crew, so I tried to figure out who that person was. I had narrowed it down to who I thought it was. But I was wrong. I found out only about three or four years ago who it actually was. It was a department head and I never would have guessed that. He made hundreds of thousands of dollars off of giving secrets.

Michael: Hundreds of thousands?

Jason: Hundreds of thousands. $50,000 a pop, $70,000 sometimes.

Steve: This was the *Enquirer* back in the day.

Jason: Yes, mostly the *Enquirer*. I don't remember any other tabloids.

Michael: Did you get approached by the press and get asked for information or offered money?

Jason: No. I was a little nervous at one point thinking, "Does HBO think I'm doing this?" because, of course, I had the keys to the whole kingdom.

Michael: I have a feeling who it was. I think I know who it was. I'm not going to say, but I have my suspicions.

Jason: You would connect the dots. You would look at the photograph of who was on set that day, who was that close to the main actor.

Michael: Who's a scumbag.

Jason: Yes, who might be a scumbag. It really drove David crazy.

————

Steve: Michael, there were some really terrific cameos in Season Six. In the "Luxury Lounge" episode you got to play against two great ones, Lauren Bacall and Ben Kingsley. What's it like to mug Lauren Bacall?

Michael: I actually knew her before *The Sopranos*. I met her in Paris in the mid-nineties. She was doing Robert Altman's *Prêt-à-Porter*, and my girlfriend at the time was also in the movie, so I was in Paris for six weeks. A lot of the cast would go out for dinner or drinks, and Lauren Bacall always had to sit between two young guys. Very often, I was one of the young guys that would sit next to her. My claim to fame.

I enjoyed working with her on this episode. The cool thing about her was she was really into the show and totally down to play herself in a comedic way. There was no ego about it. You would think someone like her would be a lot more protective over her own image.

Steve: She was certainly the biggest movie star in the world at this time, the most famous, the most glamorous.

Michael: Yes, she's a legend. But she was just game. She was no-nonsense.

Steve: And how about Ben Kingsley?

Michael: Ben Kingsley was very game, too, to play himself as kind of a douchebag. I really respected that a lot. I had a blast, doing that episode. Listen, whenever you get to be a fish out of water, it's gonna be funny. The "Pine Barrens" is the ultimate fish-out-of-water thing, but here you have Christopher and Little Carmine in Hollywood with these movie stars, dealing with showbiz, and they're outsiders looking in. We had a blast. You know what I love about playing that character, which comes out in this episode? There's no middle ground with Christopher. He goes all in. In relationships, in the mob, in the movie business, when he's in, he's all in. When he's addicted to drugs, he becomes a really bad addict, and then when he's sober, he's Mr. AA, Mr. Recovery. For an actor, it's really a pleasure to get to go to those extremes.

RAY ABRUZZO, *who played Little Carmine, did those scenes with me.*
—*Michael*

Steve: What was that like? Did you call him Sir Ben? Michael didn't. Did you?

Ray: Yes, I called him Sir Ben. We were warned that he might be difficult, but I thought he was warm and open. When we were getting ready for the pool scenes, we were just three guys sitting around by the pool waiting for those shots. We just had a lot of fun. I remember walking down the hallway before we go in, he's standing behind me, massaging my shoulders. It was nothing like you thought it would be. It was just another actor having fun, and I loved those scenes.

Michael: He certainly had a sense of humor about himself.

Ray: We called him Sir Ben Fucking Kingsley at some point.

Michael: [*chuckles*] Something like that. And Lauren Bacall was an incredible class act.

Ray: The beauty is, there's a shot when you and I first see her, I think that's the least bit of acting you and I ever did. We really were just like [*gasps*]—"There's Lauren Bacall!" It's probably our most honest moment in the show. I ran into her in the lobby the day before we shot, with a little dog under her arm. And I introduced myself. This is what she said: "Is this the ugliest fucking hotel you've ever seen?" That was the first thing she said to me and I just thought, "Oh, this is going to be fun. This is going to be great."

EVERYTHING WITH *The Sopranos had gotten really big-budget by this time. The other day I came across the invitation for the first-season premiere "at the State Theater on Broadway, buffet supper following at John's Pizza on 44th." (Bruce Springsteen showed up, by the way, to support his band member Stevie Van Zandt.) But since Season Three, we were having the season premieres at Radio City Music Hall and then a huge dinner at Rockefeller Center. Thousands of people were showing up, just to watch a TV show!*

That kind of big budget extended to the production, of course. I really enjoyed the episode we did at the Feast of St. Elzéar, "The Ride." People think we shot that at a real feast, but believe it or not, they built that whole festival in Newark, at a big cost. By this time, they were sparing no expense. We shot there for days. It was a blast. —Steve

Michael: It was one of my favorites because of that whole sequence when Christopher is high and that song, "The Dolphins," is playing. There's no dialogue. I also loved your fight with Tony Sirico. Bobby and Paulie really go at it. What did you draw on for that scene?

Steve: You know I love Tony Sirico. But Tony has no filter. Tony could say some things that could get under your skin. Am I right, Michael?

Michael: That's putting it mildly.

Steve: So I thought of all those things, like a Rolodex in my head, honestly. I used that to build myself up to a frenzy, to the point where Tony said to me, "Take it easy, would you?" People were holding me off him, and after the take, he said, "Slow down a little bit." He said that, one, because he thought maybe I was going to slip and really break free—which was never going to happen—and two, he's got a thing, he doesn't want Paulie to look bad.

Michael: Oh yes, that was a big thing.

Steve: Tony is one of those guys that mixes his character with himself. Anyway I did it a bunch of times, and I didn't have to worry about keeping the energy up. I was steamed. Speaking of Paulie in that episode, there's a really nice scene at the very end. With his mother. It's been a hard episode for him. He was rejected by everyone for being cheap. He's got a lot going on, and he's angry with his mother, because he found out she's not really his mother, she's his aunt. But at the end, it's a very poignant moment where he's sitting on the couch with her. Watching Lawrence Welk. That's from his real life. Tony used to enjoy watching Lawrence Welk with his own mother. He was very close with her.

Michael: It's a very touching scene. Frances Ensemplare is the actress who plays Tony's mother throughout the series. And then of course we find out that the woman Paulie thought was his aunt, all his life, was really the mother.

Steve: Played by Judith Malina, a famous acting teacher.

Michael: Judith Malina, who started the Living Theatre, along with Julian Beck, her husband. She was a huge figure in Off-Broadway avant-garde theater in New York. She also played Al Pacino's mother in *Dog Day Afternoon*. I got to work with her on *Household Saints*. Malina and Beck were very political. They were doing street theater in little villages in Brazil, they got arrested and were in jail in South America, they were real radicals.

Steve: But one more thing about Paulie in this episode. There's a scene where he wakes up in the middle of the night. The cancer scare. When he looks at the clock, when he wakes up to call the doctor, it's three A.M.

Michael: That's right.

Steve: Here we go again with the three A.M. You gonna tell me about that now? When are you gonna come clean?

Michael: Never.

Steve: Are you bullshitting or is there really something to it?

Michael: I can't ever talk about it.

Steve: Oh, you're full of shit. I'll find out. I'm going to make a few calls.

THERE'S A scene in "The Ride" where Christopher is in a car in a parking lot with the junkie Corky; it's a real turning point for Christopher, because he's making a long speech about the house he's going to buy, and the Christmas traditions he'll have there, and how happy his kid will be. It's the imagined life he wants to build for himself. But as he's talking about it, Corky is shooting up, and Christopher teeters between those two lives. And then winds up snorting heroin with Corky. I remember that scene very well—because we almost didn't get it. Alan Taylor, the director, remembers it too. —Michael

Alan: Christopher was in the car with one of his druggie friends. It was pouring down rain like I've never seen before. It was a monsoon. We're in the parking lot, and the water started to rise, and was closing around the car, and apple boxes were floating by.

Michael: We should explain, apple boxes are the wooden boxes with holes on the sides that you always see all over film sets. They're used for a million different things.

Alan: So they're floating by, the water is rising. By the time we got to turn around for your close-up, we really only had one take to get this three-page essential monologue. You did a perfect take. I kept listening to it and watching it. Every breath was where it should be. Every flutter of the eyelids was where it should be, and you blew me away. It was good because by the time you were done the water was slowly rising up to the windows on the car and we had to wrap. It showed me that you actually know what you're doing.

Michael: Thanks. At least on that day, I knew what I was doing.

Steve: Alan, what was your experience working with Jim?

Alan: It would have been so easy to be intimidated by him, but he never gave me that feeling, which is amazing. He owned this character. He had his own process. He was working with his drama coach to develop the character. He had a tight relationship with David Chase, but even then, on set, he would be open to direction. In this episode, "The Ride," there's a great example of that. Remember, there's a scene between Jim and you, Michael? It was the scene where you guys steal the wine from the bikers?

Michael: Yes. That was in the beginning of "The Ride." That was fun.

Alan: Afterward, you guys are having a conversation in Vesuvio or some restaurant. You guys did it, and it just didn't sound right. It felt like you weren't really where the characters would be at that point. I went over to talk to both of you, and he said, "Oh yeah, right, right," and he adjusted. And I'm thinking: This is a guy who's been doing this character for all these seasons, and he's a god, he knows this character, but he was still very receptive to hearing the director's voice. That's my experience: when you work with really strong, good actors, they understand and like direction.

EVEN AS *we started filming the twelve episodes of Season Six, we had no idea if there would be a seventh season. I felt, as I know a lot of the others did—we trusted David Chase to make the right decision. Of course we hoped our jobs would continue, but we also knew that they should only continue if there were still good stories to tell.*

Fortunately for all of us, David did make that decision. In the summer of 2005, HBO announced that there indeed would be eight more episodes. Not another full season, but a kind of "Season Six, Part Two." We were all happy to hear that the show would go on. And happy to know that, as Ilene Landress told us, David stuck to his guns. —Michael

Steve: It all coulda ended after Season Six, Part One, right? That Christmas card scene, everybody sitting together like the end of a Hallmark movie, that coulda been it?

Ilene: Yes, it could have ended at Six A. HBO wanted more episodes, but David took some time with the writers because he didn't artificially want to just take the plot he had and just drag it out. So he did take the time, by himself first, then with Terry and Matt, and talked through: if we're gonna do more episodes, what would that look like?

Steve: So they came up with this mini-season, eight episodes. How did that become nine?

Ilene: In the middle of production of Season Six B, David had plotted everything out, but he said, "I need one more episode." And HBO was saying, "Yeah, we don't want to give you one more episode. We want one more season." They would have kept going.

David's attitude was always like, "I want to stop while people still like it." You didn't want to stop when people look back and go, "Oh yeah, remember *Sopranos* when it was good?" He always wanted to leave on a high note. So everybody respected him for that.

SEASON SIX *Part Two started with probably my favorite episode to shoot. We had a fantastic time doing this one. —Steve*

Michael: "Sopranos Home Movies," the first episode of Six B, that episode was basically just the four of you, Edie and Jim, you and Aida. You shot that up in Putnam County, Lake Oscawana. You were there for what, two weeks?

Steve: We stayed in a big hotel in Tarrytown, New York. We shot it at Roy Scheider's old lake house. It was right on the water. We had another house on the property that they said belonged to Babe Ruth in the thirties. Babe Ruth used to bring showgirls up there in the winter. That was kind of our dressing room. But people lived all along that lake. We shot the birthday scene where we're singing "Happy Birthday," and of course you gotta sing it over and over, take after take, and somebody across the way went, "Shut the fuck up already!"

OF COURSE, *the good times were not contained to what you saw on the screen. Cinematographer Phil Abraham remembers it all too well. —Steve*

Steve: Phil, remember we had a big party one night? We were in the bar, and we sent one of the PAs out to get liquor because the bar was closed. Remember what they did to you?

Phil: It was all [director] Tim Van Patten. I was in a conversation with Ilene Landress and we were off to one side, and all of a sudden, the waitress would be bringing shots of tequila, and Tim Van Patten is over at the bar and he's got one. So we did the shot. Ten shots later, I find out he's drinking water, and he's sending me over tequila. That was crazy. And this is embarrassing to say but I'm going to say it anyway, that I had to take a leak and I'm meandering through the bar and I come up to Jimmy Collins, one of the teamsters. He's playing pool, and I go, "Jimmy, where's the men's room?" He goes, "Just past the second pool table," and I walked smack into a mirror. Boom.

Steve: You were wounded for a couple of days. [*laughs*]

Phil: I was wounded, yes. We were all wounded.

Michael: You weren't the only one, that's for sure.

Phil: No, there were a lot of stories for Jim and Tim as well.

Steve: A lot of parties in those two weeks. A lot of parties.

JIM AND *I had a lot of fun with Aida on-screen—there's a deleted scene, you could see it on YouTube if you want, where we grab her hat and blow it up with firecrackers. But there was another incident between Jim and Aida offscreen that we all thought was pretty funny. Aida, not so much. —Steve*

Steve: There was another incident with you and Jim that we laugh about to this day.

Aida: The chicken salad.

Steve: The chicken salad. You broke down something big-time over that.

Aida: Let me just preface it a little bit about why I had a breakdown with it. I find out a little bit before this that I'm diabetic. As a diabetic, you need to make sure you eat, and you don't want to eat a lot of sugar, you need your protein. We go away where there's no stores, or restaurants, or anything.

Steve: At the lake house. It's July, it's hot, and we're by the lake, and we're having fun. The crew, everybody's swimming at lunchtime, they're riding speedboats and everything, but because we had makeup and hair, we couldn't do it.

Aida: Right, they're swimming, we're sweating. So I go to the craft services people, I make a whole thing about it. "Could I have some protein there? I'm diabetic, I'm trying to eat well."

Now, on *Sex and the City,* if they said boo, there'd be pounds of freaking chicken salad, but on *Sopranos,* "Hello, can I get a tub of chicken salad?" No, my blood sugar was dropping a little bit because we're filming, it's time for lunch, and I realized I need something to eat. I was just asking for some food, and they never brought any protein. That's when Aida became a psycho. Just like Janice. I was like, [*evil voice*] "Where's . . . my . . . chicken . . . salad?"

Steve: You were calling yourself "Mommy," you were yelling, "Mommy wants chicken salad! Mommy wants chicken salad!"

Aida: I flipped out.

Steve: Later that night, we're doing the karaoke scene where Carmela and Janice are singing, and Jim and Bobby are on the couch, and Jim starts breaking your balls going, "Mommy wants chicken salad," like a parrot. He kept saying it, "Mommy wants chicken salad."

Aida: Did I kick his ass or something?

Steve: You teed off on him. I mean, you totally went bananas on him. You go outside, Jim follows you to go apologize, we're all hysterical.

Aida: Oh, my God, but now everyone is going to think I'm a bitch. I'm so not a bitch.

Steve: No, no. When you're working sixteen hours, eighteen hours, it gets like that. They could have brought you a little prosciutto and fixed the whole thing.

Aida: A little prosciutt'. Not so much to ask.

BUT OF *course, as we've said, David Chase being David Chase, you can't have a serious episode without some humor, and you can't do a fun episode like this without some real drama. In this case, it was more real than the viewers knew about. "Sopranos Home Movies" includes a huge fight scene with Tony and Bobby. When you watch it, it looks like I head-butted Jim hard enough to break his nose. The reason it looks like that is simple: I accidentally head-butted Jim hard enough to break his nose. —Steve*

Michael: I think there were two great fight scenes that involved Jim Gandolfini. We talked a lot about the first one, with Ralphie. This was the other great fight scene. Tell me about it.

Steve: We go to shoot the scene and Jim had gotten knee surgery in the off-season. He said, "My knees aren't good. I'm not going to be able to do this. It's going to look like shit." Six months later, they build that cabin on a soundstage at the cost of $250,000. It was eerie. When I stepped onto the soundstage, I thought I was back in the cabin. It was an exact replica.

Michael: How did you prepare for the fight?

Steve: Jim said, "Look, we're good friends. Let's go as far as we can. Let's make this look as real as we can. Do anything to me. Choke me, pull my hair, do whatever you got to do." It was choreographed.

With that stuff, you walk through and you walk through, and then you speed it up and speed it up.

We had the fight. It was two fat, sweaty, out-of-shape guys fighting. That's why it looked real. Jim is much stronger than me. We did 95 percent of the stunts ourselves.

At one point, I zigged, he zagged, and I cracked him with a headbutt in his nose. He was supposed to go right, and he didn't, and I hit him and he went down like a ton of bricks. I was praying he doesn't get up and beat me up for real. He legit broke the cartilage in his nose. You could hear it—it was loud, like a bunch of twigs snapping. But we took a break for an hour and he came back. He looked okay, actually. It was a little swollen, but nothing crazy. I apologized, but really it was just one of those things that happens. And then we went back at it. When you watch it, the real headbutting was kept in the episode. I was sore for weeks afterward, but it was worth it.

Michael: It was very realistic. A fantastic fight scene.

Steve: I got pretty good at it. It's something you don't learn in acting class. I got pretty good at ADR, too, which you don't learn in acting class either.

Michael: "Additional dialogue replacement." We should explain, it's when something didn't record well, or they want to change a line. You go into a studio and you sync to what you already shot, to redo or add to the dialogue.

Steve: Also around this time they sold *The Sopranos* to A&E, and every curse word was taken out and redone. Instead of "fucking" you say "freaking."

Michael: Sometimes you have to get very creative, like if it's a cock-sucking motherfucker, you may have to do cork-screwing, duck-humping whatever. They also did it with the Bada Bing. The strippers. They did alternate takes where they had clothes on.

A REALLY cool part of Season Six Part Two, for me, was the whole story line involving Cleaver, the movie that Christopher is trying to make. I can relate to his desire to make it in the movie business, of course—took me a while to get there myself—but David and the writers took Christopher's attempts at starting a movie career to incredibly absurd lengths. It gave me a lot to work with. —Michael

Steve: The whole *Cleaver* thing, that almost goes back to the beginning of the series, right?

Michael: In the pilot, Christopher talks about, "My cousin Gregory, his girlfriend's a development girl in Hollywood, I could sell my story." We have the episode "D-Girl," where we meet her, and they're interested in his life and what he knows about the mob. He loves all that, and here's his opportunity. He takes it very seriously, and he wants to write a story that's part mob movie and part horror movie. It becomes absolutely ridiculous.

Christopher gets involved with Little Carmine, who has done porn, and *Girls Gone Wild*–type videos down in Florida. They put this project together. Christopher goes all in, to the point where he basically just forgets the rest of his business. He's preoccupied this season with this movie business, as if everybody should be on board with him. He almost forgets he's a mobster. There's lots of work to be done in the mob all the time: he's got to kick up to Tony, there's the gambling, the loan-sharking, the clubs, all the family business. And he feels that everybody should fall in line with his passion to make a movie, and nobody really gives a shit. Tony just tolerates it. But that to me is the essence of Christopher's character, all the way back to the beginning—the way he gets so completely absorbed and obsessed with whatever he's doing. It reaches a pinnacle here, and it makes for great comedy.

Steve: But like we said before, you play it straight. Nobody knows it's funny. That's what's funny about it.

Michael: Exactly.

Steve: I honestly don't think the story line is that far-fetched. You have a guy, he gets cut up. His body is in all pieces in dumpsters. It's no different than any of these other silly, crazy zombie movies. But there's such great scenes. Like when Christopher and J. T. are trying to explain the story line to the guys, trying to get them to put money into the movie.

Michael: And they're all chiming in with their opinions. Like they all know about making movies.

Steve: That's a very real thing with mob guys, they think they know everything about everything. Because if you've ever sat with some of them, and you and I have, Michael, they know everything. They know politics, they know sports, they know movies. These guys know everything, according to them.

Michael: According to them. But my favorite scene was the movie premiere. I find it really funny. It's a really good thing for his character, because he actually made a movie.

Steve: He thinks he's the next Martin Scorsese.

Michael: I also love that he's unaware that he's writing about his and Tony's relationship—that the guy in the movie is a very thinly veiled version of Tony Soprano, and he's basically portraying Tony as a greedy son of a bitch.

Steve: But then Carmela notices the similarity between the love triangle in the film and the whole business with Christopher and Tony when they thought Tony had slept with Adriana.

Michael: And she thinks the movie is about Christopher's fantasy about killing Tony out of revenge. It just gets more and more absurd: Christopher wants the writer to say that it was all his idea, and he refuses, and Christopher hits him over the head with his Humanitas Prize trophy. Which is another nice little detail, because the Humanitas Prize is an award for film or TV writing intended to promote human dignity and meaning. How perfect is that.

Steve: On YouTube somebody showed me a little fake documentary you made, as Christopher, about the making of *Cleaver*. What was that about?

Michael: It's me as Christopher, and Ray Abruzzo as Little Carmine, being interviewed for an electronic press kit video, one of those behind-the-scenes things. It's really funny.

Steve: Did you improv that?

Michael: That was all improv, yes.

Steve: What was that like, getting to improv as Christopher? Because as we've said, there was no improv on the show.

Michael: We just did it on the fly. It wasn't something that we really prepared, although it was part of the promotional package for the last season of *The Sopranos*. We just improvised it and by then, I'd been playing that character for almost ten years. You know him inside and out and I really enjoyed just making it up, letting it go.

I'm going to say this, and I've never said this publicly: some actors insist on having the crew call them by their character's name and say they're going to stay in character for the whole day. I've never done that. I would be embarrassed to have the crew call me anything other than my real name. But in some weird way, a lot of us were in character for a lot of that ten years. I'm not saying we walked around as these guys, but when we were all together, there was a little bit of that vibe that would happen. Especially when we would run around the city together.

Steve: People would relate to you as Christopher. Or come up to me like I was Bobby. And sometimes you would fall into that a bit. Like we talked about how Jim was naturally the leader. One time Jim went to pick up the check when I took a bunch of us out to Il Cortile, and I already had picked it up, and he went, "No, no, no, give him his money back." He got irate. And I said, "This isn't the show. You don't fucking tell me what to do. I'm not Bobby. This isn't how it works. This is real life." I picked up the check.

Michael: Right. So after all those years, having to improv in character was not a big stretch. But we shouldn't take that too far. We don't want people to think we're our characters.

Steve: No. Am I a nice guy like Bobby? No. I am what I am.

Michael: But they did keep bringing parts of our own lives into the show. You got to play basketball in one scene. In the episode "Mr. & Mrs. John Sacrimoni Request . . ." How did that come about?

Steve: Terry Winter wrote that. He knew me. He knew I played at Brooklyn College. I had lost about twenty-five pounds when I came back at the beginning of the season. One of the producers says, "I think you've lost enough." He didn't flat-out tell me to stop losing weight, but just subtly said, "I think you've lost enough weight." I had been working out, getting myself back into somewhat of a shape. But I'll be honest—that was not a legitimate basket, that was a nine-and-a-half-foot basket. And they built a ramp, so I ran up the ramp when I'm dunking. We were all playing that day outside the pork store. Just messing out there before the scene started. Michael, you were playing.

Michael: Yes. Jim was playing too. And Joe Gannascoli.

Steve: We were playing a two-on-two. Jim could play. I think Jim played in high school.

Michael: I can't play. You were the best.

Steve: I could still play at that point in my life.

Michael: And what about the trains? Bobby has this obsession with trains in Season Six. Was that from your life also? Are you a train guy?

Steve: No. I have nothing to do with trains. But I guess they figured it was a good fit for Bobby, that it was something that he and his son could do together, which, of course, doesn't work out. The son rejects him and laughs at him about it.

Michael: That's something we can all relate to. Those moments when it feels like your children are pulling away from you. That always hurts.

Steve: Absolutely. I've been very lucky with my daughters. But when your kid doesn't want to do something with you, that always stings. Bobby bought this train set so they can bond, and the son just takes off with his friends. He wants nothing to do with it at all. Bobby was extremely hurt.

Michael: Have you had moments like that yourself, with your girls?

Steve: When my youngest daughter was four years old, it was Season Three on *The Sopranos*. I was living in Staten Island, and my wife was homeschooling my older daughter. I had been away so much, working. I was away for a couple of months doing a movie, and before that I was away with *The Sopranos* for Season Two. When I came back, I would take my daughter out for a walk, the little one, holding her hand, going to the store, and she didn't want to go with me. She would cry. She was afraid to go with me. She wanted to stay there with her mother, and that made me feel really bad. So I can only imagine how Bobby felt. My daughter was only four, and these things happen. His son is a teenager. So that's gonna sting a lot more.

ONE OF *the most heartbreaking moments in the entire series occurs in "The Second Coming," near the end of Season Six. A distraught A. J. tries to take his own life by putting a bag over his head, tying a cinder block to his leg, and tossing the cinder block into the swimming pool. Stunt coordinator Pete Bucossi told us how he made that scene happen.* —Michael

Michael: That scene—for Steve and I, as parents, it's probably the most difficult to watch in the whole series. And one of the reasons it's so hard is that it goes on so long, and it's so believable. How did you create that illusion?

Pete: We had a couple of safety divers on one end of the pool. We had a stunt double, Kevin Rogers, who was doubling our young actor, Robert Iler. Most of it was Kevin going down to the bottom of the water with the bag over his face. And you never really did get a clean, clean shot at seeing if it was our actor or not. But it was all pretty much done as real. There were no tubes going up into the plastic bag so he could breathe.

Steve: I just watched it again. I could swear you see Robert with the bag over his head underwater.

Pete: That was for maybe a few seconds. He would have gone in the water with the divers and he put the bag right over his head, and

the diver stepped out and you count three, two, one, let the cameras roll for a second, and then we bring him back up to the top. So
it's done very quickly and very safely.

AS WE'VE *been saying all along, at* The Sopranos, *when you gotta go, you
gotta go. Well, with one exception: Ilene Landress told us that Steven
Van Zandt talked David into letting him stay alive—albeit in a coma—
"just in case there's a spinoff," Steven said. Ilene called it Steven's "stay
of execution."*

*But as the end of the series approached, the bell was tolling for all of
us. —Michael*

Michael: You got killed off in "The Blue Comet," the second-to-last
episode of the series. Did you know ahead of time that they were
killing you off?

Steve: No. Usually I could get shit out of people, but nobody was
budging. I had been asking for years, "You hear anything? I want
to buy an apartment, you hear anything?" No one was talking. Not
even you. Did you know I was getting killed?

Michael: I don't think I did, because at that point in the last season
I was not in the writers' room. So how did you find out?

Steve: I was in my apartment, my wife, Laura, was in the shower,
and I got a call from David. He says, "Hey, what's happening? Where
are you? Are you at the old apartment or the new apartment?" How
he knew I bought an apartment, I have no idea.

Michael: He knew every move you made. [*laughs*]

Steve: I said, "I'm in the old apartment." He said, "I'm on my way." I
said, "You are coming here?" Which is strange—we didn't have that
kind of relationship.

Michael: Completely out of character, never happened before, not even close.

Steve: We got along just fine, but there was no visiting each other's homes, so it was like the CEO of Apple, Steve Jobs, is coming to your house.

Michael: You know it's something important. It's not just, he wants to shoot the shit.

Steve: Fifteen minutes later the doorman calls him up. I open the door. It's the end of January, he's wearing one of those green parkas with the fake fur. Swear to God, he says, "I guess you know why I'm here." [*chuckles*] It was like a fucking hit for real. I said, "I guess so, come on in."

He sat down, and he took a pencil that I had on the dining room table, and he was just drumming it on the table. Just kept tapping it. And I said, "So?" He went, "Well, we're going to kill you off at a train store." He was very vague. It was awkward. There was a lot of long pauses, and I said, "Well, I want to thank you for changing my life. I hope I did a good job for you." "Oh, absolutely," he said. "I couldn't see anyone else playing Bobby." Small talk, long pauses, a lot of awkwardness, not much detail, and that was it, out the door.

Michael: How did you feel about it?

Steve: I felt it didn't matter; it was always about what's the best way to end the story. On a personal note, I was getting paid for all of the last episodes anyway, at that point, all bets were off. Whatever flows, flows. I wouldn't have felt that way if I got killed in Season Three or Four, but this was the end for everyone anyway.

I will say this: Even before that, when we came back from Christmas break, 2007, it started to really hit me. This is the last time we are shooting in Vesuvio. It's going to be the last time we are shooting at the Bada Bing. The back of the Bada Bing. And I was thinking, "This is coming to an end, man. We're not going to be doing this much longer." I started getting a little sentimental. "Wow, this is the last scene I'm ever going to have with Jim." I felt it. They killed Bobby on Valentine's Day, February fourteenth. It was snowing.

Michael: The Saint Valentine's Day Massacre of Bobby Bacala.

Steve: Yes. It was at TrainLand in Lynbrook, New York. A real train store. They killed me off in a great way. It was a great shot, a great scene. That was a big thing. If you just faded away, that was a little slap in the face. But they gave me a good send-off.

Michael: Very memorable. Did you do the whole thing yourself?

Steve: It's all me except for falling into the train set—that's a stunt-man. They asked me if I wanted to do it. They only had two train setups, and I was afraid that I would fuck it up, so I said, "Let the stuntman do it, falling on his back."

So that's my story, Michael. How about you? Christopher dies a couple episodes before me, in "Kennedy and Heidi." When did you find out that Christopher was gonna get it?

Michael: I knew a year before. David told me how it would go, and I thought it was great. I thought dying at Tony's hands was just a really shocking ending. Disturbing. It says a lot about both of their characters and their relationship. I thought it was cool. Just like you, there were three episodes after the one I die in, so it wasn't like I was getting killed off in Season Four or Five or Six, then not coming back for a whole season. That would have been rough.

Steve: Did you feel bad that they were killing you off?

Michael: I didn't feel bad. I had no ego about living to the end of the show. That wasn't the last scene I shot, by the way, so even though he kills me in the scene, it didn't have as much finality as people would think.

Steve: Same thing with me. It wasn't my last scene either.

Michael: The last scene I shot, maybe a week or two later, was on a pier with Jim and Frank Vincent, doing some kind of negotiation. Shooting your last scene was a different feeling than even dying in a way, because it was like, "That's it. I'm done."

Steve: My last scene was me driving where I parked the car going into the train store. I was already Dead Bobby. Listen, it's very sad. These are your friends. I worked with them for eight years. It was a hell of a ride, and it's all ending. You're not going to come here, you're not going to see these people. It's sad but that's part of being an actor. You move on to the next thing. But that's what made me sad.

CHRISTOPHER'S DEATH *scene, by the way, included what I think was the most incredible stunt we ever did on* The Sopranos. *An excellent stunt man named Bill Anagnos drove that car, flipped it down the hill, and it rolled three or four times. He did it in one take. We asked the director, Alan Taylor, about it. —Michael*

Michael: One of the craziest stunts I've ever seen was when we shot the "Kennedy and Heidi" episode, where you flipped the car.

Alan: It was amazing, because it was a one-take wonder. Alik Sakharov was the DP. Remember him? Excellent DP who's now become a director.

Michael: I'll never forget that. How many times did it flip, the car, four, right?

Alan: It must have flipped, probably four times, and then with cutting, it made it look like even more because we multiplied a few of those cuts. But he did it in one take.

Michael: So how did you do it?

Alan: We had at least five cameras on it, and some of them were in positions where the car really had to land in a certain spot. This is an SUV going forty miles an hour, that has to pitch and roll, go down an embankment, and land in the forest. How they did it was pretty amazing. They had a cannon in the back that fires a pole into the ground, and that's what kicks the vehicle up. The stunt man is in the SUV in a cage, and he takes his hands off the wheel and hits the button that does that. He nailed it. He landed it right on target. It flew past every camera and landed exactly where it was supposed to.

At the end, the SUV was settling down. It was a moment where you think, "Okay, that was great, but did we kill somebody?" Then his hand came up out of the window and gave a thumbs-up.

SHOOTING OUR *last scenes was very emotional. But I have to say, it didn't really sink in for me until June of 2007, when the last episode aired. It was a night we'll never forget. —Michael*

Michael: Remember the night of the airing of that last episode? About a dozen of us were together in Hollywood, Florida, at the Seminole Hard Rock. It was a special night.

Steve: You, me, Jim, Arthur Nascarella, Lorraine, John Ventimiglia, Stevie Van Zandt, Tony Sirico. Ilene Landress was with us, and our lawyer, Roger Haber. They sent a private plane for us and we all flew to Florida.

Michael: When we got there, there was a red carpet with ten thousand people, which we were totally unprepared for. It seemed to just go on and on and on. It was insane. I'd never seen anything like that.

Steve: Even Stevie Van Zandt, who obviously has seen it all with the Springsteen band, said, "Holy shit." He was impressed. We went through that red carpet, all through the casino, and there were people lined up, cheering us, going crazy.

Michael: That night we did a Q & A onstage. Then nine o'clock was airtime and we went into a private room. The audience was going to watch on a closed-circuit big-screen TV. That's when it hit me. In the middle of that episode, I realized, "I'm not going to be working with these people anymore. This chapter in my life is now over." These were my friends. We had been through a lot together: we'd been through marriages, divorces, births, deaths, awards, contract battles, illnesses—and lots and lots of fun. And it was all coming to an end. Watching that last episode, it really hit me.

Steve: You know what else people don't know—Jim bought everybody a watch. A really expensive Kobold. He got them made for everybody on the cast and crew, and forty of us got gold ones. They were all engraved "The Sopranos - 1997–2007 - Rest in Peace - Thank you—J.G." He must have spent a half million bucks.

Michael: He was just such a generous guy. I treasure that watch.

Steve: Let's talk about that last episode. The ending. We already talked to David Chase about it. I remember when it ended, I was confused. I had read the script—somebody slipped me a copy— and I knew what the ending was, the script said, "Cut to black," but when I watched it, I was confused. I think Jim was confused too.

Michael: Oh, everybody was.

Steve: Did you know ahead of time?

Michael: I once asked David, maybe more than a year before, when I was in the writers' room and I said, "How do you see this ending?" I forget exactly what he said in terms of where the plot was going—but then at the end, he said, everything just goes to black. He had that in mind for a while.

So what do you think, Steve? What happens after it goes to black?

Steve: I feel Tony Soprano is alive and well and living in New Jersey. I think he's happy.

Michael: When they finish eating, he pays the check and he goes home?

Steve: What you saw is what you saw. Nothing happened. I think the Members Only guy was a red herring. I think David built up the tension. I know when we spoke to him, he said Meadow parking the car was just a young girl trying to park. In my opinion, Tony's at peace, and that's what you see.

Michael: I just watched it for our podcast but I had not seen it since the Hard Rock when we were all together. For years, I thought Tony dies and these are the last moments of his life before he gets shot by this guy sent by Phil Leotardo. It's like Bacala says, "You never see it coming."

But now I'm not so sure. After speaking to David, my opinion now is, it's a moot point. Like I said when we talked to David, it's like a book; when you come to the last sentence of the book, the book is over. There's no wondering what happens after the book is done. That's the end of the story. It's not as complete as people wanted, and it doesn't offer closure the way people wanted, but that's it. We don't see him die, so he doesn't die.

AND OF *course, The Sopranos didn't die, either. As the song that played the show out says, "the movie never ends, it goes on and on, and on, and on." When the two of us, along with Vinny Pastore, started our Conversations with the Sopranos tour back in 2014, we were stunned at how much renewed interest there was in the show—when we did Melbourne, Australia, more than 2,500 people showed up to hear us talk about the show and take questions from the audience.*

So because we owe this book—we owe everything, really—to our fans, it seems only fitting that before we wrap things up, we let one of them get in one more. —Steve

Wayne, from Kyle, Texas: Many of us look at our career path and hope to reach sixty-five, and retire, enjoy the fact that we have worked hard, and were fortunate enough to save some money and attempt to relax a little in our later years. As actors, you guys have the ability to continue to work well beyond the normal retirement age. Do you have a mental stopping point or would you choose to work until you just can't do it anymore?

Steve: Wow. What an interesting question. Michael, what do you think?

Michael: Me? I want to die on the stage, man. I have no hobbies. Work is my hobby. I have to stay creative, and as long as I can remember my lines I want to work until I can't. Because I don't know what else I'm going to do.

Steve: There's the old saying, "You don't retire from show business." They retire you, of course. When they're done with you. Myself, as much as I love acting, and I've been very lucky and have had pretty good success, I don't know if I want to go forever because I don't want to continue to chase it. Keep going to the auditions and all that. I don't love that part anymore.

Michael: What are you going to do?

Steve: Hang out, have a few drinks, take a walk at the beach, see my kids, catch some movies, have nice dinners. I get along great with my wife. I got a lot of good friends.

Michael: Is Laura going to be okay with you hanging around the house all the time?

Steve: I guess so. She ain't going to have no choice. [*laughs*]

Michael: Maybe she does have a choice. Maybe she'll put you in a retirement home like Paulie's mother.

Steve: What do you think when we retire, me and you go to a place like Green Grove and we'll have a double room with the door in between?

Michael: We'll be like Bert and Ernie.

Steve: We'll retire together. What do you think?

Michael: We'll do a podcast from the nursing home. We don't even have to record it or broadcast it. No one will know. We'll just do it.

Steve: We go to a place like Green Grove. The food is good. Everything's there. They show movies, we sing.

Michael: But you don't sing.

Steve: They'll sing. We'll listen. It'll be fantastic. Let's think about that.

Michael: Maybe we'll start a nursing home. We can call it Talking Sopranos Elder Care.

Steve: We'll have the *Talking Sopranos* logos on the bedpans.

Michael: With our faces on it? Yes. That's good.

Steve: It's all good, my friend. It's all good.

IT'S IMPOSSIBLE *to sum up in a few words what being on* The Sopranos *meant to us—to all of us. But there is one thing we can say with certainty, and every single person who worked on the show felt the same way: We were family. We were blessed. We will never pass this way again.*

We've talked a lot about how The Sopranos *changed television forever, but we wanted to take one more moment to talk about how much it affected us, as well. We picked three of our friends to help us out here— they summed it up better than we ever could. —Steve and Michael*

Robert Iler: Michael, do you know what's funny? When we did the twenty-year anniversary, my chair was at the end. Everybody had walked offstage and I was the last person, so I was walking offstage, and you were standing right in the middle of the stage, and I put my hand on your back, I was like, "What's going on?" You looked at me and you said, "I'm just sad that we're not going to be all together again tomorrow." That just hit me so hard because I was feeling the same thing. That will stay with me forever.

Edie Falco: In retrospect, it's hard to think about how much this has meant to me over the years. Just to think that it might not have happened. Certainly, very few actors get to have something like this.

Phil Abraham: It was the experience of a lifetime, truthfully. The family aspect of it made it all the more special. As hard as the work was, there was something about this group of people that jelled in a way I've never seen. Even when we had issues with each other, and there was a tremendous amount of ball-busting, and we were as dysfunctional as you could possibly be, there was this sort of bigger sense of camaraderie and purpose that really held us together. We all felt that.

AND FINALLY, *we can't end the book without talking one last time about our dear friend Jim Gandolfini. Jim left us far too soon, and it's a hole in our hearts that will never mend.*

We saw Jim a few times just before he died. Jim threw a party at his apartment in Tribeca on the day before Easter in 2013. A few folks from the Sopranos *cast were there, but it wasn't a showbiz thing; a lot of Jim's family were there, a lot of cousins, nieces, and nephews. Jim's daughter, Liliana, had been born in Los Angeles the previous October, the day after Jim went to a screening of his new movie* Not Fade Away, *which reunited him with David Chase. So this was the first time he was bringing Liliana home to New York to meet the family, and it was a joyous affair. Jim was calm, and relaxed, and laughing, and it was like a giant weight had been lifted.*

Ever since the show ended, ever since he laid down the burden of being Tony Soprano, you could see his mood lighten. Now, watching Liliana bouncing on her mother's knee and surrounded by friends talking about anything but show business, he had become buoyant. Tony Sirico was there, and the minute Steve walked in, Tony snapped at him, "Hey, have you said hello to the boss yet?" And Steve said, "He's not the boss anymore." And Steve looked over at Jim, and you could see how happy Jim was to be free of all that.

The last time the three of us were together was on May 20 of that year, at the premiere of Steve's movie Nicky Deuce, *which we had all appeared in. Jim did a comedic turn in that movie like he'd never done before; he had a really good time doing it, and was in a wonderful mood at the premiere party. There's a photo somewhere of the two of us and Jim, smiling for the camera, looking like three guys without a care in the world.*

Which, for one brief moment in time, we were.

Jim died a month later.

We've talked often about the day we said goodbye. After the funeral at the beautiful Cathedral of St. John the Divine, we all gathered at Ma-

rio Batali's Otto restaurant on Eighth Street—Mario was Jim's roommate at Rutgers—and then a few of us went to Walker's, an old haunt of ours and Jim's. We raised a glass and said goodbye, but as Aida said, he is still with us, every day. There were so many times, whether it was doing the podcast or writing this book, that it felt hollow and incomplete to do something without being able to talk to Jim.

But we did the best we could. We hope we've done justice to him. And to the wonderful, mysterious, complicated, groundbreaking, infuriating, endearing characters he, and so many of our friends, created.

And to that kid who walked up to Michael in Central Park one day and showed him a tattoo of Christopher on his leg, we just wanna say: We get it, kid. We get it.

Some things never fade away. —Michael and Steve

Acknowledgments

THE FIRST THING WE HAVE TO ACKNOWLEDGE is that we are the luckiest guys on the face of the earth. To say we couldn't have done this alone is the understatement of the century. We had a great, great team helping us every step of the way.

Thanks first to the team at the *Talking Sopranos* podcast, starting with Jeff Sussman, our mastermind behind the scenes. Jeff, without you there would not have been a podcast. You gave us great advice from day one—you're a really smart and good guy. Andy Verderame produced the podcast, and worked tirelessly and brilliantly: You guided us through unknown turf, pal, and we will always be grateful. Thanks to Elijah Amitin for creating the grooviest podcast theme song ever. And thanks to the rest of the *Talking Sopranos* team—Ty Verderame, Ciara Schirripa, Richard Young, Kate Trapani, Bobby Hutch, Frank McKay, NYC Podcasting Studios, David Raphael, and, of course, Lisa Perkins, publicist extraordinaire.

Thanks to everyone at HarperCollins, beginning with Mauro DiPreta: Thank you for believing in this project, and for your brilliant and insightful editing. This book is so much better for your efforts. Thanks also to Vedika Khanna for all your help. Also thanks to Liate Stehlik, Benjamin Steinberg, Kelly Rudolph, Kayleigh George, Anwesha Basu, Jeanne Reina, Pamela Barricklow, Andrea Molitor, and Andrew DiCecco; and a special thanks to the meticulous, eagle-eyed Aja Pollock.

Thanks to ace writer Phil Lerman: Phil, you are now an honorary Soprano. No one could have done what you did with this book. We are forever grateful.

Thanks to Michael "The Hit Man" Harriot, who has been at our side every step of the way; to Roger Haber, our attorney, our friend, our partner in crime; Valerie Baugh, a great friend who takes care of business; and Rachel Wilder, for being Phil's binge-watching companion, and for doing a great first edit on the early chapters.

Steve would also like to thank Lorraine Schirripa, Jim and Janie (Wilma) Lemos, Bill Veloric, Steve Lovett, Barry Watkins, Dan Schoenberg, Jeff Singer, Dr. Doug Lazzaro, Brian Wexler, Gary Wexler, Phil Cuzzi, Joanna Beckson, Joe Scarpinito, Jim Nuciforo, and, of course, Willie Boy Schirripa.

Michael would also like to thank His Eminence Garchen Rinpoche; Dan, Claire, and John Imperioli; Raisa and Ryszard Chlebowski; Joe Scarpinito; Nick Solideo; Nicole Romano; and, last but not least, the dysfunctional yet fabulous family of @realmichaelimperioli Instagrammers.

Our deepest gratitude, of course, goes to David and Denise Chase and the entire *Sopranos* family. David, you managed to break through the walls that constrained what could be done on television, and in doing so allowed us all to create something unique, and timeless, and beautiful, and important. Thanks to those at HBO who took a big chance on a wild idea, all those years ago. And to the cast and crew, the writers and directors and producers and editors and sound technicians, the cinematographers and costume designers and casting directors, and all the rest: We are honored to have lived, and worked, and played, beside so many wonderful and talented people. You all made this book possible. A special thanks to all of you who shared your tales, for the podcast and for the book: This is your story. We hope we've told it well. And a special shout-out to our dear friend Tony Sirico. Keep smiling, good friend. The way you've kept us smiling time and time again.

As A. J. said to Tony, sitting with the family at the end of the final scene: "Isn't that what you said one time, 'Try to remember the times that were good?'" Well, to Jim, and to all the rest of you: This book is our way of trying to remember the times that were good.

Because you are all our family.

Index